THE
KNOW-IT-ALL

A.J. Jacobs is the editor of *Esquire Presents: What It Feels Like* and the author of *The Two Kings: Jesus and Elvis*, *America Off-Line*, and *Fractured Fairy Tales*. He is a senior editor of Esquire and lives in New York City with his wife Julie.

Also by A.J. Jacobs

THE
KNOW-IT-ALL

A.J. JACOBS

*One Man's Humble Quest to Become
the Smartest Person in the World*

arrow books

Published by Arrow Books, 2006

1 3 5 7 9 10 8 6 4 2

Copyright © A.J. Jacobs, 2004

A.J. Jacobs has asserted his right under the Copyright, Designs and Patents Act, 1988
to be identified as the author of this work

This book is an account of the author's experience reading the *Encyclopaedia Britannica*.
Some events appear out of sequence, and some names and identifying details of
individuals mentioned have been changed

First published in the United Kingdom by William Heinemann, 2005

Arrow Books
The Random House Group Limited
20 Vauxhall Bridge Road, London, SW1V 2SA

Random House Australia (Pty) Limited
20 Alfred Street, Milsons Point, Sydney
New South Wales 2061, Australia

Random House New Zealand Limited
18 Poland Road, Glenfield
Auckland 10, New Zealand

Random House (Pty) Limited
Isle of Houghton, Corner of Boundary Road & Carse O'Gowrie,
Houghton 2198, South Africa

The Random House Group Limited Reg. No. 954009

www.randomhouse.co.uk

A CIP catalogue record for this book is available from
the British Library

Papers used by Random House are natural, recyclable products made from
wood grown in sustainable forests. The manufacturing processes conform
to the environmental regulations of the country of origin

ISBN 0 09 948174 X

Printed and bound in Great Britain by
Bookmarque Ltd, Croydon, Surrey

To my wife, Julie

ACKNOWLEDGMENTS

I want to thank Rob Weisbach, who is not only the smartest editor in the world, but a great, kind, and absurdly supportive friend. Thanks also to Peter Breslow and Scott Simon and all the big brains at NPR. I'm grateful to Ted Allen, Shannon Barr, Ginia Bellafonte, Steve Bender, Brian Frazer, Stephen Kory Friedman, David Granger, Andrew Lund, Rick Marin, Victor Ozols, Tom Panelas, Brendan Vaughan, and Andy Ward. I'm indebted to my family and my wife's family who, instead of objecting to this massive invasion of their privacy, were nothing but encouraging. And of course, thanks to my wife Julie, who, when she agreed to marry me, made me the luckiest man in the world.

INTRODUCTION

I know the name of Turkey's leading avant-garde publication. I know that John Quincy Adams married for money. I know that Bud Abbott was a double-crosser, that absentee ballots are very popular in Ireland, and that dwarves have prominent buttocks.

I know that the British tried to tax clocks in 1797 (huge mistake). I know that Hank Aaron played for a team called the Indianapolis Clowns. I know that Adam, of Bible fame, lived longer than the combined ages of the correspondents of *60 Minutes* and *60 Minutes II* (930 years, to be exact). I know that South America's Achagua tribe worshiped lakes, that the man who introduced baseball to Japan was a communist, and that Ulysses S. Grant thought Venice would be a nice city "if it were drained."

I know all this because I have just read the first hundred pages of the *Encyclopaedia Britannica.* I feel as giddy as famed balloonist Ben Abruzzo on a high-altitude flight—but also alarmed at the absurd amount of information in the world. I feel as if I've just stuffed my brain till there are facts dribbling out of my ears. But mostly, I am determined. I'm going to read this book from *A* to *Z*—or more precisely, *a-ak* to *zywiec.* I'm not even out of the early *A*s, but I'm going to keep turning those pages till I'm done. I'm on my way. Just 32,900 pages to go!

How did this happen? How did I find myself plopped on my couch, squinting at tiny font about dwarf buttocks and South American lakes? Let me back up a little.

I used to be smart. Back in high school and college, I was actually considered somewhat cerebral. I brought D. H. Lawrence novels on vacations, earnestly debated the fundamentals of Marxism, peppered my conversation with words like "albeit." I knew my stuff. Then, in the years since graduating college, I began a long, slow slide into dumbness. At age thirty-five, I've become embarrassingly ignorant. If things continue at this rate, by my fortieth birthday, I'll be spending my days watching *Wheel of Fortune* and drooling into a bucket.

Like many in my generation, I've watched my expensive college education recede into a haze. Sure, I remember a couple things from my four years at Brown University. For instance, I remember that a burrito left on the dorm room floor is still somewhat edible after five days, as long as you chew really hard. But as for bona fide book learning? Off the top of my head, I recall exactly three things from my classes:

1. When my comp lit professor outed Walt Whitman.
2. When the radical feminist in my Spanish class infuriated the teacher by refusing to use masculine pronouns. "*La* pollo." "No, *el* pollo." "*La* pollo." "No, no, no, *el* pollo." Et cetera.
3. When the guy in my Nietzsche seminar raised his hand and said, "If I listen to one more minute of this, I'm going to go crazy," then promptly stood up, walked to the back of the class, and jumped out the window. It was a ground-floor window. But still. It was memorable.

My career choices are partly to blame for my intellectual swan dive. After college, I got a job as a writer at *Entertainment Weekly,* a magazine devoted to the minutiae of movies, TV, and music. I crammed my cranium with pop culture jetsam. I learned the names of 'N Sync's singers—as well as their choreographer. I could tell you which stars have toupees, which have fake breasts, and which have both. But this meant anything profound got pushed out. I could talk confidently about the doughnut-eating Homer, but I'd forgotten all about the blind guy who wrote long poems. I stopped reading anything except for tabloid gossip columns and books with pictures of attractive celebrities on the cover. In my library, I actually have a well-thumbed copy of Marilu Henner's autobiography. Things improved slightly when I got a job as an editor at *Esquire* magazine (I now know that Syrah and Shiraz are the same wine grape), but still, my current knowledge base is pathetically patchy, filled with gaps the size of Marlon Brando—whose autobiography I've read, by the way.

I've been toying with the idea of reading the *Britannica* for years. Since I haven't accomplished anything particularly impressive in my life, unless you count my childhood collection of airsickness bags from every major airline, I've always thought of this as a good crucible. The tallest mountain of knowledge. My Everest. And happily, this Everest won't cause icicles to form on my ears or deprive me of oxygen, one of my favorite gases. I'll get a crash course in everything. I'll leave no gap in my learning unfilled. In this age of extreme specialization, I will be the last guy in America to have all general knowledge. I'll be, quite possibly, the smartest man in the world.

I've actually dabbled in reference books before. After college, I spent a couple of days poring over Webster's dictionary—but mostly I was looking for two-letter words that I could use in Scrabble to make annoyingly clever moves. (I was kind of unemployed at the time.) And that turned out to be a very successful experience. You can bet your bottom *xu* (Vietnamese monetary unit) that I kicked the butt of my *jo* (Scottish slang for girlfriend) without even putting on a *gi* (karate outfit).

But the encyclopedia idea I stole from my father. When I was a freshman in high school, my dad, a New York lawyer, decided he was going to read the *Britannica*. My father is a man who loves learning. He went to engineering grad school, then to business grad school, then to law school. He was about to enroll in medical school when my mom told him that maybe it'd be a good idea to get a job, since jobs earn money, which is kind of helpful when trying to buy food. But even with a day job, he continued his book addiction and scholarly writing. Back in 1982, he decided the *Britannica* was a good way to become an instant expert on all subjects. He made it up to the mid-*B*s—I think it was right around *Borneo*—before giving up, blaming his busy schedule. Now I'm going to take up the cause. I'm going to redeem the family honor.

I called up my dad to tell him the good news.

"I'm going to finish what you started."

"I'm not sure I follow," he said.

"I'm going to read the entire *Encyclopaedia Britannica*."

A pause. "I hear that the *P*s are excellent."

I figured he'd have a wisecrack. That's his way. He's got a universe of information and wisdom in his head, but with my sister and me, he'd rather tell jokes and play silly games, like filling our water glasses to the very top, making it impossible to drink without spilling. He saves his serious talks for work—or for the other lawyers in the family, of whom there are a good dozen. Maybe that'll change soon. Maybe when I start telling him about the intricacies of the Phoenician legal system, he'll include me in the adult circle.

I tried the idea out on my wife, Julie, that night as we started scrubbing a mound of dishes.

"I think I need to get smarter," I said.

"Why? You're plenty smart." Julie motioned for me to hand her the sponge.

"I think I need to cut down on reality TV," I said.

"We could probably limit ourselves to two or three hours a day."

"And I think I'm going to read the encyclopedia." No response. "The *Encyclopaedia Britannica,* from *A* to *Z*."

I could tell Julie was skeptical, and with good reason. I met her when we were both working at *Entertainment Weekly.* She was on the business side, selling ads and chatting up clients, as comfortable in social settings as I am awkward, as practical as I am unrealistic. The romance was slow to start—mostly because she thought I was gay—but she's stuck with me for five years now. In that time, she's heard me announce plenty of other grand schemes—like the time I tried to start a magazine-wide Ping-Pong league, or my plan to write a screenplay about a president with Tourette's syndrome (working title: *Hail to the Freakin' Chief*)—only to see them fizzle.

"I don't know, honey," she said finally. "Sounds like kind of a waste of time."

Make that skeptical and slightly concerned. Julie has enough trouble dragging me out of the apartment to interact with actual, three-dimensional human beings. The encyclopedia, she no doubt surmised, would give me one more excuse to stay pinned to our comfortable couch. "What about eating dinner at every restaurant in New York?" Julie suggested. "You can start with the restaurants with *A* names, and work your way to the *Z*s. Wouldn't that be fun?"

A valiant try. But I'm dead serious about Operation Encyclopedia.

I got no more enthusiasm when I told my friends. "Can't you just read the Cliffs Notes?" was a popular response. One friend suggested that I read every volume of the children's book *Encyclopedia Brown* instead. Some wondered if maybe the *World Book* wasn't more my speed. At least that one has lots of pictures. No, it has to be the *Britannica,* I told them.

And it does. Last night, I did some preliminary research on encyclopedias. The *Britannica* is still the gold standard, the Tiffany of encyclopedias. Founded in 1768, it's the longest continually published reference book in history. Over the years, the *Britannica*'s contributors have included Einstein, Freud, and Harry Houdini. Its current roster includes dozens of academics with Nobels, Pulitzers, and other awards with ceremonies that don't feature commentary from Melissa Rivers. The *Britannica* passed through some tough times during the dot-com craze, and it long ago phased out the door-to-door salesman, but it keeps chugging along. The legendary eleventh edition from 1911 is thought by many to be the best—it has inspired a fervent, if mild-mannered, cult—but the current editions are still the greatest single source of knowledge.

Yes, there's the Internet. I could try to read Google from *A* to *Z*. But the Internet's about as reliable as publications sold next to Trident and Duracell at the supermarket checkout line. Want a quick check on the trustworthiness of the Internet? Do a search on the words "perfectionist" and "perfestionist." No, I prefer my old-school books. There's something appealingly stable about the *Britannica*. I don't even want that newfangled CD-ROM for $49, or the monthly *Britannica* online service. I'll take the leatherette volumes for $1,400—which is not cheap, but it's certainly less expensive than grad school. And anyway, at the end of this, maybe I can go on *Jeopardy!* and win enough to buy a dozen sets.

A couple of days after I placed my order, my boxes arrive. There are three of them, and they're each big enough to hold an air conditioner. I rip open the cardboard and get a look at my new purchase. It's a handsome set of books—sleek and black, with gold embossing on the spine that spells out the first and last entries in that volume. An actual example: *Excretion/Geometry*. Another: *Menage/Ottawa*, which somehow confirms what we've all heard about those wanton Canadians.

Seeing the *Britannica* in three dimensions not only causes Julie to panic that it'll eat up most of our apartment's shelf space, it also drives home the magnitude of my quest. I'm looking at 33,000 pages, 65,000 articles, 9,500 contributors, 24,000 images. I'm looking at thirty-two volumes, each one weighing in at a solid four pounds, each packed with those giant, tissue-thin pages. The total: 44 million words.

As a clever procrastination device, I pile all the volumes on the floor in one big stack. It reaches past my nipples. Four foot two! Practically a Danny DeVito of knowledge. I do a little shadowbox with my new adversary, feint a right jab, then step back and look at it again. It's a disturbing sight. Is this whole endeavor really a bright idea? Is this the best use of my time? Maybe I should try to accomplish something easier, like taking a

A

a-ak

That's the first word in the *Encyclopaedia Britannica*. "A-ak." Followed by this write-up: "Ancient East Asian music. See gagaku."

That's the entire article. Four words and then: "See gagaku."

What a tease! Right at the start, the crafty *Britannica* has presented me with a dilemma. Should I flip ahead to volume 6 and find out what's up with this gagaku, or should I stick with the plan, and move on to the second word in the *AA* section? I decide to plow ahead with the *AAs*. Why ruin the suspense? If anyone brings up "a-ak" in conversation, I'll just bluff. I'll say, "Oh, I love gagaku!" or, "Did you hear that Madonna's going to record an a-ak track on her next CD?"

a cappella

A lovely surprise. I know exactly what this is—an ex-girlfriend of mine belonged to an a cappella group in college. They sang songs from Def Lepard and called it Rockapella. One for two. Not bad.

Aachen

The next few entries destroy my average. I don't recognize the names of any Chinese generals or Buddhist compendiums. And I've never heard of Aachen, the German city that's home to Schwertbad-Quelle, the hottest sulfur spring in the country. I try to memorize the information. If my goal is to know everything, I can't discriminate, even against obscure Teutonic landmarks.

Aaron

I move on to Aaron, the brother of Moses. Seems he was sort of the Frank Stallone of ancient Judaism. The loser brother, the one Mom didn't talk about too much. "Oh, Aaron? He's doing okay. Still finding his way. But back to Moses. Did you hear about the Red Sea?"

This is good stuff. I'm Jewish, but I never got any religious training, never got a bar mitzvah. I know most of my Jewish lore from Charlton Heston movies, and I wouldn't call myself observant, though I do have a light lunch on Yom Kippur. So the *Britannica* will be my savior, my belated Hebrew school.

Abbott, Bud, and Costello, Lou

After a bunch of Persian rulers named Abbas, I get to these two familiar faces. But any sense of relief fades when I learn about their sketchy past. Turns out that the famed partnership began when Costello's regular straight man fell ill during a gig at the Empire Theater in New York, and Abbott—who was working the theater's box office—offered to substitute. It went so well, Abbott became Costello's permanent partner. This is not a heartwarming story; it's a cautionary tale. I'm never calling in sick again. I don't want to come back after a twenty-four-hour flu and find Robbie from the mail room volunteered to be the senior editor. It's a tough world.

ABO blood group

Stomach cancer is 20 percent more common in people with type A blood than those with type B or type O. That's me, type A. This is even more disturbing than the tale of the backstabbing Costello. Clearly, I have to be prepared to learn some things I don't like.

Absalom

Absalom, a biblical character, has the oddest death so far in the encyclopedia. During a battle in the forest, Absalom got his flowing hair caught in the branches of an oak tree, which allowed his enemy, Joab, to catch him and slay him. This, I figure, is exactly why the army requires crew cuts.

Acoemeti

A group of monks who provided nonstop choral singing in the 5th century. They did it with a relay system—every few hours, a fresh monk would replace the exhausted monk. I love this image, though I am glad I wasn't their neighbor. We're talking twenty-four-hour entertainment long before MTV went on the air. Quite possibly before Mick Jagger was born.

Addled Brain Syndrome

Okay, I made that up. There's no such thing as addled brain syndrome. But I'm definitely suffering from something. As I vacuum up this information hour after hour, I find myself so overwhelmed that I have to take frequent breaks to walk around the office. Walk it off, as my gym teachers used to say. You only sprained that brain. It's not a fracture. Walk it off, son.

The reading is much, much harder than I expected. But at the same time, in some ways, it's strangely easier. In some ways, it's the perfect book for someone like me, who grew up with Peter Gabriel videos, who has the attention span of a gnat on methamphetamines. Each essay is a bite-sized nugget. Bored with Abilene, Texas? Here comes abolitionism. Tired of that? Not to worry, the Abominable Snowman's lurking right around the corner (by the way, the mythical Snowman's footprints are actually produced by running bears). Reading the *Britannica* is like channel surfing on a very highbrow cable system, one with no shortage of shows about Sumerian cities.

The changes are so abrupt and relentless, you can't help but get mental whiplash. You go from depressing to uplifting, from tiny to cosmic, from ancient to modern. There's no segue, no local news anchor to tell you, "And now, on the lighter side." Just a little white space, and boom, you've switched from theology to worm behavior. But I don't mind. Bring on the whiplash—the odder the juxtapositions, the better. That's the way reality is—a bizarre, jumbled-up Cobb salad. I love seeing the prophet Abraham rub elbows with Karl Abraham, a German shrink who theorized about the anal expulsive and phallic stages.

Oh yes, that's another thing. Sex. This came as a pleasant surprise to me. The *Britannica* may not be Cinemax, but it's got its fair share of randiness. I've learned, for instance, that Eskimos swap wives. Plus, the Achagua men have three to four spouses and flowers in the Acanthaceae family are bisexual. Yowza! That's some racy stuff. Hot. Hotter than the Schwertbad-Quelle sulfur spring. I expected the *Britannica* to be prudish, but it seems quite happy to acknowledge the seamy world below the belt.

And speaking of titillating R-rated material, my God—the violence! It's extraordinary how blood-soaked our history is. One Persian politician was strangled by servants, another suffocated in a steam bath. Or consider poor Peter Abelard, an 11th-century Christian theologian who, judging from his miniature portrait, looks a bit like Steve Buscemi. Abelard came up with some interesting ideas—namely that deeds don't matter, only intentions; in other words, the road to heaven is paved with good intentions. But how can I give much deep thought to that idea when the entry also discusses Abelard's love affair with his student Heloise, which ended rather badly: Abelard suffered castration at the order of Heloise's outraged uncle. Sweet Jesus! I'm guessing Heloise didn't get asked on a whole lot of dates after that one.

Sex, violence, MTV pacing—all this makes my quest much more palatable. But I don't mean to give the wrong idea. As I said, it's hard. Excruciatingly hard. First, the vastness of it. I knew there was an ocean of information out there. But I didn't really comprehend what I was up against until I started trying to drink that ocean cup by cup. I'll be reading about Addis Ababa, the capital of Ethiopia, and I'll get a list of the seven different ethnicities that make up that city: Gallas, Gurages, Hareris, Tigres, Walamos, Somalis, and Dorses. Should I even try to memorize those? Six ethnicities I could handle, but seven? That's daunting.

The *Britannica* is not a book you can skim. This is a book you have to hunch over and pay full attention to, like needlepoint or splinter removal. It hurts my poor little head. Until now, I didn't realize quite how out of shape my brain had become. It's just not accustomed to this kind of thinking. I feel like I'm making it run a triathlon in ninety-degree heat when it's used to sitting in a hammock drinking *mojitos*. The math and science parts of my brain have gone particularly flabby since college. At most, I have to calculate the number of subway rides I have remaining on my little electronic Metrocard. That rarely requires quadratic equations. At my job, the toughest science I've encountered was the time I had to edit a few sentences about Botox for men. So when I read about acid-base reactions with conjugate bases and nonaqueous solvents, I'm mystified. I generally read this type of stuff again and again and just hope it'll sink in. It's the same strategy that American tourists in Europe employ when confronted with a non-English-speaking store owner. *Umbrella. Um-brella! Um-BREL-la!* Say it often and loud enough, and it'll click. But I forge on.

Alcott, Bronson

The father of novelist Louisa May Alcott was famous in his own right. A radical reformer full of unorthodox ideas, he opened several schools for children. The schools had a particularly unusual discipline system: teachers received punishment at the hands of the offending pupil. The idea was that this would instill a sense of shame in the mind of the errant child. Now, this is a brilliant concept. I have a long list of teachers I wish I could have spanked, among them my fifth-grade instructor, Ms. Barker, who forced us to have a sugar-free bake sale, which earned us a humiliating $1.53.

Alger, Horatio

I knew he was the 19th-century author of the famous rags-to-riches novels. I didn't know he turned to writing after being kicked out of a Massachusetts church for allegations of sexual misconduct with local boys. I told you—the *Britannica* can be a gossip rag.

amethyst

One of my biggest challenges is figuring out how to shoehorn my newfound knowledge into conversations. Naturally, I want to show off, but I can't just start reeling off facts or I'll be as annoying as an Acarina, a type of mite that, incidentally, copulates by transferring little packets of sperm called spermatophores.

And since I've read only entries in the very early *As*, my new topics of expertise don't come up that often. You'd be surprised at how many days can go by without one of my friends mentioning aardvarks, much less aardwolves—an African carnivore that the *Britannica* generously describes as "harmless and shy."

But today I had my first successful reference. Well, I don't know if it was actually successful. Okay, it was spectacularly unsuccessful. A total failure. But it was a start.

I'm in my office with a writer, and I need to give him a deadline for his piece.

"Can you get it to me Tuesday?"

"How about Wednesday?" he says.

"Okay. But Wednesday is the latest. Otherwise, I'll be angry. I'll have to rip you more assholes than an abalone."

Puzzled look.

"Abalones are a type of snail with five assholes."

Silence.

"They've got a row of holes in their shells, and five of them serve as outlets for waste."

Silence. Annoyed look.

I thought it was an amusing little tidbit, a nice twist on the cliché, a clever way to make it clear that I really needed the article. Instead, I came off like a colossal outlet for waste.

I figure it'll be easier to show off my increasing intelligence in a relaxed social environment. So when Julie and I go to her friends' house for dinner that night, I am prepared to dazzle. We arrive at Shannon and David's apartment, exchange cheek kisses and "Great to see you's."

"Brrrrr," says Julie as she unbundles her several layers of winter wear.

"A little nippy out there, huh?" says Shannon.

"Not quite as cold as Antarctica's Vostok Station, which reached a record 128 degrees below zero," I reply. "But still cold."

Shannon chuckles politely.

We sit down in the living room and Shannon starts telling Julie about her upcoming vacation in Saint Bart's.

"I'm so jealous," says Julie.

"Yeah, I can't wait to get some sun," Shannon says. "Look how white I am."

"Albinism affects one in twenty thousand Americans," I say.

Shannon doesn't quite know how to respond to that one.

"Anyhoo," says Julie, "where are you staying?"

I probably shouldn't have said my albinism fact, but I can't help it. I'm so loaded up with information that when I see a hole—even if it's a small hole, even a microscopic hole, the size of an abalone's butt hole—I have to dive right in.

David returns from the kitchen with a bottle of wine.

"Anyone want some cabernet?"

"I'll have a glass," says Julie.

"I'll have some too," I say. "And an amethyst if you've got one."

David cocks his head.

"Amethysts protect against drunkenness, according to the ancients," I say.

"Is that so?" says David.

"Yes. I don't want to end up like Alexander the Great, who died after getting ill from a drinking bout."

"No, I suppose not," says David. He laughs. Nervously, I think.

Julie turns back to Shannon, hoping to resume the vacation talk. "So, which hotel?"

"We've got reservations at this place I found in *Conde Nast Traveler*—"

"Also, speaking of alcohol consumption," I say, "what country do you think has the highest per capita rate? I'll give you a hint: it's not Ireland."

"Hmm. Is it France?" asks Shannon. She's very polite.

"Nope. Not France. The residents of Luxembourg are the biggest boozers in the world."

"Huh."

"Who woulda thunk?" I ask. "Luxembourg! But seriously, do not get between a Luxembourgian and a bottle of whiskey!" I say, shaking my head and laughing.

Part of me is hoping Shannon and David won't notice that all my facts start with *A*. But at the same time, I'm also kind of longing to be exposed. I've already logged thirty hours reading my encyclopedia, and I want them to ooh and aaah at my accomplishment. Maybe Julie senses this, or maybe she just wants to avoid further embarrassment, but she decides to spill my secret.

"A.J.'s decided to read the encyclopedia," she tells Shannon. "And he's only in the *A*s, so you'll be hearing a lot of *A* facts."

"The encyclopedia?" says David. "That's some light reading."

"Yeah, it'll be good on the beach," I say.

"Seriously, why are you reading the encyclopedia?" says Shannon.

I had prepared for this. I had my answer.

"Well, there's an African folktale I think is relevant here. Once upon a time, there's this tortoise who steals a gourd that contains all the knowledge of the world. He hangs it around his neck. When he comes to a tree trunk lying across road, he can't climb over it because the gourd is in his way. He's in such a hurry to get home, he smashes the gourd. And ever since, wisdom has been scattered across the world in tiny pieces. So, I want to try to gather all that wisdom and put it together."

"I guess you're not up to *P*, for 'Please shut up,' " says Julie.

They all laugh at that one.

Arabian horses

Next morning, it's back to my daily dose of *Britannica*. Arabian horses have twenty-three vertebrae instead of the twenty-four found in most horses. I spend a moment trying to think of a situation in which this information might be useful. Maybe I could write a mystery story where the identification of an Arabian horse skeleton is a major plot point. Maybe I could win a bar bet with a moderately—but not overly—knowledgeable equestrian. Who knows?

Asimov, Isaac

I was aware that Asimov was a major figure in American literature, the author of numerous science fiction and science books. I didn't know just how many books: about five hundred. The man wrote five hundred books. I don't think I've written five hundred Post-it notes. He wrote so many books, even his biographers are reduced to the vague "about five hundred." The *Britannica* can be depressing that way. As you read accomplishment after accomplishment, Nobel after Nobel, you are reminded just how little you've done with your life. My entry—if written today—would look something like this:

Jacobs, Arnold "A.J." (b. March 20, 1968, New York, N.Y.)
A minor figure in 20th-century American journalism. Jacobs attended Brown University, where he studied philosophy, attracted to the discipline because it required the lowest number of course credits necessary to graduate. Upon receiving his degree, he began his career writing articles for *Dental Economics*, the leading publication covering financial matters for dentists and orthodontists. He later established his reputation with a prescient sidebar in the pop culture magazine *Entertainment Weekly* comparing O. J. Simpson and Homer Simpson, which received great acclaim across America, or at least within the home of his parents. He met many of the midlevel show business figures of his day, including Bill Maher and Sarah Michelle Gellar, neither of whom knew his name.

In 2000, Jacobs married Julie Schoenberg, a vivacious advertising sales representative also working at *Entertainment Weekly*. The marriage was apparently a happy one, despite the fact that Jacobs whined whenever Schoenberg suggested maybe he should put on pants because they were going to a nice restaurant.

Jacobs's other achievements include folding napkins into such shapes as a rabbit and a hat. See also: hypochondria and germaphobe.

I think the Asimov entry stings all the more because I have a quasi Asimov in my own family. My dad—in his spare time, just for fun—writes legal books, and has so far published twenty-four of them. These are serious volumes, books with titles like *The Impact of Rule 10b-5* and *Disclosures and Remedies Under the Securities Law*. He specializes in laws on insider trading, the kind that Martha Stewart was investigated for breaking, launching a thousand riffs on ways she might redecorate her jail cell.

The other day, I was over at my parents' house for lunch, and I figured, since I am trying to finish my dad's quest, I should take a look at his books. So after the meal, I wandered into his study and was confronted with those twenty-four tomes. A big, sagging shelf of them.

I haven't picked one up in years, not since I was fourteen. Back then, I used to enjoy the first volume of *The Impact of Rule 10b-5*, mainly because my dad had inserted a *Playboy* centerfold into a half dozen copies to send to friends as a joke. He had kept one of these customized copies for himself. So that was probably the closest I came to going to law school—studying the case of Miss January's missing ballet tutu.

This time, I figure I should read words other than "Turn-ons: champagne, walks on the beach, and men who can help my acting career." I pick up *The Impact of Rule 10b-5* and read a sentence thick with words like "fiduciary" and "annuity plan" and "corpus." No comprehension; it could be random ink splatters on the page and I would have had the same level of understanding.

I flip to the middle of the book. As expected, the pages are heavy with footnotes. Really heavy. Some pages have just a couple of lines of regular text floating at the top, then a sea of footnotes all the way down. I guess footnotes isn't the right word when they get this abundant—more like shouldernotes or foreheadnotes.

My father is proud of his footnotes. A few years ago, he broke the world's record for most footnotes in a legal article, coming in at an impressive 1,247. Soon after that, a California legal professor topped my dad's record with 1,611 footnotes. My dad didn't stand for that. He wrote another legal article and just crushed his opponent. Squashed him with 4,824 footnotes, ensuring his status as the Wayne Gretzky of footnotes. My dad tried to get the *Guinness Book of World Records* interested, but legal footnotes apparently don't get the same respect as fingernails the size of adult rattlesnakes. So he had to settle for a mention in *Harper's Index*.

I flip to Dad's own index to see if I recognize any words. More dense Latinate legalese. And then I spot this entry: "Birds, for the, 1–894." My mother had once told me about that joke of Dad's, but I had forgotten about it. One of his better ones. But my Lord, 894 pages of text in just one volume—that's no joke. No wonder he gave up reading the *Britannica*—he was writing his own encyclopedia.

This investigation into my dad's oeuvre wasn't particularly good for my self-esteem. The scope and denseness of his work—those were both envy inducing. But that's not to mention that my dad has made himself the expert on insider trading. Not *an* expert. *The* expert. What had I made myself an expert on? The plot lines of the various *Police Academy* movies? Not even that. Though I haven't read the *Britannica*'s write-up of psychoanalysis, I figure my dad's accomplishments have something to do with my quest to finish the encyclopedia. If I can't beat my dad on depth, at least I can get him on breadth.

assault and battery

They're always lumped together, but there is a difference. Assault is the *attempt* to apply force, battery is the actual application. Look at that—I'm already getting a legal education. Almost ready for the bar exam.

atrophy

A very troubling entry—all the ways my body is crumbling. The bones are becoming lighter and more porous. Muscles are shriveling. And worst of all, age leads to a striking decrease in the number of living cells in my cerebral cortex. Every day, my brain's surface ridges shrink and the skull fluid swells to fill the space.

The *Britannica*'s passages on evaporating cortexes would disturb most people, but I'm particularly rattled; oddly enough, I've had a long history of grappling with a fear of brain damage. I might as well get this out on the table now. I mentioned earlier on that, growing up, I thought I was smart. Well, that wasn't exactly the whole story. I didn't just think that I was smart. I thought that I was *really* smart. I thought that I was, in fact, the smartest boy in the world.

I'm honestly not sure how this notion popped into my head. My mom probably had something to do with it, seeing as she was only slightly less enamored of me than I was of myself. And it's true, I did pretty well on tests, sometimes notching up the highest score in the class. As my mom likes to remind me, on one geography quiz, I got so cocky, I wrote "New Joizy" instead of "New Jersey." Ha! In any case, with my handful of good fourth-grade test scores as evidence, I somehow made the logical deduction that no other ten-year-old on planet Earth was my intellectual equal. It's a leap, yes. But in my defense, I hadn't taken any high-level statistics courses. At the time, it just somehow made sense. I could just feel that I was unique in some way (again, my mom told me so). And since I wasn't the best-looking boy or the best hockey player or the best glee club singer, that left intelligence. So what if I didn't always get the highest score? Or even very often? That could be explained away. Maybe I wasn't trying, or maybe the other kids cheated. Deep down, I knew I was top intellectual dog.

Let me tell you, though: being the smartest boy in the world wasn't easy. I didn't ask for this. I didn't want this. On the contrary, it was a huge burden. First, there was the task of keeping my brain perfectly protected. My cerebral cortex was a national treasure, a masterpiece, the Sistine Chapel of brains. This was not something that could be treated frivolously. If I could have locked it in a safe, I would have. Instead, I became obsessed with brain damage.

Danger lurked everywhere. If my skull was touched, that might jostle the brain and squash a few valuable dendrites. So no one was allowed contact with anything above my neck—that was the holy of holies. No friendly pats on the head. No soccer, with its insane practice of bonking the ball on your pate. And if Grandma came in for a kiss on the forehead, I would dart my head like Sugar Ray Leonard. If I'd known then about the annelid worm—which can turn its skin cells into brain cells—I would have been extremely jealous.

Even seeing other people get brain damage flustered me. When I was eleven, I went to the movie *Hair* with my mother at New York's Ziegfeld Theater, and was horrified to watch Treat Williams and his unshowered cohorts smoking pot in a Central Park tunnel. I could almost hear their poor brain cells scream for mercy. "Can we go?" I asked my mom before the first "Aquarius" refrain. "I don't feel so good."

Drug-addled musicals aside, the thing that really unhinged me was car rides. My fourth-grade biology teacher told us that the carbon monoxide produced by cars can cause brain damage. That was it, just a throwaway line inserted into a lecture on mammalian bloodstreams. But to me, carbon monoxide became the number one enemy, my white whale, the Joab to my Absalom.

I became a window Nazi. A window had to be cracked at all times so that my brain could get fresh oxygen to dilute that nefarious carbon monoxide. It could be forty below zero and we could be driving through Vostok Station; I'd still roll down the glass in the backseat of the Plymouth Valiant.

"Can you please shut that? It's really cold," said Mom.

"Just a little fresh air, Mom," I'd say.

"That fresh air is freezing my eyelids together."

"Roll up the window, A.J.," my dad said.

I'd roll it up. I'd wait about two minutes, till the conversation had drifted to some other topic, like which fast food chain most deserved our patronage, then I'd slowly—in barely noticeable spurts—lower the window again.

"Dammit, A.J.!" my mom would say, as her lower lip turned cobalt blue. "Please put up the window."

I was smart enough to know that I shouldn't tell anyone the reason I needed that icy air. No need to spill the secret that I was the genius of all geniuses, the Leonardo da Vinci of the 1980s. That would just inspire envy and skepticism. So I'd just stare at the closed window and stew. If ten minutes went by without my lungs getting fresh air, I panicked. I needed to make sure the monoxide hadn't eaten my cranium. For some reason, and this continues to baffle me, I thought the best way to test whether my mind was still in peak form was to create new and bizarre racquet sports. That was my homespun IQ test. So I made up racquet sports involving big racquets, tiny racquets, balls the size of refrigerators, balls the size of pencil erasers. There were racquet sports involving garage doors, bathroom sinks, and telecommunications satellites. Strange, I know. But it made me feel better.

Not counting my vigilance against brain damage, there were plenty of other strains associated with being the smartest boy in the world. It was a huge responsibility, nurturing this amazing organ of mine. I knew someday soon I'd have to invent something, cure something, or write something of grand significance. I knew I should be feeding my mind the highest-quality nourishment, like physics textbooks or Dostoyevsky, but instead I was keeping it on a starvation diet by watching *Gilligan's Island* reruns. Even back then, I had trouble resisting pop culture's pull. I felt guilty every time I watched those hapless castaways. Not that it stopped me, but I just couldn't enjoy Thurston Howell's lockjaw one-liners like my lucky bastard classmates with their slightly above-average intelligence.

I remember the day I decided I wasn't the smartest boy in the world. I was watching TV—not sitcom reruns, for once, but a documentary on Hasidic Jews. The footage showed a room of young Hasidic boys about the same age as I was, at their desks, their noses buried in books. The narrator intoned that these boys studied for sixteen hours a day. I was blown away. Sixteen hours a day! My God. Even though I knew I had the initial advantage of the highest-quality brain, these boys studied so much, they must have pulled several lengths ahead of me in the intelligence horse race. I just couldn't compete with sixteen hours a day. This was an immense relief. A whole new day. I started watching Gilligan and Ginger and all the rest with impunity.

In the years that followed, I became increasingly less impressed with my own intelligence. My perceived place on the bell curve drifted farther and farther to the left. I went from being, in my mind, much smarter than my dad to a little smarter, to just as smart, and then, finally—if I had to guess when, it'd be somewhere in my freshman or sophomore year at college—less smart than my dad, the author of those imposing twenty-four books.

In retrospect, the revelation about my intelligence—the one inspired by the studious Hasidic boys—wasn't exactly the product of flawless logic. There's not a perfect correlation between hours of reading and intelligence. Perhaps there's very little correlation at all. Of course, I do realize I'm committing the same fallacy right now, twenty-three years later. Deep down, I know that reading the encyclopedia and jamming my brain full of facts won't necessarily allow me to reclaim my title as the smartest person alive. I know my quest is a bit of a lark. I know it's got a whiff—or maybe more than a whiff—of the absurd.

And just in case I didn't know, I'm constantly being told this by friends and family. My aunt Marti, who lives in Berkeley and is always ready to voice her skepticism, whether it's about our phallocentric government or our reliance on oppressive Western medicine, confronted me in a phone call the other day.

"Now, why are you reading the encyclopedia again?"

"I'm trying to become the smartest man in the world."

"And how are you defining intelligence? Just the amount of information you have?"

"Yup."

"Well, that's not very intelligent."

"Well, I haven't gotten to the letter *I*."

It's an easy response, but there's something to it. I'm not so deluded that I think I'll gain one IQ point for every thousand pages. I don't honestly think that the folks from the MacArthur genius grant will be kicking down my door. But I also believe that there is *some* link between knowledge and intelligence. Maybe knowledge is the fuel and intelligence is the car? Maybe facts are the flying buttresses and intelligence is the cathedral?

I don't know the exact relation. But I'm sure the *Britannica*, somewhere in those 44 million words, will help me figure it out.

augury

You can predict the future based on dice (cleromancy), dots on paper (geomancy), fire and smoke (pyromancy), entrails of sacrificed animals (haruspicy), animal livers (hepatoscopy), or shoulder blades of animals (scapulimancy). They had me up until the crazy shoulder blades part.

Aztec

The *A*'s have been lousy with Aztecs. They popped up under all sorts of headings, including *American Peoples, Arts of Native* and *Alcohol and Drug Consumption* (they called magic mushrooms "God's flesh"). And here they are again, under plain old *Aztec*. Thanks to the *Britannica*, I now know the Aztecs prophesied the destruction of the earth followed by an age when humans become monkeys. Hey, that's the plot of *Planet of the Apes*! Damn you, Hollywood! You stole the idea from the Aztecs. Damn you to hell!

I polish off the monkey-fixated Aztecs, and just like that, I'm done with the *A*'s. It's been two weeks, and I am now one twenty-sixth of my way to the summit. I have absorbed 3.8 percent of all the knowledge in the world. I slam my *Britannica* shut and do a little touchdown dance. Yes! I am the alpha male.

And yet, do I feel smarter? Have I proved my skeptical aunt Marti wrong yet? Well, I do know a lot more information, but in a way, I'm feeling more insecure than ever. I'm worried I'm not intelligent enough to process all my data into some coherent conclusion or worldview. I'm worried I'm not focusing on the right things. Take Aristotle. Here's one of the great philosophers of all time. I should be drinking in his theories on morality and epistemology. Instead, I'm fascinated by Aristotle's obscure maxim about marriage: that men should be thirty-seven and women should be eighteen when they take their vows. Aristotle came up with that theory because—now here's an odd coincidence—when he was thirty-seven he married an eighteen-year-old woman. I like that he rationalized his dirty-old-man behavior with a grand philosophical statement. There are a lot of Aristotelians in Hollywood, I chuckle to myself. So that's the profound conclusion I draw from the essay on Aristotle. That he likes young ladies.

Maybe by the end of the *B*s I'll be smart enough to concentrate on the Big Picture.

B

Bacon, Francis

I am making sacrifices in my quest for knowledge. No one can argue with that. I wake up early, about 7 A.M., which is the middle of the night for most journalists. I read in the morning, I read at night. I'm on the verge of losing a half dozen friends because I've got no time to call them back. And worst of all, I've missed several hours of crucial television, including what Julie tells me was a particularly riveting *Real World* episode in which an enraged girl throws a fork at another cast member.

So it's tough, this pursuit of intelligence. But I feel humbled by Sir Francis Bacon, who made the ultimate sacrifice. He died in the quest for knowledge, a martyr to the cause.

I hadn't remembered much about Bacon from school, except that he's suspected by some to be the real Shakespeare. Also, he wore a huge ruffled collar. So, as you can see, it was nice to get a refresher course.

I learned Bacon—a 17th-century intellectual and politician—had a troubled public life. He was convicted of taking bribes in 1621 and thrown in the Tower of London. His defense: yes, he took the bribes, but they didn't affect his judgment (not his best moment). As a scholar, he wrote cleverly about language and the philosophy of science.

But my favorite fact about Bacon, the one that will stick with me, is how he died. It happened in March of 1626, north of London. Bacon was riding along in his horse and carriage when he suddenly decided he needed to know whether snow delays putrefaction. So he abruptly stopped his carriage, hopped out to buy a hen, and stuffed it with snow.

Unfortunately, this caused him to be seized with a sudden chill, which brought on bronchitis, and he died soon after at a friend's house.

This, to me, is a noble anecdote. Okay, it's a little embarrassing that his death involved frozen poultry. And maybe he displayed a touch of sadism—I'm just hoping the poor hen wasn't alive when he rammed snow into its gullet. But there's also something great about it. Bacon had such an itch for knowledge, he was so giddy about an idea, that he just went bonkers and bolted out of his carriage. The man couldn't wait another *second* to find out more about antiputrefaction techniques. I find this inspiring. If you're going to give your life for a cause, furtherance of knowledge has got to be in the top two or three. In Bacon's honor, I put down the *Britannica* and go defrost a frozen bagel in the microwave.

baculum

This is the official name for a penis bone. The baculum can be found in hedgehogs, shrews, and bats. Interesting. I had no idea. The only time I'd ever even encountered the concept of a penis bone was during conversations with my college friend Ileana. Ileana had a very casual relationship with the truth. She liked to tell me stories about the pet llamas in her New York apartment, and her father's love affair with singer Robert Goulet. And once, she told me a detailed story about how her brother had broken his penis bone. He had been standing naked in front of an open window admiring the view from his hotel room, when—whoom—the window slid down and snapped his penis bone right in half.

"It's been three months, and he still has to wear the penis cast," she told me. "I was the first one to sign it."

"But Ileana," I said, "the penis doesn't have a bone."

"Oh," she said. That was it—no apology, no attempt at backtracking, just an "oh." Now, after reading about the baculum, I realize that Ileana's brother was probably a hedgehog.

baldness

My newfound knowledge bubbles up in my brain at strange times. In the elevator up to work, I stood behind an Asian man who happened to be bald. That's odd, I thought to myself. According to the encyclopedia, baldness in Asians is rare. It's rare in Asians and Native Americans. I guess what we have here is one of the unlucky few Asians who couldn't hold on to his follicles. I feel like giving him my condolences.

Barnum, P. T.

When he was eighty-one, Barnum fell gravely ill. At his request, a New York newspaper printed his obituary in advance so that he might enjoy it. That's brilliant. In fact, that could be a nice new revenue stream for newspapers—they could sell obits to people on their deathbeds. The encyclopedia is giving me lots of good ideas.

bearbaiting

A popular form of entertainment in 16th-century England. A bear was tied to a stake, and trained dogs were set upon it. Other variations included a bull tied to a stake and a pony with an ape tied to his back. Sounds like Fox has itself a new TV show!

bedlam

My growing collection of facts keeps overlapping with my life. I knew it would happen, but I'm surprised at the frequency. Several times an hour, a little internal "ding" goes off in my mind. I step into the bathtub for a shower, and I flash to the 17th-century health clinics where people stayed in baths for days at a time. I have my cereal, and I'm reminded of the world's longest breakfast table, in Battle Creek, Michigan. I read about a Boy Scouts controversy in the newspaper and I think of the scout movement's founder, Robert Baden-Powell, who also, incidentally, pioneered the use of hot-air balloons in military spying.

These little sparks happen so often that I couldn't possibly work them all into conversation. Which, I'm sure, is a great relief to those around me. But I can mention some of them—and I do. Like today at the office.

I wander in to chat with my fellow editor Mark. Mark is the office intellectual—a tall, brilliant Texan with a floppy Hugh Grant haircut. He's been working at *Esquire* an astounding fourteen years, a fact that causes plenty of amusement among the rest of the staff. "Mark, weren't you Hemingway's editor?" "Mark, were you at the Rita Hayworth photo shoot?" That kind of thing.

So I make my way into Mark's office, which is difficult, since he hasn't thrown away a book in his fourteen years. The floor is covered with waist-high piles of volumes by Philip Roth and Saul Bellow. It's bedlam in there (a word, by the way, that comes from Bethlehem Royal Hospital, a notorious London insane asylum).

"So that was a great event last night," I say.

"A really great event," agrees Mark.

The previous night we had been to an *Esquire* function that featured a speech by a budding politician named Cory Booker. Cory spoke passionately about the inner city, and ended his speech with a long, inspiring quote from James Baldwin.

"God, you have to love that James Baldwin quote."

"One of *Esquire*'s own, that James Baldwin," says Mark. Having been at *Esquire* since the quill pen era, Mark has also become the office historian.

"Really?" I say. "I didn't know that."

"Yes, *Esquire* published 'The Fire Next Time.' "

Huh? I had just read the Baldwin essay in the encyclopedia, and I happen to remember that "The Fire Next Time"—Baldwin's groundbreaking article on civil rights—first appeared in *The New Yorker*. Usually, I keep my mouth clamped and listen in awe to Mark. He's a great talker—he often speaks in full paragraphs— and he knows his stuff, especially about magazine history. But this particular fact he did not know. And this was an opportunity I couldn't pass up.

"Actually, I think that appeared in *The New Yorker*," I say.

"No, it was *Esquire*."

"No, I'm pretty sure it's *The New Yorker*."

"It wasn't *The New Yorker*," says Mark. Then he wavers: "Well, maybe it was *The Progressive*. But it certainly wasn't *The New Yorker*."

I scurry back to my office and look up Baldwin on the Internet. Yup. "The Fire Next Time" appeared in *The New Yorker*. I e-mail Mark the news, concluding my note with some helpful advice: "Also, if you have any questions for Bavarian cream pie or beavers, just let me know."

So I had done it. I had made my first correction, and I corrected a brilliant man, to boot. I felt great. Well, actually I felt like kind of a dick. But also great.

bell

Back to the books. The world's largest bell was built in 1733 in Moscow, and weighed in at more than four hundred thousand pounds. It never rang—it was broken by fire before it could be struck. What a sad little story. All that work, all that planning, all those expectations—then nothing. Now it just sits there in Russia, a big metallic symbol of failure. I have a moment of silence for the silent bell.

Bentham, Jeremy

The British ethical philosopher—who advocated the greatest good for the greatest number of people—died in 1832. "After Bentham's death, in accordance with his directions, his body was dissected in the presence of his friends. The skeleton was then reconstructed, supplied with a wax head to replace the original (which had been mummified), dressed in Bentham's own clothes, and set upright in a glass-fronted case. Both this effigy and the head are preserved in University College, London." Not sure how that contributes to the greater good of mankind. The greater creepiness, yes.

Berserkers

Savage Norse soldiers from the middle ages who, it is said, went into battle naked. Hence "going berserk." So to truly go berserk, you should take off your pants. Noted.

Beuys, Joseph

A German avant-garde performance artist whose most famous piece was entitled *How to Explain Pictures to a Dead Hare*. For the piece, "Beuys covered his head with honey and gold leaf, wore one shoe soled with felt and one with iron, and walked through an art gallery for about two hours, quietly explaining the art therein to a dead hare he carried."

Huh. And for this he gets himself written up in the encyclopedia. Maybe I'm a philistine, but I don't see the brilliance of this. If he explained pictures to a dead hamster or a dead iguana—yes, *that* would be ingenious. But a dead hare? Eh. Feels lazy.

birth control

The condom, according to legend, was invented by a British physician named Dr. Condom, who was alarmed by Charles II's growing flock of illegitimate offspring. That's the legend, anyway. The sober *Britannica* instead endorses the theory that the condom is named for the Latin word *condus*, which means a receptacle. The condom, the pill, the IUD, the vasectomy—they all get their proper due in this section. But I prefer the creativity of the earlier birth control techniques, which ranged from the delicious (using honey as a spermicide) to the aerobic (jumping backward seven times after coitus).

Those are good to know. Very relevant. I tell Julie not to jump backward seven times after sex and to keep honey safely above her belt. We can't afford any mishaps. For the past year, Julie and I have been trying to have a baby. We're getting a bit desperate. It doesn't help that all of Julie's friends are breeding like the female octopus, which lays and cares for 150,000 eggs. They're frighteningly fertile, her friends. They seem to get pregnant if they brush up against their husbands in the hallway. Which means there's a growing platoon of diaper-wearing creatures stomping through our lives, and an accompanying fleet of fold-up strollers and car seats. Meanwhile, Julie and I have nothing. Zilch. It's infuriating.

And it's not for want of effort. We follow her ovulations like a day trader follows the Nasdaq. She takes her temperature every morning, she makes charts and notes and annotations. Spreadsheets are involved. Still, bubkes. The *Britannica* points out that despite the widespread myth, women don't need orgasms to conceive. Which is a very good thing for us, because at this point, our sex life has become about as erotic as artificial respiration (which, by the way, should be given at a rate of twelve breaths per minute).

I suppose the world isn't screaming out for another child. Each week, the *Britannica* says, 1.4 million more people are born into this world than leave it. But I can't help it—I really want one of those little drooling, burping eight-pound creatures. I didn't expect to want a kid this badly, but I do. I yearn to be a dad.

Not that I'm ready. I'm pretty sure I'm way too self-absorbed and im- mature—and ignorant. When I was growing up, my father knew the an- swers to all the Frequently Asked Children's Questions: How far down does dirt go? Why don't the Chinese fall off the earth? Why do the leaves change color? He knew how things worked—why the fridge was cold, how the water got to our sink. I've forgotten all that knowledge. Maybe I'll feel better at *Z.*

bobsledding
The name comes from the early—and probably mistaken—belief that if the sledders bobbed their heads back and forth, it would increase the speed. Okay, ready for the sports bar.

book
The United Nations defines a book as a text that is at least forty-nine pages long. By that definition, the *Britannica* equals 673 books. Unsettling.

Braille, Louis

Just as unsettling: the number of prodigies in the *Britannica*. Braille developed his writing system for the blind at age fifteen. Bentham—the one who later had himself mummified—was studying Latin at the age of four. (When I was four, I was studying the effects of shoving bananas up my nose.) At age five, Aleksandr Blok was writing memorable Russian poetry. If I had known about these whiz kids back when I thought I was the smartest boy in the world, I wonder if I would have seen them as compadres, or if it would have snapped me out of my dream.

brain

Here, the ovoid tangle of neurons that, I hope, will be encoding every mountain range and vice president and 15th-century Icelandic bishop. The *Britannica*'s brain-related highlights so far: the Greeks believed that it produced mucus, which gives new meaning to blowing your brains out. Also, if I ever take up boxing, I should do the old bare-knuckle style, which ironically causes less devastation to the neurons. (Bare-knuckle boxers rarely hit on the head for fear of breaking their hands.) With my mortal fear of brain damage, this is important information.

brandy

This liquor was allegedly invented when a Dutch shipmaster concentrated wine, planning to add water to it when he arrived on shore. He never got a chance. Everyone started dipping into the concentrate. Impatience has its advantages.

broccoli

Julie and I arrive at my parents' apartment for the holiday gift exchange. It's sort of Hanukkah-related, but since we're not so religious, we throw a nod to New Year's for good measure.

Mom greets us at the door.

"Happy Holidays!" she says, giving us each a kiss on the cheek. "And Happy 2003."

"Actually, technically, it's probably 'Happy 2007,' " I say.

"Really?" says Mom. "Why is that?"

"Well, because scientists believe Jesus was actually born between 4 and 6 B.C."

By this time, Julie has long since departed for the safety of the living room. But Mom, being my mom, is stuck listening. She's supportive of everything I do, not counting the time my sister and I took hang gliding lessons from a Deadhead or all those open car windows in arctic temperatures.

I explain to Mom that the Bible talks about Jesus' birth coinciding with the Star of Bethlehem, which wasn't a star at all, but an astronomical phenomenon. It was either a nova that occurred in 5 B.C. or the combined light of Mars, Jupiter, and Saturn, which all nearly lined up in 6 B.C.

"Well, then, Happy 2007," she says.

God bless Mom. I have to remember to hang out with her more often.

As for the gift exchange, I get a sweater and some pants. My sister Beryl and her husband, Willy, give me a couple books that I can't even imagine reading until 2008 or so.

Julie—a master gift buyer—had scoured catalogues and stores to get my family exceedingly appropriate presents. I was happy to take partial credit. In my defense, I did help write the cards, including my masterpiece, the one to Beryl, which started: "Dear $Be_3Al_2(SiO_3)_6$."

"This is for me, right?" Beryl asks.

"Yep. That's the chemical symbol for the beryl mineral."

"I thought that might be it."

"One of the largest beryls was found in Brazil—two hundred tons. So compared to that, you're very skinny."

That came out wrong. I had somehow just called my sister fat, which she isn't, and which I would like to take back, but it's too late.

After the gift exchange, we all clean up the mess of wrapping paper and ribbons that has accumulated on the floor.

"So I've officially passed you," I say to my dad, as we take out the holiday detritus. "I'm in the late *B*'s."

"Anything interesting?" he asks.

"I was just reading about broccoli. You know, it's officially classed as a type of cabbage."

My dad nods his head. "I've got a good fact for you," says my dad. "You know the speed of light, right?"

"Yes. 186,000 miles per second."

"Yes, but do you know it in fathoms per fortnight?"

"What?"

"Do you know the speed of light in fathoms per fortnight?"

"Uh, don't think I do."

My dad tells me that he has calculated the speed of light in fathoms per fortnight so that he can be the only person in the world who knows that particular piece of information. That, as my mother would say, is "very Arnie."

"It's 1.98 x 10^{14}" he says.

"Wow. Really fascinating." My tone is definitely snappish, aggressive. My dad looks a little hurt. I'm not sure why I said it the way I did—I guess I felt he'd one-upped me—but it wasn't in the holiday spirit, that's for sure.

bruise

My left eye has turned a bright lobster shell red. I'm not positive it's tied to my exhausting marathon reading sessions, but I like to think it is. I consider it my first *Britannica*-related injury, and I wear it proudly. Though I don't want to go blind like your average early blues singer (Blind Willie McTell, Blind Boy Fuller, Blind Lemon Jefferson), a little manly eyestrain seems appropriate.

Julie got concerned and has bought me several bags of baby carrots to help my rods and cones. Carrots, by the way, are a close cousin of hemlock (both in the Apiaceae family), so I'm hoping Julie didn't mix the two up.

Brutus

I was familiar with Brutus, the one featured in Shakespeare's classic line *"Et tu, Brute."* But what I didn't know was that there were two Brutuses who took part in Caesar's assassination, Brutus Albinus and Brutus Marcus. But only one Brutus—Marcus—gets all the headlines. That poor sap Brutus Albinus—also a protégé of Caesar's—needed a better publicist. *"Et tu, Brute. Et tu, Brute,* too?" I can't be certain, but the forgotten Brutus seems to have been the more powerful one at the time. After the assassination, this Brutus led an army against Antony; he lost, and was killed by a Gallic chieftain on Antony's orders. Ignored by history or killed by a Frenchman—I'm not sure which is sadder.

burial

Here's something I'm learning: what a shockingly conventional thinker I am. Despite my liberal cross-cultural education at Brown, despite my delusion that I can think creatively, I'm realizing that I've been trained to look at life in a very particular way.

Consider burial. I always figured, when you are buried, your body is lying down on its back in the sleeping position. It just seemed natural. It never occurred to me that there were other options on this particular menu. But there are.

The *Britannica* reveals that some early cultures buried their dead in a crouching or squatting position. Also, North American Indians buried their dead in a fetal position, with the knees tucked under the chin and the body neatly tied in a bundle. Other cultures have opted for upright burial, especially for warriors.

This was startling to me. Without even realizing it, I'd always bought into the metaphor that death was the long sleep. But maybe it's not. Maybe it's the long gestation, so you should be in the fetal position. Or maybe it's the long bus ride, so you should be standing.

I like uncovering the cultural prejudices that I didn't even know I had. Maybe these revelations will have a practical application someday. Maybe I'll opt to be buried in the sitting position, remote control in hand. But for now, I feel that I've widened my perspective. And frankly, I feel ever so slightly superior, not only to my former self but to all those losers who think of burial as a horizontal affair. A small but important victory as I finish letter number two.

C

_____

cappuccino

Every once in a while I'll know something more about a topic than the *Britannica* does. Such was the case with with cappuccino. I happen to know that cappuccino got its name from the Capuchin monks, whose robes were light brown, the same color as coffee with steamed milk. Hence cappuccino. This fact was not in the *Britannica*; I learned this from an Italian cab driver when Julie and I went on vacation to the Amalfi coast last year. It's a little thrill to feel like I've got the edge on the *Britannica*—a feeling that vanishes quickly in the ensuing pages, as I'm reminded of my epic ignorance.

Caravaggio

A great, groundbreaking, prolific 17th-century painter—and also a complete jackass. Caravaggio had a terrible temper, sort of the Sean Penn of his day. He got in trouble for tossing a plate of artichokes at a waiter's face. He was arrested for throwing stones at the Roman Guards. And during a brawl over the score of a tennis match, he killed a man. After the murder, Caravaggio fled Rome, hopped from city to city, was arrested, escaped jail, was attacked at the door to an inn, pleaded for clemency from the pope—all the while continuing to paint his great, dark religious paintings. Finally, Caravaggio died of pneumonia—just three days before a document granting him clemency arrived from Rome.

I hate the cliché of the tortured genius, of the temperamental artist—but unfortunately, maybe there's something to it. Is that why I'm not a great artist? I'm not temperamental enough? I don't throw enough plates of vegetables at waitstaff? There's another mystery I hope to crack in the next 31,000 pages.

Casanova

The famous 18th-century lothario ended his life as a librarian. Librarians could use that to sex up their image.

chalk

Chalk used in classrooms is not actually made of chalk, but a manufactured substance. More reason to distrust my teachers, those weasels.

Chang and Eng

The original Siamese twins share a write-up, which is only appropriate. Just as appropriate: the write-up is twice as bizarre as the average *Britannica* fare. I learn that Chang and Eng were born in Siam in 1811 of a Chinese father and a half-Chinese mother. They were joined at the waist by a tubular band about three inches long and one inch in diameter, approximately the size of a D battery. Even as kids, that tube turned them into celebrities, winning them an audience with the king of Siam. In 1829, Chang and Eng went on tour, hitting the United States, Canada, Cuba, and Europe with a British merchant who kept their earnings, as you'd expect of a British merchant who would take anatomically deformed children on tour. After Chang and Eng turned twenty-one, says the *Britannica,* they took charge of their own tours and made themselves a small fortune.

So far, so good—pretty much what I expected. But the next part I wouldn't have guessed: with their money, Chang and Eng settled in Mount Airy, North Carolina, bought some land, adopted the surname Bunker, and took up farming. I like that image—just two farmers named Bunker who happen to share a liver. Their assimilation continued. In April 1843, Chang and Eng married a pair of sisters, Adelaide and Sarah Yates. They had a nice, functional system going. Chang and Eng maintained separate households 1.5 miles apart and alternated three-day visits with their respective spouses. The *Britannica* doesn't explore the bedroom logistics—did Chang pretend to read the sports pages while Eng and Sarah were getting busy? Or did he get to peek if he stayed real quiet? Whatever the routine, it worked—each twin fathered several children. And that wasn't the only physical activity they did—Chang and Eng were expert marksmen, could run quickly and swim well. There was talk when they first arrived in the States about getting surgically separated. Chang and Eng decided against it, not just because of the dangers, but because they adapted so remarkably well to their condition.

During the American Civil War Chang and Eng lost much of their money, and in 1869 they once more went on tour in Europe. Chang, who was moodier than Eng, had begun boozing heavily. And then "in 1870, while returning to the United States from their successful tour, Chang had a paralytic stroke. Some four years later, during the night, Chang and Eng died, Chang preceding Eng by about three hours."

This is all very humbling. My sister and I used to complain about having to share the backseat of my parents' Plymouth Valiant. The territorial squabbling got so intense that we had to mark off our respective sides with masking tape. (Inevitably, I'd try to provoke her by inching my pinky over to her side.) We whined about having to share motel rooms, a TV, a phone. And here are these two siblings who had to share a body, no less, and yet they made it work pretty well. The photo in the encyclopedia shows them wearing dapper waistcoats, leaning against Victorian furniture, their arms around each other's shoulders, looking relaxed, content, and mildly aristocratic. It's a touching photo. When I have kids—God willing—and they complain about having to share an Xbox, I'll show them this photo. I've got three words for you two, I'll say: Chang and Eng.

character writer

In 17th-century England, writers such as Sir Thomas Overbury and Joseph Hall drew up character sketches to exemplify a quality such as vanity or stinginess. I'm no Tom Overbury, but there's someone in my life who calls out for a little character sketch. It's Julie's brother Eric, and the quality he exemplifies is brilliance. Or cockiness. Or smart-aleckness. Or some combination of the above. He's a big part of the reason why I felt I needed to get smarter, so here goes . . .

Eric is shockingly bright—as he's happy to let you know. He went to Harvard, talks at a rapid clip, and quotes Latin aphorisms in his e-mails. After college, he took the Foreign Service exam because it was reputedly the hardest test in the world. He passed, but took it again because he wanted the highest score in the class. He got it.

Eric's the kind of guy who never needed braces, has rock-bottom cholesterol, and whose hair stubbornly refuses to recede. He's even moderately good-looking, along the lines of a John Cusack.

When Eric looks at me (his eyes, incidentally, are 20/20), it's the same way I might look at a golden retriever. No matter how clever the golden retriever—even if it learns to flush the toilet or bark along to "Happy Birthday"—it's still a golden retriever. A different species. And just as I get a chuckle from watching a golden retriever chase its tail, Eric has found amusement in my lack of knowledge about the Crimean War and my confusion between fission and fusion.

This is something I'd never had before—a condescending older brother. When I was growing up with my sister, I was considered the scholar. Beryl had other advantages—friends, for one thing. But I was the acknowledged bookworm. Then, at age thirty-one, I suddenly inherited this brother-in-law who not only was far more knowledgeable than I was, but who loved to emphasize that point whenever he saw me.

He's the intellectual star of the family, and he knows it. At holidays, Eric sits at the table, his arms folded across his chest, holding forth on the big issues of the day. He'll talk about the historical precedents for John Ashcroft's crusade or dissect the psychology of investing in a 401k. He says everything with such confidence, we all just nod our heads, taking mental notes for some imaginary quiz. I hate that feeling. I want to be the one giving the lecture. Or at the least, I want to be the one who knows enough to heckle Eric.

And that's not to mention another humiliation: games. My wife's family loves a good board game. So whenever they gather, Scrabble, Boggle, and Balderdash sets materialize in the room, and you can count on Eric to rack up a half dozen victories before the day is through. The most recent Thanksgiving was a particularly brutal one. It was a few weeks ago, just days before I started my encyclopedic adventure, and for reasons I still don't understand, I agreed to play Eric in a one-on-one game of Trivial Pursuit.

"You're lucky," said Eric. "In this game, you only have to roll one die. So you won't have to do that pesky addition that comes with two dice."

Eric's piece began jumping around the board, filling up alarmingly fast with those multicolored wedges. How many feet in a fathom? Six. Who wrote "Stardust"? Hoagy Carmichael. Who discovered Victoria Falls? David Livingstone. Eric occasionally had to think a bit. He'd tilt his head and look at the ceiling, as if the answer were written there. Which it apparently was. Because he'd almost always figure out that Varig Airlines is from Brazil and the like.

My piece, on the other hand, remained empty. Hollow. If you listened closely, you could hear a tiny echo in it.

"How many equal sides are there on a scalene triangle?" asked Eric. I sat there trying to remember what the hell my geometry teacher had taught me in ninth grade, but could recall only that he had a thick German accent and a comb-over.

"I'll give you a hint. It's about the same as your IQ."

"Two?" I tried.

"Zero," said Eric, snickering. He actually snickered.

My next turn, he asked, "What movie character was Elmo Lincoln the first to portray?"

I drew a blank. I was even flubbing the entertainment category, my supposed strong point. The irritating Trivial Pursuit people loved to ask about old-timey entertainment, the kind before DVDs and stalkerazzi.

"This character has the same-sized vocabulary as you do," said Eric.

I knew what he was driving at. "Frankenstein," I said.

"Nope. Tarzan."

And so it went. In the end, Eric beat me six wedges to two, but not before asking me if I wouldn't prefer a game more suited to my intellect, like Go Fish.

I know Trivial Pursuit is just that—trivial. Still, this was a disturbingly effective reminder of my patches of ignorance—which now included politics, economics, literature, history, geography, and anything else you wouldn't find on the E! channel.

That was five weeks ago. Now Eric's back in Manhattan—along with Julie's mom, her other brother, Doug, and their families—and we're at an Upper West Side restaurant for lunch. I've got two and a half letters under my belt. It's a whole new day. As we sit down, I decide to break the big news to Eric. I tell him about Operation Britannica. I want his approval—and I also want him to feel threatened. But my revelation doesn't seem to affect him either way. It's as if I'd just told him that I enjoy wearing corduroy pants.

"Yeah, I knew a guy at Harvard who did that," he says.

"Good, maybe I can compare knowledge with him."

"You could," says Eric, "except he committed suicide. But I'm sure you'll do just fine."

The conversation moves on to the choices of appetizers and entrees. Crab cakes seem particularly popular.

"Ah, crabs. The true aristocrats," I say.

"What?" asks Doug.

"Crabs have blue blood. You know, blue bloods. Aristocrats."

The laughter wasn't quite as deafening as I had hoped.

"I read it in the *blood* section," I said.

"Tell us something interesting you've learned," Julie's mother says.

"*That* doesn't count?"

"No, that wasn't interesting."

Wow. Tough crowd.

"Well, do you like a nice macabre story?" I ask.

"Sure," says Julie's mom.

"How about the story of Burke and Hare?"

"We're listening," says Doug.

"Okay, then. William Hare and William Burke," I say, putting down my menu. "These were two Irishmen who met at a hotel back in the 1820s. One day, an old pauper died in the hotel. But instead of having the corpse buried, Burke and Hare sold the body to the local surgeon for about seven pounds."

"Merchants of death, eh?" says Doug.

"But wait. It gets better. That first corpse gave them a savvy business idea. They started enticing travelers into the hotel, getting them drunk, smothering them to death, and selling the corpses to the surgeon. Killed at least fifteen people. Their neighbors finally busted them, but it took a year."

"And they went to jail?"

"Hare ratted out Burke and was released. But Burke was hanged. And Knox—that was the name of the surgeon—never got thrown in jail, but had a wee bit of a PR problem."

I sat back. It was a lively tale, and I told it well. Even Eric had to admit that, which he did.

"It's a good story," says Eric.

"Thanks."

"And of course, you know the poem about it, right?" he asks.

"Um."

"You don't know the poem about Burke and Hare?" asked Eric.

Dammit. I can't believe this. "No."

"Oh, that's the best part. It's a poem that British schoolboys used to say. It goes like this:

Burke's the butcher,
Hare's the thief,
Knox the one who bought the beef.

The family laughs.

"That's wonderful!" says Julie's mom.

"You're scary," says Eric's wife, Alexandra.

Eric sits back and crosses his arms on his chest, one of his favorite gestures. He looks at me and smiles. He knows he's beaten me. I'm annoyed at the *Britannica* for not having that poem in it. I'm annoyed at myself for picking Burke and Hare. Mostly, I'd like to smother Eric and sell his body to an anatomist for seven pounds.

I'll have to keep reading. I'll find things he doesn't know about. I'll find things so obscure he won't know how to pronounce them.

Charles

Here's a tip: if you meet a king and can't remember his name, you might as well guess Charles. You've got a pretty good shot. I've arrived at the *Charles* section and it's a disturbingly long one—forty-eight Charleses, to be exact, spread over twenty-four pages, hailing from just about every European country that could afford a cape with some ermine trim, including Germany, Italy, Spain, Portugal, Sweden, Holland, Hungary, and Austria.

It's sort of helpful that a lot of the Charleses have nicknames, which I consider trying to turn into some sort of Dr. Seuss–like poem as a mnemonic device:

There's Charles the Good
and Charles the Bad.
There's Charles the Lame
and Charles the Mad.
There's Charles the Bold
and Charles the Fair.
Don't forget Charles the Bald.
So many Charleses are there!

But I can't think of anything to rhyme with "Charles the Well-Served." So I just read carefully and hope for the best.

One thing that strikes me is that this is not an overwhelmingly inspiring group of men. In fact, these twenty-four pages seem a fine argument against monarchy as a governmental system.

There are the occasional Charleses who founded universities or made judicial reforms—the Swedish ones in particular seemed better than average. But overall, this is a sorry lot of war-loving, greedy, mentally unstable, gout-infected rulers. Not to mention randy. Consider Charles II of England—the man who regained the throne after the downfall of Cromwell. Charles is quoted as saying God would not "make a man miserable only for taking a little pleasure out of the way." Charles II took enough "pleasure out of the way" to produce fourteen illegitimate offspring (and if you recall, inspire the legend of the concerned Dr. Condom). One of the few who did remain faithful was Charles the Whipped (not his real name), who concluded a treaty in Brittany in 1693, only to be persuaded by his wife to break it, which led to his death in battle. He would have done better to sire fourteen illegitimate kids.

I'm trying like hell to remember which Charles is which, but it's a task that would make anyone as loopy as Charles VI of France, who suffered forty-four attacks of insanity in the late 1300s and early 1400s. I wish the monarchs had a little more creativity when it came to names—though my family isn't much better. My full name is Arnold Stephen Jacobs Jr., after my father, A.S.J. Sr. My father—the jokester—tried to name me Arnold Stephen Jacobs IV, skipping right over the intermediate steps, but my mom put the kibosh on that one, so Junior it is.

Chaucer, Geoffrey

The author of *The Canterbury Tales* was apparently fined for beating a Franciscan friar in a London street. Again with the temperamental artists.

Cheney, Dick

Our vice president dropped out of Yale—or was kicked out; it's not clear—and finished at the University of Wyoming. Do the Democrats know about this? Seems like they could have made a bigger deal out of it.

chess

I wasn't very interested in chess growing up. I'm not sure why, though I think it might have had something to do with all the kings and queens. Even before I read about the barrel of reprehensible Charleses in the *Britannica,* I was no fan of monarchy. Maybe if the pieces had been presidents and first ladies, or Starskys and Hutches, then I'd be hooked. But as it was, I never caught chess fever.

Still, it seemed like something that smart people did. So in my quest to boost my intelligence, I made sure to pay close attention to all facts in the *Britannica* about the ancient black-and-white board game. In my spare time, I started playing electronic chess on my Palm Pilot. After about sixty-three games, I finally beat the computer. Granted, it was on the lowest skill level, the one reserved for first-graders in remedial math courses and Anna Nicole Smith. But that didn't bother me. I beat the damn thing.

Buoyed by my success, I thought it might be fun to take my game downtown and test it out against the big boys at the Marshall Chess Club. Now, I'm a moderate agoraphobe, so this was an uncharacteristic idea. But I had decided that—for the duration of this project, during this year of self-education—I would try to put my knowledge to the test, to see how it helped me interact with the best and the brightest, so off to the chess club it was.

The Marshall Chess Club, as I expected, has lots of chess tables and stacks of chess magazines. But I was a little surprised by the makeup of the crowd, which is an odd and varied lot. You've got a minyan of old potbellied Jewish men with their pants hiked up to their armpits; a handful of twenty-something black men; a smattering of Eastern European guys; and a dash of cocky, knapsack-toting chess prodigies in the third grade.

I introduce myself to the man in charge, Larry, who seems to fall into the old-Jewish-guy category, and inform him I'm here to prove myself. He replies that I picked the wrong night.

"Tonight is a big tournament," Larry says, shuffling through his paperwork. "You came on glamour night!" I look around. This type of glamour isn't quite the paparazzi's dream, but I know what he's saying.

"I can't play in the tournament?"

"No," Larry says. He puts down his paperwork and leads me through the tournament players and into a back room. The Club Room. "Here, you can play in here," he says. "You could play with her." He points to the Filipina nanny of one of the third-grade chess prodigies. Larry then chuckles and leaves.

Not counting the nanny, there are, in fact, a few potential rivals in the Club Room. Two of the prepubescent players are here, capturing pawns in between bites of their Subway sandwiches.

"Can I play winners?" I ask.

They nod, without looking up from the board.

In the meantime, I spot someone from the high-waisted-pants squad, a man with a Jew-fro to rival the hairdos of any member of vintage Earth, Wind & Fire.

"Care for a game?" I say.

"Why not," he says.

Before we start, I silently review what I've learned from the *Britannica*: develop knights before bishops, anticipate enemy threats, try to form an overall goal—like a kingside attack—that coordinates the forces. I consider a postmodern opening move—jumping the knight over my line of pawns—but settle instead for a classical opening, and move my pawn two squares. After a couple of moves, the Jew-fro man takes my pawn. I tell myself this is good. A gambit, a sacrifice. But over the next couple of moves I do a tremendous amount of sacrificing. It's not exactly clear to me what the greater purpose of my sacrificing is. But I do have a knack for sacrificing.

As I'm figuring out where I move my one remaining knight, I put my index finger on square e4 to mark an option. My opponent looks physically pained, as if his toe had been run over by a cab.

"You shouldn't do that," he says. "You shouldn't touch the board. It's bad form."

"Oh," I say, removing my finger.

"It's not genteel. It's not sophisticated."

I promise no more board fondling. I decide to attack with my bishop, which I hope will earn his respect. That, and some chess knowledge: "You know, the bishop used to be called an elephant, and it was limited to a two-square diagonal jump."

He nods. A couple of turns later, he takes my former elephant.

Caissa, the patron goddess of chess, would be proud, I think to myself.

According to Nimzowitzsch, you should voluntarily surrender the center. I have surrendered that. I have also surrendered the sides and front. I move my queen. "This used to be called a counselor, and could only move one square in any direction."

He nods again, and puts his hand in his chin. Good, I'm making him think.

"You know, I'm considering underpromoting later in the game," I say. I knew it was a long shot, but I thought maybe he didn't know the definition of underpromoting and I could inform him. He knew. It's when your pawn gets to the other side and you choose not to queen it, but instead turn it into a knight or a rook or bishop.

And then he mates me. He mates me with authority, like the squid that uses a fourth arm to deliver its sperm cells.

He shakes my hand. The match over, Jew-fro man turns out to be very nice. He takes the time to dissect my game for me, pointing out my many errors, but managing not to be condescending. He even tells me why the hell someone might want to underpromote—if a queen will cause a stale-mate, but a castle will force a checkmate, you underpromote to castle.

And for some reason, after throwing out a dozen chess facts, I finally do impress him.

"You know, medieval Muslim chessboards were monochromatic."

"Really? I knew some early boards were monochromatic, but I didn't know they were Muslim." He isn't being sarcastic. He is actually interested.

"They were Muslim," I say.

I turn to the third-graders at the board next to me. I'm ready for my match. Problem is, after having seen my lack of chess chops, they've lost interest. I'd be a waste of their time. So I pack my bag and go. I probably knew the gap between information and know-how was big, but I had got-ten a firsthand lesson in just how big it can be. On the way home, I kick my Palm Pilot's butt, then explain to it all the mistakes it made.

Child, Julia
She once worked in the OSS, the precursor to the CIA. Sounds like a good movie: Chef by day, spy by night. I should option that now.

Children's Crusade
Here, a major contender for the saddest entry so far. About thirty thousand kids—led by a French shepherd boy—set out to conquer the Holy Land from the Muslims by love instead of force. They never made it, instead falling victim to disreputable merchants, with most being sold into slavery in North Africa. When Julie and I have kids, they will not be allowed to go to the Middle East without supervision. That's a promise.

choreography
Julie and I were watching TV—well, sort of watching. I was reading the *Britannica* and she was doing the *New York* magazine crossword, from which she looked up to ask:

"Hey, you know Fred Astaire's real name?"

"As a matter of fact, I do."

It's Frederick Austerlitz, I told her. I helped my wife fill in 42-Down—which may not justify an entire year of reading the encyclopedia, but nevertheless makes me feel like spinning Julie around the room in an elegant waltz. I'm a knight with shining information coming to the rescue of my damsel in distress. Excellent.

Christmas

Tonight is the *Esquire* Christmas party. (By the way, Christmas in Armenia is celebrated on January 6; so if you're ever late with presents, just say you're Armenian.) I'll be going to the *Esquire* party solo, since Julie is working late. Her new job is an interesting one—she works for a company that puts on scavenger hunts around New York City—but it requires night duty once a week. So, alone it is.

Esquire's party is for our writers and friends in the literary community. But it's not a fancy affair—it's held in our eighth-floor offices, the cubicles draped with red-and-white checkered tablecloths and a wine bar set up by the Xerox machine. I arrive late—it's a long walk from my office on the seventh floor, after all—and I spot my old friend Rick a couple of cubicles down. He's talking to a tall woman I don't recognize, but who apparently has a lot to say.

Rick motions me over. My arrival doesn't do much to stop the tall woman's monologue, which seems to be about how she prefers to read plays instead of novels. Right now, she's going through a Strindberg phase. He's much more complex than his more famous counterpart Ibsen, she explains. I can't be sure, but I think she used the words "criminally overlooked."

Rick looks less than enthralled. In fact, he looks like he might, at any moment, pull a pillow out of his pocket and curl up on the floor for a quick nap.

"A.J.'s smart," says Rick, as she pauses momentarily to inhale. "He's reading the encyclopedia."

"Really," says the woman.

"Yep, from *A* to *Z*."

"And where are you now?"

"I'm up to *C*."

"But how much are you retaining?"

I hate that question. Especially the way she asks it, which makes it sound more like an accusation than a question, like maybe I've violated the Mann Act or something. *How much are you retaining?*

I respond: "There are a couple of rivers in Bolivia that I'm a little hazy on, but everything else I've got down cold."

I figured that would shut her up. Of course, I'm retaining slightly less than that. There are also a couple of rivers in Chad that I'm hazy on. And a few other bits as well.

But honestly, my retention rate is far higher than I imagined it would be. My best gauge of this is those internal *dings*—the ones that happen whenever my life intersects with the encyclopedia—which have only increased. It's a constant symphony in my head. I'd say at least two per minute.

So I feel good that something's sinking in. My main concern, however, is that my retention is not evenly spread out among the facts. Instead, my new knowledge is clustered around several themes and trends—and those trends aren't always the most elevated ones in the world. Like syphilis. I'm retaining an awful lot about syphilis. I could tell you that Al Capone's and Winston Churchill's fathers both had syphilis. I could tell you that the French poet Baudelaire had syphilis—and that he caught it from a Jewish prostitute named Squint-Eyed Sarah. I could tell you that some Bedouins have a nonvenereal form of syphilis called *bejel*, which could be a handy excuse for those trying to explain to their spouses an unpleasant positive test result. "I'm Bedouin, you see. It's not venereal." In a way, syphilis is an appropriate example. These themes that keep popping up are like a disturbingly contagious disease. I don't feel I have control over them. They just sneak their way into my brain, and all of a sudden I'm keeping a tally on the mentions of cannibalism, or following the recurrences of men blinded in one eye.

But anyway, back to our Strindberg aficionado, who doesn't seem to be buying the rivers-in-Bolivia line. She looks quite severe.

"What do you know about Samuel Beckett?" she asks. Beckett, Beckett. I'm frantically searching my internal CD-ROM for a good Samuel Beckett fact. But I'm coming up blank. "If you want to talk writers, I actually found Balzac much more interesting," I say. "Did you know he was a huge perfectionist, and he kept making changes to his books way after deadline, and the printer's bills almost ruined him? You got to let it go, you know? A good lesson for us all."

That is evasion strategy number one. If you don't know something, deflect, distract, razzle-dazzle them with another fact, and hope they forget. This time, it seems to have worked.

"Okay. What about cauliflower?" she says.

"Not up to it yet. I think it's under *V* for 'vegetables.' "

That's strategy number two. The old I'll-get-back-to-you trick. Of course, this tactic's got a built-in expiration date. It'll become harder and harder to rely on as I keep polishing off the letters. But for now, I've got twenty-three letters to choose from. "Speaking of which, I think I'll make my way over to the canapes," I say.

And that's strategy number three. Leave. I abandon poor Rick to what will no doubt be more searing insights on Scandinavian theater.

Civil War

Before I waded into the *Britannica,* I knew enough about the Civil War to make sure I wasn't a complete embarrassment to my country. I watched that Ken Burns documentary a few years ago, or at least a half hour of it, before I flipped back to something in color with a zippier sound track. Also, I knew that Denzel Washington led a black regiment to a victory at the historic Battle of the Oscars.

But I was missing just a few details. I was missing, for instance, any knowledge of a woman named Belle Boyd (who got her very own entry back in the *B*s). I'm glad I filled in that particular gap because, having read about her, I've decided her tale is worthy of a summer blockbuster (Movie Idea Number Two) and much-needed proof that romance exists in the real world.

Belle Boyd was born and raised in Virgina. At the start of the Civil War, Boyd gained fame after she and her mother refused to let some Union soldiers into their house. When one of the men in blue attempted to force his way through the door, Boyd shot him dead. She was put on trial, but acquitted on justifiable homicide.

Instead of retiring quietly back to rural life, Boyd just got deeper into the war. While staying in the same house as some Union officers, she eavesdropped on their plans to destroy the bridges in the town of Fort Royal, Virginia. "She undertook a hazardous journey through the lines to inform General T. J. 'Stonewall' Jackson of the Union plans," says the Britannica. It turned out to be a key piece of intelligence. This led to her stint as a courier and scout for J. S. Mosby's guerrillas. She was arrested by Union forces, but released from prison after a bout with typhoid fever.

A pretty good yarn so far—your average tough-girl secret-agent thriller. But here's where any Hollywood agents out there should pay attention, because this is where the romance comes in—an unlikely meeting between a Confederate lady spy and a Union navy officer. In 1864, Boyd was sailing on a Confederate ship to England bearing letters from

Jefferson Davis. Boyd's boat was intercepted by a Union vessel, and a Union officer named Hardinge boarded the ship. Hardinge was utterly distracted by Boyd. That's what the *Britannica* says, "utterly distracted." It doesn't say what that means. Did she flutter her eyes? Compliment him on his big saber?

Regardless, Hardinge was so distracted by Boyd, he allowed the Confederate ship's captain to escape. For this snafu, he was court-martialed and discharged from the Union navy. Then in August of 1864, Officer Hardinge sailed to England, where Boyd was now living and—cue music—married his former enemy. Hardinge and Boyd lived happily ever after, or at least until he died a year later.

This makes me wonder what the hell my high school history teachers were thinking. I remember my Civil War lessons being bone dry. We talked a whole lot about King Cotton and the economic rationale for the Civil War, which are important, no doubt. But couldn't they have spiced things up with a nice romantic tale between a Union fellow and a Confederate lady? What's wrong with a good old-fashioned love story? It'd certainly have skewed well with the girls in class.

clammyweed

This is a first. I fell asleep while reading the encyclopedia. Just drifted off somewhere around *clam shrimp, clam worm, clambake,* or *clammyweed,* I can't be sure which. I was reading it while lying down on the couch—a dangerous proposition, I now realize—and could only fight off shut-eye for so long. Did I mention my schedule is fucking exhausting?

Anyway, I woke up when Julie came into the room. I felt like I'd been caught doing something naughty, like masturbating or selling idealistic Christian kids into slavery.

claque, aka canned laughter

It's becoming increasingly clear that there's nothing new under the sun (a heavenly body, by the way, that some Indian ascetics stare at till they go blind). I knew that some things had a history—the Constitution, rhythm and blues, Canada—but it's the odd little things that surprise me with their storied past. This first struck me when I was reading about anesthetics and I learned that, in the early 1840s, it became fashionable to hold parties where guests would inhale nitrous oxide out of bladders. In other words, Whip-it parties! We held the exact same kind of parties in high school. We'd buy fourteen cans of Reddi-Wip and suck on them till we had successfully obliterated a couple of million neurons and face-planted on my friend Andy's couch. And we thought we were so cutting edge.

And now, I learn about claque, which is essentially a highbrow French word for canned laughter. Canned laughter was invented long before Lucille Ball stuffed chocolates in her face or Ralph Kramden threatened his wife with extreme violence. It goes back to the 4th century B.C., when Greek playwrights hired bands of helpers to laugh at their comedies in order to influence the judges. The Romans also stacked the audience, but they were apparently more interested in applause than chuckles: Nero—emperor and wannabe musician—employed a group of five thousand knights and soldiers to accompany him on his concert tours.

But the golden age of canned laughter came in 19th-century France. Almost every theater in France was forced to hire a band called a *claque*—from *claquer,* "to clap." The influential claque leaders, called the *chefs de claque,* got a monthly payment from the actors. And the brilliant innovation they came up with was specialization. Each claque member had his or her own important job to perform: There were the *rieurs,* who laughed loudly during comedies. There were the *bisseurs,* who shouted for encores. There were the *commissaires,* who would elbow their neighbors and say, "This is the good part." And my favorite of all, the *pleureuses,* women who were paid good francs to weep at the sad parts of tragedies. I love this idea. I'm not sure why the networks never thought of canned crying. You'd be watching an *ER* episode, and a softball player would come in with a bat splinter through his forehead, and you'd hear a little whimper in the background, turning into a wave of sobs. Julie already has trouble keeping her cheeks dry, seeing as she cried during the *Joe Millionaire* finale. If they added canned crying, she'd be a mess.

Cleveland

I had always figured the Ohio town was named for Grover Cleveland. No, the real story is that it was named for Moses Cleaveland, an employee of the Connecticut Land Company, who arrived with his surveyors in 1796. His mission was to speed up the sale of land in Ohio, and in his honor, the town was called Cleaveland.

That day must have been the proudest day in the life of this real estate salesman. No doubt he wrote a letter to his mom: "Dear Mother, the family name shall not be forgotten. There is a town in this fair state of Ohio that bears the glorious name of our family, the magnificent Cleaveland!"

Then, in 1832, the *a* in "Cleaveland" was dropped because "Cleve-land" fit better on a newspaper masthead. That was the reason. His name was bastardized to fit a newspaper's masthead? They couldn't have reduced the font? Did they consider changing "Ohio" to "Ohi"? That would save some ink, too.

Fame is a fleet-footed hussy. It's not the most shocking lesson I've learned, but it sure gets driven home every day. I've learned of hundreds of people who were huge in their time, adored by millions, but now totally forgotten except by freaks who read the encyclopedia. And even if your name is remembered, it'll probably be spelled or pronounced incorrectly. Cleaveland can have a support group meeting with Dutch explorer Cornelius Mey, for whom Cape May is named. It's discouraging. If I ever do achieve anything and become famous, within a couple decades, I'll become R. J. Jackobz.

climate and weather

Lightning goes up. It shoots right up from the ground and into the cloud. This is what the encyclopedia says in the section on climate and weather. I reread this passage a couple of times to make sure I hadn't gone batty—but no, lightning goes up.

To be technical, it does first go down—there's an initial bolt called the "leader" that zips from the cloud to the ground. But the bright part, the part that flashes, is the "return stroke," which goes from the ground back to the cloud.

This is profoundly unnerving. When I didn't know the history of canned laughter or the existence of a sexy Confederate spy, that was mildly vexing. But this is unnerving. This is a whole new level of ignorance. I've been looking at lightning all my life, and its sky-to-ground direction seemed about as certain as the slightly asymmetrical nose on my face. To be confronted with this totally counterintuitive information—it makes me paranoid. What other incorrect ideas do I have? Is the sun actually cold? Is the sky orange? Is Keanu Reeves a brilliant actor?

coffee

I obviously need to be drinking more coffee (which was discovered, according to legend, when a goatherd noticed his flock acting strangely after eating the beans). Or maybe I need more sleep. Or something—because I'm screwing up on the job. My latest was a particularly embarrassing bungle. I was helping to edit an article in which a supermodel gives relationship advice to men. My boss had sent it back to me, pointing out that was a little bland. So I figured I should try to spice it up.

The supermodel had suggested that men, when they compliment a woman, should choose something besides the eyes. Too clichéd, she said. Flatter another body part, she said. Something unexpected, like the cheeks or knees. Good advice. I simply tacked on the sentence "Men who compliment a woman's eyes should be taken out back and whipped by a Bulgarian dog trainer." Okay, maybe it wasn't worthy of Mark Twain or George Bernard Shaw, but it was something. And it worked. My boss liked it better.

The problem was, I completely forgot to send the piece back to the supermodel to make sure she was okay with my little addition. I had meant to—I know you can't just insert something without the writer's approval. But I forgot. A dunderheaded move—both bad etiquette and bad journalism.

And now my dog trainer line has bitten me in the behind. I get in today and there, in the gossip column, the supermodel is complaining that *Esquire* put words in her mouth, and that she's getting lots of angry e-mails from the Bulgarian community. Jesus! Who knew there was a Bulgarian community? And who knew that community had an antidefamation league! But I feel terrible. I should be whipped by a big Bulgarian man (whose average life expectancy, by the way, is sixty-eight years).

I'm hoping this little scandal will blow over, which I think it will. And I'm even more confident that my career blunder won't be written up in the *Encyclopaedia Britannica*. That makes me feel better. Because there are people whose entire place in history rests on a screwup, who are famous for nothing other than their failure.

I'm thinking, in particular, of poor James Challis. You've got to feel for this unfortunate 19th-century fellow. As the *Britannica* says in its very first sentence about him, Challis was a "British clergyman and astronomer, famous in the history of astronomy for his failure to discover the planet Neptune."

Here's the sad planetary tale: Challis's career was going along at a nice clip. Born in 1803, he published dozens of scientific papers in his twenties and early thirties, and got himself named director of the Cambridge Observatory. Not bad. Then came the fateful September of 1845. A fellow

Cambridge astronomer had been making calculations of the perturbations of the orbit of Uranus, and asked Challis to look for an unknown planet in a specific position. Challis was apparently not impressed, and put it pretty far down on his "To Do" list.

Finally, on further urging, Challis started looking closely in July of 1846. Every night he looked, and every night he found nothing new. Then on September 23, Challis was scooped. The Berlin Observatory made international headlines by announcing the discovery of Neptune. Challis went back and checked his calculations, and realized he had actually observed the planet one night in August, but because he didn't compare his notes from that night with those of the previous night, he didn't realize it.

I pity the man. He must have gotten some serious ribbing from his astronomer buddies over that night's sherry. "Say, James old chap, I lost my pocket watch. Would you help me look for it? Oh, I just remembered. Never mind." And they'd all burst out laughing. Then another royal astronomer would pipe up, "James old sport, do tell us what happened. Where was your head? Was it perhaps . . . up Uranus?" Then they'd all laugh so hard they'd spit up their cucumber sandwiches.

I try not to revel in other people's failure, but this does make me feel better about my Bulgarian debacle. So I'm embarrassed for a couple of days. Who cares? Everyone makes gaffes at work, and it's not the end of the solar system. At least I'm not James Challis.

I know it's a mixed bag, this comparing your life to historical figures. Naturally, it can be incredibly dismaying—as when you realize how uneventful or unimpressive your life is. But it can also be inspiring, or energizing, or—in this case—comforting. I thank poor Mr. Challis and move on.

Cortés, Hernán

More syphilis. A lusty man "much given to women," the conquistador contracted the disease in the 1500s, which caused him to miss an ill-fated expedition to South America in 1509. Luck is a weird thing. Sometimes getting an STD can save your life.

cosmos

In the entry on *cosmos,* the *Britannica* tells us the universe will end either as a "cold, dark and virtually empty place" or as a "fiery crucible." So, which is it? Fire or ice? That's a pretty big difference. Take a stand, *Britan-*

nica! I want to know what lies in store for me, assuming I exercise daily and eat low-fat muffins and live another few billion years. Information can be maddeningly imprecise. If I had to bet, I'd go with ice, since I vaguely remember some magazine article saying that's the current leading contender.

But either way, it's not an uplifting end to all of existence. Unlike a well-timed STD, there's no way those could turn out to be a lucky break. I'm only in the *C*s and already I've reached the horrible end to all existence.

courtship

I can't believe what a bunch of sleazeballs these animals are. That's what strikes me whenever I read about courtship rituals in the animal kingdom. These critters—at least the male ones—are some slimy, deceitful operators. Consider the shameless debauchee known as the swordtail characin fish (whom I first encountered in the *animal behavior* section). The male swordtail characin, you see, has long stringy bits that dangle from his gills—bits that are designed to look exactly like the daphnia worm, the characin's favorite snack. When a hungry female characin sees this tantalizing daphnia, she naturally approaches, anticipating a nice meal. Instead, when she's close enough, she gets an unpleasant surprise: the male shtups her. A literal bait and switch.

There are dozens of such stories. Here's just one other, for variety. The female cichlid fish are called "mouth breeders," which means they incubate eggs in their mouth. The females swallow up any stray eggs and keep them stored safely between the cheeks. The male cichlid fish knows all about this, so he's developed his fins to look exactly like an egg—same size, same mustard color. The poor lady cichlid spies one of these so-called eggs, and paddles over to try to swallow it up. But as soon as she opens her mouth, bam, the male sprays her with sperm. Just like that.

I guess I shouldn't be all that surprised about the level of deceit in courtship behavior. Humans aren't exactly 100 percent guileless when it comes to romance. If they were, Wonderbra would be out of business, and match.com ads would read, "Short, pudgy guy with no discernible income and acne scars that resemble the constellation Ursa Minor seeks beautiful woman to share his rent-controlled apartment." So I shouldn't be all high and mighty.

In fact, Julie loves to tell me that I engaged in shameless deceit when wooing her. "For the first three months, it was Dr. Jekyll, Dr. Jekyll, Dr. Jekyll," she says. "Then you had hooked me, and all of a sudden, here comes Mr. Hyde!" I had my own version of the tantalizing daphnia-shaped gills, says Julie. Namely, I pretended to like parties, dancing, dinners at fancy restaurants, even the occasional Broadway musical. Over one early dinner, we made ambitious plans about all the places we'd like to travel: Sweden, South Africa, Portugal. Now Julie knows my actual list of places I want to travel: kitchen, bathroom, and bedroom. And as for Broadway musicals, I haven't been within five hundred yards of an orchestra pit since she accepted my engagement ring.

I, on the other hand, don't see it as deception. I tell her: "It wasn't a conscious change from Dr. Jekyll to Mr. Hyde. It's just that I found the woman I love and I figured I didn't need to go out to parties anymore." That one always causes a half laugh, half scoff.

After I read about the characin, I padded out to the living room to share it with her. "Hey Julie," I say. "You know how you say I deceived you and tricked you into marrying me?"

"I sure do."

"Well, look at this."

She reads it. "Makes sense," she says. "Makes a lot of sense." She seems pleased.

I take back my *Britannica* and pad back into my office. I'm not sure why I just shared that with her. It certainly didn't help my cause. In fact, now I'm pretty much screwed in all future arguments. I think I have to be a little more careful with the information I share.

couvade

Couvade is a custom wherein the father goes to bed during the birth of his child and simulates the symptoms of childbirth. He pretends to undergo painful labor, just like the baby's mother. In fact, the mother sometimes gets to her feet hours after giving birth and waits on the father. Couvade's social function, says the *Britannica,* is to emphasize the role of the father in reproduction. It was most recently practiced in the early 20th century in the Basque country.

No offense to the Basques, but couvade seems—how do I put this?—*insane.* In the first few letters of the alphabet, my gender has come off like a bunch of selfish tools. First the duplicitous cichlid fish, now these

Basque fathers who—it's pretty transparent—are crying out for attention. The wife is getting all the sympathy and limelight for creating a human life. *Hey, look at us, we can make faces too!*

Well, at least I won't be jealous of my wife's contractions anytime soon. Last night, Julie and I took yet another early pregnancy test. It was aggressively negative. For the past few weeks, Julie had been popping fertility drugs, so I was thinking I'd maybe get a litter of Jacobses, but no. Nothing. In my darker moments, I rationalize that maybe it's a good thing. This isn't the greatest world to introduce another human being into—it's got civil wars and corpse-dealing murderers and temperamental artists and carbon monoxide. So maybe it's okay not to have a kid.

Czetwertynski

I knock off the Czetwertynskis—a Polish princely family—and I'm done. Three out of twenty-six. Now I know my ABCs. Where do I stand? I'm still dazed by the amount of knowledge in the world—but I've noticed two things that make me just the tiniest bit better. First, the *Britannica* does tend to repeat itself. I got a lesson on the Hundred Years' War in the *A*s, then in the *B*s, and then again in the *C*s. So maybe half a million of those 44 million words are unnecessary. Second, I occasionally read about something that rings a bell, a very faint bell, one barely more audible than the broken two-hundred-ton Russian bell—in other words, a fact I knew when I was a kid but that has long ago faded. Once, long ago, I knew that baseball was based on the British game of rounders—a less genteel version of the game, where you could get the runner out by beaning him with the ball (a rule also employed by that depraved bully in third grade). But I hadn't thought about rounders in maybe twenty years. Still, knowing that it was buried deep in my memory—somehow, that was a little reassuring.

That's the happy news. The bad news is that I'm still having a hell of a time figuring out what all this information—old, new, half forgotten—means. I feel my mind isn't fundamentally different. I may have given it a new paint job and fixed the screen door, but it's still the same shotgun shack.

D

dance

In a tribe on the island of Santa Maria, old men used to stand by with bows and arrows and shoot every dancer who made a mistake. The perfect way to raise the stakes on *American Idol*.

Darwin, George

Poor George. When your dad is Charles Darwin, you might get a couple of perks—free mutton at the poshest Victorian restaurants, say—but you're pretty much screwed from birth. You'll always be a loser Darwin—unless, of course, you also happen to totally revolutionize science and shift our worldview. Well, that didn't quite happen for George. George Darwin did go into science like his father—he became an astronomer—but his Big Idea was this: the moon was formed when molten lava was pulled free from the earth by solar tides. It's an idea now considered unlikely to be true. Scientists now believe the moon was formed when a mammoth asteroid smashed into the earth, splitting off a moon-sized chunk. So George Darwin's moon idea ain't exactly the theory of evolution. Though to be fair, George Darwin did have another interesting theory—namely, that a pear-shaped rotating fluid body shows stability in space. Oh, wait. Also incorrect.

George is actually the second Darwin descendant I've read about in the encyclopedia. There was also Frances Cornford, Charles Darwin's granddaughter. Her accomplishment? She wrote a poem called "To a Fat Lady Seen from the Train," which went like this: "O fat white woman whom nobody loves, / Why do you walk through the fields in gloves?" And so on.

It's enough to make you want to lie down in front of that train. These loser relatives of history always depress me. They probably wouldn't even have made it into the encyclopedia without their pedigree, and now that they're here, they cast serious doubt on the notion that greatness is inherited. I've read about Bartholomew Columbus, Christopher's tagalong brother, and about a whole bunch of obscure Bachs who are Baroque versions of Tito and Jermaine Jackson.

It's depressing on a personal level as well, because it brings up a recurring theme in my own life—the fear that I'm a modern-day version of Frances Cornford. No one in my family has created a new scientific paradigm, but I've got my dad with his above-mentioned twenty-four books and his reputation as an expert in his field. And I've got my grandfather, who is also a genuinely great man. He's a lawyer named Ted Kheel and he spent the 1960s and 1970s solving strikes, meeting with presidents, working on civil rights. He tells stories about meals with LBJ and Martin Luther King Jr. He's eighty-eight years old, but he still goes to the office every single day, plugging away on a bunch of causes—conflict resolution, biodiversity, sustainable cuisine, Internet for the third world. He actually makes people's lives better. And then there's me, who, uh, chooses whether we should run the cleavage shot or the butt shot of the actress of the month in *Esquire*. Helps choose, anyway.

I'd like to say that everyone's successful in his or her own way, that you can't spend your life comparing yourself to others. But then I read about someone like Emily and Charlotte Brontë's brother, Patrick Branwell Brontë, a drunkard and opium addict who was fired from his job as a tutor after "making love to his employer's wife."

Dasnami sannyasin

Dasnami sannyasin were naked Indian ascetics who engaged in battles with other Hindu sects. First the Berserkers, now this. I seem to have stumbled on what has got to be one of the stranger little leitmotifs in the *EB*: naked soldiers.

As a journalist, I've got a dozen years of training in spotting trends. Officially, in my profession, you need three instances to qualify something as a trend. If there are two movies coming up about pet astrologers, you pray that someone, somewhere, is developing a third so it can become a trend. At *Entertainment Weekly*, I eventually got tired of looking for trends of three, and started a feature called "trend of two," which my bosses promptly killed. So anyway, naked soldiers is, as of now, a trend of two.

death

A Russian nobleman patented a coffin that allowed the corpse—if he regained consciousness after burial—to summon help by ringing a bell. Another good idea. Because that could really screw up your week—to wake up and find yourself in an airless coffin. I guess nowadays they could put cell phones in there.

Descartes, René

René Descartes had a fetish for women with crossed eyes. That's what it says, right there in the venerable *Britannica*. The French philosopher loved a lady whose pupils had migrated toward her nose.

I feel a little sorry for Descartes when I learn this, because I can't imagine there were tons of cross-eyed women in his circle of 17th-century European intellectuals. He should have been a Mayan. Or he should have been born in our era, because nowadays, I'm sure there is a plastic-wrapped magazine called *Cross-Eyed Vixens* and a subscription-only Web site called hotcrossedeyes.com. But back then, it must have been hard to find an outlet for his fetish. I just hope I don't learn in the *H*s that Thomas Hobbes liked ladies with a harelip.

There is a reason, though, that this cross-eyed fact is in the encyclopedia. Strangely enough, it has profound philosophical implications. In his *Principles of Philosophy*, Descartes argues that he was attracted to cross-eyed women because, as a child, he loved a cross-eyed playmate. He says that as soon as he realized the origin of his fetish, he was freed from it and could, once again, love women with normally spaced eyeballs. This insight, says the *Britannica*, "was the basis for Descartes's defense of free will and of the mind's ability to control the body." Jesus. I wonder if his cross-eyed playmate knew she had such a profound effect on Western thought.

I've got to respect Descartes (who, incidentally, gets the *Britannica*'s coveted double treatment, with writeups in both *Descartes* and *Cartesianism*). I'm sure when he made his cross-eyed confession, it caused some gentlemen at the local French philosophy club to snicker about René "Le Freak" Descartes. But it's a nice notion. I like that Descartes has such faith in the power of the mind that he places such high value on self-knowledge. There's *Cogito ergo sum,* and apparently there's also "*Cogito* about my kinky side, *ergo sum* free from it." He was doing Freudian therapy on himself 250 years before Freud bought his first couch.

It's a nice thought, but I don't really buy it. I don't think that you can flip off a passion just because you know where it comes from. If that were the case, there would be a lot fewer bullwhips and fuzzy handcuffs sold in Greenwich Village.

Regardless of whether I agree with Descartes, I'm happy to be pondering heady topics about the power of knowledge, instead of what I used to ponder, which was *Wasn't it funny when that guy on Blind Date last night lost his bathing suit in the hot tub?* And if that's not enough of a good thing, consider this: Descartes liked to stay in bed till 11 A.M.—good ammunition the next time anyone gives me flak about sleeping late.

Deseret News

I always thought the name of Utah's major newspaper was some sort of weird misspelling of the word "desert." But no, Deseret is the "land of the honeybee," according to the Book of Mormon. I guess I should have figured they would have caught a typo in the masthead after 154 years.

diction

As in the correct choice of words in writing or speaking. Samuel Johnson, for one, believed that great thoughts were of a general nature. He said it is not the business of poets to "number the streaks of the tulip." I couldn't disagree more. I'm all for numbering the streaks of the tulip. Isn't that what they tell you in writing class? Write the specifics. Once you've put in some time numbering the streaks, then you can draw some grand conclusion about tulips or botany or life. Great thoughts don't just appear out of nowhere, I think. That's right. Damn, it feels good to disagree with the towering minds of the past.

Dionysus

Maybe it's time to join Mensa. This, as most people know, is the society for bona fide geniuses and also Geena Davis. So in my quest to become at least one of those two things, I decide it'd be good to start hanging around some heavyweight brains.

Of course, I'm terrified that I'll be rejected. In fact, I'm pretty sure that they'll send me a letter thanking me for my interest, then have a nice hearty laugh and go back to their algebraic topology and Heidegger texts and *Battlestar Galactica* reruns. But if ever I have a chance of sneaking in, it's now, when my brain is plump with information.

I log on to the Mensa Web site, and after several minutes of clicking, I discover something strange. You don't need to take the famously difficult Mensa admissions test as long as you have what is called "prior evidence." And what is prior evidence? IQ tests, GMAT scores, SAT scores, that kind of thing. I check the SAT scores. If you took the SATs in 1986 as I did, you need a 1250 or above to qualify for Mensa. Twelve-fifty? That doesn't seem so high. You get 800 just for mastering the art of inhaling and exhaling. I scored a respectable 1410 combined, seeing as I took the test way back when I was still genuinely bright. That's way over 1250. So either I'm not smart enough to decipher the Mensa Web site or I will soon be discussing Proust with Geena Davis over vodka tonics at the annual meeting. This is far too easy. I feel like I've found a huge loophole.

I order my SAT scores and send them to Mensa, and sure enough, a couple of weeks later, I get a bunch of paperwork. I'm in! Well, at least I'm in if I can figure out how to fill in these damn forms, which are about as intuitive as the blueprints for a supercollider. I was particularly careful in totaling up my membership and subscription fees—$49 plus $14 plus $21 equals $84. I did that seven or eight times. A math mistake on the Mensa form would be grounds for blackballing. I look at it one more time. Eighty-four bucks. Jesus. That could explain why they're eager to bring in new members, even if their SAT scores are 1250.

Regardless, this is huge news: A.J. Jacobs, Mensa member. I start dropping that fact at every opportunity. At work, when Sarah, the copy editor, questions my overuse of capital letters in a story, I say, "Well, you know, I *am* a Mensa member." At home, I trot it out during arguments with Julie, like the time we got in a squabble over the Thai food delivery. I'm on the phone with the restaurant and I've forgotten what she wants, even though she's told me three times.

"Coconut shrimp," she repeats. Then sticks out her tongue and rolls her eyes, making the universal sign for "nitwit."

"That was not constructive," I say, after clicking off the phone.

"What are you? A retard?" she asks.

"Uh, how many retards are members of Mensa?"

"Just one," she says.

Cute. Well, at least I can retreat to my surprisingly large stack of Mensa literature. I love curling up with the monthly *Mensa Bulletin,* especially the little announcements in the back for Mensa's special interest groups. There are Mensans who like tennis, cats, scuba diving, the parody songs of Weird Al Yankovic—any hobby you can think of. More disturbing, there's M-Prisoned, for Mensans who are incarcerated, as well as a eugenics group, for Mensans who are interested in manipulating the gene pool, if, of course, they ever have the opportunity to breed. But most unsettling of all is the naturist group, which is for geniuses who like to frolic nude. I don't have firsthand knowledge yet, but I'd say the percentage of Mensans that I'd like to see naked hovers around—let's see now, carry the seven, okay, right—zero percent. And that's counting Geena Davis.

There are plenty of other joys available in the Mensa literature. Looking for typos, for one thing. That gives me a special immature thrill, as when I found this question on the Young Mensa Web site: "In what movie does Robbin Williams star as Mensan Adrian Cronauer?" Robbin Williams? Ha! Just one *b*, Einstein. And it's *Good Morning Vietnam*. If I'm bored with that game, I can browse the Mensa catalogue, enjoying the Mensa T-shirts, Mensa baseball caps, and Mensa critter stuffed animals, which are supposed to look like Beanie Babies to everyone but Beanie Baby lawyers.

But after a month of this, I start to feel cheap. I don't feel like a real Mensa member. I feel I'm a loophole-loving fraud, that I'll always have an asterisk next to my name in the great Mensa logbook, that I'm the Roger Maris of geniuses. I decide I should take the official Mensa test.

I call up the Mensa organization and leave a message that I'm interested in knowing test times. If someone could call me back, I would be "much appreciative." Much appreciative? Jesus. They should take my membership card away for crappy grammar. But who wouldn't get nervous when calling the national headquarters?

A few weeks later, I'm in a fluorescent-lit classroom in Chelsea awaiting the start of the official Mensa test. I'm sitting next to a guy who's doing a series of elaborate neck stretches, like we're about to engage in a vigorous rugby match. He's neatly laid out four types of gum on his Formica desk: Juicy Fruit, Wrigley Spearmint, Big Red, and Eclipse. I hate this guy. I hope to God he's not a genius.

Our proctor—a large woman with an accent I couldn't place—checked our photo IDs to make sure we didn't hire a Stephen Hawking to take the test for us, then handed out an exam. It's seven parts, each about five minutes. I feel okay about the first three parts because they consist of looking at a bunch of cute little pictures, sort of like a very sophisticated version of something you'd see on *Sesame Street*. Which one of these is like the others—King Tut, or the Easter Island statues? I find myself asking questions like, what's the opposite of an Asian woman—Western woman, or an Asian man?

I do okay on the vocabulary section—I know what "propinquity" means—but the math quizzes send my score scurrying south. I have the unpleasant realization that, despite my *Britannica* reading, I have forgotten how to do long division. The accented proctor tells us to put our pencils down when I have finished only a third of the math section.

"That was way too easy," I say, trying to break the iciness between me and the gum fetishist.

"You found that easy?" he says.

"No, just kidding. Why—did you?"

"Well, I finished it without too much problem." At this point, I would like to wring his well-stretched neck.

I feel the *Britannica* failed me thus far, which is annoying. But finally, in section seven, the trusty *EB* gives me a little boost. This part tests the memory; the proctor reads us a story and then asks lots of questions about it. The story, luckily enough, is about Dionysian rituals and Dionysus being born from the thigh of Zeus. Since the *EB* loves its Greek history, I feel at home, and even know that Dionysus crawled out of Zeus's leg. I rule section seven! I hand in my test and leave as my neighbor is still packing up his gum collection. I can't tell whether I squeaked by or not.

A few days later I get a call from a very nice but confused woman at Mensa HQ. She doesn't understand why I took the test when I am already a member.

"I just wanted to see if I was still smart," I say.

"I'm sending you your test fee back."

"But how'd I do on the test? Would I have gotten in on my Mensa test score?"

She pauses. A very long and painful pause. "Be glad you got good SAT scores."

disease

I think about disease a lot. Some people—namely my wife, friends, coworkers, family, and strangers I've just met—call me a hypochondriac. And I admit, I am careful. I avoid handshakes, preferring the head nod or, if necessary, the hug (backs of shirts seem far less likely to harbor germ colonies). I wash my hands till they're chapped white. When I clink glasses for a toast, I make sure to clink the base of the glass so there's no bacteria transfer. So yes, I'm a tad more observant than your average man.

But I wouldn't call myself a hypochondriac, for one reason: I actually do get sick at least twice a month. I swear. My immune system puts up about as much of a fight as your typical French general, such as Achille Bazaine, who surrendered 140,000 troops during the Franco-Prussian War, a strategy that got him sentenced to twenty years in French prison. Viruses, bacteria, funguses—my white blood cells welcome them all. One of my proudest accomplishments at *Entertainment Weekly* was to catch several colds from celebrities, including one from Ellen DeGeneres and another from Ernest Borgnine. I felt just as crappy, but at least I had celebrity germs, which had no doubt lived a glamorous life, probably doing some replicating at an awards ceremony or at Jack Nicholson's pool.

The *Britannica* isn't necessarily very good for someone like me. Even before the *disease* section itself, every two or three pages I learned about some horrible new way to die. This set of books harbors enough illnesses to infest a million petri dishes.

A couple of days ago, right on schedule, I got sick. I shuffled into the living room.

"I'm sick again," I said.

"I'm sorry, honey," said Julie.

"Do I have a waxy pallor?"

"What?"

"A waxy pallor. Do I have one?"

"Not more than normal."

"Good. Because that would mean I have aplastic anemia, which I really don't need right now."

I was sort of joking. But at the same time, I have all these symptoms and diseases floating in my brain. And without really wanting to, every time I start to feel my health go south, I start on a mental checklist of the afflictions I've most recently read about.

Is my urine black? No. Then I probably don't have blackwater fever. So that's a relief.

My joints don't ache, so I don't have bursitis in any of its forms—tennis elbow, housemaid's knee, soldier's heel, or the dreaded weaver's bottom.

I look at my hands. My fingers aren't involuntarily flexing in a slow and purposeless manner, therefore I probably am not suffering from athetosis. All right.

I pinch my skin. It isn't loose about my face, so I don't have cutis laxa.

I feel good about my chances with Chediak-Higashi syndrome, an immune disorder, since only two hundred cases have ever been reported.

I also probably don't have stinking smut, since it's mostly confined to wheat and rye. But I do like it, because it's the dirtiest-sounding disease thus far. It sounds like something Tony Soprano would say to one of his wayward captains: "Don't you ever fuck with me again, you stinking smut!"

I might, on the other hand, have Andersen's disease, which causes lethargy. But I probably just have a cold.

So this is the problem. I have all this new information to worry about—including some new ones in the *disease* entry itself—and yet I end up doing the same thing: eating some low-fat chicken soup, swallowing some zinc pills, and getting better two days later.

Sometimes I try to look at the ocean of diseases out there in a positive light. I tell myself, sure, I get sick more often than I change my razor, but I should be proud of my immune system for all the evil organisms it does manage to keep out. At least it has denied entry to Malta fever, also known as brucellosis, which causes excessive sweating. Go, microphages! But then I start to focus on Malta fever, which does sound horrible, and I get all worried again. So many diseases, so few white blood cells.

Disney, Walt
Disney's early collaborator was Ub Iwerks—perhaps the *Britannica*'s best name so far. Ub and Walt's first creation was Oswald the Rabbit, but they had to abandon him in a copyright dispute. Another reminder of how different life could be: Rabbiteers, thousands of kids wearing rabbit hats, Oswald-the-rabbit politics.

divorce
The easiest divorce around: Pueblo Indian women leave their husband's moccasins on the doorstep and—that's it—they're divorced. Simple as that. No lawyers, no fault, no socks, just shoes.

dogs
Dogs have a third eyelid to protect the eyeball from irritants, which seems like a damn good idea, and makes me quite jealous.

Incidentally, my own eyes and their paltry two eyelids have become a subject of much concern among my family. My bloodshot left eye has faded to its traditional white, thanks no doubt to Julie's carrots. But my mom is still worried about my extreme reading habits. She's bought me a lamp called Happy Eyes. It's an imposing device—ivory-colored, mammoth, with several moving parts, it looks like it would be right at home in an ob-gyn exam room. But I've come to love that lamp. Its rays are supposed to mimic those of the sun—hence the Happy Eyes label—though it reminds me more of the light I used to have over my pet turtle's tank when I was a kid. Regardless, if I'm going to push my pupils to the limit, if I'm going to force them to run a marathon every day, the least I can do is give them the equivalent of a good pair of Nikes. I recommend Happy Eyes to anyone undertaking this task.

While we're on the subject, I've learned some other important reading techniques. First, the proper stance. Since the *Britannica*'s a cinder block of a book, you can't treat it like your average Patricia Cornwell novel and hold it in the air. I tried, and my wrist paid the price. You need support. After much experimentation, I've found the best method is to lay the encyclopedia on your lap and grasp the edges with both hands, sort of like a steering wheel.

As for the equipment, you'll want to wear loose, comfortable clothing, nothing that will constrain your page-turning ability. An old college sweatshirt is fine. You should drink lots of fluids, load up on protein, and—I can't stress this enough—make sure to take frequent breaks. You've got to give your brain a rest from the heavy lifting. I like to keep some *Us Weekly*s nearby, so that I can relax with an article discussing Julia Roberts's midriff.

I do most, maybe 90 percent, of my *Britannica* reading on a fluffy white couch in the extra bedroom of our apartment. But I've read it all over: in the bathroom, a car's backseat, a car's front seat, a movie theater, a restaurant, a bar, a lobby, an office, a doctor's waiting room. I've got shoulder strain from lugging the thing around New York in a black bag.

I've taken it on the Manhattan subway, and though the lighting isn't ideal, I was pleasantly surprised that I got no strange looks from my fellow passengers. When there's a homeless guy in the same car shouting that Pat Sajak is the second coming of Christ, a man reading an oversized book with some gold embossing on the spine isn't going to attract a lot of attention. New York taxicabs, on the other hand, are much less hospitable. The jouncing over potholes will make you sick. I also strongly recommend against reading the encyclopedia on the Stairmaster. You can strain your mind or you can strain your body, but it's not a good idea to do both. Plus, getting sweat drops on the *Britannica* is just plain wrong.

Everyone asks me, do I skim? Well, it depends on how you define skimming. This I can assure you: I have cast my eyes on every word in the encyclopedia so far. I have not *comprehended* every word, but I have *seen* every word. Sometimes, yes, I zone out and merely sweep my eyes swiftly from left to right across the lines as I think about whether we need to get some more Tropicana orange juice or that I forgot to call my sister back, only to snap to attention a few minutes later.

I'm particularly susceptible to this autopilot mode while reading the *Macropaedia.* For those who don't pay proper attention to encyclopedia structure, the *Britannica* is divided into two main sections: the *Micropaedia* and the *Macropaedia.* The *Micropaedia* accounts for twelve volumes, and it contains thousands of little snippet-sized articles—a couple of paragraphs, maybe a page or two maximum. The *Macropaedia*—which clocks in at seventeen volumes—takes a handful of the *Micro*'s articles (*accounting, China, evolution*) and offers the extended dance mix. The *Macro* articles can be brutal, impenetrable, and they take just shy of a Cryptozoic eon (3 billion years) to read. The one on *digestion and digestive systems* droned on for thirty-nine pages. The one on *continental landforms* had me pleading for mercy at fifty-six pages.

I rotate between the two—I'll read a few hundred pages from the *Micropaedia*'s Bs, then a couple of hundred from the *Macropaedia*'s Bs, after which I'll switch back to the *Micropaedia* for still more Bs. Of the two, I much prefer the *Micro.* It's more like the front section of a magazine—the section I work on at *Esquire*—as opposed to the daunting features in the middle. Right now, I'm in the *Micro,* and am going to dive into the section on the . . .

dragonfly

It can eat its own weight in thirty minutes. Just like Roger Ebert.

Damn. I should be beyond Ebert jokes by now—I'm in the *D*s, for crying out loud—but those pop culture references die hard.

dress and adornment

One of the sad ironies of my life is that I work at *Esquire,* an arbiter of men's fashion, and yet I'm a shockingly bad dresser. I've got all the fashion sense of agricultural zealot Johnny Appleseed, who liked to wear an old coffee sack with holes cut out for arms.

It wasn't always this way. At one point in my mid-twenties, I paid a lot of attention to clothes. I got myself a closet full of tight trousers, some even in primary colors, and a bunch of fancy shirts with buttons made of things like mother-of-pearl. Then I got married. My only criterion now is that all my clothes should feel like pajamas, which can cause some problems at work. I wear these sneaker clogs around the office that would barely be acceptable at a beach cabana. Of course, when I go in to meet with my boss—an appropriately natty man—I make sure to change into my professional black leather shoes. One day last year, I got confused by all the trips back and forth to his office, and ended up taking a meeting with my fancy black shoe on my left foot, and my sneaker clog on the right, like a scene out of a seventies sitcom. And you wonder why I haven't gotten a promotion in three years.

All of this is to say that I took some twisted pleasure in the life of Beau Brummel, the biggest dandy in the *Britannica,* who gets a special shout out in the *dress and adornment* section. I had vaguely heard of Brummel, but knew practically nothing. Here's what I found out: Brummel became famous for his good fashion at Eton, then added "wit" to his résumé at Oxford. He moved to London in 1799, befriended the Prince of Wales, set up a bachelor establishment, and was soon recognized as high society's arbiter of good taste, parading about town in his cravats and silk stockings and pantaloons. Brummel "was so concerned with style that he had his coat made by one tailor, his waistcoat by another, and his breeches by a third. . . . His neckcloth was so elaborate and voluminous that his valet sometimes spent a whole morning getting it to sit properly." The prince himself copied Brummel's look.

Then, in 1812, things started to unravel. Brummel quarreled with the prince (his tongue was "too sharp," says the Britannica), blew through his thirty-thousand-pound inheritance on gambling debts and those damn white cravats. And on the night of May 16, 1816, Britain's most celebrated fop fled to France to avoid his creditors. Brummel struggled on for years in France, and was briefly imprisoned there, also for debt.

And here's the sentence I know I shouldn't enjoy, but I do: "He soon lost all his interest in dress; his personal appearance was slovenly and dirty, and he began to live in fantasies of the past." I feel bad for him, but it's a good fact to have in my plumed hat: even the quintessential dandy eventually gave up on fashion. This I can tell Julie next time she tells me I look like a homeless man.

duality

So far, the Britannica has been intermittently useful. It's given me perspective on my life—sometimes for the better, sometimes for the worse—loaded me up with cocktail party conversation, and helped Julie solve 42-Down. But what about the stuff my old boss at the *Antioch Ledger* newspaper called "news you can use"? What about good, solid how-to hints?

Well, to its credit, the *Britannica* isn't entirely lacking in handy suggestions. For instance, there's a nice write-up on how to protect yourself from painful g-forces when in a spaceship (just turn sideways to the rocket's thrust). And there's another on how to toss a boomerang properly (throw it downward, snapping your wrist right before release). And if you ever see a snake but aren't sure whether it's the deadly coral snake, just remember this poem about its coloring ("Red touching yellow, dangerous fellow"). But so far this winter, I've had minimal contact with boomerangs, acceleration stress, and coral snakes.

Which brings me to tonight's dinner. Finally, a breakthrough I've been waiting for, the first truly practical application of my knowledge. It's a good feeling. Jolly good, even. Here's what happened: My assistant Genevieve, a proud native of Anchorage (she smiles condescendingly whenever we whine about New York winters), sent me Alaskan crab legs as a Christmas gift. Julie is delighted, and has invited her friend Anna over for some crab soup.

"You know," I say, hovering around the kitchen as Julie puts the finishing touches on the soup, "the giant crab in Japan can grow to over twelve feet long."

"Wow, twelve feet," says Julie. Her tone is that of a mother whose four-year-old has toddled in to display a particularly large strand of drool. Anna nods her head, pretending to be impressed as well.

"Okay, soup's on!" says Julie. She ladles out bowls for each of us. "Now the recipe suggests coriander on top. You want?"

"Sure, I'll take some," says Anna.

"Wait," I say. I pause dramatically. "I think 'coriander' is the British word for cilantro."

"Really?" says Julie.

"I think so," I say.

As Julie and I both know too well, Anna despises cilantro with an intensity most people reserve for war criminals or David Arquette, a fact we've learned from several unpleasant guacamole incidents at Mexican restaurants. Julie dips her finger in her bowl—which she has already sprinkled with chopped coriander leaves—and puts a little on her tongue.

"He's right. It's cilantro."

"Read about that just the other day."

"Huh. I never knew," Julie says. "I thought it looked familiar."

Julie had asked the grocery guy for fresh coriander, and he had shown her the cilantro leaves. And now, I had cleared up the confusion. I had exposed this duality.

"Thanks, A.J." says Anna.

" 'Tis a pleasure, guv'nor!" I respond.

"Good job, honey! I'm proud of you."

This is a big moment. Huge. My newly acquired knowledge has actually had a beneficial impact. It has saved a close friend from an unpleasant herb-related experience and earned the respect of my wife.

"Blimey, I need a spoon!" I say.

"Okay," says Julie, "enough with the British talk."

Dundatree

This the Britannica defines as "the mythical country where large-footed dictators come from." Huh. That's an strange concept, I think to myself. I've never even heard of it.

The reason I've never heard of Dundatree is that . . . I dreamed it. I read so much that it's invaded my sleep. I can't escape those endless descriptions and dates, that little ten-point Times font text, the fancy gold embossing, not even when I close my eyes. And now I'm making up my own facts, which I'm worried I'll confuse with actual facts.

Dyer, John

I'm relatively sure I didn't dream this British poet up. He was born in 1699 and he wrote the following verse:

A little rule, a little sway,
A sunbeam in a winter's day,
Is all the proud and mighty have
Between the cradle and the grave.

Jesus. That's disheartening.

On the one hand, I suppose it's a wisely humbling poem. So what if Donald Trump has dozens of menservants to dust his gold-plated toilet plungers? All he really has is a little rule, a little sway, between the cradle and the grave. But on the other hand, the verse plays to my cynical side, the whatever-you-do-doesn't-matter-because-you'll-eventually-die side, which isn't a healthy mind-set. I need better wisdom.

E

Earth

It's Friday night, and Julie and I are out to dinner with our friends Lisa and Paul. Julie met Lisa at camp, and they've remained close for a couple of decades. Lisa looks a bit like Audrey Hepburn, and Paul looks a bit like Lisa, which I guess makes him a male Audrey Hepburn with less hair.

It's always good to see them, even if we all agree the restaurant's chef needs some more focus—he's offering sushi, French food, blintzes, everything but bird's nest soup (a dish made from the saliva of tiny Chinese birds). The main thrust of our conversation is that we're all way too busy. This, I've found, is one of the absolute favorite discussions of East Coast urbanites in my age bracket, along with real estate prices, smoking laws, and the inexplicable career of bow-tied PBS satirist Mark Russell. Well, maybe that last one is my own little obsession.

In any case, my dinner companions are all complaining about their overloaded schedules. Lisa—who never leaves the house without a camera—has a dozen shoe boxes bulging with photos.

"I just don't have time to put them in photo albums."

"I'll do it for you," says Julie. She's the single most organized woman in the world. If given the choice between organizing a closet and going on vacation, she'd have to think about it.

"I might take you up on that," says Lisa. "I'd do it myself, but I just need more hours in the day."

"There really should be at least thirty hours in a day," says Paul.

And here—like a great running back who sees a hole in the offensive line—I make my move. "You know, if you just wait a bit, there will be more hours in the day."

No one responds, so I continue.

"The days are getting longer because of the drag on the earth. So just wait a few million years. I mean, you're lucky you didn't live half a billion years ago. There were only twenty hours in a day."

"You sure do know a lot," says Paul.

I have to say, he's right. I learned that fact in the entry on our planet Earth. It was a fascinating essay—but also more than a bit disconcerting.

It's not just the length of our days that is shifting. There's also a disturbing phenomenon called "polar wandering." Apparently, the North and South Poles are restless little buggers. The magnetic South Pole cruises about eight miles to the northwest each year. Give it a couple decades and it'll make its way to Baton Rouge. After that, I hear it's heading to the Jersey shore.

This I don't get. Stray cats are supposed to wander. Maybe dazed hippies in search of a Phish concert. But the poles? They're supposed to be stable and solid and frozen, like the red-and-white striped poles I used to see on Rankin/Bass Santa Claus specials.

That's not to mention what's known as the precession of equinoxes: the earth is wobbling on its axis every 26,000 years. And there's more. The earth's magnetic field reverses direction every 300,000 to a million years. There's something called azimuthal drift, which involves shifting particle streams. And many other things I barely understand.

The point is, the earth's not solid as a rock. The earth's not firm. The earth is a big wobbling, wandering, reversing, shifting sphere of Jell-O. I suppose I should have known from elementary school that my world wasn't completely stationary. I knew about the revolving and rotating and had a passing acquaintance with plate tectonics.

But the volume of instability and flux—that's what threw me. It makes me feel like I'm walking on a half-melted ice pond.

And by the way, in case you're under the impression that the earth is a sphere, you're wrong. It bulges in the middle, like Alfred Hitchcock after a couple too many helpings of kidney pie. It's a wobbling, wandering, reversing, shifting sphere of Jell-O with a weight problem. But it's all we've got.

After dinner, as we walk along the rickety West Side streets, Julie says: "Honey, I think you need to restrain yourself a little with the facts."

Damn. I was riding high from my cilantro victory. Now I've gone and blown that goodwill. "But I did restrain myself," I say. "I had a lot more facts about the earth I didn't mention."

"Well, thank you for that."

"You didn't find that interesting at all?" I ask. "That our days are getting longer?"

"I'm just saying, you seem to be losing your ability to interact with human beings."

"So you're saying I once *had* ability to interact with human beings?"

I got her there. Ha! But Julie does have a point. Maybe I need to control myself a little more. It's just so hard—I've crammed so much info into my brain, I feel that I need to get it out whenever I can. It's so damn cathartic (as are certain noxious members of the buttercup family when ingested).

Ecclesiastes

This is a book of the Old Testament. I don't believe I've ever read this section of the Bible—I know my Genesis pretty well and my Ten Commandments (I like lists), but I'm hazy on a lot of the other parts. Here, the *Britannica* provides a handy Cliffs Notes version of Ecclesiastes:

> [The author's] observations on life convinced him that "the race is not to the swift, nor the battle to the strong, nor bread to the wise, nor riches to the intelligent, nor favor to the men of skill; but time and chance happen to them all" (9:11). Man's fate, the author maintains, does not depend on righteous or wicked conduct but is an inscrutable mystery that remains hidden in God (9:1). All attempts to penetrate this mystery and thereby gain the wisdom necessary to secure one's fate are "vanity," or futile. In the face of such uncertainty, the author's counsel is to enjoy the good things that God provides while one has them to enjoy.

This is great. I've accumulated hundreds of facts in the last seven thousand pages, but I've been craving profundity and perspective. Yes, there was that Dyer poem, but that was just cynical. This is the real thing: the deepest paragraph I've read so far in the encyclopedia. Instant wisdom. It couldn't be more true: the race does not go to the swift. How else to explain the mouth-breathing cretins I knew in high school who now have multimillion-dollar salaries? How else to explain my brilliant and kind friends who are still stuck selling wheatgrass juice at health food stores? How else to explain Vin Diesel's show business career? Yes, life is desperately, insanely, absurdly unfair. But Ecclesiastes offers exactly the correct reaction to that fact. There's nothing to be done about it, so enjoy what you can. Take pleasure in the small things—like, for me, Julie's laugh, some nice onion dip, the insanely comfortable beat-up leather chair in our living room.

I keep thinking about Ecclesiastes in the days that follow. What if this is the best the encyclopedia has to offer? What if I have found the meaning of life on page 347 of the *E* volume? The *Britannica* is not a traditional book, so there's no reason why the big revelation should be at the end. Will *zywiec* be even more profound than Ecclesiastes? Maybe, but I doubt it.

ecstasy

I learn that ecstasy was patented as an appetite suppressant by Merck in the 1920s. Incidentally, I took Merck's appetite suppressant when I went to visit Brown University as a high school senior trying to figure out where to go to college. Damn, that was a great visit. Brown should give out ecstasy to all prospective applicants.

I couldn't believe how wonderful everything at the school was. "I love this cafeteria! This is the most beautiful cafeteria I've ever seen. And this baked ziti—this is fucking delicious! You get to live in these dorm rooms? They're palaces. And your library carrels are so well designed. What beautiful fluorescent lighting! God, look at that pile of bricks in the yard. That's the most gorgeous pile of bricks at any college I've ever seen." I think I gave out about fifteen hugs to surprised and apprehensive students who made the mistake of wandering within a twenty-foot radius of me.

Unfortunately, the ecstasy had worn off by the time I actually became a freshman at Brown and learned that the baked ziti actually tasted like Styrofoam dipped in ketchup.

eggplant

It's our apartment-warming tonight—we moved in six months ago, but never got around to throwing a party till now. It'll be our first catered affair. A real adult party with men in tuxedos passing out skewered coconut chicken and grilled eggplant roulade (eggplant's name, by the way, comes from the white egg-shaped variety, which I've never seen). We spend the day cleaning up. I, for one, make sure my *Britannica* volumes are neatly lined up, ready for their debut in polite society.

The party seems to go well. People love the skewered coconut chicken, and the dreaded mixing of friends seems to be going along without incident.

Midway through the party, I see Dad talking to one of Julie's former coworkers, a banker named Jeff. Jeff motions me over.

"When's your birthday?" Jeff asks.

I look at Dad. His face is poker serious, but I can see it in his eyes. The glint. I know what I'm supposed to say. I'm supposed to say February 29.

My father has been telling Jeff one of his classics, namely, an elaborate story about how the entire Jacobs family shares the same birthday: leap year day. My dad has no doubt informed Jeff that his own birthday is February 29, 1940 (he was actually born on February 26), and that he met my mom at Cornell because they were both members of a club for students born on leap year day, and that she was born exactly four years after him (she was born on February 3). In the story, they got married and timed the conception of my sister and me so that we too were born on leap year day. Well, they had to do cesareans on us, but we still qualify as February 29 birthdays. So we were, he told Jeff, the only family in the United States with all four members born on leap year day. The odds of that, my father has calculated, are 4.6 trillion to one.

Jeff is no doubt conflicted. On the one hand, my father—a man he barely knows and who has no reason to lie to him—is telling this story without a hint of a smile and in remarkably convincing detail. On the other hand, it sure seems like a crock.

"What's your birthday?" says Jeff again.

I just couldn't do it. "March 20th." I say.

I think this is my father's greatest disappointment with me—that I don't collude with him on his practical jokes. Those jokes are his favorite form of social interaction. He tells them at every opportunity in his low-decibel voice, two notches above a mumble.

Sometimes they can be simple, these jokes: he'll introduce himself to strangers at a party by saying, "Hello, I'm Sam." Or Harvey or Edgar or whatever name strikes him.

But those are just throwaways. My dad prefers the more complex ruses. When asked his occupation, my father will say, "I sell cemetery plots." And then he'll describe a nice space he can offer his conversation partner, something with a lovely view of a lake.

Then he might ask what his conversation partner does for a living. Whatever the answer, my dad will always feign ignorance about the firm.

"Time Inc.? Is that a clock company?"

"Harvard? Is that in Pennsylvania?"

No, the person will patiently explain. It's a magazine company or it's a college in Massachusetts, or what have you.

"Oh, yes," my dad will say. "I think I've heard of it."

And then there are the carefully premeditated jokes. My father is a teetotaler, but if he's at a dinner party—preferably hosted by someone who doesn't know him very well—and offered a drink, he'll inevitably order a Yellow Lightning.

"Yellow Lightning?" the host will say.

"Yes, please."

"I'm sorry, I'm not sure what a Yellow Lightning is."

"Oh, it's two parts lemon Kool-Aid and one part tequila."

My dad has concocted the Yellow Lightning on the theory that no one in America has both necessary ingredients. The apologetic host will inevitably return from the kitchen to explain that they can't find any lemon Kool-Aid in the cupboard.

"Well, nothing for me, then," my father will sigh. "Thanks anyway."

And then, at the far end, are those lies that are so byzantine, so full of twists and nuances, that I can never remember how they go, even though I've heard them recounted a dozen times. I know, for instance, he somehow convinced a fellow lawyer that her tip at a restaurant hadn't been big enough, which caused the waiter to go postal and punch out all the eatery's windows, which got him arrested and ruined his life. M&M's were somehow involved. So were wooden boards. She called the restaurant to apologize, and the maitre d', of course, was baffled.

As I said, I never play along with Dad's games. Like when he introduces me as his son-in-law Willy, I just say, "Hi, I'm A.J." He always looks a little crestfallen. I'm not sure why I do it. Maybe it's because I know that I can't compete with him in this arena. Or maybe it's a remnant of my adolescent rebelliousness—my dad puts so much energy and thought into these fabrications, I just want to throw cold water on them.

But anyway, back to Jeff, who is shaking his head and chuckling politely. He knew something was fishy.

"Your dad almost had me there," he says.

Well, I tell him, he can always be sure of one thing: if a stranger says he was born any day between October 4 and October 15, 1582, he's lying. Why? Because there were no such dates. That's when the Western world switched to the Gregorian calendar, and they skipped those ten days. Never happened. Jeff makes that face that I've come to know well from other people: he purses his lips in a sort of half frown, raises his eyebrows, and nods his head. The universal symbol for "Isn't that something."

My dad and I are similar in that respect—we've each found a way to deal with our innate social awkwardness: he with his practical jokes, I with my facts. We're quite a duo. We even look alike—lanky, brown-haired, bespectacled. And our combined conversational tactics have apparently given Jeff an appetite. He excuses himself to get some more eggplant roulade.

elf

Not the cute creatures we've been spoon-fed by the media. Elves in traditional folklore sat on people's chests while they slept to give them bad dreams. They also stole human children and substituted deformed fairy children. Wonder if Santa is really a crack dealer.

embalming

I'm still worried about myself. Remember that problem I had with Aristotle? That I was more interested in how he chased young girls than in his metaphysics? I'm still suffering from that same handicap. I should be grappling with quasars or learning secrets behind the human genome, and yet, here I am, fourteen thousand entries in, and my favorite article so far is this one—the history of embalming. And yet I can't help it. I find it fascinating.

First off, the embalming article has plenty of new uses for the basic items found right in my own kitchen. For instance, Alexander the Great's body was returned from Babylon to Macedonia in a cask of honey. And when British admiral Lord Nelson's body was shipped back to England from Trafalgar, it was pickled in brandy, much like Lee Marvin's.

Second, since everyone likes easy-to-follow recipes, the *Britannica* offers this one, courtesy of Egyptian mummifiers: Remove the brain and intestines, wash in palm wine, and place in vases. Fill body cavity with perfumes. Stitch incisions and place body in potassium nitrate for seventy days. Remove. Wash and wrap in cotton bandages. Enjoy.

But my favorite part of the embalming entry was a man named Martin Van Butchell and his ingenious loophole. Before I get to that, a quick detour, because loopholes deserve a little attention of their own. I've been keeping track of loopholes, and have come to the conclusion that humans are a sleazy, slippery, tricky, untrustworthy species. The Bible says that men of the cloth cannot take up the sword. So what'd medieval bishops do? They took up the club. They figured, apparently, that it's perfectly okay with Jesus to bash in the head of the enemy, as long as it's not with a long metallic blade. Speaking of religious men, monks were banned from eating meat on Friday. Somehow—and there's no explanation of the logic behind this one—the monks decided that baby rabbits were fish. And in colonial America, legend has it that the authorities outlawed nine-pin bowling. So what'd bowling fans do? They added another pin and invented ten-pin bowling. Voilà! That's not illegal.

So as you can see, if there's a law, rule, or order, someone's going to find the loophole. Which brings us back to Martin Van Butchell. Van Butchell was a widower in 18th-century England. His wife—a wealthy lady—had specified in her will that Van Butchell could have access to her money only as long as her body was aboveground. I suppose she didn't want him spending it on gold snuffboxes for his second wife. Problem is, when Mrs. Van Butchell died, her husband found perhaps the best loophole in the history of wills. He hired a man named John Hunter to perform one of the first arterial embalmings ever, then placed Mrs. Van Butchell's fashionably dressed body in a glass-lidded case in a sitting room and held regular visiting hours. Her body remained, technically, aboveground, and he was free to frolic in her bank account.

emotion

Despite the enjoy-life-while-you-can wisdom of Ecclesiastes, I've been mildly depressed lately. Partly it's because I'm exhausted—this early-morning schedule is a killer. I know I brought it on myself—no one's threatening to kneecap me if I don't read a hundred pages a day. Still, it's a killer. Journalists just aren't meant to wake up to the sunrise and Al Roker's relentlessly cheery voice. But the real reason I'm down is that we got slammed with another negative pregnancy test the other day. I hate it. It makes life's little annoyances—my commute, the line at the drugstore, etc.—seem especially unbearable.

I've taken the offensive against the depression—I've become annoyed at it. I've decided 98 percent of depression has long outlived its Darwinian value. You ingest a dozen pages of biology every day—the evolution of crustaceans and bacteria and blood types—and you start to see everything in a Darwinian light. Even emotion. I'm not sure what the original evolutionary value of sadness was, but I can guarantee you this: mine is not helping me survive or reproduce. My freezer will still have plenty of microwave veggie lasagnas regardless of whether or not I get upset at the fourteen-minute wait for the subway. Unfortunately, this realization—brilliant as it may be—hasn't helped me shake off the funk.

As I dive into the *Macropaedia* article on *emotion,* I'm hoping to find some more helpful information. And sure enough, I do. There's a snappy section on something called "facial feedback." This is when your brain senses that your facial muscles are in a happy position, so the brain figures, Hey, I must be happy. (The brain can be remarkably stupid sometimes.) As the *Britannica* puts it, there is "some scientific support for the old advice 'smile when you feel blue' and 'whistle a happy tune when you're afraid.'"

For the rest of the morning, as I plow through the *Es,* I test out some facial feedback. I force my lips into a slightly exhausting, two-hour-long fake smile. On a bathroom break, I check out my face in the mirror. It frightens me. It looks like I have electrodes in my cheeks that are zapping my face into an unnatural approximation of happiness. I look like a deranged elf in a horror movie about an axe-murdering Santa. But I have to say—I think it might be working. I am feeling just the tiniest bit better.

In addition to facial feedback, I also paid close attention to the section on dealing with anger. The *Britannica* lists several strategies, among them:

1. Confrontative coping ("stood my ground and fought")
2. Distancing ("didn't let it get to me")
3. Planful problem solving ("changed or grew as a person")
4. Positive reappraisal

Studies show that the first two methods—confrontation and distancing—just make people more upset. The second two—planful problem solving and positive reappraisal—make them happier. I've always been a distancer, a stereotypically stoic male. This is good. I'm going try out this planful problem solving.

I decide to start with yesterday's dustup with the Verizon phone company. That pissed me off. It involved forty-seven minutes on hold, several forms that I had filled out twice before, and an extremely patronizing tone of voice from a woman with the IQ of a five-assed abalone. How could I planfully solve this problem? After less than a minute's thought, I figured it out. Get my assistant Genevieve to call next time. Nothing makes me feel better than delegating.

encyclopedia

The *Britannica* does not suffer from any self-esteem issues. This book is not ashamed of itself. In fact, one of the favorite topics in the *Britannica* is . . . the *Britannica. Britannica* editors, *Britannica* publishers, *Britannica* Chinese editions—they all get their very own entry. I wouldn't be surprised if the guy I talked to at *Britannica*'s CD-ROM tech support gets his own write-up soon. (Yes, it's true—I buckled and got the *Britannica* CD-ROM, which I use occasionally for its search function).

That's not to mention the way the *Britannica* manages to insert itself the unlikeliest of places—as with its discussion of the hand grenade pioneer who began his hand grenade obsession after reading about the weapons in his *EB*. In short, if the *Britannica* were a teenage boy, it would be in serious danger of growing hairy palms.

But right now, I've arrived at the most onanistic moment of all—the encyclopedia essay on encyclopedias. If I'm going to be spending a year with these thirty-two clunky volumes, I might as well pay attention to where the hell they came from.

The word "encyclopedia" is derived from Greek—as you'd expect—and means a circle of learning. Plato's nephew wrote perhaps the first circle of learning, with Pliny the Elder polishing off his own version soon after. (By the way, Pliny the Elder died investigating the eruption of Mount Vesuvius in 79 A.D. Another martyr to knowledge—we salute you!)

Over the millennia, humans have produced an estimated two thousand encyclopedias. The award for the longest goes to China's Yu-Hai encyclopedia, published in 1738, at a disturbing 240 volumes. The most lyrical is probably the French one from 1245, written in octosyllabic verse. The most creatively organized—I'd give that to the Spanish encyclopedia from the 15th century that was written allegorically, with a young man getting lessons from maidens named Grammar, Logic, Rhetoric, and so on.

The most historic, though, is not a matter of debate. It has to be Diderot's *Encyclopédie,* which made its debut in Paris in August of 1751. I knew this was a controversial pile of books, but I had no idea exactly how big a ruckus it had made. Editors were jailed, the volumes themselves were locked up in the Bastille alongside murderers and madmen, and police scoured Paris in search of manuscripts to burn. The *Encyclopédie*—written

by the intellectual rock stars of the day, including Voltaire and Rousseau—
went out of its way to squash myths and needle the clergy, even featuring a
quasi-flattering write-up of atheism. And it might have been censored
completely if not for a chance dinner table conversation at King Louis XV's
palace. The king got into a squabble with his guests about the correct composition of gunpowder. The solution: they dispatched someone to track
down a copy of the illegal *Encyclopédie*. After that, according to Voltaire, the
king grudgingly tolerated the pesky volumes.

Less than twenty years later and five hundred miles to the north—
and with a lot less hullabaloo—the first edition of the mighty *Britannica*
came off the presses in Edinburgh, Scotland. This 1768 edition had three
fathers: an obscure printer named Colin Macfarquhar; an editor named
William Smellie, who in his spare time was an accomplished drunk (he
liked to toss back pints with poet Robert Burns); and a buffoon named
Andrew Bell, who stood four foot six and had a huge nose—but liked to
wear an even bigger papier-mâché nose as a joke. Ha! Incidentally, he
could pay for his wacky nose with the fortune earned from engraving
fancy dog collars for the rich. They shared an interest in learning and, apparently Greek-inspired spelling (hence the *ae* in encyclopaedia).

The work they produced is an odd and fascinating cocktail. I ordered
a set from *Britannica*—you can buy reproductions, complete with fake
age spots. Dip in anywhere, and you'll get a taste of what was important
to the average 18th-century Scotsman. As Herman Kogan points out in
The Great EB—a remarkably detailed history of the *Britannica*—the first
edition devotes seven lines to drama and dispenses with poetry in five
hundred words. But cures for horse disease? That fills a riveting thirty-
nine pages. Apparently, the Scots had some seriously unhealthy horses.

Not counting veterinary tracts, the first *Britannica* can be great reading—opinionated, eccentric, occasionally cranky. Suicide, the *Britannica*
informs its readers, is "an act of cowardice disguised as heroism." For excessive gas, the *Britannica* prescribes almond oil and tobacco smoke
blown up the anus. Cold baths should be taken for melancholy, madness,
and the bites of mad dogs. And cats? My God, these Scotsmen were not
cat people. The poor feline species inspires several hundred words of venomous prose. To give you an idea:

Of all domestic animals, the character of the cat is the most equivo-
cal and suspicious. He is kept, not for any amiable qualities, but

purely with a view to banish rats, mice and other noxious animals from our houses.... Constantly bent upon theft and rapine, they are full of cunning and dissimulation; they conceal all their designs; seize every opportunity of doing mischief, and then fly from punishment.... In a word, the cat is totally destitute of friendship.

Wait, there's more. The cat is overly "amorous" (that is, horny), "torments" his prey, and generally "delights in destroying all kinds of weak animals indifferently." Cats often pretend to sleep when "in reality they are meditating mischief." Oh, and cat mothers "devour their offspring."

Well. As an unabashed cat lover, I have to disagree. Cats may not have the wide-eyed unquestioning loyalty of dogs, but they're also not the feline equivalent of Josef Mengele. Plus, they won't go mad and chew on your leg, forcing you to take cold baths. (By the way, the current *Britannica* seems to have gotten over its cat issues; the 2002 edition says that "the cat's independent personality, grace, cleanliness and subtle displays of affection have wide appeal." Much better spin.)

The first edition of *Britannica* clocks in at only three volumes. Oddly, the erudite Scottish boys had an obsession with the letters *A* and *B*; those two get an entire volume all to themselves. The rest of the alphabet is crammed into the remaining two volumes. Apparently, Smellie and friends got a little bored of their project midway through and decided it would be more fun to go to the tavern with Robert Burns. The letter *Z* is lucky to get mentioned at all.

The first edition became a moderate hit, selling about three thousand copies, according to *The Great EB*. Soon after, pirated editions were printed in America, available to the colonists for $6. Among those who bought a set were George Washington and Thomas Jefferson. The official second edition came out in 1777. Smellie declined to edit this one, so his replacement was another hard-drinking Scotsman, named James Tytler. Tytler's other claim to fame: an early fan of hot-air ballooning, he reputedly made love to a dentist's daughter on a flight, thus earning himself what some say is the very first membership in the Mile High Club.

Since then, the *Britannica* has climbed its way on up to the fifteenth edition—an edition being defined as a top-to-bottom rewrite—which debuted in 1974. That's the edition I have on my mustard-colored shelf right now. Sales of the fifteenth have dropped since the glory days of the eighties. And astute home owners will notice that *Britannica* salesmen no longer tap on their doors—they were nixed in 1994. (Incidentally, star salesmen of yore include the founder of Sharper Image and the father of comedian Mike Myers.) But sales have stabilized recently, thanks mostly to schools and libraries, which replenish their sets regularly.

As you might expect, the big growth spurt has come on the electronic side—the Internet, CD-ROM, and DVDs—which now make up about half of the *Britannica*'s business. Yes, Microsoft's *Encarta* is the market leader, the Nike sneakers of the encyclopedia world. But the *Britannica*'s business is big enough to support a staff of five hundred worldwide who diligently revise the articles. In the last couple of years, they've tweaked about a third of the 65,000 entries in ways large and small.

The shifting *Britannica* text is fascinating to me. The first couple of editions are works of art, but I love to read any and all vintage editions. They're always a snapshot of the age, each revealing its own delightful and disturbing prejudices. My friend Tom, a writer at *Esquire*, has volumes *A* through *Q* of the 1941 Britannica. He rescued them one day when he was poking around the garbage dump at Shelter Island, but had to abandon volumes *R* through *Z* because they were too stained with burrito juice. In that edition, Herman Melville got a dismissive little write-up—some minor American writer with a weakness for turgid prose who squeezed out a couple of decent nautically-themed books. Apparently, the Melville renaissance hadn't hit the *Britannica* offices in 1941.

You can find good stuff even in those editions from just twenty years ago. The library at *Esquire* has the 1980 *Britannica,* which I peeked at, only to find what is probably the strangest passage ever published in *Britannica*'s history. It's about John Adams, in the section on his retirement, and it says he spent his old age "enjoying his tankard of hard cider each morning before breakfast" and "rejoicing at the size of his manure pile." Now, it's moderately strange that the second president of the United States was sloshed before breakfast. But that he derived joy from the size of a pile of excrement? I just don't know how to interpret that. It occurs to me, though, that this might make for a nice monument to this American hero—a marble replica of his twenty-foot-high manure collection. Take that, Mount Rushmore!

And speaking of classic *Britannicas,* we can't neglect the most classic of them all: the eleventh edition, from 1911. As any book-obsessed dweeb will tell you, this was the greatest encyclopedia ever produced. This is the edition that has not one but two Web sites devoted to it—1911encyclopedia.org and classiceb.com. Granted, Ashton Kutcher has a few more, but still, for cyclopedia, that's not bad.

What made it so momentous? Partly, it was the contributors. This edition was written by hundreds of heavyweight experts, including scientist T. H. Huxley, philosopher Alfred North Whitehead, poet Algernon Swinburne, and revolutionary Peter Kropotkin, who wrote the *anarchy* entry from his jail cell. But the impressive roster alone doesn't quite explain the cult of the eleventh—especially since many of those essays were left over from previous editions. Plus, the real blockbuster names wouldn't come until the thirteenth edition (Houdini wrote on magic, Freud on psychoanalysis, and Einstein on physics).

You could also argue that the eleventh's appeal comes from its literary style—the prose is wonderful, occasionally worthy of a novel. Consider Lord Macaulay's essay on Samuel Johnson, which contained passages like this one, about Johnson's depression: "The light from heaven shone on him indeed, but not in a direct line, or with its own pure splendour. The rays had to struggle through a disturbing medium; they reached him refracted, dulled and discoloured by the thick gloom which had settled on his soul, and, though they might be sufficiently clear to guide him, were too dim to cheer him." The man could *write*.

Still, the literary style doesn't quite explain the eleventh's unique appeal, either. To really understand what's going on, your best bet is to consult a 1981 *New Yorker* article by Hans Koning called "Onward and Upward with the Arts: The Eleventh Edition." This was when magazine articles were almost as long as the *Britannica* itself; if his piece appeared today, it would probably be squeezed into a three-sentence photo caption. Koning starts his opus with a primer on encyclopedias in general (part of which I referred to above). He then makes his argument: that the eleventh was the culmination of the Enlightenment, the last great work of the Age of Reason, the final instance when all human knowledge could be presented with a single point of view. Four years later, the confidence and optimism that had produced the eleventh would be, as Koning puts it, "a casualty in the slaughter at Ypres and the Argonne."

The eleventh edition was a work in which civilization would soon conquer every corner of the earth, a book that predicted the "lessening of international jealousies." This was a book, says Koning, where reason ruled and great deeds were done by great and logical men, not the result of irrational forces or luck. Having read a bit of the eleventh, I think he's right. That's where the real appeal lies—nostalgia for a world where it all made sense, where all was knowable, where one point of view was the correct one.

Of course, as Koning points out, this point of view had an ugly side: it was racist as all hell. "The negro would appear to stand on a lower evolutionary plane than the white man, and to be more closely related to the highest anthropoids." Haitians are "ignorant and lazy" and the natives of the Philippines are "physical weaklings . . . with large clumsy feet."

The *EB* has since weeded out racism. But having read eight thousand pages, I still notice the tone that Koning talks about. The volume has been turned down, but it's still there: the world of the *EB* is still one that treats everything rationally and sensibly, that still believes in the overall progress of civilization. As worldviews go, it may be deluded—but I like it. It's better than the alternative.

Engels, Friedrich

Back to my 2002 edition, and Friedrich Engels. I'd always thought of Engels as the lesser half of the Marx–Engels team, sort of a 19th-century revolutionary Garfunkel. But in a way, Engels is more interesting than his better-known compatriot.

What I love about Engels is his capacity to lead a double life. Born to a plush existence—his father owned a cotton plant in Manchester and a textile factory in Prussia—Engels spent the better part of thirty years in the family trade. During the day, he was an effective German businessman, crunching his numbers, closing his deals. But after hours, Engels wrote spittle-emitting articles against the evils of capitalism.

To outward appearances, he seemed quite well adjusted. As the *Britannica* says, "He joined a choral society, frequented the famed Ratskeller, became an expert swimmer and practiced fencing and riding (he outrode most Englishmen in the foxhunts)." That has got to be one of the most startling images I've encountered in *Britannica,* second only to John Adams's manure pile: the cofounder of modern communism astride a gelding, all decked out in a red jacket and jodhpurs, shouting "Tally ho!" with a German accent. Then, presumably, Engels would go home, take a bath, and scribble screeds urging textile factory workers to string up their evil foxhunting capitalist bosses. Eventually, Engels got promoted to partner in the Manchester cotton plant, where he continued to bring home the knockwurst, "never allowing his communist principles and criticism of capitalist ways to interfere with the profitable operations of his firm." By the way, in between his fomenting and his foxhunting, Engels found time to learn twenty-four languages.

So there's Engels for you—the ultimate limousine liberal. It reminded me of this guy I knew in college. He was an avowed manifesto-quoting communist, but his dad was some fancy Washington lobbyist. You could just tell this guy grew up in an enormous house filled with Latin American domestics and an intercom system to connect the various wings. When I first visited his dorm room, I remember complimenting him on his lovely colossal poster of Vladimir Lenin. He thanked me, then told me how proud he was of the frame he had selected—it was mahogany, if I recall correctly. A professionally framed poster of Lenin. For the same price he could have bought three tractors for a Minsk turnip farm.

In Engels's case, though, his ability to live with a surreal contradiction worked out nicely. If Engels wasn't a corporate drone by day, he wouldn't have had the cash to send to that moocher Marx. Without his allowance, Marx wouldn't have had the time to formulate his revolutionary theories, Russia might never have gone communist, and Warren Beatty would never have written the screenplay for *Reds*. So the *Britannica* has taught me that hypocrisy can be effective. Of course, it might have been better if Engels hadn't endorsed a totally flawed social system, but you can't have everything.

Enigma

"Device used by the German military command to encode strategic messages before and during World War II. The Enigma code was first broken by the Poles in the early 1930s." See? The Poles aren't so dumb. Another stereotype busted by the *Britannica*. (A stereotype, by the way, is a printing plate. I never knew that one).

eraser

Good thing I didn't take more ecstasy during my college years. I need all the brain cells I have. This became apparent during a conversation with Julie a couple of days after our party. She asked me how I was liking the Hanukkah present she had given me.

"Which one?" I asked.

"The one at your office."

I blanked. A Hanukkah present I brought to work? What the hell was it?

My mind is so packed with bauxite formations and Cameroonian cities and 19th-century composers that it's elbowing out everything else in my life.

"I'm loving it!" I said.

But I gave myself away with that two-second delay.

"You don't know what it is, do you?"

"Yes, I do."

"What?"

"Um, a Frisbee?" I guessed.

She laughed—which was a relief.

"You got too much in your *keppe*."

Turned out it was an aromatherapy candle that smelled like grass. And I was liking it quite a bit—that much I remembered.

It's not just Hanukkah gifts I'm forgetting. It's my beloved facts. The new ones are pushing out the old ones. Here's a demoralizing story: Back in the early *E*s, I read about the scientist who pioneered the study of how humans forget information over time; he invented a curve to describe the phenomenon. When I read that entry, I said to myself, I'm going to make an effort not to forget this man's name.

Well, yesterday—about two weeks after I'd made that vow—I tried to remember his name. I couldn't come up with it. I knew it was an *E* name, but nothing else. Ironic, no? I looked in my notes and figured it out. It's Ebbinghaus. Hermann Ebbinghaus and his famous "forgetting curve."

I said before that I was remembering a lot more than I thought I would. That's true. But I'm also forgetting a lot more. This seems paradoxical, but you have to understand—I just didn't grasp the huge cubic volume of information I'd be ingesting. So I both remember more and forget more than I anticipated. There's that much information.

But man, what a world I've forgotten. I've forgotten more than many people have learned their whole lives. I've forgotten a small stadium of historical figures. I've forgotten a couple of zoos' worth of animals. I've forgotten a continent's worth of towns, and equations to fill a thousand blackboards.

Of course, forgetting is not a black-and-white issue. The information doesn't suddenly disappear like a pencil marks under an eraser (which, incidentally, is made of rubber, pumice, vegetable oil, and sulfur). It doesn't vaporize in a flash of gunpowder. It fades like the color of a sofa in the sun. So I'm left with hundreds of half facts, missing a correct detail here, a name there.

I remembered that the author of *Peter Pan* had an unconsummated marriage, but I couldn't tell you the asexual man's name. I remember the publisher of some magazine built a secret subway underneath New York sometime in the 1800s—but which magazine? I remember that there's a movie where the actor playing an Egyptian pharaoh wore sneakers, but which movie? Don't know. (It was *The Ten Commandments*—I just looked it up in the *anachronism* section.)

ethical relativism

This I knew about. I discovered ethical relativism way back in high school. I had been reading something pretentious—perhaps Roland Barthes, maybe a logical positivist of some sort—and I unearthed this amazing truth: there is no such thing as absolute morals! I've since come to believe that teenagers and profound philosophical doctrines are a bad mix, as dangerous as nitroglycerin and kieselguhr (Alfred Nobel's original recipe for dynamite). And this philosophical doctrine practically exploded in my face, leading to an absurd and humiliating moment in my career as a young know-it-all.

It was my senior year at Dalton, the New York private school I attended from kindergarten on up to graduation. You may remember Dalton from its not-so-flattering cameo in Woody Allen's *Manhattan*. It was the school where Mariel Hemingway's 17-year-old character studied algebra before going home to have sex with Woody's character, who was about eighty-three at the time. I don't believe that too many of the girls in my Dalton class were having sex with eighty-three-year-olds after school, though if they were, it would help explain why none of them ever had sex with me. In any case, Dalton is a very hoity-toity institution, attracting the offspring of lawyers and bankers and the occasional celebrity. (Robert Redford's daughter! Jonas Salk's niece!) And thanks to its embarrassingly large endowment, the academics were demanding.

Such was the case with my senior year physics course, which I took with my friend Nick Panetti. Since I was marginally better at physics than Nick—who admittedly wasn't going to be the next Heisenberg—I decided to let him cheat off my exam. Which wasn't smart to begin with. But then I made things much, much worse by committing a stupid error: I wrote "$f = m + a$" instead of the more traditional (if slightly clichéd) equation "$f = ma$." Nick duplicated my error. As we used to say back then, we were so busted.

The head of the high school—a pudgy bearded guy who pretended to be loosey-goosey and liberal, but who was actually a total hard-ass—scheduled a meeting with me and my parents for the next day. I went home and spent several hours scribbling a three-page, single-spaced, brilliantly reasoned defense. My argument boiled down to this: all morality is relative. I have my own moral system. In my moral system, letting Nick cheat off my exam was not wrong. Therefore what I did was not wrong. Therefore the Dalton School cannot punish me. QED.

In preparation for our meeting, I presented my argument to my parents. You know, just to see if they had any little suggestions. "And therefore," I read to them off my yellow legal pad, doing my best to speak from the diaphragm, "the Dalton School has no philosophical grounds on which it can punish me. You must let me go."

I looked up. My dad's face was very stern. Even my mom—who almost always supported me, who loved to boast about my brilliance, who knew I was special ever since I mastered that Tonka dump truck before any of my classmates—even Mom seemed unhappy with me. Her face was scrunched up, as if she'd just wandered into a big patch of arales (a flowering plant that emits a fetid odor that attracts flies).

"I think that's a very bad idea," said my dad. "Just go in there and say you're sorry."

"No, I'm saying this. It'll work. Trust me."

I brought the notes for my speech to the meeting with the administrator. But as I studied his unsmiling face and listened to his lecture on the honor code, I began to suspect my parents were right. It would take more than a well-organized five-minute speech on ethical paradigms to radically alter his moral philosophy. And if I decided to try, I might well find myself applying for educational opportunities at high schools not featured in Woody Allen movies. So instead, the administrator got to hear how sorry I was that I let Nick cheat off my paper. Truly, awfully sorry. "It was wrong letting Nick cheat off my paper," I said, shaking my head in disbelief at the blackness of my soul. "I'll never do it again."

Whenever I think of this story, I'm always amazed at my initial level of delusion. Nowadays, I know that beautifully crafted philosophical arguments will not get you out of trouble at work, get you a raise, or land you a table at Nobu. And if I were that bearded administrator today, it sure wouldn't work on me. Ethical relativism—even if I still clung to it intellectually in the years that followed—has little impact on my postschool life.

Reading the *Britannica*, though, had an odd effect on me: it actually made me much less of an ethical relativist. I had a vague idea from high school and college that I shouldn't be judging other cultures, especially preliterate ones. They have their own customs, and who are we to critique them with our biased Western eyes? A few thousand pages of the *Britannica* will cure you of any fuzzy idealization of preliterate societies. I've read about culture after culture with traditions that strike me as wrong—evil, even.

Just try to refrain from judgment when you read about, say, the customs of the Native American Kutchin people. When a Kutchin girl had her first menstruation, she was sent to live for a year in a special shelter away from the tribe, wore a pointed hood that forced her to look down at the ground, had a rattle that prevented her from hearing anything, carried a special stick if she wanted to scratch her head, and had a special cup that could not touch her lips. No doubt in my mind. That's not only crazy, it's just wrong.

I've even come to a conclusion that would get me blackballed from ever setting foot in liberal education circles again. That is this: colonialism wasn't 100 percent evil. More like 96 percent evil. Sometimes the colonizing culture actually made moral improvements in the native culture. I came to this conclusion while reading about the abolition of the Indian custom of widow burning. In pre-British India, a man's widow was burned alongside his corpse. The British imperialists put a stop to that. So yes, they criminally oppressed an entire people. But like a robber who fills up the ice trays while he steals the TV, they did a smidgeon of good.

Etruscan alphabet

Etruscans sometimes wrote boustrophedon style, in which the direction of writing alternates with each line—right-to-left, then left-to-right. Brilliant! The eye doesn't waste time trekking back to the left side of the page after every line. If the *Britannica* were written boustrophedon style, I'd be in the *F*s by now.

eunuchs

Julie's not pleased with the *Britannica*. She had a few minutes to spare and decided to see what it had to say about her favorite movie star, Tom Cruise. She slid out the *C* volume and found the answer: nothing.

"What kind of business is this?" she says, pointing to a page with illustrator George Cruikshank and a cruise missile. "No Tom Cruise? He's had a huge impact on our culture. Huge."

"They're a little light on the pop culture," I say.

"Weird," she says.

What about one of her favorite musicians, George Harrison? She got out the *H*s, to discover that the Beatle didn't rate his own entry either—though there was a nice write-up of George Harrison, noted church organ designer from the 19th century. He's a musician too, in his own way.

"That's a weird book you got there," she says.

The *Britannica* may seem a little peculiar in its choices at times. But the good news is, once you've read several thousands of its pages, you get a sense of what it takes to get behind these velvet ropes. I'm proud to say I've cracked the code. And as a service to you, the reader, here are the ten best ways to get your own entry in the *Encyclopaedia Britannica*:

1. *Get beheaded.* This is perhaps the surest path to getting written up. The *Britannica* loves nothing more than a person—preferably a noble one—who has had his or her neck chopped in two. One of my favorite games involves reading a biographical squib that begins with the words "French revolutionary" and then guessing how many years it takes before he finds himself under the guillotine.

2. *Explore the Arctic.* It helps if you can go on an ill-fated expedition, but pretty much any Arctic adventuring will do. If you travel anywhere north of Banff, you'll get a careful look from the *Britannica* editorial committee.

3. *Write some poems.* Surrealist and Russian formalist poets are especially welcome, but almost anyone who has ever written a quatrain or rhymed more than a dozen words seems to get into the club. At times, it gets almost as absurd as an early Paul Bowles poem. A two-page spread in the early *B*s that is only slightly atypical features no less than three of 'em: Carl Bellman, Andres Bello, and Hilaire Belloc—a Swedish poet, a Chilean poet, and a good old Anglo-French poet.

4. *Become a botanist.* Scandinavian ones seem particularly popular. Also, the study of mosses and peat deposits shouldn't be underestimated.

5. *Get yourself involved in commedia dell'arte.* The *Britannica*'s obsession with the Italian 18th-century comedies borders on the unhealthy. The *EB* has great enthusiasm for commedia dell'arte actors, whether they happened to play the pretentious but cowardly soldier Capitano, the saucy maid Columbine, or the madcap acrobat Zanni.

6. *Win the Nobel Prize.* Economics, physics, peace—the category's not important, as long as you've got the medal.

7. *Get castrated (men only).* If you're really committed, the word "eunuch" is a good thing to have on your résumé. And don't despair, just because you have lost a pretty important source of testosterone, it doesn't mean you'll be powerless. On the contrary. Maybe it's a compensation thing, but many of these eunuchs over the years have had impressive clout. Like Bagoas, a Persian minister in the 4th century B.C., who led an army in conquering Egypt, looted the temples, made a fortune, killed the king, killed the king's sons, then tried to poison the new ruler he appointed, only to be forced to drink the poison himself. A good run while it lasted.

8. *Design a font.* Apparently, coming up with a new typeface is a more impressive feat than I had previously thought. The *Britannica* especially likes controversial typefaces that are initially dismissed haughtily, only to be revived later and recognized as brilliant, like Baskerville, designed by font hero John Baskerville.

9. *Become a mistress to a monarch (ladies only).* This seems a pleasant and painless way to get in. If I were a woman, I'd start working on that as soon as possible, since there are fewer and fewer monarchs every day.

10. *Become a liturgical vestment.* I know this is easier said than done, but since every garment ever worn by a religious figure gets a nice picture, I thought I'd throw it in, just in case.

Ezekiel

The biblical prophet Ezekiel ate a scroll to symbolize his appropriation of its message. Now, that's a committed reader. Maybe I should eat the entire encyclopedia to symbolize my appropriation of its message, but I don't think my stomach would react well to the leatherette covers.

I like this image of Ezekiel and the scroll as snack. It's the literal version of the metaphor linking eating and reading—he's a voracious reader, he devours books, he's hungry for knowledge, et cetera. It rings true to me. After my four-hour reading stints each morning, I feel like I've stuffed my mind full of very rich food, like a Thanksgiving dinner for my head every day. I wish that I could unbutton the pants around my brain and let out my cerebral cortex a little.

I'm wondering if—to continue Ezekiel's metaphor—I bit off more than I can chew when I announced this *Britannica* project to the world. Because I have to tell you, I'm not sure I can go on. I'm not sure I can hear another one of those tissue-thin pages crinkle while turning. Or see another black-and-white picture of an old man with elaborate facial hair. Or learn about the average cubic meters of water discharged by another African river. Or crack open another volume with a spine emblazoned with the Scottish thistle—a plant with sharp thorns that serves as *Britannica*'s weird-looking and aggressive logo. Why exactly did I think this was a good idea again?

F

fable

Julie and I spend the afternoon at my mom and dad's apartment. They're throwing a brunch for their friends, and we've been invited to have some smoked turkey and try to make a good impression. I sit on the couch next to their friend, a lawyer named Bob. When he learns about my project, he tells me an encyclopedia-themed fable. I haven't heard too many of those, so I'll repeat it here.

"Did you hear about the Middle Eastern potentate?" he asked me. "This potentate called a meeting of the wise men in his kingdom, and he said, 'I want you to gather all the world's knowledge together in one place so that my sons can read it and learn.' The wise men went off, and after a year, they came back with twenty-five volumes of knowledge. The potentate looked at it and he said, 'No. It's too long. Make it shorter.' So the wise men went off for another year and they came back with one single volume. The potentate looked at it and said, 'No. Still too long.' So the wise men went off for another year. When they came back, they gave the potentate a piece of paper with one sentence on it. A single sentence. You know what the sentence was?"

Bob looked at me. I shook my head.

"The sentence was: 'This too shall pass.'"

Bob paused, let it sink in. "I heard that when I was very young and it has always stuck with me."

It's a good story. And it's some good wisdom, too: "This too shall pass." So far, the *Britannica* has backed that sentiment up. The Black Plague passed, the Hundred Years' War passed, the vogue for codpieces passed. Maybe Bob's sentence is, in fact, the secret of life. I wonder if I'll be able to come up with anything better by the end of my journey. What will be my mind-blowing one-sentence distillation of all knowledge? René Descartes had a fetish for women with crossed eyes? The French had not only canned laughter, but canned weeping? Needs some work.

Fahrenheit, Daniel

My anger toward 18th-century German physicist Daniel Fahrenheit is all out of proportion. I went into the living room just now and started ranting to Julie about this brainless jackass Fahrenheit. She tilted her head, concerned. "Is there maybe something else going on here?" She's right. Our babyless marriage continues to darken my mood—and Herr Fahrenheit is taking the brunt of it. Still, he genuinely pisses me off.

Born in 1686, he spent most of his life in the Netherlands, where he invented the mercury thermometer in 1714, which is fine. I don't begrudge him that. I do, however, find his temperature scale completely absurd. For zero on his scale, Fahrenheit chose the temperature of an equal ice-salt mixture. For 30, he chose the freezing point of water, and 90 was supposed to be the human's normal body temperature.

There's so much wrong with that, I'm not sure where to start. First of all, Fahrenheit bungled the measurements. As I've been forced to remember all my life, the freezing point of water is actually 32 degrees and body temperature is 98.6. So he's an inaccurate moron. Second of all, why choose 30 for the freezing point of water in the first place? What's wrong with starting it at zero? Oh, that's right. He's reserved zero for the temperature of an equal mixture of ice and salt. Huh? Where'd he come up with that one? How about an equal mixture of ice and tomato juice? Or how about one-third ice and two-thirds baking soda, with a dash of paprika?

I'm astounded by the inertia of bad ideas. Once they take hold, it's a bitch to root them out. Now, three hundred years later, we're stuck with Fahrenheit's ill-thought-out, badly executed system. It makes my blood boil, which happens at about 100.1 degrees Celsius.

Family, The

A hippy Christian cult in the sixties whose female members were instructed to engage in a practice called "flirty fishing." In other words, they spread the gospel by having sex with men. Unfortunately, while spreading the gospel they also spread herpes, and flirty fishing was discontinued.

Farinelli

Remember what I was saying about eunuchs? Here's another one. Born Carlo Broschi, Farinelli was the most famous castrato opera singer of the 18th-century. In 1737 he went to Spain, where his singing alleviated the melancholia of Philip V. Every night for ten years he sang the same four songs to the king. I hope he at least shuffled the order.

Farnsworth, Philo

The Utah engineer who helped develop television. In 1927, after many years of research, Farnsworth successfully broadcast the first image in the history of the American TV: the dollar sign. He couldn't have come up with a more appropriate image for his invention. Somehow, deep down, Philo knew that Lisa Kudrow would earn $1 million per episode for singing songs about her smelly cat.

Fellini, Federico

The movie *8 ½* got its name from the number of films Fellini had directed up till that time: seven features plus three shorts. That answers a question that I had never, ever wondered about.

Fertility and infertility

According to the *Britannica*, Julie and I are officially experiencing infertility. "Infertility is defined as the failure to conceive after one year of regular intercourse without contraception." We're up to fifteen months now.

The *Britannica* says that one in every eight couples is infertile. That's a pretty high percentage, and it would make me feel better if the anecdotal evidence in my life provided any support. Instead, our friends just keep pumping young 'uns out.

As for medical advice on beating infertility, the *Britannica* hasn't provided much I haven't gotten from our ever-growing stack of how-to-get-pregnant books. But that's not to say we aren't enlisting the *Britannica*'s aid—by which I mean Julie and I have become experts in ancient fertility rites. Every time I read about a preliterate society's rituals, I tell Julie, who makes a note of them. We know it's highly unlikely any of these will have any effect, but what's the harm in trying? Nothing else seems to be working.

So we have adopted a Fertility God of the Week. First came Anahiti, Iranian goddess of fertility and agriculture. Then it was Baal, the god of fertility worshipped by Canaanites. After that, Dumuzi, the Sumerian goddess of fertility and marshes. We don't actually worship these gods, and we have yet to sacrifice any small mammals to them, or even offer up our ficus tree. But we do like memorizing their names. It gives us something to do.

"Who is it this week?" Julie will ask.

"This week we've got good old Earth Mother."

"Oh, yes. Earth Mother."

"And unlike other female fertility goddesses, she doesn't undergo periodic sexual intercourse with a male god."

I also bought Julie a stuffed rabbit, because in the section on Easter, I learned that rabbits are a symbol of fertility. The Easter bunny was imported from pagan rituals, and did not actually have much interaction with Jesus.

"You know, some cultures believe that flagellation promotes fertility," I say, as we read in bed one night.

"I'm gonna have to pass on that one."

"Just one whip?" I say.

"No thanks."

I lightly whip her with the comforter, just for luck.

Fillmore, Millard

The thirteenth president was born in a log cabin. Why doesn't poor Millard ever get press for this? Lincoln hogs all the log cabin spotlight.

Fitzgerald, F. Scott

In 1920, after marrying Zelda and publishing *This Side of Paradise*, Fitzgerald wrote: "Riding in a taxi one afternoon between very tall buildings under a mauve and rosy sky, I began to bawl because I had everything I wanted and knew I would never be so happy again."

Jesus. That one stops me. What a sad quote. I find it particularly haunting because I've had that same feeling. During those few times in my life when I've been exceedingly happy, I've only gotten stressed out because I figured that my happiness would be fleeting. Fitzgerald's life didn't end so well—a spiral of drunkenness and commercially unsuccessful novels and a heart attack at forty-four. Not a good role model.

Fleming, Ian

He not only wrote the Bond books, but also the flying-car novel *Chitty Chitty Bang Bang*. And it's there you can find the line that summarizes Fleming's philosophy of life: *"Never say 'no' to adventures. Always say 'yes' otherwise you'll lead a very dull life."* Huh. That's actually moderately profound. It's not quite Ecclesiastes, but it's pretty good advice. A much better way of thinking than Fitzgerald's, anyway.

fondue

Legend has it that this dish originated during a Swiss truce in the 16th century, when the Protestants brought the bread and Catholics brought the cheese. Or the other way around—no one's sure. It's a nice story. Sort of Reese's Peanut Butter Cups, but with more war and religion.

fowl

Technically, the term "duck" should be used only for a female. The proper term for a male duck is "drake." So Daffy Duck's true daffiness: gender identity disorder.

French literature

I e-mail my favorite high school teacher to tell him about Operation Britannica. I figure I've done him proud. He agrees to meet me for lunch.

My butt has barely touched my chair at the Chat 'n' Chew diner when he starts in on me. "You know, this is a ridiculous project. A complete waste of your time." Oh boy. He's got the same tone as when he handed me back my paper comparing James Joyce to prop comedian Howie Mandel. I've just gotten a D minus, but this time it's my life.

Mr. Bender was my English teacher in sophomore and junior years. Now, fifteen years later, I call him Steve, even though every time I say it, I feel like I'm playacting as an adult. Steve—a large, bearded man who looks a bit like Abe Lincoln without the sunken cheeks or stovepipe hat—was the cool, funny English teacher. He told us stories of his former life as a stand-up comedian alongside Eddie Murphy. He could play a mean ukulele. And he introduced us to surreal filmmaker Luis Buñuel, which was like catnip to our fuzzy rebellious high school brains. Since I graduated, Steve had gotten into Buddhism, which at this very moment he is using to attack my endeavor.

"From the Buddhist position, you're actually dumber," Steve says.

"You're taking an original, pure mind, which is a crystal reflection of the soul, and you're making it dirty and crusty, so you won't be able to see anything. You're cluttering your mind."

"I disagree," I say, as I desperately try to flag down a waitress. Any distraction—a list of daily specials, perhaps—would help my cause. But the waitresses are as hard to find as Indonesia's glory-of-the-sea cone shell (fewer than a hundred known to exist).

"Being a Buddhist, my relationship to knowledge has changed. It's more about genuine inquiry than about the accumulation of facts."

"Why can't I have both?" I ask. "Like, did you know that Daniel Defoe went bankrupt thirteen times? That's a good one for your English class, huh?"

Steve shakes his head. "You're probably retaining a huge amount of superficial knowledge, and since we live in a superficial culture, you will impress people with your facts. But what about wisdom?"

"I'm not up to the Ws yet," I say. It's my cheap, fallback answer, and Steve is disappointed. I seem to have disturbed his Buddhist calm. In an effort to deflect any more attacks, I get Steve talking about Buddhism. He tells me how much he loves meditating. He says he's attracted to Buddhism because it's peaceful—Buddhists don't kill people.

"Actually, they do!"

This is an exciting moment. I get to correct my former teacher. I tell Steve that the prime minister of Ceylon was shot by a disgruntled Buddhist monk. And that's just one example. Steve nods. He knows all about that, and isn't impressed. I am failing to see the big Buddhist picture.

"Do me a favor and read *Bouvard and Pécuchet* by Flaubert. I think you'll find it very relevant."

When your high school English teacher gives you an assignment, it's best to follow it, even if you've already got a 33,000-page book weighing down your nightstand. So I picked myself up a Penguin Classics edition and dipped into this almost-forgotten novel.

Steve was right. This was relevant. Way too relevant. I was dismayed to learn that Gustave Flaubert had stolen my life a full 150 years before I was born, and was taking great delight in mocking it, the absinthe-drinking schmuck! In *Bouvard and Pécuchet,* Flaubert tells the tale of two 19th-century Frenchmen—bumbling, sexually inept, and dumb as hunks of Camembert—who decide they want to learn everything. They begin to read obsessively. They are enamored of chemistry, so they set up an experiment—which ends up blowing up their house. They read up on medicine, only to become quack doctors who almost kill their patients. Same story with politics, religion, philosophy, and on and on. These two would make a nice buddy comedy starring Jim Carrey and Adam Sandler. Just as disturbing, Flaubert ridicules some of the very same insights I've had. Remember Absalom? I noted to myself that he should have gotten a crew cut so he wouldn't get his hair stuck in the tree. Flaubert says he should have put on a wig. I console myself that my crew cut observation is much more clever.

I know what Flaubert's saying. He's saying that a little knowledge is a dangerous thing. He's saying that you can't learn the secrets to life from reading textbooks. And I know that he and Mr. Bender have a point. At face value, my quest teeters on the absurd. Still, it is a quest—and that in itself has some merit. I've never embarked on a quest. Who knows where it might lead, what I might discover?

In fact, I like to think of Bouvard and Pécuchet as heroic. At least they're trying to do something instead of sitting around eating pastries, ignoring basic hygiene, and persecuting Jews, which is what your average 19th-century Frenchman did. And some of Bouvard and Pécuchet's so-called comical ideas—that women should be emancipated, that light indoors will one day be stored—turned out to be not so comical after all. Nice going, *hommes*.

I hate Flaubert, that superior bastard. Why should the pursuit of knowledge be the monopoly of so-called experts? Hooray for dilettantes. And anyway, earlier in the *F* section I learned that Flaubert fell in love with a woman but didn't tell her about it till thirty-five years later. Which leads me to the conclusion: what the fuck does he know?

Freud, Sigmund

I've never been a big fan of Freud's. I think I know why—if I may indulge in a little self-analysis. When I first read Freud's theories, I was a freshman in high school, and I wasn't having an awful lot of sex. By which I mean no sex at all. So the idea that sex was the driving force in human behavior just increased my already dangerous level of frustration. It was like a color-blind person reading that the meaning of life lay in the joys of multihued flowers. No, I preferred Marx. Not that I'd had much experience with factories or proletarians or chains, but at least I could use Marx to take a self-righteous stance against my parents, those oppressive, bourgeois tools. As for Freud, I took great joy in repeating a quote I read somewhere: "Psychoanalysis is the disease for which it purports to be the cure." That was nice. A dismissal of an entire system of thought with a single witticism. Brilliant!

Those early prejudices die hard, so I'm still not much of a Freudian. But if I had to choose one doctrine of Herr Doctor's to embrace, I'd have to go with the Oedipus complex. That just might have some validity. In fact, now seems as good a time as any to lie back on my couch, rest my head against the analyst's napkin, and dissect my lifelong competition with my dad.

It began early. Every night when I was a kid, we played the same game: a modified version of handball that involved my wall, my cantaloupe-sized green Nerf ball, and my bed (the obstacle that made the game interesting). We called it, imaginatively enough, Wall Ball.

The game took on enormous importance to me. I would practice with my Nerf ball—whose name, by the way, was Seymour—for hours after school. My dedication would have impressed Bjorn Borg. It was monotonous work. Thump, thump, thumping that ball against the wall, trying to land it in the hard-to-reach corner by the radiator. The only enjoyable break in my regimen came when the ball semiaccidentally rolled into my sister's room across the hall, eliciting a glass-shattering shriek. With good reason, actually. I had developed the habit of drooling on the Nerf ball for good luck (don't ask). So Beryl would be doing her Spanish homework and all of a sudden this spongy green *moist* thing would roll up against her ankle—well, it couldn't have been very pleasant.

When bedtime rolled around, Dad would come to my room and we'd play two or three games. To me, it mattered. I threw tantrums to rival John McEnroe, if not Caravaggio. I would shout and scream and use whatever bad words I thought I could get away with—"retarded" being a particular favorite. If there was a Wall Ball referee, I would have kicked him in the shins.

Thanks to my rigorous practice schedule, I'd occasionally win a game. My dad would congratulate me, seeming genuinely happy for me. And I'd take the opportunity to do something mature, like pump my fist and shout, "I am the Wall Ball king!"

If we weren't feeling athletic, my dad and I had another option for competition—a board game version of hockey. I liked this game a lot, mostly because I had invented it. And since I was the inventor, I was also the expert on the rules. Interestingly, the rules turned out to be remarkably flexible. Especially when my father was winning.

"When the puck bounces off two walls at a forty-five-degree angle, you actually have to roll a nine or it's automatically my turn," I'd say.

"Is that so?" my father would say. He never argued. He just went along with it, happy to be interacting with me.

As I've gotten older, my dad and I have continued to play games, though we've moved on to those invented by other people: croquet, Boggle, Scrabble. I've become a slightly better sport. I no longer throw things, and I've phased out "retarded" in favor of more mature words, like "dammit."

I think I now know why I've had this thirst to beat my father. It's not—sorry, Dr. Freud—fear of castration or desire to have sex with my mother. And it's not that my dad is particularly competitive with me. You won't find him bouncing a basketball off my forehead as Robert Duvall did to his son in *The Great Santini*. No, it probably stems from cognitive dissonance that started in my childhood. Namely, this dilemma: on the one hand, I believed quite firmly that I was the smartest boy in the world, but on the other, here was a person in the same apartment who was clearly far smarter than me. Here was a man who knew all the answers. Who knew why the fridge was cold and what made the Lexington Avenue subways run and how far dirt went down. Here was a man who made the smartest boy look dumb. This caused plenty of confusion and frustration in my prepubescent mind—which still lingers today. I needed some area where I could clearly reign supreme; I hoped Wall Ball was it. And if not, then maybe hockey or croquet or encyclopedia reading.

frigate birds

I find out my fellow *Esquire* editor Andy is looking for a writer to interview Alex Trebek, host of *Jeopardy!* I plead with him for the assignment. How could I not? I mean, *Jeopardy!*—the pot of gold at the end of my project. And Alex Trebek! The world's most famous know-it-all.

"I'm a big Trebek fan," I tell Andy. "Huge Trebek fan." Andy—who eventually relents—is no moron. He knows I'm reading the encyclopedia and have an ulterior motive: me versus Trebek. A knowledge showdown.

Truth is, I have conflicted feelings about Trebek. On the one hand, I love *Jeopardy!* and respect the way he runs the show with stern colonel-like authority—not a moment wasted on buffoonery. On the other hand,

I want to pop Trebek in his smug Canadian mouth. I mean, this is the man who pretends to know every potent potable and every presidential pet, who oozes faux sympathy for mistaken contestants with his famously condescending "sorry," who pronounces "burrito" as if he went to kindergarten with Fidel Castro and "Volkswagen" as if he grew up on the banks of the Rhine. Plus, my friend who writes about TV says that in real life Trebek is kind of rude. All the better. This will be my chance to expose him for what he is: some guy with a ridiculous mustache who reads the answers off the cards. That's right, folks: he has the answers already!

That was the plan, anyway. But if I was hoping to impress Trebek with my superior intelligence, things didn't get off to the best start. The day after I flew to Los Angeles, I drove my rented compact to Trebek's Beverly Hills mansion and rang the bell.

Trebek's son answers, and tells me his dad is out back, waving vaguely in the direction of the yard. The yard in question is an elaborate landscape, with lots of trees and walls and bushes and paths, and after a brief walk, I run into a Mexican gardener. "I'm looking for Alex Trebek," I say. He waves me back. I pass another Mexican gardener, who waves me even farther back. I get to a third Mexican gardener. He is on his knees, a look of intense concentration on his face as he digs a hole. By this time, I'm getting a little frustrated. "I'm looking for Alex Trebek," I say, a bit too sharply. I am about to clarify with a *"Donde esta Señor Trebek?"* but I don't have a chance.

"You found him," says the gardener. He stands up, takes off his thick soiled glove, and comes to shake my hand.

This is not good. As an experienced journalist, I probably should have been able to pick out Alex Trebek inside the perimeter of Alex Trebek's own property. But in my defense, Trebek is wearing a baseball cap, his hair is grayer than I thought—and where the hell is his mustache? Turns out he shaved it off a few years ago. Okay, a little more research might have been advisable. It's about five seconds into my alleged know-it-all showdown, and I'm feeling about as clever as, say, Jennifer Love Hewitt on Celebrity Jeopardy.

I'm not sure what Trebek thinks of my lack of reporting skills, but he's cordial enough not to dwell on them. "Let's go to my office," he says. We enter the house, which has a blue-and-yellow *Jeopardy!* rug the size of a large surfboard in the entry hallway. His office walls, as you might imagine, are lined with books—Russian textbooks, Civil War tomes, the illustrious *Encyclopaedia Britannica* itself. As you also might imagine, the books are well organized into thematically linked sections. This is a man who, according to press reports, puts his dress shirts on light-colored hangers and his sport shirts on dark-colored ones.

I ease into the interview with some small talk—gardening, rental cars, that sort of thing. And when he's feeling comfortable, I hit him with my real question: if he's so damn smart, how would *he* do as a contestant on *Jeopardy!*

Well, Alex says, he'd do okay among senior citizens, but against someone my age, he'd get his butt whipped. Just doesn't have the recall anymore. "I flew from New York to Los Angeles recently," Trebek says, "and I entertained my first serious thoughts about coming down with Alzheimer's. They brought out the food and I said, 'Oh, this is my favorite vegetable.' And I looked at it, and I looked at it, and I looked at it, and I could not come up with 'broccoli'. And that's when you realize that, hey, you're starting to lose it. But so what? It's not important. Knowing everything is not the most important thing."

Alex Trebek showing signs of early senility? And he doesn't even care? What kind of know-it-all nemesis is this?

As we talk, I'm confronted by a Trebek I never expected. No prissy milquetoast, he goes out of his way to swear like Uncle Junior on *The Sopranos* ("bullshit" and "asshole" are two favorites). No cold-blooded Spock, he tells me he's an impulsive romantic—he left military college after four days to chase a girl.

I won't say that Trebek is entirely without pretension. Occasionally the pompous side of him peeks through—he tells me that he speaks English, French, some Spanish, and that he can "fool around in other languages," which strikes me as very annoying for some reason. He also uses the word "escarpment" in casual conversation. And he relates to me an elaborate pun he once made on the names of Edith Cavell and Enos Cabell, a moderately well-known British nurse and first baseman, respectively. But overall, he's a decent guy.

About halfway into our interview, Trebek tells me the following story.

"I was at a college tournament in Ohio recently, and I was telling the audience about my trip to Africa, and I got teary-eyed. I started to cry. This is kinda dumb. I'm in front of three thousand people and I'm getting weepy talking about Africa."

Alex Trebek crying? That is a hard image to conjure up. That's like

Henry Kissinger giggling or Vladimir Putin yodeling. Makes no sense.

"And what the hell's Africa to me?" Trebek continues, asking the very question I was wondering. "Well, I go to Africa—to Kenya, Ethiopia, Tanzania—and I stand there and I am overwhelmed by the thought that this is where I'm from. I came from here. And I feel comfortable."

Huh. I'm not sure how to respond to this. Is Alex Trebek black? He sure doesn't look black. He looks pretty white to me. He looks like the quintessence, the very incarnation, of whiteness.

"You mean . . . because it's the cradle of civilization?" I ask, taking a shot.

"Yeah. It's like, hey, I'm home."

It's a strange story, and I'm not certain why he'd share it with a journalist, but it has an odd effect on me: it makes me like him more. That clinches it. Trebek isn't a mustache-twirling villain, especially since he doesn't have a mustache. He's a guy who's not afraid to look vulnerable, even a little ditzy. My plan for a showdown is in full meltdown.

If I'm not going to try to humiliate him, maybe I can bond a little. Here we are, two men who spend their days swimming in facts. I tell him that I'm reading the *Encyclopaedia Britannica*. He seems mildly impressed, if not blown away. He tells me that as soon as *Jeopardy!* goes off the air, he's going to retire and try to read every book in his house, "even the ones I've read before, because I can't remember them."

I ask him, of the quarter million clues over the last thirteen years, what's the favorite fact that he's learned?

"Oh God," he says. After a struggle, he comes up with one: You know how in nautical law, a country has jurisdiction over the first three miles from its coast? (Actually I don't, but I'm not up the *N*'s.) Well, that came about because a cannon's range was three nautical miles. "That's fascinating," I say, though it probably wouldn't be my first pick.

My favorite line in our two hours together comes when I ask him for his philosophy of knowledge. Trebek thinks for a moment, then responds: "I'm curious about everything—even things that don't interest me." I love that sentiment. It's totally contradictory, but I know what he means. And so, at the end of our talk, I climb in my rented compact and drive back to the hotel to read about friendly societies (the 17th-century forerunners of insurance companies) and frigate birds (they've got eight-foot wingspans and often catch fish in the air dropped by other panic-stricken birds) and other things that don't interest me. At the very least, they could come in handy if I decide to return to L.A. in a suit and tie and become a beloved five-time champion of Alex Trebek's quiz show.

Fux, Johann

I'm proud of myself. When I saw the name Johann Fux—an 18th-century Austrian composer—I didn't giggle. Sure, there was a faint smile, but I'm getting better, I tell you. I didn't ask myself whether Johann Fux on the first date or whether Johann Fux while wearing proper protection. I didn't secretly think that "Fux You" would make a cool T-shirt.

The more I progress in the alphabet, the more successful I am at stifling that eleven-year-old boy inside of me, the one that still thinks a good Beavis-and-Butt-head-style scatological pun is cause for great joy.

It's not easy. Just the number of asses alone will tempt even the most evolved mind. I've learned about *The Golden Ass* (a book by a Platonic philosopher) and *The Wild Ass's Skin* (a novel by Balzac). I've read about the half ass (a type of mule in Asia) and Buridan's ass (an animal in a philosophical parable). But it goes way beyond asses. Asses are just the start. You can also take a trip to the river Suck (in Ireland), where you could fish for crappies (a freshwater bass) while you drink some Brest milk (the town in Belarus is known for its dairies). If you're bored, you can have a stroke-off (while playing bandy, a version of ice hockey) and fondle a bushtit (a small bird). If you're feeling smart, you might want to argue the impact of Isaac Butt (an Irish leader), or debate the merits of the Four Wangs (Chinese landscape painters), who might have been collected by the Fuggers (an art-loving family). Or else, just take a flying Fokker (a German airplane).

I know this is wrong. This isn't why I'm reading the *Britannica*. I'm reading it to get smarter, better, more enlightened, not to make dirty puns. Maybe it's because I've read so many of them, or maybe it's because the *Britannica* is actually making me more enlightened, but I've cut way down on these Beavis moments. The Four Wangs, though—that is kind of funny.

G

gagaku

At long last, the wait is over. If you recall, the word "a-ak," the very first word of the *Encyclopaedia Britannica,* had no definition, only the recommendation that the reader "see gagaku." I showed remarkable willpower and decided not to flip ahead, but to continue reading the *As,* figuring I'd get to "gagaku" in good time. Well, three months later, I am here. I have arrived.

That's got to count for something. That is, without a doubt, an accomplishment. The mystery is about to be solved! Unfortunately, the actual definition of "gagaku" does not provide quite the huge payoff I was hoping for. Not exactly a shocking twist you might find in an O. Henry story or an M. Night Shyamalan movie. "Gagaku" is the Japanese term for a type of East Asian music that was prominent during the 5th to 8th centuries ("a-ak" is its name in Korean). Gagaku involves flute, drum, and strings, and sometimes accompanying dances. The notations remain obscure, but some form of gagaku can still be heard in Japan. And that's about it.

Huh. Well, there's always "zywiec" to look forward to.

gal

It's Valentine's Day. We don't make a big deal about this holiday in the Schoenberg-Jacobs household. We were both single for so many years that we have residual resentment from all of the date-free Valentine's Days we suffered through. It's a cruel concept, Valentine's Day. It's as if they had a holiday to celebrate rich people or attractive people. Miserable and alone?

Sorry, this isn't your day. So in mini protest, Julie and I spend the night at home. We order in Thai and watch some romantic TV—the scene of the coroner on *CSI* removing a pancreas was particularly enchanting.

Cards, however, are allowed. Julie gives me a lovely one about how these last five years with me have been the best in her life. In response, I give her my card, which I'd typed that day at work, hovering over the printer as the paper came out. Don't want this one leaking out.

Julie reads it aloud.

"You make me suffer tachycardia," she reads. She cocks her head.

"It's when someone has an irregularly fast heartbeat," I say. "I'm just saying you make my heart beat faster. Keep going."

"I'm glad we practiced assortative mating together," she says. She looks at me again.

"It's when you pick a mate who's similar to you. Like fat people mate with fat people. I'm saying we're similar."

Julie looks back at the printout.

"You are worth much more than twenty spears," she says.

"That's the traditional bride price among Africa's Azande tribe."

She finishes up: "You are my gal—and I don't mean the unit of measurement."

"Yeah, a gal is a change of rate in motion of one inch per second per second. Or one centimeter. That's right, one centimeter. Anyway, you really are my gal. So what do you think?"

"A little show-offy," she says, "but the sentiments are nice."

I'm relieved. It could have backfired, but she seems to have enjoyed it. Which emboldens me to tell her that, though the encyclopedia is taking a bunch of my time and putting a little strain on our marriage, it's made me realize how lucky I am. There just aren't many happy marriages in the encyclopedia. Marriages in history are loveless obligations, something to suffer through in between affairs. The French, of course, raised out-of-wedlock sex to perfection, even creating an official position for mistress to the king. I knew kings had mistresses, but I didn't know that they practically had business cards and an office.

A surprising number of marriages are unconsummated, and an even greater number end in bloodshed. Once in a while, maybe every couple of hundred pages, I read about a happy marriage. But even these are often tainted with oddness—as in the unlikely union of brilliant poet William Blake and an illiterate peasant woman. I hope they had amazing sex, because I can't imagine the conversations were too lively. I tell Julie the Blake story, adding that I'm glad she's not illiterate, which she takes in stride.

gall

Julie's brothers are in town, their families in tow, and they've all congregated at our apartment in preparation for a visit to the Museum of Natural History. Doug has taken out the *A* volume, and is flipping through it. Doug is smart—he owns a software company, for one thing—but he's not the information freak that Eric is, and he only mocks me half the time.

"You remember anything from the *A*s?" he asks.

"Pretty much everything."

He flips to a random page. "Ankh," says Doug.

"Egyptian symbol of life," I say. I didn't mention that I actually knew that before reading the *EB*.

He flips some more. "How many Aleutian Islands are there?"

"Four hundred and twenty-three," I say.

"No, fourteen large islands, fifty-five smaller ones," he says.

I try to deflect with a lame joke about how I was counting in the Mayan base-twenty system.

"What is Archimedes' screw?"

This I knew! It's a helix inside a cylindrical pipe, a piece of equipment used to lift water up in ancient times.

Doug seemed moderately impressed.

"And why did they want to lift up water?" he asks.

A low blow. I already got the definition—why is he pressing me for more details? I admitted I didn't know.

"They used it to lift water out of the holds of ships," Doug says.

"Let me see that," says Eric. He grabs the volume from his brother and reads it quickly. "This is wrong. The Archimedes' screw was first used for irrigation."

I couldn't believe it. First, Eric concluded that the *Britannica* omits key information (see Burke and Hare). Now, he says it's just plain wrong. How am I supposed to deal with this blasphemy? He's questioning the authority of the mighty *Encyclopaedia Britannica*. Like he's an expert on the early uses of Archimedes' screw? The unmitigated gall ("gall" is also the word for a plant swelling, by the way). I tell Eric to take it up with the editors.

I need a break, so I go into the office, where my nieces and nephew are playing a game of Sorry! Doug's kids are adorable, no surprise there, and so are Eric's—Gap-ad cute and sweet as butterscotch (named for scorched butter). Eric may treat me like roadkill, yet I have to admit, much as it pains me, that he's a good, caring father and has done a re- markable job raising his kids.

"Who's up for Simon Says?" I ask.

They seem up for it, and since I have seniority, I appoint myself Simon.

"Simon says, raise your right hand," I say. We all raise our right hands.

"Simon says, touch your toes." We all touch our toes.

"Simon says, turn around and around and around."

My nieces and nephew and I start twirling. This wasn't a spontaneous twirling, mind you. I had been planning this twirling for quite some time. I had plotted this twirling ever since I had read about the secret Blasis technique, invented by ballet teacher Carlo Blasis, in which a dancer pre- vents dizziness by snapping the head around more quickly than the body so as to maintain focus on one spot.

I knew this was potentially extremely useful information. But how? Since we rarely put on employee shows of *Swan Lake*, I seldom find an ex- cuse to twirl at work. And I don't run into many dervishes on the Upper West Side. The only thing I could come up with was Simon Says.

So there I was, spinning around and around, snapping my head, keeping my focus on Julie's painting of Ray Charles. And it worked in a sense. I kept myself from getting overly dizzy, even as my nieces and nephew tumbled to the ground.

I didn't feel nauseated, but afterward, I sure felt like a bully and a jackass. I was so desperate to put my knowledge to some sort of use, I forced it into a semicruel game of Simon Says. This wasn't organic. This wasn't like when I saved Anna from eating cilantro. What was I thinking?

I confessed my sin to Julie that night. She wasn't even impressed. She said anyone who had taken a modern dance class knew about the head- snapping technique.

gamete

Another one of Julie's friends just got pregnant. Her and her partner's gametes (sex cells) are now a diploid zygote. These friends of hers are frighteningly fertile. We're in bad moods. I spend the day with my lips frozen in a fake smile, trying some facial feedback. It fails to comfort me.

Gandhi

I don't have teenage kids, as is abundantly clear. But someday, God willing, when I do, I'm going to do my best to remember the postpubescent Gandhi. When my kids go out and chop down a telephone pole or put a stink bomb in their friend's locker, I'm going to recall this paragraph: "[Gandhi] went through a phase of adolescent rebellion, marked by secret atheism, petty thefts, furtive smoking and—most shocking of all for a boy born in a Vaishnava family—meat eating."

Gandhi—that little thug! I wonder if other parents in Porbandar told their kids, "For the last time, I don't want you hanging around that bad seed Mohandas!" This gives me Movie Idea Number Three: *Young Gandhi,* with Frankie Muniz as the cigarette-sucking, burger-eating pickpocket who eventually accepts his fate as the most saintly man alive.

Not to make too much of one paragraph, but it does give me a little more hope about human nature. As I've gotten older, I've gotten crankier, and have started to think that personality traits don't change through a person's life. Once a bully, always a bully. But now I'm confronted with Gandhi. You can't get a much bigger transformation than that, unless, unbeknownst to me, Mother Teresa went through a phase as a loan shark.

Garibaldi, Giuseppe

I knew Garibaldi had something to do with uniting Italy. I could probably have come up with the fact that he led an army of Red Shirts. (Incidentally, someone needs to write a history of the world according to colored clothing. In addition to Italy's Red Shirts, I've read about the Yellow Hat Order in Tibet; the Black and Tan police force used against the Irish; the feared Seneca leader Red Jacket; those fascist scum the Brown Shirts; the Great Yellow Turban rebellion in China; and, for a little variety, the Shirtless Ones, who supported Argentina's Juan Perón. I think it would make a great doctoral thesis, or at least a lovely spread in *Harper's Bazaar.*)

Back to Garibaldi. I'm ashamed I was so ignorant of this man, because he led an inspiring life, one that intersected in a surprising and—to me, at least—profound way with the life of Abraham Lincoln.

The sixty-second Garibaldi:

Born on the fourth of July, Garibaldi first got into trouble as a sailor in the Piedmont navy. After taking part in a socialist-inspired mutiny, he fled to South America to avoid a death sentence. There, among other things, he eloped with a married Brazilian woman and led a group of Italian soldiers in Uruguay's revolt against Argentina. These were the first Red Shirts. In other fashion news, Garibaldi adopted the gaucho costume he'd wear for the rest of his life.

Garibaldi returned to Italy in 1848 to help in its fight for independence from Austria. He scored some astounding underdog victories before being exiled again, landing in, among other places, Staten Island. But Garibaldi was a tenacious man. He returned to Italy and in 1860, he fought his most famous battle: he conquered Sicily and Naples with his tiny band of a thousand Red Shirts and the support of the local peasants, who, taken by his charm, saw him as a god who would deliver them from feudalism. By 1862, he had effectively united the country.

Garibaldi's love life wasn't so successful. In 1860, says the *Britannica*, he married a woman named Giuseppina, but abandoned her, within hours of the marriage, when he discovered she was almost certainly five months pregnant by one of his own officers. A shorter marriage than most of Shannen Doherty's.

By the end of his life, Garibaldi had become a pacifist, a champion of women's rights, racial equality, and religious freethinking. Not bad. The most likable revolutionary I've encountered so far.

But I haven't even brought up my favorite fact about Garibaldi, which is this: in July of 1861, an embattled Abraham Lincoln offered to make Garibaldi a Union general in the American Civil War. Garibaldi turned Lincoln down, partly because Lincoln wasn't ready to abolish slavery yet, and partly because Garibaldi wanted supreme command of the federal troops.

This is an appealing tidbit. Not just because it raises the question, what if an Italian had led the Union troops to victory? Would the South hold a grudge against his country? Would there be no pizza parlors in Alabama? It also appeals to me because I would never have guessed Honest Abe was going to make a surprise cameo in the life of Garibaldi. I love when this happens. It's always exciting, like when there's a special guest star on a sitcom. The *Britannica* is packed with weird ways that great lives intersect. I love reading how Arthur Conan Doyle had a venomous feud with Harry Houdini (the occult-hating Houdini thought Conan Doyle's seances were a sham.) Or that Winston Churchill wrote the obituary for Ian Fleming's father. Or that Bach and Handel were both treated by the same quack doctor. I like the more random connections as well, like the one between Esso and Erte and Eminem (all have names derived from the pronunciation of letters). The *Britannica* reminds me of the Six Degrees of Kevin Bacon game, but for all of life. In the words of Donne, John (1572–1631), no man is an island. I find it comforting to know that I'm not alone, that I'm part of the big fabric, and that it's a lovely fabric, like the intricate carpets that Abbas commissioned in Persia.

Garrick, David
Famed 18th-century Shakespearean actor who also managed the Drury Lane Theatre. He fought to "reform" the audience, discontinuing the practice of reduced entry fees for those who left early. I don't like this guy. His reform is terrible. We need to go back to the old system: You stay an hour at a movie, you pay half price. You stay a half an hour, quarter price. Leave after ten minutes, the theater has to pay you for your trouble.

gazpacho
I'm feeling overwhelmed by the reading. I'm spending way too much time on it. The font is too small, the pages are too big, the words too polysyllabic. It's the literary equivalent of trying to hike in the dense underbrush of a jungle (though not the Amazon rain forest, which has a curiously sparse ground level; the canopy doesn't let light get through). In any case, it's excruciatingly slow going. I need a machete to chop my way through.

So I do something drastic: I enroll in a speed reading course from the Learning Annex, New York's adult education outlet. The $44 class promises to make me a literary speed demon, to double my intake. It's held on a Tuesday night in a nondescript classroom with an instructor named Les. Les is one of the founders of the Evelyn Wood speed-reading courses, which, he boasts, have trained more than 2 million people, among them Presidents Kennedy, Johnson, Nixon, and Carter. "Carter got the Nobel Prize," he says. "We're not going to take credit for that."

The class chuckles dutifully. There are about twenty of us. We've been told to bring our books with us, so there's an odd assortment of reading material scattered around. One woman has brought *Earth in the Balance* by Al Gore, someone else has *The Prince* by Machiavelli, and one guy has brought his copy of *Maxim* magazine, presumably because he wants to learn to masturbate faster (it turns out *Maxim* is just for the midclass break; he also has a novel that features fewer models in nurse outfits). I pull the *Britannica* out of my bag and drop it on the desk with a manly thud. Sadly, no one seems to notice.

Les looks to me like a turtle. A large turtle. I feel sorry for the buttons on his striped shirt, which seem to be under a tremendous amount of pressure from his stomach. They seem like they could pop any moment and shoot into the unsuspecting eye of a would-be speed reader. I'm glad I have my glasses on.

The first thing I learn is that Les can talk. He talks about a one-eyed executive he once taught. He talks about a housewife who sold the paperback rights to her book for $3 million. And, yes, he talks about the topic at hand. "The slower you read, the more you're going to remember, right?" he asks in his thick New York accent. "Uh-uh . . . the slower you read, the *worse* your comprehension." Les looks around to see if there are any Skeptical Sams. No one takes the bait. "Your brain is so powerful, it's like driving a brand-new Ferrari at thirty miles per hour. Or the way my daughter drives—one foot on the brake and one foot on the accelerator. We're going back and forth, back and forth, and she can't figure out why until I tell her. The faster you read, the greater your comprehension . . . If you read slow, your brain gets bored. You daydream about going to Bloomingdale's or to a party."

I nod, hoping he'll see. Got it. My Ferrari-like mind has comprehended. Ready to move on. But Les lingers on this theme for what seems like a very long time, making me wish I was at a department store or a party or anywhere else. Les may be a fast reader, but he sure is not a fast teacher.

Finally, Les tells us to pick up the gadget he handed out to all of us at the beginning of class—a silver cigar-shaped laser pointer. "This is a revolutionary thing," announces Les grandly. "We call it the Raster Master. I'd like you all to introduce yourself. Say, 'Hello, Raster Master.'"

The class actually says, "Hello, Raster Master." We all start clicking the button and shining the red dots around the classroom. Les explains that the Raster Master's name is derived from the Latin word for rake, adding that it's "a technical term."

"It didn't fall out of the sky," he continues. "We did research for ten years." The secret, he explains, is that "the eyes follow a moving object. Why? Because our ancestors in the savannah in Africa who just fell out of the trees didn't want to get killed." They had enemies—lions and tigers and other cavemen (though not dinosaurs, he points out, since they had gone extinct)—and needed to spot the dangers. "Whoever made us—

God, evolution, take your pick—gave us peripheral vision to survive." He's worried he's lost the class. "Too much? Too complicated?"

No, we think we've got it. "I teach fourth-graders. I tell them, do not put the Raster Master up your nose. So they put it in their ears." I smile and nod. I will not put the Raster Master in any orifice whatsoever. The Raster Master, Les tells us, widens the peripheral vision and lets us read more than one word at a time. He tells us this a lot.

We finally get to test out the famed Raster Master. I open to the *G* section and read with the rest of the class for sixty seconds. I move that red dot across the lines. I try to read clumps of words, not single words. I read about "gazebo" (a joke word that combines "gaze" with the Latin suffix *ebo,* meaning "I shall") and "gazpacho" (Arabic for soaked bread). I'm about to dive into Gbarnga (a Liberian city) when he tells us to stop. Honestly, I can't tell whether I read faster with the help of the Raster Master, but I don't want to get in trouble, so I say that I did.

Les pleads with us to be careful with the Raster Masters. They're not ours to keep, but they are available on his Web site for about $20. He continues telling the class about peripheral vision and the Raster Master until finally, after what seems like an eon or two, a Russian woman in purple pants raises her hand. "You're repeating this over and over. You're not telling us anything new."

Yes! Someone's said what I was too timid to say. She has challenged the mighty Les. Hallelujah!

But Les shoots right back. "Most people can't handle more than one strategy at one time," he says. His tone is sharp. "You can leave if you want. But you're not ready for a second strategy. It'll overwhelm you."

She says nothing. I scan the class for some outrage among my fellow students, praying the Russian woman was the Trotsky in a revolution that would sweep the classroom. But no luck. The others are looking at her as if she's some sort of nogoodnik troublemaker. I just don't get it. People are way too accepting of authority, even if that authority is some blowhard with a Latin-named gadget.

After a short break, Les does get around to teaching us new strategies. Unfortunately, none of them have to do with speed reading. One is a learning method that involves tracing an outline of your hand on paper the way that kindergarteners draw Thanksgiving turkeys. Another is a meditation technique using the mantra "Men Hay Sheen," a sound he likens to the name of *West Wing* actor Martin Sheen. "The Hindus have been doing this for twenty-five hundred years, and look how smart they are." Les pauses. "Well, I don't know if they are or not. But they're skinny. You ever notice how skinny Hindus are?"

We nod. Yes, we've noticed. Hindus *are* skinny.

Oh, and we learn one other lesson, the most important lesson of all: if you *really* want to learn how to read fast, you can enroll in Les's weekend course, where many other secrets will be revealed. That one's only $395.

When I hear that, the clouds part. All becomes clear. Tonight's seminar is just a teasing infomercial for the real—aka expensive—course. Dammit! I toss my *G* volume manfully into my bag, shaking my head.

As I walk out, I can't resist getting in one sharp dig at Les. I inform him that the first sentence of his xeroxed handout contains a typo. The handout warns that if you read while on automatic pilot, it "wrecks havoc."

"It should be 'wreaks havoc,' " I tell him.

"You think so?"

"I know so."

"No, you're right. *W-r-e-e-k*?"

"No, *w-r-e-a-k*."

"You're right. I'll tell my secretary."

I thought that would feel good—showing up Les. But it didn't. It just felt cheap and dirty. I took the number 9 train home annoyed, playing with my Raster Blaster on the subway posters. (Yeah, I'm a sucker; I bought one of the damn things.) For the next few days, I tried to read my Gs using the red dot method. But it felt so dorky and unnatural and awkward, I gave up. I figured that even if I sped up my reading a bit, the total saved time would never equal the three hours I wasted in that class.

General Grant National Memorial

I am desperate for someone to ask me the dusty classic "Who is buried in Grant's Tomb?" Because now I can say, "Ulysses S. is buried in Grant's Tomb, but so is his wife, Julia Dent Grant. Also, it cost a remarkable $600,000 for 1897, and reaches a height of a hundred and fifty feet."

Genghis Khan

I pay special attention to this one, seeing as my father is obsessed with Genghis Khan. His bookshelf has an all-Genghis-all-the-time section that stretches at least a yard, maybe more. I'm sure he knows all the *Britannica*'s facts on Genghis. I'm sure he knows that Genghis was born clutching a clot of blood, which was taken as a sign of good luck. I'm sure he knows that when Genghis conquered the Tartars, he had all Tartars taller than the height of a cart axle put to death, which reminds me of some horrible, bloody twist on a Disneyland ride. *You must be this tall to live.*

The Genghis fixation is an odd one, since my dad is the least warrior-like man I know. The most violent I've ever seen him is when he staples a big wad of papers. If my dad were somehow transported back to Genghis Khan's army, he'd no doubt get in trouble for failure to meet his decapitation quota. In all my years, I've never seen him ride a horse, much less hurl a plague-infested body over an enemy wall.

The *Britannica*'s write-up of Genghis doesn't help much in illuminating my father's obsession. To me, the man seems like just another run-of-the-mill pillaging tyrant, if a very successful one. So the question remains: why Genghis? Since my quest is ostensibly to learn everything, I suppose I should try to solve the Genghis mystery as well. Maybe I can—in this year of knowledge gathering—also figure out my dad. So I do something I rarely do: I call my dad and ask him a serious question point-blank.

"I like the way he dresses."

No, really.

"Um, he's a very good dancer. You should see his fox-trot."

I'm not letting my dad off the hook. No, really. I want to know. This is a highly unusual demand in our father-son relationship, and he probably hates it. But after my pleading, my dad does think about it a bit. And finally comes up with two reasons. First, not too many people know about Genghis, so that's appealing to him. And second, despite the tyrant's ruthless and murderous ways, he did help spread civilization—his Pax Mongolia opened trade from East to West.

Now I understand. And the reasons are, in fact, illuminating. My own interests are—not so coincidentally—fueled by similar motives. Just like my dad, I like carving out a quirky, little-explored territory of knowledge. And just like my dad, I'm drawn to counterintuitive information. I feel I have made some progress. I thank my dad, and tell him that I'm not plotting to kill him, the way Genghis's son Jochi did.

George III

The British king ended his sentences "rhetorically and fussily with the repeated words 'what, what, what?'" I considered trying the "what, what, what?" thing out on Julie, especially after we had a fight over where exactly the paper towels should go in the pantry closet, but even I realized it was way too annoying.

gerbil
Some say that the African variety of gerbils carry the bubonic plague. The gerbil—of all rodents—does not need more negative publicity. There's enough antigerbil Hollywood gossip out there.

Gettysburg Address
Like everyone with an IQ over two score and three, I knew the phrase "four score and seven years ago." But I hadn't read the rest of Lincoln's speech since high school. The *Britannica* printed it in full, and for that I am grateful. It's a beautiful speech, worthy of its reputation. Maybe it's even too good. Lincoln says, "The world will little note, nor long remember what we say here, but it can never forget what they did here." Whereas, in truth, the world did note and did long remember what Lincoln said, perhaps even more clearly than the details of the battle itself. Did I recognize that little irony in high school? I must have, but I had no recollection of it.

Still, that wasn't the most surprising thing I learned (or relearned) about the Gettysburg Address. I learned that despite being president of the United States, Lincoln wasn't the main speaker that day. The big attraction was a two-hour speech by Edward Everett, a former Massachusetts congressman and president of Harvard, who was considered the greatest orator of his day.

Poor Everett. He probably spent weeks working on his speech, tweaking it, trying it out on his wife. On the big day, he went up to the podium, gesticulated and orated and exhorted for two straight hours, mopping his brow, maybe pausing to take some sips of water, finishing with a big rhetorical flourish. He probably thought he blew everyone away. Then Lincoln goes up to the podium. Two minutes later, Lincoln steps down and Everett is a historical footnote, some guy who gassed on before the Gettysburg Address.

Two hours versus two minutes. This is fantastic. Now I've got the perfect historical anecdote to back up my oft-mocked contention that shorter is better. Even 140 years ago, before attention spans shrunk to the size of the pygmy shrew (the smallest mammal, weighing less than a dime)—even 140 years ago, people liked the quick take. I've been on board this bus for years. I can't sit still when a movie drags past ninety minutes. By the time the entrees are served, I'm ready for the check. I have such trouble watching even a half-hour sitcom, I've figured out a secret, which I share with you now: if you put on the closed captioning and press fast forward on the VCR or TiVo, you can still read all the dialogue. I read sitcoms in eight minutes flat. So now, when my colleagues at *Esquire* make fun of me for preferring the bite-sized item to the four-thousand-word magnum opus, I've got poor old Edward Everett in my quiver. But I've droned on about this topic enough. So let's move on.

giraffe
"The voice has so rarely been heard, that the animal is supposed to be voiceless; but it is capable of low call notes and moans." Good to know next time I'm playing with kids: "A cow says *moo,* a cat says *meow,* the giraffe says [imitate nonsexual low moan here]."

glottal stop
In phonetics, this is a momentary stoppage of the airstream, caused by closing the glottis. When those with Brooklyn and Cockney accents pronounce "bottle" as *bah-ul,* they are using the glottal stop. There's a cruel little irony here—those who use the glottal stop can't even pronounce it correctly. They say "glah-ul stop." I wonder if the people who named the glottal stop did this on purpose, the scamps.

Glyndwr
A district in Wales. Please buy a vowel.

Goethe
Once in a blue moon (a blue moon, by the way, is caused by the dust in the air following a forest fire), I'll read a section or two from the Britannica CD-ROM. Such was the case with the Goethe entry. I was at the office, I had my laptop, I had some rare free time at lunch—the temptation was just too great. I always feel a little cheap afterwards, as if I've had an affair with a younger, flashier woman. I feel like apologizing to my good old crinkly-paper-and-ink volumes when I get home, maybe bring them some flowers.

But anyway, Goethe. Before the *Britannica* I knew, at least, the semi-proper pronunciation of his name. For a couple weeks in high school, I thought there were two people—a German writer named Gerta that Mr. Bender kept talking about, and some guy named Goethe (Go-eetha) I was reading about in my textbook. I figured out they were the same person when it turned out they both wrote *The Sorrows of Young Werther*. That was a tip-off even for me.

What I didn't know was Goethe's curriculum vitae. When Goethe wasn't busy explaining to people how to pronounce his name, he found time to be a critic, journalist, lawyer, painter, theater manager, statesman, educationalist, alchemist, soldier, astrologer, novelist, songwriter, philosopher, botanist, biologist, color theorist, mine inspector, and issuer of military uniforms.

Well, at least he didn't supervise irrigation schemes, that slacker. Oh wait. My mistake. He was also a supervisor of irrigation schemes.

I was familiar with the phrase "Renaissance Man," but Goethe is like a Renaissance Man with access to amphetamines. I can't figure out how he fit all these jobs into a single life, much less the one-page single-spaced résumé that employers generally request. He makes Leonardo da Vinci look like a lazy bum.

And he makes me extremely jealous. I've always wanted to be a generalist, to snack off the pupu platter of life without committing to any particular entree. In college, I specialized in introductory courses—intro to sociology, anthropology, math, whatever. By senior year, when my friends had all progressed to taking seminars like "The Semiotics of Ornithology in Cervantes's Oeuvre," I was sitting with a bunch of freshmen in "Psychology for Those Who Can Barely Speak English." After college, I became a journalist partly because I could remain something of a generalist. That, and I had no other job offers. But even journalism is a long way from the life of a Renaissance Man. In my ten years in the business, I have yet to do any deep thinking on color theory and I rarely get asked to supervise an irrigation system.

My dad wanted to be a Renaissance Man too, as evidenced by his overabundance of diplomas—diplomas he'd still be getting if my mom hadn't put her foot down and made him get a job.

My dad and I live in the wrong era, apparently. Everyone before the 20th century held at least one second job that had absolutely nothing to do with the first. Witness these actual job combinations I've read about thus far:

poet/meteorologist
lawyer/astronomer
shipowner/sociologist

lyricist/mollusk scientist
typographer/puppeteer
buccaneer/scientist

Nowadays, not only do you have to specialize, but you have to specialize within your specialty. There probably aren't any general mollusk scientists anymore. You have to be a Northeastern digger clam reproductive scientist. I suppose my encyclopedia adventure is an attempt to fight the forces of specialization, to reclaim the title of Renaissance Man. But I read about Goethe, and I realize I'd be lucky to have 4 percent of his range, which is sad.

Did I mention that Goethe's writings on science alone fill fourteen volumes? And that he also found time to write fifteen hundred passionate letters to Charlotte von Stein, the wife of a court official whom he had a crush on? I did know enough about Goethe from high school to remember that his *Faust* was all about the dangers of the quest for knowledge. But judging from his life, he had an insatiable thirst for knowledge and did just fine.

gospel

Sometimes my day job can be exhilarating. I'm thinking, for instance, of when vineyards send me free bottles of wine hoping for coverage in the monthly wine column. That's always interesting. (By the way—in case any vineyard owners are reading this—*Esquire*'s address: 1790 Broadway, 13th floor, New York, NY 10019. I'm partial to sauvignon blanc.) But a lot of times, my workday can be boring. Dull as watching the grass grow, even grass with cool names like creeping bent grass or turkey beard.

This is one of those times. As an editor, I have to read each of the articles in my section about forty-three times, until the sentences are sucked of all meaning and become weird little black marks on the page. Today's article—a man's guide to shining shoes, military style—has long ago passed into the nonsensical state. "Whorl"? That's a strange word, I think to myself. Whore-l. Wore-ell. Wooorl.

But at least the *Britannica* reading has given me some new perspective on my job. It's given me awareness of the power of editing. I'm thinking, for instance, of the Ems telegram in 1870. Prussian chancellor Otto von Bismarck edited the report of a diplomatic meeting to purposely offend the French and start the Franco-Prussian War. I'm not saying that as an editor, I want to start a war, but it's nice to know I could.

Or better yet, there's the Wicked Bible, which I learned about back in the *B*s. This was an infamous edition of the Bible from 1631. The problem? It omitted the word "not" in Exodus 20:14, resulting in the commandment "Thou shalt commit adultery." See that? One small editing error and you get a whole country fornicating with their neighbors' wives.

The average British peasant no doubt read the Wicked Bible and thought to himself: Okay, I'm not going to kill anyone. Won't worship a false idol. I'll make sure to have sexual congress with a married woman. Adultery. Now that's a commandment I can get behind. I wonder if God would rather I beget with Farmer John's wife or Parson Jebediah's wife.

I'm curious whether the editors of the Wicked Bible—who, incidentally, were fined three hundred pounds for their error—made an honest mistake, or if they were playing an immature little practical joke with God's words. Maybe they thought of changing "Thou shalt not kill" to "Thou shalt not spill"—which would have caused a lot of very carefully poured glasses of tea and a few hundred more homicides—but settled on the adultery commandment instead.

I ponder all this as I read *Esquire*'s own shoe-related commandment: use "small circles that tighten the whorl." What if I changed "small" to "large" circles? I'd be sending hundreds of *Esquire*-reading men into their offices with improperly polished shoes. The power! I cross out the word "small" in the sentence, then stet it, newly aware of my responsibility.

graham crackers

Another in the thousands of forgotten controversies: Sylvester Graham, inventor of the graham cracker, was an eccentric health guru of his day who preached the virtues of hard mattresses, cold showers, and homemade bread. That last one got him attacked by a mob of outraged bakers.

Grateful Dead

I'm no Deadhead—I attended one Dead show, which I found about as interesting as the diagram in the *fungi* article charting the life cycle of bread mold. Still, I know enough about the classic stoner band to hold my own. I know about Jerry Garcia, LSD-laced punches, Terrapin Station, etc. And I certainly know more than my mom, who called me the day Garcia died to ask me if I knew who "Jerry" was. She came home to a barely coherent ten-minute message on her answering machine from a Deadhead at a gas station. He had just heard the news about Jerry and was apparently too bummed out to dial the phone correctly. In any case, I probably already know everything the *Britannica* has to say about the Grateful Dead.

I start to read: "In folktales of many cultures, the spirit of the deceased person ..." Well, I'm not even through the first sentence and I feel like quite the moron. I had always figured Jerry and Co. had come up with the name the Grateful Dead out of their acid-addled heads. But no, it's a sly allusion. Just so you know, the grateful dead folktale goes like this: A traveler finds a corpse of a man who was denied a burial because he had too many unpaid debts. The nice traveler pays for a burial, and goes on his way. Sometime later, the spirit of the corpse appears to the traveler in the form of an animal and saves him from some danger. Finally, the animal reveals himself to be the grateful spirit of the dead man and offers the traveler two free tickets to Red Rock and some really awesome hash brownies. Well, I embellished there at the end. But you get the idea.

The Grateful Dead bait and switch is not unusual. I have a similar forehead-slapping revelation every few pages, and they always make me feel dumb as a box of extrusive igneous rocks. It's making me paranoid. I'm realizing there are dozens, hundreds, thousands of allusions I'm missing every day. They're hiding everywhere—in my medicine cabinet, on my bookshelf, on my TV screen—just waiting to make me look stupid. I'm not talking about *Finnegans Wake*. I wouldn't feel too bad about missing a couple of Joycean allusions to druidic runes. I'm talking about everyday things like Lorna Doone, which I thought was a Nabisco cookie, but turns out to be a famous swashbuckling novel by English novelist Richard Blackmore. Or corvette, which isn't just a car but a small naval vessel.

Sadly, the Grateful Dead isn't even the first band name I learned about in the *Britannica*. I got the same feeling when I read about Eurythmics—which isn't just Annie Lennox's eighties band, but was originally an early 20th-century method of teaching music involving the tapping of feet and clapping of hands. Or about Supertramp, which came from the title of a William Davies book called *The Autobiography of a Super-Tramp*.

I'm not up to *N* yet, but I figure 'N Sync is a revolutionary faction in the Ottoman Empire or something.

grease
Have I gotten across the mind-blowing diversity of everything? Whatever the topic—bottles, lakes, rodents—the *Britannica* seems to have hun-

dreds and hundreds of varieties you never knew about. It's like discovering for the first time that there's a world beyond chocolate and vanilla, like walking into a Ben & Jerry's-type ice cream boutique to gaze upon its buckets of mango-loganberry sorbets, rutabaga fudge, and so on.

Consider grease. I figured, as I venture most of my friends and family do, that grease is grease. But no, there's a whole marvelous, disgusting world of grease, with endless flavors to choose from. There's white grease, made from inedible hog fat; yellow grease, made from darker parts of the hog; brown grease, containing beef and mutton fats; fleshing grease, from the fatty material on pelts. And don't forget bone grease and garbage grease! And that's just your fat-based greases. You've also got your mineral greases, which consist of a liquid lubricant such as petroleum mixed with soap or inorganic gels. Delicious.

There's always more diversity than you think. Even if you figure you've got a good grasp of a topic, the *Britannica* still manages to surprise you. Back in high school, I memorized the various ways of classifying organisms: kingdom, phylum, class, order, family, genus, species—a list I still remember thanks to the mnemonic "King Philip came over from Germany Saturday." So I was feeling pretty good until I got to the *Macropaedia* entry on *biological sciences,* where I was disturbed to find out that I knew exactly squat about taxonomy. In addition to my precious phylum and friends, there's also brigade, cohort, section, and tribe. There are also subphyla and superclasses and suborders. You get the idea. There's a lot of freaking diversity.

Since I'm on the topic of taxonomy, let me talk about that for a second. Because here's something I've realized: the *Britannica* is doing for my mind what Julie has done for the rest of my life. By which I mean organizing it.

As I've mentioned, Julie is the single most organized person in America. She lives in a world of four-color notebooks, Post-it notes, Magic Markers, hanging files, and three-hole punchers. She keeps an Excel spreadsheet charting every movie we've seen, and whether we saw it on DVD, tape, or in the theater. She has, in the past, kept lists of every outfit she's worn and every celebrity she's spotted (Monty Hall in a Tel Aviv hotel!). She still remembers our entire wedding list. One night a few months ago she spent twenty minutes breaking down the guests by first name: five Davids, three Michaels, et cetera. Our kitchen is a thing of beauty. On our counter, there's a three-ring notebook containing the menus of every restaurant that will deliver to our house, organized with color tabs listing the various cuisines. I once pointed out to her that the cuisines were not properly alphabetized; the Italian menus came before the Indian menus. She told me that she had organized it geographically, with the westernmost countries first, and then working east.

At first, I laughed at Julie's organizing fetish. But slowly, over the last couple of years, without even trying, she's converted me. I now put things in folders and make endless lists. At work, I have a four-color notebook of my own, though I hide it whenever my boss comes by my office, since I feel it's embarrassingly unmanly, akin to the practice of putting smiley faces over *i*'s. But it makes me feel better. Everything in its proper place. Life may be chaotic, and the second law of thermodynamics (discovered by Rudolf Clausius) will win out in the end, but we can fight it while we're here.

But back to the *Britannica*. Thanks to my reading, I feel like my brain is becoming beautifully organized, filled with little hanging folders inside my skull. The *Britannica* has helped me organize the world into rational categories. It excels at taxonomy. Consider card games. There must be hundreds of them, but the Britannica points out that they all fall into one of two categories: those based on rank (such as bridge) and those based on combinations (such as poker). Maybe this is obvious, and maybe I'm a mouth-breathing moron, but I'd never thought of it. The world of card games suddenly seems more manageable—just two neat categories. Same has happened with cereals (which come in just four varieties: flaked, puffed, shredded, and granular), cakes, fires, types of abbreviation—all sorts of things. Even the subject of taxonomy itself has its own taxonomy, but don't get me started.

Greek system

I shelved my *G* volume long enough to join Julie at the movies. We chose *Old School*, a comedy about a bunch of thirty-something guys who start their own fraternity. (By the way, the first true frat was Kappa Alpha, begun at Union College in 1825.) I figured it was a good choice: it had the word "school" in the title, so it sort of related to my quest for intelligence.

We get there half an hour early, as we always do. Usually, this is a smart idea—we avoid getting stuck in the front row and staring at the actors' manhole-sized nostrils for two hours—but in this case, it backfires in a spectacular fashion. As soon as we take our seats, a couple sits down behind us. I take an immediate dislike to the male half of the couple. He is young and cocky and loud as an emu in heat (they have a specially constructed trachea for noisy vocalizations).

He feels it necessary to make a business call on his cell—he works for a record label, I surmise—during which he makes it clear that everyone in his office but him is a complete dimwit who couldn't operate a spoon. He hangs up, and whines to his girlfriend for making him come to this movie, which he knows is going to be stupid. He segues into a complaint about the Grammy Awards, which he has been pressed into attending, the poor man, and which he knows will be chock-full of morons and jack-asses (well, maybe he is right about that one). He makes another cell phone call, during which he abuses another colleague. At which point his girlfriend makes—in my mind—the heroic suggestion that he stop treating everyone like peons.

"You don't even know what 'peon' means," says the guy.

"It's a servant or lowly person," says his girlfriend.

Good for her, I think to myself. He thinks differently.

"No, that's wrong," he says. "It has nothing to do with social position."

"What is it then?"

"It means a small person. Small in stature. Like a midget." He has a fine mixture of condescension, confidence, and ennui going.

"Really?" says his girlfriend. "I could swear it's a servant."

"Nope. The actual definition is 'small in stature.' People misuse it all the time."

He is not joking.

A peon is a midget? Is this true? I'm not up to the Ps, so I haven't yet read about peons and yet I am 96 percent sure that he is wrong. I am almost positive that the only thing small in stature is his cerebral cortex. But that 4 percent of uncertainty keeps me from turning around and telling him to please use his cell phone as a suppository device. Well, that and a lifelong aversion to confrontation. I flash to that scene in *Annie Hall* when Woody Allen pulls Marshall McLuhan out from behind a display and gets him to personally dress down the offending gasbag. I don't need Marshall MacLuhan. All I need is a dictionary.

When Julie and I get home from *Old School*—which turned out to be entertaining, though a little light on academic rigor—I look up "peon" in my dictionary. No mention of midgets, dwarves, hobbits, or Dustin Hoffman. "Peon" means farm laborer, servant, or poor person. The etymology is from Spanish *peon*, or peasant, which in turn is from the Latin word for a man who goes on foot.

Another reminder that many of your everyday know-it-alls are complete and total imbeciles. I vow that when I become smart again, I will use my knowledge for good, not for evil—for enlightenment, not for conde-scension.

Green, Hetty

The Witch of Wall Street they called her. Not a beloved woman. Hetty lived in the late 19th and early 20th centuries, and through clever, and sometimes vulturelike, investments, she became the richest woman of her day. Also the cheapest. She wore shabby clothes, lived in a small apart-ment in Hoboken, and allegedly refused to hire a doctor to treat her son's hurt leg, a decision that eventually led to its amputation. Which she prob-ably liked, since that meant fewer socks to buy.

Personally, I've never been a cheapskate. I'm not a free spender, mind you, but I do buy decent clothes from midlevel chains like Banana Repub-lic, would probably pay a doctor to save my son's limbs if the kid asked nicely, and unless the waiter spills cappuccino on my lap or tells me I look like Lyle Lovett, have always given a respectable, 15 percent tip.

I'd say I'm right in the middle on the stinginess scale. Or I was. The *Britannica* has nudged me to be ever so slightly less cheap. For the last few weeks, I've started tipping more, in the range of 20 to 25 percent. That's one clear-cut—if very small—way the *Britannica* has changed me, proba-bly for the better. I noticed the change after reading about marginal utility theory in the *economics* section. I probably learned all about marginal utility theory in college, but it didn't sink in, just as most things in college didn't sink in, unless they involved new and more efficient ways to get hammered.

For those foggy on their microeconomics: marginal utility theory says that consumers differ in the amount of satisfaction they derive from each unit of a commodity. When a man with only seven slices of bread gets of-fered another slice, that one extra slice gives him a lot of happiness. But if a man has a couple of hundred slices of bread—enough bread to keep him waist deep in sandwiches for months—another slice of bread won't send his spirits soaring.

In short, money means more to those who don't have it. I know this verges on common sense. But there's something about seeing it in the *Bri-tannica,* expressed as a rock-hard economic law, that makes it more pow-erful to me. So, for instance, today, when I took a cab home in the snow, even though the driver tested my nerves by spending the entire time telling me about his favorite Dunkin' Donuts flavors (he's partial to crullers), I gave him $6 instead of the usual $5. I probably have more money than he does in my bank account, so the dollar will provide him greater happiness than it would me. A simple, logical conclusion. I know it smacks of noblesse oblige, of extreme condescension. But I don't care— it makes me feel better. Of course, the real right thing to do would be to give away 90 percent of my bank account, but what can I do? I like my Banana Republic khakis and my cappuccinos.

Greenland

A mystery solved. I've always wondered why Greenland—which is basically a massive sheet of white ice—is called Greenland. Turns out the country's name was coined by an Erik the Red, who had been banished from Iceland in 982 A.D. for manslaughter. He called his new home Greenland in order to entice more people to join him there. In other words, it was all a shady PR ploy by a felon. Shady, but smart. No doubt he got more takers than if he'd gone with something more accurate, like Bleakland or Depressingland or Youllstarveland.

gymnasium

The literal Greek translation is "school for naked exercise." Which made toweling off the stationary bike even more important.

H

haboob

The haboob is a hot wind in the Sahara Desert that stirs up huge quantities of sand. The sand forms a dense wall that can reach a height of three thousand feet. Jesus. It kind of reminds me of my life. It's my own damn fault, but I've found myself in an information haboob. A dense wall I can't see out of. I'm not even a third of the way to those glorious *Z*s, and my life consists of work and reading, reading and work, with a little sleep and a bowl of Life cereal in between.

I found a couple of minutes to call my parents for a brief catch-up. My mother spent most of the time telling me about her new crusade against multitasking. She hates when people check their e-mails while talking on the phone. It means they're not listening. "Uh-huh," I told her, "that's interesting," as I opened another of my AOL e-mails.

Hanson, John

He's sometimes referred to as the first president of the United States, thanks to his role as president of the Continental Congress in 1781. The first president wasn't George Washington—that's a good fact to mention at the bar, assuming you want to get kicked in the groin and have your glasses broken.

Harrison, William Henry

The ninth president—or the tenth if you count John Hanson—campaigned by passing out free hard cider to voters. The man basically bought his way into the presidency with booze. It backfired on him, though; he died a month into office.

Harvard

As if I needed reminding that everyone who is important in world history went to Harvard. My alma mater, Brown, isn't a bad school, but when it comes to famous attendees, I can only think of S. J. Perelman, a couple of Kennedys, and, uh, let's see, Kara Dukakis, the daughter of former presidential candidate Michael Dukakis, who lived in my dorm and whose roommate had very loud sex in the dorm shower. But Harvard, my God. Presidents aplenty, countless members of Congress, and pretty much every great American writer. The *Britannica* lists just some of the graduates who went on to literary fame: Henry James, T. S. Eliot, E. E. Cummings, Robert Frost, John Dos Passos . . .

Whoa, nelly! Wait just an Ivy League second. Robert Frost as a graduate of Harvard? I flip back to the *F*s, because I distinctly remember that—yes, it's true, right there next to his picture—Robert Frost dropped out of Harvard. Attendee, yes. But graduate? I think not, you nutty gold-embossed volume.

This is a very exciting moment for me. In fact, it's embarrassing how exciting this is for me. I find mistakes rarely—maybe once every four hundred pages—but when I do, I feel like an astronomer spotting a comet (perhaps even the Tago-Sato-Kosaka comet, which, by the way, passes by earth only once every 420,000 years). I feel like the middling student with a C average who has somehow busted the smartest kid in the class as he was writing an equation on the blackboard. I still remember fondly when I discovered that the entry on Dvur Kralove, a Czech city, had a backward quotation mark.

And this find is disputable, but I throw it out anyway because it made me proud: The *Britannica* was discussing grammar, and mentioned something called an "infix," which is a cousin of the suffix and the prefix, except that it occurs inside a word. The *Britannica* stated that the infix occurs in Greek and Tagalog, but not in English. I somehow summoned up from my college linguistics course the fact that there is, actually, one infix in the English language: "fucking." As in "in-fucking-credible," or "un-fucking-believable," or "*Bri*-fucking-*tannica*." It may not be polite English, but it still counts, at least according to my liberal college professor.

Since it's the work of humans—even if they are high-IQ humans—

the *Britannica* has a long history of mistakes. I came across a 1999 *Wall Street Journal* article by Michael J. McCarthy that gives an entertaining peek at the foibles of fact checking such an immense product. The first edition was particularly riddled with misinformation and half-truths, such as this entry on California: "California is a large country of the West Indies. It is uncertain whether it be a peninsula or an island." Ha! Even your average movie star knows this is absurd, at least after you explain to him the definition of a peninsula.

The *EB* has since fixed *California* but other errors have popped up, as readers have been delighted to point out. Apparently, there's a whole group of people—and by people I mean losers—who also comb the *Britannica* looking for mistakes. The *Journal* article reports that, for years, the *Britannica* bought into the widely held myth that the emperor Caligula appointed his horse to the Roman Senate. After researching classical sources at the suggestion of a reader, the *Britannica* nixed the reference. Caligula's steed never held government office, though he did have an ivory manger and a marble stall, which isn't too bad. Another victim of close inspection: the story of Martin Luther nailing his ninety-five theses to the church door. Turns out he just passed the pages around. The *Britannica* also caused a hubbub in Scotland recently when its CD-ROM mistakenly reported that the country had no parliament. A British newspaper headlined its article about the gaffe "Encyclopedia Twit-annica." Tough stuff. Of course, not all complaints have merit. One misguided reader wrote the editors an outraged, obscenity-packed missive claiming the Ostrogoths—an obscure medieval ethnic group—did *not* assimilate, as the *Britannica* claimed. Perhaps he believed he was an Ostrogoth-American.

To be fair, the *Britannica* is admirably anal in its attempts at accuracy. The fact-checking department got a photocopy of Houdini's birth certificate to prove he was born in Budapest, not Wisconsin, as he had claimed. And in 1986, they barely avoided a massive factual meltdown. That was the year a disgruntled laid-off editor tampered with the database, inserting a reference to his boss as Rambo and replacing all references to Jesus with Allah—a real howler. When the *Britannica* threatened legal action, the editor fessed up to all his unauthorized tweaking.

Still, for all their thoroughness, bloopers slip through. And thank God. It's good to know that even the brainiest among us, even the weightiest institutions, make mistakes. Just to be sure on the Robert Frost situation, I run him through Nexis. He did drop out—but later got an honorary degree. Huh. I decide that still does not make him a graduate. Though I could be mistaken.

Hawthorne, Nathaniel

I may have known quite a bit about Hawthorne at one point in high school. As an adult, I know only the very basics: (1) He wrote *The Scarlet Letter.* (2) That letter was *A.* (3) The book had a sad ending. (And I only remember that last one thanks to Demi Moore. When she turned the book into a movie and slapped a happy ending on it, she justified it by saying, "Not many people have read the book." Which, in my case, was sadly true.)

Turns out that Hawthorne had an unhappy life, even for a 19th-century writer. His dad, a ship captain, died at sea when Hawthorne was four. Hawthorne was weighed down with guilt because one of his forefathers was a judge at the Salem witch trials. He had a complicated friendship with Herman Melville that ended badly—Melville thought Hawthorne was too distant, so Melville wrote a poem satirizing him. Hawthorne was bitter about being fired from his job at the customhouse. And toward the end of his life, "he took to writing the figure '64' compulsively on scraps of paper."

I reread that sentence several times. That's what it says, right there in the encyclopedia—Hawthorne compulsively wrote the number 64 on scraps of paper. There's no explanation, no mention of why he wrote 64 instead of, say, 65 or, even crazier, 63. I'm thinking some ambitious grad student needs to explore this topic and write a thesis called "The Scarlet Number: Hawthorne and the Eschatological Implications of the Repeating 64."

In the meantime, this strange fact stays with me. Maybe it's because I've got plenty of my own compulsions. I don't have any special affinity for the number 64, but I do like to swallow in pairs. If I take a bite of a peach, for instance, I make sure to gulp half the pulp in one swallow, but save half of it for a second swallow. Or there's my radio ritual. When I turn off the radio, the last word I hear has to be a noun. No verbs, no prepositions, no adjectives—I need a noun, preferably a good, solid noun, something you can hold in your hands. So I'll stand over my shower radio, dripping, pushing the power button on and off and on and off till I catch Nina Totenberg saying something like "bottle" or "car." Only then can I get out of the shower and get dressed.

I'd prefer to kick these tics altogether, but since that's not going to happen without some time-consuming therapy, I'm delighted to learn about other people's compulsions. So reading the encyclopedia is good for me. It's packed with personality quirks, and we're not just talking the compulsions of John Q. Obsessive. We're talking about the compulsions of the most brilliant men and women in history.

head flattening

This is just what it sounds like: the ritual deformation of the human skull, as formerly practiced by some Pacific Northwest Indians. The desired flat-head effect is achieved by fastening the infant's skull to the cradle board. Some Indians from the Southeast practiced another method: placing a bag of sand against the infant's forehead.

I actually remember head flattening from back in the Bs. It made a cameo in the article on body modifications and mutilations, which, if I may reminisce a bit, was one of the weirdest entries in the *Britannica*. The variety of ways that humans have found to distort their bodies is truly remarkable. It makes your jaw drop, assuming the jaw hasn't been deformed by some ritual.

Over the centuries, cultures have put bands on various parts of the skull to squeeze it into an hourglass shape. Humans have gone to town on their own teeth, chipping them, putting pegs in them, blackening them, carving relief designs into them. The Mayan Indians considered crossed eyes beautiful, and induced the condition by hanging an object between the baby's eyes.

The tongue has seen some rough times, getting slashed (some Australian tribes) and having a cord of thorns pulled through it (the Aztecs). Labia have been elongated. Necks have been stretched like a mound of pasta dough (the Padaung woman wear a fifteen-inch brass neck ring that pulls four vertebrae into the neck).

The breasts have been compressed (in 17th-century Spain), distended (in Paraguay)—and systematically enlarged by the tribe members of the modern United States.

That was a jolt. I was reading along, thinking to myself how mystifying these primitive cultures are with their need to squeeze and pull the human body into contorted shapes. And then, bam—a sentence about gel implants and boob jobs. We're not so different. We're just another of the world's cultures with our own weird fetish—one that happens to involve boobs the size of female blue whales (the largest recorded animal, weighing in at two hundred tons, with a heart of fifteen hundred pounds).

Heisman, John

The man who gave his name to the Heisman trophy was a famed football coach for Georgia Tech. During the off season, however, Heisman supported himself as a Shakespearean actor, a job that inspired him to use Elizabethan polysyllabic language in his coaching (for example, he called the football a "prolate spheroid"). Why aren't there any Shakespearean football coaches nowadays? Now all we get is Bill "the Tuna" Parcells and his love of Henrik Ibsen. Okay, we don't even have that because I made that up. My point is, John Heisman is proof—just in case you needed it—of how far we've slid into dumbness.

heroin

Heroin was first developed by the Bayer company. That'll whisk your headache away faster than a couple of dozen aspirin. Take two syringefuls and call me in the morning. Or late afternoon.

hip-hop

"Influential early deejays include DJ Kool Herc, Grand Wizard Theodore and Grandmaster Flash." I've heard of Grandmaster Flash, but Kool Herc? Grand Wizard Theodore? Holy shit—I don't recognize either. Let me tell you: it's a sad, sad day when the *Encyclopaedia Britannica* is hipper than you. I'm annoyed I've never heard of those guys. Back in high school, I was actually an early fan of rap music, thanks to the influence of my friend Eric, who called himself M. C. Milano. (Get it? White on the outside, black on the inside.) But obviously, we weren't listening to the authentic stuff, because we missed Kool Herc and Grand Wizard Theodore.

And yet just as I was feeling pathetic and totally un-phat, I read the *Britannica*'s assertion that Public Enemy and Wu-Tang Clan "were among the popular purveyors of rap during the 1980s and 1990s." Purveyors of rap? Now that's got to be the whitest phrase I've ever read. Yo, what up, dawg? Just hanging with my posse, drinking my Chivas, purveying some rap.

Hogan, Ben

Hogan was the most famous golfer from the forties. The *Britannica* says: "His exceptional will enabled him to play winning golf after an automobile accident in which he was injured so severely that he was not expected to walk again."

What a sentence.

I need this sentence. I need some positive overcoming-hurdles stories. I've got hurdles aplenty in my own life, the tallest of which seems to be whatever is preventing Julie and me from getting pregnant. We try not to talk about it too much, but it's always there, permeating our apartment. The apartment has three bedrooms, one for us and two for the kids that don't exist. So those empty rooms are an ever-present and expensive reminder of our infertility. Oh, and then there's that little apocalypse hanging over our head: it looks like we're going to war with Iraq, and God knows what's going to happen.

So thank the Lord for Ben Hogan and his exceptional will. And thank the Lord for all his fellow overcomers. There are heaps of dismaying stuff in these volumes, but there are also these incredibly inspiring stories compressed down to a paragraph or a single sentence. It's like watching a particularly sappy Robin Williams movie in ten seconds.

The great Greek orator Demosthenes suffered from a speech defect—he stammered and had terrible pronunciation—but he overcame it by speaking with pebbles in his mouth. John Fielding—one of the founders of the London police—was blind but could identify three thousand thieves by their voices, sort of a primitive but effective fingerprinting system. It's like chicken soup for the soul, the microwave version. Francis Ford Coppola got interested in directing when he was laid up with polio and put on puppet shows for himself. Chester Carlson, inventor of the Xerox machine, was turned down by more than twenty companies before he finally sold it. And on and on. Did you know that Che Guevara had asthma? So you shouldn't let wheezing stop you from leading a violent revolution.

I've got to have exceptional will like Ben Hogan. No matter what, Julie and I are going to have a child—and if we can't biologically, then we'll battle through the paperwork and adopt one.

Holland Tunnel

Here, some good, calming information. One less thing to worry about. The Holland Tunnel—which connects Manhattan and New Jersey and which, by the way, was not named for the country, but for an engineer, Clifford Holland—has a remarkable ventilation system. It refreshes all the air in the tunnel in ninety seconds. Remember my mortal fear of carbon-monoxide-induced brain damage? Well, it still lingers, twenty years later, and I tense up whenever we drive through a tunnel. So this information is good stuff.

Hollywood

This was founded by a man named Horace Wilcox, "a prohibitionist who envisioned it a community based on his sober religious principles." Well, I know that a lot of Hollywood types are in AA. But other than that, Mr. Wilcox would probably not be overjoyed.

hoop skirts

In the 18th century, some hoop skirts were an astounding eighteen feet wide. And satirists talked of hoop skirts that were twenty-four feet wide. Frankly, I think those satirists need a little punching up. Adding six feet just doesn't do it for me. Maybe they could have gone with twenty-eight or twenty-nine feet. Then they'd be funny.

Hoover, Herbert

We were walking along Columbus Avenue, and I asked Julie to quiz me today, to see how my memory was doing. She gave me Gibraltar. I had a good response: it's the only place in Europe to have wild monkeys. She nodded her head, sort of impressed. She asked me about Herbert Hoover. I replied he was president—and an orphan. Raised by an uncle. She asked me about Halifax. This one was a little foggier.

"It's a town in England," I say.

"Noooo," she says. She looks at me, concerned.

"Is it one of the Carolinas? A town in North or South Carolina?"

"No."

"I don't know. Where is it?"

"It's a town in Canada. You didn't know that?"

Oh, yes. I knew that, I tell her.

When I got home, I looked up Halifax. There were three separate entries for Halifax. There's a Halifax, England; a Halifax, North Carolina; and a Halifax, Canada. I had just filled my brain up with the two piddling Halifaxes and neglected the big Halifax, the one everyone knows. My mind is working in strange ways.

hummingbird

Hummingbirds beat their wings up to eighty times a second, which is astounding. But even more astounding: they are extremely territorial, and have been known to chase off crows, hawks, and even humans. They've got what my father's mother called chutzpah. These birds the size of grapes take on humans—and *win*. An inspiration to tiny organisms everywhere, including my wife's favorite actor.

humor

You had to be there. That is what I've learned from the history of humor. If you don't believe me, try to tell this Japanese joke from the 1700s in the locker room: "The boss of the monkeys orders his one thousand monkey followers to get the moon that's reflected in the water. They all try and fail. Finally, one of the monkeys gets the moon in the water and respectfully offers it to the boss. 'This is what you asked for,' he says. The boss is delighted and says, 'What an exploit! You have distinguished yourself!' The monkey then asks, 'By the way, Master, what are you going to do with the moon from the water?' And the master says, 'Well, yes . . . I didn't think of that.'"

I tried it on my fellow *Esquire* editors Andy and Brendan, who coined a new name for me: the Great Conversation Stopper.

hunting

People sure do love to kill animals. Kings of Central European countries seemed especially fond of the practice. The *Britannica* says that John George II the ruler of Saxony in the 17th century, killed an astonishing total of 42,649 red deer. "He refused the crown of Bohemia not for political reasons but because Bohemian stags were smaller than Saxon ones"— and he erected a fence between Saxony and Bohemia to keep out those stunted Bohemian mammals. Louis XV of France was another fan of the chase: in 1726, he spent a total of 276 days hunting. He worked fewer days than George W. Bush.

I've never been a fan of hunting myself—for one thing, I don't like loud noises or sports that require a lot of equipment. Also I try to avoid removing mammal innards in my leisure time.

But in my bleaker moments, I feel like hunting is the most appropriate metaphor for my quest. I'm worried I'm not much better than John of Saxony. I'm just trying to fill my wall with the stuffed heads of deer and lions and bears, though in my case, my wall would be filled with *facts* about lions and bears (e.g., bears are not true hibernators—their body temperature doesn't dive and they are easily awakened. You want true hibernators, think bats and hedgehogs and squirrels.) Is this all a macho accumulation?

hurling

My friend Jamie has invited me to come with him to the American Crossword Puzzle Tournament. This is an invitation I wasn't expecting. I met Jamie years ago—he was my editor at *Entertainment Weekly*—and I thought I knew his secrets. I knew he had seen and enjoyed the Spice Girls movie. I knew he had a handful of stalkers—he writes a funny sex column for a local magazine that inspires overzealous fans. I even knew he liked atonal jazz. But his crossword puzzle hobby—that was new to me.

Jamie tells me he's been a fan for a long time. He's spent dozens of Saturday nights at home deciphering clues. "It's easier than meeting people," he tells me, "and more enjoyable." (He pretends to be a misanthrope.)

I decide to accept his invitation. I'm no crossword expert. I've sampled maybe three in my life—nothing against them, I just never got in the habit, the same way I never got interested in racquetball or methamphetamines. But I did have that glorious victory with Julie and Frederick Austerlitz, so I figure this will be an excellent test of newly acquired knowledge. I'll teach these pencil-pushing dorks a thing or two.

On Saturday morning, Jamie and I take the 8:10 train up to Stamford, Connecticut, and it is then that I began to realize I am in some serious trouble. Jamie has brought me a copy of the Saturday *New York Times* crossword, and I am having difficulty with a couple of clues. Namely, 1- through 57-Across and 1- through 53-Down. I look at Jamie, who is sitting next me, confidently scribbling away.

"I have a question about strategy," I say.

"Yes?"

"How do you know which letters to put in which boxes?"

Jamie isn't quite sure how to answer that. And I'm not sure what I'm saying. I just know that my knowledge—vast as it is—does not include 29-Down: "Character in Chesterton's 'What's Wrong with the World.'" At least I eventually figure out 32-Down: "Relative of hurling." Since I recently read about the Irish stick-and-ball sport, I deduce the answer is lacrosse.

When we get to the Stamford Marriot, we join four hundred other crossword competitors milling about the lobby and coffee shop. The first thing that impresses me is the variety of crossword puzzle accessories. There are crossword ties, crossword tote bags, crossword notebooks, crossword scarves, and crossword T-shirts ("Real Women Use Pen"). One particularly gung ho competitor is wearing a crossword bandanna around his head, *Deer Hunter*–style. This man would later threaten to poke his pencil into Jamie's neck because Jamie was taking too long at the pencil sharpener. He pretended to be kidding, but I'm pretty sure he wasn't. I noticed he didn't blink very much.

The only other people in the hotel lobby are, oddly enough, a team of high school lacrosse players in town for a big match. They are looking at the crossword crowd with a mixture of fear and bewilderment.

"Good luck with your 'relative of hurling'!" I shout across the room. Jamie and I giggle—that's the only word to describe it—then realize that we are a couple of six-letter words beginning with *L* and ending with O-S-E-R-S.

We end up talking shop with a woman who looks remarkably like Rhea Perlman. Apparently we missed some good puzzling last night. (The competitors love to use "puzzle" as a verb. Also, "puzzler" is a very popular noun, as in "I'm just a leisure puzzler.") The head of the French crossword puzzle society had given a hilarious post-dinner lecture on French puzzling. He had told them that French tournaments are held only in towns with two letters in the name. Jamie and I smile blankly.

"Because two-letter towns show up a lot in French crosswords," she says, annoyed at our thickness.

"Ohhh," we say.

She walks away in search of smarter people. But no matter, there are plenty of other puzzlers to mingle with. We meet a *New York Times* puzzle constructor—"constructor," I learn, is the preferred term—who tells us it's not an easy life. The complaints kill him. He had a clue that said "24 hours" and the answer was "rotation," as in the rotation of the earth. Someone wrote an angry letter pointing out that, actually, the rotation of the earth is just 23 hours and 56 minutes and 9 seconds, because the earth is simultaneously revolving around the sun.

As I try to process this, we are approached by a balding, bespectacled man whose jacket is blanketed with buttons. One says, "I used to procrastinate but now . . .", another says, "Knowledge Is Power. Power Corrupts. Study Hard and Be Evil." He's not a competitor, just here to observe and volunteer as a proctor.

We ask why he decided not to compete.

"I don't do crosswords," he informs us in a brisk staccato. "At least not the American kind. They aren't difficult enough in an interesting way. I prefer the British cryptic."

The British cryptic?

Well, he just happens to have one with him. He unfolds the paper and shows it to us: "Okay, the clue is 'Late bloomer, finally flown, in back.' Aster is a flower that's a late bloomer. *N* is the last letter of 'finally flown.' And a stern is in back. So the answer is 'astern.'"

He looks at us expectantly, as if we should burst out laughing and shake our heads in wonder. First Benny Hill, now this! Those Brits are brilliant.

Luckily, before we have to respond, we are told the first of several tournament puzzles is about to start.

"Let's hit the grids!" says Jamie.

"Let's cruciverb it up!" I respond.

We realize that we might just have made the button-wearing cryptic guy look cool by comparison. But that's okay—we are ready. We file into the grand ballroom and sit at a long table in the front, placing our arsenal of Sanford American pencils carefully in front of us. I'm trying to feel cocky, hoping my debacle on the train was some sort of weird anomaly. After all, I know 28 percent of all knowledge.

The director of the tournament—the velvet-voiced, mustachioed Will Shortz, the man who edits the *New York Times* crossword puzzle and who, to this crowd, is cooler than Lou Reed—tells us that we will be judged on speed and accuracy. We have fifteen minutes. Now puzzle!

Okay, here's one I know: "Radar screen indicator" is a blip. *B-L-I-P*. Let's see, let's see. "Roswell sightings" are *U-F-O-S*. Okay. Let's see. At which point I notice that hands start shooting up all over the ballroom. That means the person attached to the hand is finished with the cross-word. Who are these people? A couple of minutes later Jamie slams down his pencil and raises his hand. Shit! After what seems like significantly less than fifteen minutes, Will Shortz instructs those who haven't finished to put their pencils down. I look at all the white boxes in my unfinished puzzle. A lot of white. As much white as the Vostok Station in Antarctica. This is bad. I'm not sure why the *Britannica* is failing me, but I'm not pleased.

The second puzzle is even more of a disaster. What the hell is the river to the Bristol Channel? One of Jupiter's smallest moons? I'm blanking. Must be because I'm not up to the *J*s. I've finished barely a third of puzzle when Will Shortz tells us with his gentle, pediatrician-like voice that time's up.

I decide I'm going to blame my failure on the woman next to me and her extremely distracting and persistent cough. It wasn't just your average cough, it was a deep gurgling cough involving lots of viscous fluid and several internal organs. How can I puzzle with that around me? Jamie and I agree there should be a separate section for consumptives.

The third puzzle is a little better, the fourth is about the same, but the fifth—with its "'Uncle Vanya' character" and "Former Bud Grace comic strip"—plunges me into a black mood. I should have known it would be bad: when the name of the constructor was announced, the crowd let out a respectful "oooh."

So what went wrong? Why was my crossword puzzle adventure such an aggressive failure? If anyone could give me an insight, it would be John Delfin. John is the Tiger Woods of the puzzle set, a seven-time champ and the winner of the tournament in which I placed an impressive 510 out of 525. He's polished off a Monday *New York Times* puzzle in two minutes flat. He's done a Sunday one in six minutes. He owns fifteen dictionaries.

John is disturbingly ungeeky. He seems perfectly socially adept, looks a bit like Paul Simon, and makes his living as a pianist. And instead of gloating, he's graciously comforting about my loss.

"Crossword is a language," he tells me. "And once you learn that language, you'll be able to speak it fluently."

The point is, general knowledge rarely comes in handy in crosswords. You need a very specialized knowledge. Namely, you need to know nouns of about four letters with a high percentage of vowels. You need rivers named Aere or Uele. You need the African antelope called an eland. You need to know all your Aidas and Oonas and Ermas—whether it's Erma Bombeck or Erma Franklin (Arethra's sister). So I may know almost everything in *A–I*, I just have a little weakness in vowel-heavy nouns. That's what I tell myself, anyway. And it's true—generally, I'm not a fan of vowels, they seem so soft. Give me a good hard consonant. I long for the days when alphabets—like the Etruscans'—had no vowels at all.

I'm ready to take the train home with my lepton-sized shred of dignity intact, but Jamie wants to stay for a night of word games—namely, a crossword-puzzle-themed version of the TV show *Family Feud*. Somehow I agree, somehow my name is chosen from a hat, and somehow I find myself onstage in the grand ballroom in front of four hundred competitive puzzlers. I'm a member of the Cross family and am facing off against the Downey family. Jamie, the lucky bastard, just gets to sit in the audience.

The question is, "Name another type of puzzle that crossword puzzlers enjoy." My teammates do admirably—they guess anagrams and find-a-word, both of which are correct. It's my turn now. The host repeats the question. The pressure's on, my team is counting on me—and my mind is a blank. Nothing. Blank as the upper right corner of my answer sheet to puzzle three. I feel I've got to say something. So I lean into the microphone and give my answer: "Puzzles involving card games."

Huh. Puzzles involving card games. I'm not even sure what that means and I'm the one who said it. The host looks at me as if I'd just said something in the rare Andamanese language (which, by the way, has words for only two numbers—one and more than one). I turn around to gauge the reaction of the crowd. Four hundred faces of confusion and concern. They're all wondering why I didn't say "Jumble" or "Cryptics"— or anything that makes a glimmer of sense.

"Ooooooooookay," says the host. He turns to the answer board. "Puzzles involving card games." A big fat buzzer.

I slink back to my seat. "Puzzles involving card games?" says Jamie. I don't know what to say. My brain just froze. I was so desperate to impress, I put so much pressure on myself, I temporarily lost all ability to carry out simple mental functions. "When we leave," asks Jamie, "can you walk out fifteen feet ahead of me?"

I

identity

I'm told it's a good thing to know thyself.

Nowadays, I know myself better than I've known myself ever before. I've become quite intimate with myself. I know dozens, hundreds, maybe thousands of facts about myself that I never knew before.

I know that I'm a collection of seventy-five trillion cells, which seems like an alarming amount. (Worse, since I barely ever use the Stairmaster anymore, I think I've added another hundred million cells to my midsection). I'm 60 percent water by weight. I'm a bipedal mammal, a distinction unique to humans (kangaroos don't count because their tails act as third legs). I have about a hundred thousand hairs on my head that grow at a rate of a half inch per month. My phylum is Chordata, which was a shocker. I knew my kingdom and species and probably could have come up with my class and order. But my phylum was news to me.

If I went into boxing, I'd be a junior middleweight (148–154 pounds). When I was born I had 20/800 vision—and I had gill slits in utero. When I breathe, I suck in trace amounts of fun-sounding gases like krypton and xenon along with boring old oxygen. As for my address, you can find me in the Local Group of galaxies, in a spiral galaxy about a hundred light-years across. I live on Earth, a planet about twenty-five thousand miles in circumference and tilted at 23.5 degrees. More specifically, I'm on North America, a continent supported by the Canadian Shield.

Along with 350 million other humans, I speak the English language, specifically the Inland Northern dialect (unlike those pompous British Received Pronunciation folks, I pronounce the *t* in motor like a *d*). I'm a member of the Ashkenazi tribe of Jews, which started out in what is now Germany and France (though that doesn't make me French, mind you). I work in magazines, the first of which was the British *Gentlemen's Magazine,* founded in 1731, which had the familiar-sounding motto *"e pluribus unum."*

On the one hand, I like this. There's something comforting about being defined within an angstrom of your life. The stuff that freaks me out is the biology. I haven't thought this much about the workings of my seventy-five trillion cells since high school. I probably should be in awe at the miracle that is my life. But instead I'm terrified. Last week, I spent ninety minutes lying awake in bed, worrying about my bodily organs. Especially the heart. Mine beats at seventy beats per minute. Seventy beats per minute seems so many—not as many as canaries, with their thousand beats, but far more than elephants, with a pathetic twenty-five. It's been going on for thirty-five years without stopping—but how many more beats can it continue without something going wrong? It's got so many delicate moving parts—the sinoatrial pacemaker, the papillary muscle, the tricuspid valve. I stayed motionless in bed for ninety minutes with my hand on my heart, making sure it kept pumping and that I was still alive, until slowly, finally, I dropped off to sleep.

illusion

We went to the wedding of Julie's family friend. It was a happy occasion, but one made much happier by a conversation I had with Eric's wife, Alexandra.

Alexandra is a great woman. Julie and I have canonized her Saint Alexandra for putting up with Eric. They met while Eric was doing foreign service duty in Colombia, and when Alex moved to the United States a couple of years later, she spoke about fourteen words of English. Now, she talks fluently, despite her accent and the occasional word mangling (she thought "homely" meant pretty, which caused some problems when she complimented the neighbors on their very homely children).

Anyway, at the cocktail party, over our little plates of grilled asparagus, I was complaining to Alexandra that I'd never catch up to Eric, knowledge-wise. He has too much of a head start in that head of his.

Alexandra told me a story to make me feel better.

A couple of years ago, Alexandra and Eric went out to dinner with another couple. After their waitress took their order and left, Alexandra was all atwitter.

"That's a Colombian accent on that waitress," she said. "Not just that—I think she's from my hometown of Cali."

Eric shook his head emphatically. "That's not a Colombian accent. That's a Slavic accent." After which he proceeded to give a speech about the linguistics of the Balkan states.

When the waitress came back with their appetizers, Alex said, "Where are you from?"

"Colombia," said the waitress.

"Which town in Colombia?"

"Cali," said the waitress.

Alex was floating on air. Eric shrugged it off.

It's a fascinating story. Not just because Eric was wrong, which is nice, no doubt. I'm fascinated by the fact that he pooh-poohed his Colombian-accented wife on the topic of Colombian accents—that takes some *cojones*.

No doubt he declared the waitress's accent to be Slavic with absolute confidence. Not a moment of hesitation. The same tone he'd use to state his eye color, or that the Battle of Hastings occurred in 1066. Now, I'm not saying that Eric doesn't know a lot. He's accumulated an obscene amount of data. But what about those rare occasions when he's not sure of something? Well, he's not going to let a little detail like that stop him.

It's confirmation of something I've been toying with for a couple of months: one secret to being a successful know-it-all is extreme confidence. Just state your fact loud and proud, even if, as is the case with me, the details are often faded and jumbled up. As my friend the financial analyst once told me about his line of work: sometimes right, sometimes wrong, always certain.

The other day, someone at the office brought up twins. I had a beauty of a fact for him. "Did you know that in traditional Vietnamese society, boy-girl twins were forced to marry?" I said. "Because it was assumed they had sex in the womb." A good story—but it was actually Balinese society. I knew it wasn't Vietnam, but I couldn't remember the country of marrying twins. So I just made it up. I guessed my conversation partner did not have a doctorate in East Asian obstetrics. I guessed right.

Indian Mutiny

This was a failed rebellion against the British regime in 19th-century India. The Indian Mutiny was notable for the strange way that it began. In

1857, the Brits employed Indian soldiers—called sepoys—to serve the British East India Company. But the Brits made the mistake of introducing the new Enfield rifle to their Indian troops. This gun required the soldiers to bite off the ends of lubricated cartridges. The lubrication in question? A mixture of pig and cow lard, which managed the neat trick of offending both Muslim and Hindu soldiers, who were prohibited from eating pig and cow, respectively. The Indians rose up and killed British officers, but the English put down the rebellion with biblical ferocity. To quote the *Britannica*: "In the end the reprisals far outweighed the original excesses. Hundreds of sepoys were shot from cannons in a frenzy of British vengeance (though some British officers did protest the bloodshed)."

First, the image of people being shot from cannons has to be one of the most disturbing things I've run across. But also, I noted the parenthetical remark: some British officers did protest the bloodshed. That's classic *Britannica*. The *EB* is the single most fair, even-handed book in the history of publishing. Everything has two sides. Even the most evil deeds, the most dark-hearted people have their redeeming qualities.

The Black Death, admittedly, wiped out a third of Europe, but it also raised wages for those still breathing by opening up the labor market. You take the good, you take the bad.

Attila the Hun? Sure, he was a vicious barbarian with the decidedly uncuddly nickname of Scourge of God. Yes, he murdered his older brother Bleda so that he could rule alone. And there's his résumé, which includes raping and pillaging pretty much every inhabited acre of eastern Europe. Oh, and when Attila died, the saps who buried his body were later put to death so the location of his grave would never be discovered.

Fine. He's got his flaws. And yet, and yet . . . you catch him on the right days, and he could surprise you. Attila "was by no means pitiless," says the *Britannica*, and at banquets he was "served off wooden plates and ate only meat, whereas his chief lieutenants dined off silver platters loaded with dainties." See? He ate off wooden plates. Would you eat off wooden plates if you had worked up a hearty appetite conquering all of Europe? Probably not.

It may not be much, but it's something. The *EB* is very proper, a perfect gentleman. I imagine if it bumped into you, it would say, "Terribly sorry, old chap." Read it for five hours a day, and you start to be brainwashed by its constant pro/con tone. Yes, you'll think to yourself, Rush Limbaugh can be a bullying jackass, but he's also got some fine points about the importance of patriotism and a clear speaking voice.

industrial engineering

Big news. The *Britannica* has inspired me to change the way I load the dishwasher. The revolution began with a passage on mass production, where I learned the most important thing is to carefully divide the operation into specialized tasks. Namely, "simple, highly repetitive motion patterns and minimal handling or positioning of the workpiece. This permits the development of human motion patterns that are easily learned and rapidly performed with a minimum of unnecessary motion or mental readjustment."

I realized—when I was in the kitchen later that day—that I was doing some serious unnecessary motion and mental readjustment while cleaning up after dinner. I used to scrape a dish, rinse it, put it in the dishwasher, scrape another dish, rinse it, put it in the dishwasher, and so on. Crazy, I know. No specialization, no division, pure chaos.

Now, I've become a beautifully efficient poet of motion. Now, I scrape all the dishes using the same precise swipe of the fork. Only then do I rinse the stack. And after that, I load them all with an economy of motion.

I love it. I am trying to live up to the example of those early 20th-century efficiency experts like Frank Gilbreth, who descended on factories with stopwatches and clipboards. (By the way, Gilbreth had twelve kids, and was the inspiration for the book *Cheaper by the Dozen*.)

I'm telling you, my new system is faster. I may be wasting a year of my life reading the encyclopedia, but at least I'm shaving time off my daily tasks. Over a lifetime, this method may well save a full two to three minutes.

inherited traits

I've been reading a lot of intriguing theories about heredity recently. The ancients believed in something called "maternal impressions"—that the baby's personality is affected by experiences the woman undergoes while pregnant (this is why Eskimo mothers eat ducks' wings while carrying; they hope to make their babies good paddlers). Aristotle endorsed the theory of telegony, which says that an infant's inborn traits come not only from his biological father, but also from other males who mated with the mother in the distant past. My mom once dated the great-grandson of William Howard Taft, so if I become enormously fat and start supporting higher tariffs, we'll know whom to blame.

But today, I got a close-up lesson in heredity. It happened over lunch with my dad. Since my dad and I both work in midtown, we occasionally meet at a deli for sandwiches.

As soon as we're seated, I start in on him. "Let me see if I've learned enough legal stuff in the encyclopedia to help you with one of your cases."

Dad looks very uncomfortable.

"Just tell me one of your cases and I'll see if I can solve it," I say.

"How about the case of the disappearing waiter. That's a good one to solve."

I could have pushed him but I sensed this one was better left alone. There *is* that attorney-client privilege thing.

"What about nonlegal questions?" I ask him. "You have any of those?"

"How about 'What are you ordering?'"

"No, like factual questions."

Dad thinks about it for a few seconds, and comes up with one: "-What's the most southern state?"

I pause. Is this a trick question? "Hawaii."

"Yes. Most northern?"

"Alaska."

"Right. Most western."

I try to picture the map of the United States. It's either Alaska or Hawaii.

"Alaska is the most western."

"Good. Most eastern?"

"Maine."

"Nope. The most eastern state is Alaska."

What? That's crazy talk. I give him a disbelieving scowl.

"A couple of the Aleutian Islands cross the 180th meridian. So it's officially the most eastern state."

Huh. I hate to admit it, but that is pretty good.

"Did you get that from the *A* section back when you read the *Britannica*?"

"I'm not sure where I picked that up," says my dad.

I'd never pressed him about his recollections of reading the 1974 *Britannica*. I know he says he didn't remember much, and the Alaska section may not have stuck with him, but there must be something he retained, right?

"I remember most of the words started with *A* or *B*," he says.

"Come on, really."

"Not much. A little here and there."

Shit. That doesn't bode well.

"I actually remember more from the *World Book* set I had when I was a kid," my dad says. "I remember doing a big report on Australia. I really got into Australia, became obsessed with it. I wanted your grandfather to move the family to Australia, and he had to sit me down and explain that he was a lawyer in New York."

This gives me a jolt. Back when I was a kid, I became obsessed with the very same island continent. I used to spend hours tracing maps of Australia with the manic single-mindedness of Richard Dreyfus in *Close Encounters*.

"I loved Australia as a kid too."

"Yes, I remember," says Dad.

I'm not sure how I feel about this information. Could there possibly be a gene that specifies adoration of particular geographical locations? Or did my dad somehow subtly influence me to choose Australia as my beloved continent? Either way, it's left me frazzled. Along with being the smartest boy in the world, I also fancied myself completely unique. I wanted to be totally different from other humans, perhaps spontaneously generated like the primordial giant of Norse mythology formed from drops of water. Which is partly why I chose Australia—I was the only boy in my class who knew his didgeridoo from his dingo. And now, here's more evidence that I'm not different at all. I am practically a replica.

intelligentsia

I've got big weekend plans. After nearly a month of waiting, I will be attending the semiannual Greater New York Mensa Club Regional Gathering in Staten Island.

I invited Julie, since spouses are welcome, but she had a previous engagement involving sitting on the couch and reading magazines. So stag it is. This will be my first Mensa convention, and I'm a bit nervous. Will they be impressed with my knowledge? Will they sense that I weaseled my way in on my measly SATs? Will they spend the whole time talking about bioethics? Will Geena Davis be there?

I did attend one other Mensa event a couple of weeks back—the Fun Friday Dinner at a Chinese restaurant downtown—but it wasn't quite as fun as advertised. I ended up sitting in the corner and had trouble wedging myself into a conversation. The only highlight was watching one Mensan carefully arrange ice around the exterior of his bowl of won ton soup.

"Can I ask what you are doing?" I said.

"It's to cool the soup without having to water it down," he said.

"Oh," I said.

"At home, I use plastic ice balls."

"Why don't you bring the ice balls here to the restaurant?" I said.

"And where would I store them at work all day?"

He was startlingly unimpressed with my intellect. He studied me, no doubt wondering when Mensa began accepting people who spent their childhood eating lead paint. But I had to give it to him: the ice trick was pretty smart.

The convention—officially called "A New York State of Mind"—will be much better, providing me with lots more quality Mensa time. I get up early Saturday morning to try to catch the Staten Island ferry, but end up waiting in the pigeon-filled terminal for two hours. I'm not even leaving New York City, and the trip will take me at least three hours. This puts me in a dark mood. I've already skipped Friday night's activities and don't want to miss more. Who the hell has a convention in Staten Island? I think. That's not very smart. I chuckle to myself at my wit.

I get to Staten Island Hotel just in time for the Mensa pizza luncheon. It's in the Harbor Room, a space with low ceilings, an alarmingly patterned rug, and at this moment, about forty geniuses consuming pepperoni and Almaden wine. No Geena Davis in sight.

I sit down at a round table. My fellow luncheoners are busy rehashing last night's comedy show, which apparently didn't go so smoothly.

"What happened?" I ask.

"It was a disaster," says a woman wearing a denim jacket and very large glasses. "There were hecklers."

"Mensan hecklers?" I ask.

"Yes," she admitted. "Drunken Mensans. They were not acting in a Mensan way."

"What'd they say?"

"They told the female comedienne that she had a nice ass. Instead of saying, 'Nice act,' they said, 'Nice ass.'"

"Oh," I say. I'm annoyed that I have missed crass drunken Mensans. I would have liked to see that.

"It just wasn't very wise," says my friend with the denim jacket and the glass lenses that could fill a submarine porthole. "It ruined the night. It was a nice evening till then."

This wasn't the only controversy of the Mensa convention. I learned that one genius had brought two huge Bernese mountain dogs and one of them had taken a huge Bernese mountain dump outside of the game room, which the owner allegedly had neglected to clean up. So Mensans can be as immature and irresponsible as those with just average IQs. I take a bite of pizza and mull the implications of this.

I notice my lunch mate's convention badge has a circular yellow sticker on it.

"What's the yellow circle for?" I ask her.

"A green circle means, 'Yes, I want a hug.' A yellow circle means, 'Ask me before hugging.'"

I look around the room. Everyone's badge but mine has the color-coded circles, which makes me feel a bit left out. I notice one man has a badge with no less than three green circles, which I assume means he wants a hug really fucking badly. He wants a hug like a crack addict wants a fix.

"You don't like hugs?" I ask my friend.

"I'm too small," she says. "I could get crushed. There are just too many fat Mensans."

Well, I didn't want to mention it, but yes. It's true. This group may have big brains, but a shocking number of them also have enormous asses. For every IQ point, they're packing at least two, two and a half pounds. And while we're on the subject, it's worth noting that obesity isn't the only physical problem here. Remember René Descartes's fetish? Let's just say he'd be having a ball at the Mensa convention.

After a few more slices of pizza and a couple of plastic glasses of Almaden, I've made several other observations.

1. Mensans love puns. I heard about how the eating of frogs' legs makes the frogs hopping mad. A person who is interested in architecture has an edifice complex. When I met one Mensan who worked in a photo shop, he told me, "It gives me a very negative outlook on life."

"I shudder to think," I responded, which simultaneously earned his respect and made me hate myself a lot.

2. A Mensa convention is not the best place to network for a new job. Not counting the photo shop pun lover, an unusual number of the conventioneers seem to be without steady income. When asked their line of work, many responded in such vague phrases as "I work on projects" or "I do a little of this, a little of that." Eventually I learned that asking, "What do you do for a living" is bad Mensa etiquette, the equivalent of asking the average person, "How often do you masturbate?"

3. Mensans love grand theories. One fiftyish woman explained to me her Bonsai Tree Theory of Human Nature. "Plato has his cave. I have my bonsai tree." I can't repeat her theory here since I have no idea what she was talking about, but it's apparently the equivalent of Einstein's $E = mc^2$ for human behavior.

I decide to continue my own study of human behavior in the Mensan game room, which is down the hall in something called the Verrazano Room. Here I find an impressive stack of games: Scrabble, Boggle, Taboo. You name it, they got it. I watch a game where a gray-haired man is trying to get his teammates to guess a word.

"It's a space between two things," he says.

"Interstitial!" shouts a woman.

"No," he says. "A space between two things."

"Interstices!" she tries again. "Interstitial! Interstices!"

"No!" he says.

Time's up. The word was "gap." This makes me happy for some reason. This woman is throwing out four-syllable Latinate words, and the answer is the beautifully simple "gap." Some people, I conclude, try way too hard to be smart.

In another corner of the game room, two Mensans have taken a break from gaming to engage in what seems to be a fierce conversation. I drift over to eavesdrop. Now, I'm not out to reinforce stereotypes here, so I wish I could report that the argument was about post-Clintonian foreign policy or the relative merits of Mozart and Tchaikovsky. But the actual topic of their debate was *Star Trek: The Next Generation*. Specifically, Captain Jean-Luc Picard.

MENSAN ONE: I just don't understand why Picard is bald.

MENSAN TWO: What's the problem?

MENSAN ONE: Because wouldn't they have a cure for baldness by the twenty-second century?

MENSAN TWO: Yes, they would.

MENSAN ONE: So why is he bald?

MENSAN TWO: Because it's a personal style choice. He chooses to be bald.

MENSAN ONE: I still think it's strange.

Since I'm not a Trekkie, and no one's inviting me to join their game, I wander back to the Harbor Room to see if I can score another pizza slice. I sit down at a table with two men, both of whom have unorthodox hair. The topic, I'm happy to hear, isn't *Star Trek*. It's calculators.

They compare notes on what words you can spell if you punch in the right numbers and turn the calculators upside down—"Shell Oil", "hello", "hell", et cetera—before one of them takes it to the next level.

"You know what I like to do?" says the guy with the mini pompadour. "I like to get a calculator and ask for the square root of negative one and see what the calculator does."

"What happens?" asks the other guy, who has a beard that is creeping north of the cheekbones and heading for his forehead.

"Depends on the calculator. If it's a good one—over twenty dollars—it'll say it's an error. If it's under twenty dollars, it has a nervous breakdown."

The bearded guy is impressed. That's good calculator information. For the next twenty minutes, I sit quietly as the conversation turns to 20th-century physics. They talk confidently about quanta, wavicles, Max Planck, superstrings, alternate universes, quarks, the double slit experiment. I want to jump in—I know enough physics from my *Britannica* to keep up—but they never glance my way. I feel locked out.

A brunette woman sits down next to me. Fresh meat. She has just come from the game room.

"Ah, the Verrazano Room," I say. "Giovanni Verrazano."

"Yup," she says.

"You know, he discovered the Hudson River before Henry Hudson."

"No, I didn't."

"On top of that, Henry Hudson was a real bastard. He was so stingy, he took back a gift from a crew member, which led to an uprising. His crew mutinied him. Sent him off to die in a rowboat. So in my opinion, it should be called the Verrazano River, not the Hudson River."

"I hadn't heard that before," says my table mate.

Ha! I look over at the two calculator jocks, hoping they're hearing my knowledge. No acknowledgment. They're still nattering on about Neils Bohr. As for the woman, she's looking around for escape routes. I have succeeded in boring a Mensan.

Lucky for her, someone's just announced that the trivia contest will be starting momentarily in Parlor 902. I'm there. Here, a perfect chance to show off my *Britannica*-earned knowledge.

Parlor 902 is chock-full of Mensans sprawled on the couch, sitting on the floor, and passing around pencils and paper. "Does everyone have a pencil?" asks the emcee. He looks like he could be an up-and-coming orthodontist in Great Neck—but because job questions are taboo, I'll never know. "Everyone have a pencil?"

Everyone does have a pencil. And so we begin. I'll say this for the Mensan quiz: it's damn hard. A sample question: "Whose last words were 'The world has lost a great artist'?" (Nero, I would learn later.) Another: "What is the meaning of the mnemonic 'Oh be a fine girl kiss me right now sweety'?" (The spectral class of stars.) I would be freaking out about my lack of intelligence if the rest of the geniuses weren't complaining so loudly. "Who the hell wrote these questions!" demanded a woman in the corner who looked to be about the size of a star of spectral class K.

If not for the *Britannica*, I would have gotten maybe one question out of seventeen. But thanks to my diligent reading, I scored a respectable 4.5 out of seventeen, which I hoped might just be enough to give me the victory (the half point came from knowing that Ben Franklin endorsed the turkey as the national bird, though not knowing it was because he considered the eagle "cowardly").

One of my proudest quiz moments was knowing the origin of the phrase "dog days of summer." (It derives from the ancient belief that the Dog Star, Sirius, gives off the heat of a second sun, so when it's rising it causes the weather to be particularly hot.) But I also knew the punishment inflicted on Abelard: castration.

"I don't even know who Abelard was," says the emcee, as he reads the answer. The crowd murmurs and shakes their heads.

"He was an 11th-century Christian theologian," I say. This should have been my big moment—giving a history lesson to a bunch of Mensans who know less than me. But for some reason—acoustics, my tendency to mumble, a combination—no one seemed to hear me.

I say it again. "He was an 11th-century Christian theologian!" Again, nothing.

The emcee is already on to the next question: "The original definition of pedagogue is—"

"HE'S AN 11TH-CENTURY CHRISTIAN THEOLOGIAN!" Not only is my timing off, but the Mensans can sense the anger and bitterness in my voice. They are frightened. The emcee pauses and makes a mental note to put me on the handle-with-care list, right next to the guy who didn't clean up the crap of his Bernese mountain dog. Then he continued.

In the end, I lose to a guy who scored seven. He is a cocky dweeb with a haircut in the shape of a wedge and the posture of a proboscis monkey. He doesn't even acknowledge my respectable 4.5.

Soon after, I find myself on the Staten Island ferry, returning to my life on Manhattan with non-Mensans. I am in a sour mood, and not just because I've lost the genius trivia contest. After a day of intensive Mensa, I feel annoyed at the club for being so elitist and self-congratulatory—and angry at myself for so desperately wanting to be a part of it. That feeling, in turn, is tempered by pity, seeing that many of these people are even more socially maladjusted than I am, and definitely more in need of career counseling. That is then colored by bitterness, since they'd probably pity *me* if they knew that I sneaked in on my SAT scores.

The convention, I decide, brought out an unattractive side of me. I'm thinking in particular of my final few minutes, when a fellow Mensan and I were approached by a guy from New Hampshire who happened to be staying at the hotel and who had a question for us.

"You guys with that Mesna?" he asked.

"Yes, Mensa," said my fellow genius.

"Okay, I have a serious question for you: what is the fancy name for an outhouse?"

"Water closet?" I offered up.

"No, it wasn't that. It begins with *P*. I heard an interview with this archaeologist on the radio. He digs up old outhouses, and they used this word."

"Privy," my fellow genius said.

"Yes! That's it!" said the New Hampshire man.

"That's why they call it the privy council in governments," the genius said, following the Mensa bylaw that all conversations must include a pun.

The New Hampshire man was satisfied and wandered off, at which point my fellow Mensan and I laughed and shook our superior heads. Oh, the regular people. Aren't they silly with their lack of synonyms for plumbing? Yes, maybe. But at least they don't need stickers to decide whether or not to hug.

intercourse

Julie and I, in our quest to get pregnant, are having an awful lot of sex. The rumor is that sex is supposed to be fun, but we've long since passed that phase. We have purposeful sex. For us, sex is about as entertaining as taking the crosstown bus—it's merely a vehicle to take us where we want to go. This doesn't seem fair. Why can't there be a more even distribution of sex throughout a man's life? Why couldn't I have had some of this sex when I really needed it, like during some dry stretches as a single man in my twenties? Instead, it's all clumped up in my mid-thirties, like a steep bell curve, proving too much of a good thing is exhausting. At times, I wish Julie were like a queen bee, which has sex only once in her life, but stores the sperm in a pouch for use throughout the next five years.

Tonight, though, I'm going to put some spice back into our sex life. Julie is in bed already, reading her novel. At about ten-thirty, I lay down my *Britannica* and come into the bedroom. I stand at the foot of the bed and start stomping my feet—left, right, left, right—then pointing my head at the ceiling. Julie looks up from her book.

"What's going on here?"

"Are you getting turned on?" I ask.

"Oh, I'm hot."

I stomp my left, then right, foot again. "It's the mating dance of the blue-footed booby. It's called sky pointing. I thought you'd like it."

"Yes, it's extremely arousing."

"Perhaps you'd prefer a visible dung heap, as left by rabbits to indicate they're ready to mate?"

"Uh, how about you just come here and get me pregnant."

"Fair enough."

I climb into bed and we get down to business. Julie stops kissing me for a second, pulling her head back.

"Are you thinking about the *Britannica*?" she asks.

"No," I say. Which is a lie. Because I am thinking about it. I can't help it. Even in this, the least cerebral of pursuits—not counting the Jim Belushi show—I'm mulling over my new knowledge. I'm thinking about how damselflies mate in the air and amphibians have sperm packets and female button quails sleep around. I'm thinking about how engaged couples in Scotland were allowed in the same bed—but were sewn up in separate sleeping bags (the practice is called bundling). I'm thinking how male and female bony fish have sex organs oriented either to the right or left and that only opposite-oriented individuals can mate and that it'd be really sad if a male bony fish with a left-oriented penis fell in love with a female bony fish with a left-oriented vagina.

Julie returns to kissing me. She knows I'm lying, but she's come to accept it.

Iraq

It's clearer and clearer that we're going to war with Iraq. I half expect our *TV Guide* to give a time and day so we can program our TiVo to record it.

I'm extraordinarily stressed out about it. It's going to be ugly. I said over drinks with my colleagues the other night that I fear this war will open a Pandora's box of terrorism. (Though I wanted to say Pandora's jar; that's what the *EB* calls it, a jar, not a box, but I thought they'd look at me funny, so I stuck with box.)

I spend my little free time worrying and clicking on Yahoo! to check the terror alert level, and figuring out ways to avoid taking the subway.

Julie tells me to stop wasting my time. The worrying doesn't help anyone. She tells me I could either sign up for the marines or else join one of those protests where they throw Dumpsters through McDonald's windows. Then at least I'd be doing something. But fretting about terrorism doesn't help anybody. She's right, and I know it, but still I can't stop. I'm addicted to worry.

I was hoping the *EB* would help me come up with a clear solution for the Iraq crisis—or at the least clarify my opinion about the war. But that's just not happening. I read the twenty-five-page *Macropaedia* article about Iraq just now. I know a lot about those 167,975 square miles in the eastern Arab world—at least until the Ebbinghaus curve kicks in. I know it was called Mesopotamia until the 7th century. I know that aside from oil, date palms are its major export. That Baghdad has red double-decker buses, a holdover from the British occupation. I know there was a fertilizer shortage until 2000. That there's a big monument to Ali Baba's housekeeper in Baghdad. I know the Tigris and Euphrates formed one of the early cradles of civilization—which, I figure, might make for some nice closure; the world started there and might end there. And I have some historical perspective on the war: I know that this land has been sacked just about every other year for the last eight hundred years. Oh, it's Tuesday, time for another upheaval in Iraq. I know, most pertinently, about the Christian-Islamic feud that stretches back before the Crusades.

But how should we deal with Saddam? That I don't know. Frankly, I'm not sure what I was expecting. Was I expecting the *Britannica* to finish the

Iraq entry by saying, "Plus, the United States should not go to war with Iraq because it would be a disaster"? Or, "In conclusion, nuke 'em"? Still, I'm disappointed. I suppose it goes back to something I was reading about in the *ethics* entry. There is a gap between "is" and "ought." The facts are on one side of the canyon. And there, on the other side, across the river, are your ethical options. No logical syllogism can bridge the two.

The only thing I can say for sure is this: we should all go back to the type of warfare practiced by many Native Americans—counting coup. Back then, warfare was sort of an elaborate game of tag. The touching of one's enemy was considered the greatest coup. Not scalping, not murder, but touching them. That I'd like to see. General Tommy Franks going into Baghdad, poking Saddam in the ribs, then running away laughing victoriously.

irony

The French horn is from Germany. The Great Dane has no connection to Denmark. Cold-blooded animals often have warmer blood than warm-blooded animals. Softwood is often harder than hardwood. Catgut is made from sheepgut. Caesar was not born by cesarean section. A cold is not caused by the cold (Ben Franklin pointed this out). Death Valley is teeming with life (more than two hundred types of birds, several types of fish, and so on). Heinz has several hundred varieties, not its advertised fifty-seven. Starfish are not fish. The electric eel is not an eel. The anomalous Zeeman effect in atomic physics is more common than the regular old Zeeman effect.

These are all things I've been keeping in my little "Ironic Facts" file on my computer. Irony is named for "the Greek comic character Eiron, a clever underdog, who by his wit repeatedly triumphs over the boastful character of Alazon." But the stuff above is a different kind of irony. These ironies are a function of our ridiculously imprecise language. I feel we need someone to come in and clean it all up, a Rudy Giuliani of English who would crack down on all lazy, loitering, leftover-from-other-eras words. But that'll never happen. As I learned in *Fahrenheit*, the inertia of bad ideas is a powerful force.

J

Jackson, Reggie

Reginald Martinez Jackson of Wyncote, Pennsylvania. My hero. Back when I was a Yankees-obsessed prepubescent, I loved my Reggie Jackson. I had my Reggie posters, knew my Reggie stats, ate my Reggie candy bars, even though they tasted like fourth-rate Snickers and looked like a clump of guano from the Peruvian cormorant (an effective fertilizer).

I'm glad to see the *Britannica* has written him up, since my other favorite Yankee—Bucky Dent—didn't rate a mention. It's a joy to read about Reggie in these illustrious, oversized pages and how he played for Arizona State, joined the A's, excelled as a base runner, and in the momentous year of 1977, signed a five-year contract with the New York Yankees and smacked a record three home runs in a World Series game.

I remember that World Series game. I was there. This is the only piece of history in the encyclopedia that I actually got to witness live and in person. I wasn't at the Battle of Waterloo. I missed the Crusades. But I did see Reggie Jackson play that epic sixth game of the 1977 World Series at Yankee Stadium. Well, almost.

Here's what happened. When I was nine, Dad somehow scored tickets to the big game. My parents were no sports fans, but they wanted to give me an all-American childhood, so once in a while they'd suck it up and take me to the stadium. So there I was, with my mitt on my left hand, my Yankees yearbook on my lap, gloriously giddy.

My hero, Reggie, steps up to the plate in the fourth inning, and bam, hits a home run. Sails it over the right field wall. Awesome. The very next inning, crack! Another home run. Unbelievable. I'm in heaven. Two home runs! And then—Dad decided it was time to leave and beat the traffic. We wouldn't want to be jammed into a subway with all the other people, right?

"But Dad, what if Reggie hits another home run?"

"Oh, he won't," Dad assured me, as he tugged me out of the packed stands.

We were on the subway platform when we heard it—a stadium-shaking roar from the crowd. A roar like I'd never heard before. Reggie had hit his third home run. History had been made. People would be talking about that homer forever. And I would not be speaking to Dad for several days. Though we did have the subway all to ourselves, which was nice.

My attendance at two-thirds of this historical event is in one sense disappointing—like leaving Iwo Jima right before the flag was planted. But it also makes makes me think that I had an impact, ever so slight, on the *Britannica*. If I hadn't been cheering so dutifully in the stands, Reggie might not have hit those two home runs. The third I can't take credit for, as we know.

Incidentally, the Reggie era was about the last time I really had a handle on sports. I think I know less about current professional athletics than any fully functioning man in the United States, including your average Amish dairy farmer (who, by the way, runs a very high risk of inheriting knock-knees, also known as dysplasia).

I'm not 100 percent certain why I lost interest in sports back when I was fourteen. I don't think the World Series incident had much to do with it. My theory is this: I began to recognize the vast gap between my enthusiasm for sports and my ability to play them. So I stopped paying attention.

After twenty-one years, it's gotten embarrassing. I go to meetings at *Esquire*, and they'll talk about the weekend's games, and I have to avoid all eye contact in hopes I won't get called on. I'll be studying a particularly interesting floor tile, and my friend Andy, who knows that my sports awareness ended in 1982, will say, "Hey, A.J., did you see Graig Nettles hit a double this weekend?" And then everyone will crack up. I feel as emasculated as a crab after an encounter with a barnacle (barnacles consume crab testes).

As any high school football coach will tell you, the best defense is a good offense. So that's what I've started to do. I can't compete with other men on this year's stats or trades. I don't even know the names of the more obscure expansion teams (the Guam Jaguars? the Lynxes? the Cheetahs?). But thanks to the *Britannica*, I can thrash my fellow men in the history of sports. When the topic of sports comes up, I just make some noises about how athletics today are such a dirty business, just an extended Gatorade commercial. I much prefer sports from times gone by.

If it's baseball: The very first games had a second catcher behind the regular catcher, whose job it was to field foul balls. Also, before the New York Yankees, there were my favorites, the New York Highlanders and the New York Mutuals.

If it's football, I say: The 1905 college season was so violent, no fewer than eighteen players died from injuries on the field. Teddy Roosevelt called a presidential commission to investigate. From that came the legalization of the forward pass.

If the topic is tennis: Long before the Williams sisters, the Doherty brothers dominated the sport. They ruled from 1897 to 1906—and one brother lost only two matches in four years.

The reaction varies from mild interest to perplexity. But that's better than ridicule. If it were baseball, I'd call it an infield single as opposed to a strikeout.

Jacobs

I'm no more narcissistic than most Americans. Well, maybe a little more narcissistic. I get an embarrassing amount of pleasure from entering my own name into Google and seeing what turns up. So here we have six pages of Jacobses, which promise to be excellent reading for me. They start with the father of all of us Jacobses—Jacob of Bible fame. I had forgotten that he was so duplicitous (he stole his brother Esau's birthright by impersonating Esau to his blind father), which taints my name for me just a bit. But I forge on.

There was urbanologist Jane Jacobs and folklore scholar Joseph Jacobs. But even more impressive, there were no less than three Jacob movements: the Jacobins (French revolutionary extremists), the Jacobites (supporters of the exiled King James II) and the Jacobean Age (referring to art and architecture produced during the reign of King James I). I was happy to learn that Shakespeare, in his later tragedies, is considered a Jacobean playwright, which somehow, in my mind, makes Shakespeare and me related. Two Jacobean writers, me and the Bard.

In my defense, I'm not interested only in those who share the name Jacobs. I keep track of other name coincidences, as well. In the fishing entry, I learned about a Kalamazoo man who, in 1896, invented a revolutionary type of fishing reel. His name was . . . William Shakespeare. Yes, just like the Jacobean playwright. This man's parents must have had quite the sense of humor. They must have thought: "What name can we choose for our son that will ensure that he will (a) be mocked until long after puberty, and (b) always have a nice sense of failure about him, because he'll never be able to live up to the other guy?" Well, they dost hit the mother lode!

There's more. Kathy Bates was an Oscar-winning actress who hammered James Caan's ankles, but she also, apparently, wrote the text to "America the Beautiful." And the *National Enquirer*? No need to be ashamed to read it anymore. Back in the 1800s before the Civil War, there was another *National Enquirer*—a famous abolitionist newspaper that had very few articles about Jennifer Lopez's love life. So you could always say you got confused, that you thought you were buying an antislavery publication at the checkout line.

I'm not sure why I'm fascinated by these name coincidences. I don't think they reveal anything excessively profound—except maybe that names are imprecise and repetitive and arbitrary. But whatever the reason, it's another interest that I inherited from my father.

A few years ago, I was working with a friend named Albert Kim at *Entertainment Weekly*. My father was working at his law firm with an associate named . . . Albert Kim. So my father arranged a lunch between the two Albert Kims and the two Arnold Jacobses. In theory, it seemed like a good idea. We got to the restaurant, and the two Albert Kims greeted each other and we all had a nice laugh. And then they asked each other their respective middle names. And then . . . it became quite clear they had pretty much nothing else in common besides their first and last names. And we hadn't even ordered the entrees. It didn't become an annual event.

James, Jesse

The greatest robber of the Wild West died in 1882. He was shot in the back by a gang member while he was at home "adjusting a picture." That doesn't seem right. Being shot in the back is bad enough, but while adjusting a picture? A notorious bandit shouldn't end his life engaging in interior design. Well, at least he wasn't crocheting throw pillows.

Jefferson, Thomas

More confusion. With Jefferson, I'm seeing the flipside of the Attila the Hun effect. Just as Attila had his good side, even the most amazing, accomplished, original, justice-loving men have their dark side. I knew about Jefferson's hypocrisy on slaves, which is evil enough to fill a couple of lifetimes. But it also says here that Jefferson paid newspaper reporters to libel his nemesis John Adams. That I didn't know about. What a horrible fact. Do people have to be sleazy to succeed? I hope not, but if even Jefferson was, it makes me wonder.

In other news, Thomas Jefferson had very clean feet. Every morning, he rose at dawn and washed them in cold water.

joke

It's April Fool's Day today. The timing of April Fool's Day, by the way, seems related to the vernal equinox, when nature "fools" mankind with sudden changes in the weather. The victim of the practical joke is called a fish in France and a cuckoo in Scotland.

At work, people aren't quite as interested in these facts as they are in the question of who left plastic dog poop on all the editors' chairs.

Jonson, Ben

I knew a lot of things could save your life—a helmet, a good lawyer, cholesterol medication—but this one was new to me: the ability to read Latin. If you know your *E Pluribus* from your *Unum* you'll live a lot longer. At least if you're an accused criminal in 16th-century England, as was Ben Jonson.

I remembered Jonson vaguely—he was the second most successful Elizabethan playwright after Shakespeare, the Pepsi to the Bard's Coke. What I didn't know was that he was a rascal—an angry, stubborn man with a homicidal temper. In 1598, the same year he had his first big hit play—*Every Man His Humour*—Jonson killed a fellow actor in a duel.

The strange part, though, is how he escaped capital punishment. The accused playwright invoked a legal loophole called "benefit of clergy." The concept of benefit of clergy started in 12th-century England when the church convinced the king to offer immunity to priests and other ecclesiastical officials. By the 16th century, however, the definition of "clergy" had stretched to include anyone who could read the Fifty-first Psalm in Latin.

On the one hand, this is a crazy law—elitist, unjust, arbitrary. On the other hand, it's kind of nice that reading and scholarship were once so highly valued that they had the very tangible benefit of stopping a hatchet from removing your head from your shoulders. It's beautifully clear-cut: You read Latin, you live. You don't read Latin, you'll soon be experiencing a nice case of rigor mortis (though you won't know the definition of rigor mortis, you illiterate jackass).

juggling

You should know that juggling has gone through historical stages. Nowadays, your top jugglers tend to stick to three or four balls, but do their juggling from unusual and surprising places—on horseback, or on a unicycle, for example. This as opposed to 19th-century juggling, when ball quantity was king. The more the better. Back in the 1800s, Enrico Rastelli made a name for himself by juggling with ten balls, which the *Britannica* calls "an almost miraculous accomplishment."

I admire Enrico. He's my kind of man, and ten-ball juggling, that's my kind of accomplishment. Enrico's a welcome break from the usual *Britannica* fare. I get dejected reading page after page of men who created vaccines or opened trade routes. I know I'll never do anything like that. I just don't have it in me. But I can see myself doing something along the lines of Enrico. A lesser accomplishment, one that doesn't save lives or change the world, but nonetheless makes people marvel and say, "Now that is impressive." Or else, "Jesus, what a massive waste of time."

There are a handful of these types sprinkled throughout the encyclopedia. Like Peter Bales, a 16th-century Brit who was famous for his microscopic writing, and produced a Bible the size of a walnut. Or Blondin, a tightrope walker in the 1800s, who tiptoed across Niagara Falls, stopping in the middle to make and eat an omelet. Admittedly, that's not my thing, especially if the omelet wasn't egg white. But still, I love Blondin's passion and commitment.

And now, for the first time in my life, I'm feeling the same passion and commitment. I've got my own quest, one that causes a handful to marvel, and far more to ask me, "What the fuck?" I know my accomplishment of reading the *Britannica* won't get me into the *Britannica* itself. But it's a start. And maybe next time I can conquer something even more impressive, like reading the walnut-sized version of the *Encyclopaedia Britannica*.

jujube

Julie's throwing an Oscar party. Not just a haphazard, casual Oscar party. This is serious Oscar party. This is the most well-organized Oscar party on the Upper West Side. Movie posters suddenly appear on the walls. Fake Oscar statuettes frame the television. There are prizes, pools, Oscar trivia. The tables fill up with Junior Mints, Twizzlers, popcorn, Jujubes (the name Jujube, I learn, comes from a plum-sized Chinese fruit. The etymology of candy—another gap in my education I didn't even know I had).

If you attend Julie's Oscar party, you should come prepared. All the twenty guests are encouraged to wear costumes that represent a movie that was released that year. Julie has selected a red devil outfit and an accompanying pitchfork; she's *Far from Heaven.* My costume is a little less elaborate. I've got on jeans and a T-shirt and plan to sit silently in the corner. I'm *The Quiet American.*

An hour before the guests arrive, Julie flips on all three of the TVs. She likes to have each of our TVs going just in case anyone happens to be walking through another room. She doesn't want them to miss a single self-congratulatory moment. It gave me a little thought.

"We should do a past posting scam," I say, as I arrange the Twizzlers in a bowl.

"What?"

"Past posting—it's a scam I read about in the *con game* section. I'll watch the Oscars on the office TV, and you and the guests can watch on TiVo in the living room. But the trick is, you delay the broadcast a few minutes on TiVo. So I'll know who won before you do. And I'll saunter in and bet on the categories and we'll win hundreds of dollars. You know, like in *The Sting.*"

"Is that what they did in *The Sting*? I saw it when I was young and never understood it."

"Yeah, well sort of. But they faked the whole thing. But that's the idea."

"And they didn't have TiVo."

"Right, no TiVo in *The Sting.*"

"Past posting—that's interesting."

Ha! She liked that one. Nothing better than that. I love having her on my side. Maybe I should confine my facts to ones that help illuminate the plots of old movies.

The party went off splendidly, though Julie did put the kibosh on my scam because she didn't want me ruining the surprise for her. A reasonable if costly decision.

Julie

Sandwiched between *Julich* (a duchy of the Holy Roman Empire) and *Julijske Alpe* (the Alps that run near Slovenia), there's a little note in blue ballpoint pen. It reads: "Where's Julie?"

I laugh out loud when I read this. Julie has snuck into my *J* volume and done some defacing. I go into the living room and tell her that she's probably under her maiden name, Schoenberg, and they just haven't had time to update it.

jump rope

It's about midnight, and Julie's asleep. I'm in the extra bedroom, getting my daily dose of knowledge, my butt planted on the white couch, my feet kicked up on the coffee table, reading about jump rope's most popular chants (as in "Apples, peaches, pears and plums / Tell me when your birthday comes").

I look up for a second, and I see it silently cruising across the light blue rug. A cockroach. A German cockroach, to be precise, sometimes erroneously called a water bug. It's one of the most primitive living winged insects, basically unchanged for 320 million years.

And it's about to die.

I take my *J* volume—I should have grabbed volume 16 of the *Macropaedia*, the one that says *Chicago–Death* on its spine; that would have been more appropriate, but I didn't have time to be witty. I hold my *Britannica* at shoulder height and drop it, like the payload from a B-17 bomber (a plane so big it was called the Flying Fortress). It lands with a satisfying thud.

I pick up the book, and am annoyed to see the determined little vermin has survived the assault. It just keeps cruising along like a tiny tank, heading toward the safety of the radiator.

This time I slam the *Britannica* down and mash it into the floor with my foot. Victory! I must say, the *Britannica*'s leatherette covers are very easy to wipe down. No bug juice stains at all. So at the very least, even if the whole knowledge thing is a bust, the encyclopedia has come in handy as pest control.

I get a lot of that—people telling me the different uses for their encyclopedias. My cousin hurt his wrist while playing squash, and his doctor prescribed physical therapy with the encyclopedia. Another friend said that when he was young, he drove his parents crazy by using a volume of the *Britannica* as a drum in a makeshift percussion set.

I recently read an article that said that explorer Ernest Shackleton lugged the entire eleventh edition with him on his expedition to Antarctica. (So I can never whine when I lug a volume onto the downtown number 9 subway). In any case, Shackleton, while stranded over a freezing winter, ended up using the *Britannica*'s pages for kindling.

Which makes me realize there's something great about the physicality of the *Britannica*. It's not disembodied information, not a bunch of encoded 1s and 0s on a microchip the size of an Indian mung bean. It's a big old-timey book, a massive object that can squash bugs and light fires and make thuds. I know I sound like a crotchety old grandfather on the porch reminiscing about the good old days of rumble seats, but I believe in pages you can actually turn.

K

Kafka

There are few things more annoying than a busybody friend, the kind who thinks he knows what's best for you and ignores your wishes.

Like Albert. Several years ago, when we were both working at *Entertainment Weekly*, I confided to him that I had a crush on an ad sales girl named Julie Schoenberg. But, I said, that is strictly confidential; you cannot tell a single person, especially Julie. Which he interpreted to mean: "Please, feel free to tell anyone at all, especially Julie."

Within two hours of my confession, Julie and Albert were behind closed doors, dissecting my crush and laughing.

The only thing more annoying: when your friend turns out to be right. If Albert had honored my wishes for secrecy, I probably would never have acted on my crush. I'd still be single, lonely, and have no idea what a sconce is, much less have several in my home.

All this was on my mind as I was reading about Kafka, who had the biggest busybody friend in Western history.

First, some relevant background on Kafka. As I figured from what little I knew, Kafka had some self-esteem issues, most of which came from having a tyrant of a father. So Kafka, unable to commit himself fully to literature, got his doctorate in law and found a day job at an insurance company. While at law school, Kafka met a minor novelist named Max Brod. The two became lifelong friends.

While he was alive, Kafka halfheartedly agreed to have some of his strange stories—including *Metamorphosis*—published by avant-garde literary publications. But on his death from tuberculosis at the age of forty-one, full of misgivings about his work, Kafka left Brod a very clear note: Destroy all unpublished manuscripts. Which Brod interpreted to mean, "Publish all unpublished manuscripts." He even somehow interpreted it to mean "Become Kafka's posthumous publicist, biographer, interpreter, and archivist." If not for Brod, we would never have known *The Trial*, *The Castle*, or *Amerika*, to name a few.

After reading about Kafka, I decide I'm going to call my friend Albert and tell him to burn my unfinished manuscripts when I die. He'll know what to do.

Kama

An Indian angel who shoots love-producing flower arrows. His bow is of sugarcane, his bowstring a row of bees. I have to say, Kama with his fancy bow and arrow makes our Cupid look kind of second-rate in comparison. Cupid just flies around in a diaper shooting regular old love arrows. It is odd, though, that two cultures have these love archers. Does this say something profound about the human mind? Maybe about violence and love? The damn *Britannica* raises these questions in my mind but doesn't answer them.

kappa

The strangest type of supernatural being I've encountered so far: a "vampirelike lecherous creature" from Japan that's obsessed with cucumbers, resembles a green monkey with fish scales, and refuses to lower its head for fear of spilling the magic water it keeps in the holes on top of its skull. I don't know who came up with this, but I can almost guarantee those weren't shiitake mushrooms he was eating.

katydid

This member of the grasshopper family is named for its unique mating call, which sounds like a psychotic witness: "Katy did, Katy didn't, Katy did, Katy didn't."

Kennedy, Edward M.

If Reggie Jackson's home run spree was the only piece of history I witnessed, here we have the only person in the *Encyclopaedia Britannica* whom I've actually met. I never had the pleasure of chatting up Aristotle or Balzac, but Ted Kennedy and I have shared a firm handshake and some good times. Or a firm handshake, anyway.

I met him at my friend Douglas Kennedy's bachelor party. Douglas is one of the many children of the late Robert Kennedy, and he was my roommate at college. Douglas had his bachelor party a few years ago at a steak house in Boston. I flew up from New York, and arrived at the restaurant an hour and a half early. When I walked inside, I found that only one other guest was there ahead of time: Senator Kennedy. Ninety minutes with Ted Kennedy. Alone.

Some might see this as a wonderful opportunity to talk to a living legend, to probe his mind about politics and history, triumph and tragedy. I saw this as a wonderful opportunity to mumble, laugh nervously, and toss out a half dozen baffling non sequiturs. I'm not very good with powerful people. If I had known he was going to be there, I'd probably have loitered at the airport T.G.I. Friday's for ninety minutes. But there I was with Doug's uncle, the host of the party, drinking vodka tonics.

He asked me what I did for a living. I told him I worked at *Entertainment Weekly* magazine. I could see from the quizzical look on his face that he wasn't a longtime subscriber. In fact, he wasn't a huge fan of pop culture at all. Didn't spend a lot of time in *Dawson's Creek* chat rooms. But he tried. He brought up Seagram's Universal and how they were doing post-merger.

As for me, on the other hand, I knew about Dawson and his love triangle. But I knew squat about which conglomerate was having balance sheet woes. Dead end.

He brought up yachting. Another topic where I didn't know my yardarm from my winch. So that sputtered out after about three minutes. I'm honestly not sure how I got through the next eighty-two minutes. I know we spent a good amount of time enjoying the sounds of the restaurant's air conditioner and clinking silverware. But the rest is hazy. When Douglas finally walked in, I experienced something similar to what I imagine Jessica Lynch felt when those marines burst into the hospital.

The senator—who, as it turned out, was a friendly, big-hearted fellow when around those with social skills—never caught my name, but I did score a couple of points for being punctual. In fact, that became my identity: Punctual Guy. The rest of the weekend, whenever the senator saw me, he shouted, "It's the Punctual Guy!" At the photo shoot, he suggested to the Punctual Guy that he stand over here. At the rehearsal dinner, he gave a hearty hello to the Punctual Guy.

If I met the senator now, I think I'd fare a lot better. I now know a bit about health care reform and fair housing. Though I might not bring up how the *Britannica* says his "somewhat raffish personal life" dimmed his presidential prospects.

Kentucky

Julie's family's visiting again—they love to visit, these people—and her nephew Adam will be staying the night. I've been assigned to inflate the air mattress for him. It's not an easy assignment.

I've spent a good fifteen minutes pushing and pulling the little bicycle pump that attaches to the mattress, but I've made disturbingly little progress; the mattress still looks as wrinkly as a large raisin or a senator from one of the Carolinas. The problem seems to be that the air hose doesn't properly fit over the mattress's hole, and so the air keeps hissing out. My father-in-law, Larry, is watching the proceedings from a comfortable chair. He decides to chime in, telling me: "You got book-learning, but you got no street smarts, boy!" (He's from the Bronx, but for some reason likes to affect an Alabama twang.)

I thank him for his insight, then go back to my pumping. My forehead is damp, I think I've lost a couple pounds so far, and the air keeps wheezing out of the mattress. "You should spend more time reading the instruction manual and less time on the encyclopedia, boy!"

This is not an unusual comment. Over the past couple of weeks, I've begun to sense the monumental amount of crap that I'm going to receive for the rest of my life (an amount somewhere between John Adams's famous mound of manure and the debris that Hercules had to clean at the stables of King Augeas). Anytime I have a bit of trouble in the mechanical department—working a microwave, opening a lock, downloading a file at work—someone will say, "What's the matter? That not in your fancy encyclopedia?" Anytime I don't know the directions to Yonkers or whether there's a gas station nearby or when the next bus leaves, someone will say, "Guess you don't know everything after all, huh, Cliff Clavin?" Anytime I don't know the secretary of state under Eisenhower or the capital of Kentucky, someone will say "Hey, I thought you knew everything!" (That'd be John Foster Dulles and Frankfort, by the way.)

And yes, I did finally inflate the mattress. Well, halfway, anyway. But I tell Adam that it's more comfortable that way, and he believes me.

Khnum

Still trying to get pregnant. The fertility god of the week is Khnum, the Egyptian deity with a human body and a ram's head. Julie and I gave a little nod to him last night before dinner, though we don't know how to pronounce his name. (The *Britannica,* sadly, doesn't have phonetic guides.) Meanwhile, our non-Egyptian helper—Julie's ob-gyn—has recommended I get my sperm tested. Which is why I'm at a reproductive clinic studiously avoiding eye contact with the other people—mostly women—in the waiting room.

I check in with the receptionist.

"Yes, you're here for a collection," she says chirpily.

I like that euphemism—a collection. So that's what I spent so much time doing as a high schooler: collecting. I was much more dedicated to this type of collection than to my coin collection and the drink stirrer collection combined.

The nurse leads me into a room specially suited to collecting and hands me a small plastic specimen cup.

"If you need any help, feel free," she says. She points out a basket of pornos—not *Playboy* or *Penthouse,* but the really skanky variety, the kind with sweaty men and women engaging in what the *Britannica* might classify as *coition, really nasty types of.*

Speaking of the encyclopedia, I'm relatively confident that I am the only man to ever bring a *Britannica* volume into this room. It's in my computer bag, and I briefly consider taking it out.

Though it's probably not nearly as much "help" as the magazines in the basket, the *Britannica* does have a surprising amount of nudity. And not just text about nudity, mind you, but pictures containing butts and breasts and other areas that would send John Ashcroft into a foaming-at-the-mouth frenzy. And not just classical nudes, but some actual black-and-white photographs of nude women. Like the one by art photographer Bill Brandt, back in the *B*s, which, though fuzzy and dark, does upon close inspection in fact contain a nipple. Or the photo next to the entry for Chicago-born photographer Wynn Bullock, which shows a woman lying naked in the forest, also exposing a single nipple. That's two nipples within a couple of hundred pages. It's like very highbrow *Hustler.* If I had known about this as a teenager in my parents' house, I could have saved myself a lot of time searching for revealing pictures in sweater catalogues. But being an adult, I decided to refrain from flipping through the *K* volume.

I get my collection over with quickly. Being smarter doesn't necessarily help with this task. Though I will say that, having read about the Bible, I believe that, technically, what I did does not qualify as the sin of Onan. The sin of Onan means that you "let your seed fall to the ground." Since mine falls into a specimen cup, I think I'm safe.

I notice the door has a little yellow smiley face with the motto "Thank you for coming." Some angry collector has scrawled in pen next to it: "Very tacky!" I actually thought the smiley face was a nice touch. On the other hand, the layout of the fertility office could use some work. I have to drop off my specimen cup and its 3×10^8 swimmers at a nurse's station—which requires me to do a perp walk right through the waiting room filled with women reading magazines and chatting on their cell phones.

I can't believe how much work it is to have a baby. Or more specifically, how much work it is for me and Julie. It's baffling to me that all our friends actually got pregnant by having a pleasant bit of sexual intercourse. And here I am, smuggling my bodily fluids around like a felon.

Kierkegaard, Søren

Man, did the world's favorite 19th-century Danish philosopher have some problems. Self-loathing, depression, guilt, anger, father hatred. Kierkegaard was haunted by the fact that his dad—when he was a struggling tenant farmer—stood on a hill and solemnly cursed God, an act that Kierkegaard believed doomed the entire family. But that wasn't even Kierkegaard's biggest issue. In my opinion, that was his inability to say no.

Julie is always telling me I have this problem as well. I end up in all sorts of unpleasant scenarios because I don't want to offend anyone. "A nude whitewater rafting trip in the Yukon in February? Sure, sounds fun." When I was single, this translated into an inability to break up with women. I'd go out with a totally inappropriate partner for eight months too long because I couldn't figure out how to break it off. Things got so bad, I went to see a shrink, a Freudian woman who resembled Janet Reno, to learn how to confront situations like an adult. After about a dozen sessions, I stopped going. I canceled by leaving a message on her machine at 2 A.M. and then wrote her a letter that said: "Thank you for helping me with my issues about confrontation. I think we made a lot of progress." I was aware of the irony.

I thought about this as I read about poor Søren. In his late twenties,

Kierkegaard fell in love with a young girl named Regine, and the two got engaged. But then, soon after, he had second thoughts, aware of the age gap between them, not to mention the gap in their mental states. Kierkegaard wrote in his diary, "I was a thousand years too old for her. . . . If I had explained things to her, I would have had to initiate her into terrible things, my relationship with my father, his melancholy, the eternal night that broods over me, my despair, lusts and excesses, which perhaps in God's eyes were not so heinous."

So not the perfect match, obviously. Kierkegaard decided to try to break off the engagement. Problem was, Regine wasn't hearing it and clung to the skinny philosopher's side. So Kierkegaard resorted to a breakup strategy worthy of sitcom: he dropped her, then staged what the *Britannica* calls "an elaborate show of caddishness" to preserve her reputation. Nice, but way over the top.

king's evil

A swelling from tuberculosis, once thought to be curable by the touch of royalty. In England, Charles II is said to have touched more than ninety thousand victims. Another reason to be thankful I'm not a king in the 18th century. Because of my germ phobia, I hate shaking hands with anyone, even healthy people with no visible swellings. When I greet friends I do an air shake, which is like an air kiss, but with handshakes—it's a trend I'm trying to start. So to sum up monarchy: Unlimited power and untold wealth—good. Fondling TB sores—bad.

kissing

Julie's in the kitchen, chopping carrots for a vegetarian chili.

I sneak up beside her, press my nose against her cheek, and inhale deeply.

"What are you doing?"

"Just kissing you the way the Lapland people of Scandinavia kiss."

I press my nose against her cheek again and suck in through my nostrils. She stops choppng the carrots and looks at me. It's the look a dog might get if it kept trying to hump her leg.

"Uh, they also do this kind of kissing in southeastern India. So it's not just the Laplanders."

"I'm kind of busy here, honey."

Knox, John

Knox was a 16th-century Scottish priest who wrote a work with the hard-to-forget title *First Blast of the Trumpet Against the Monstrous Regiment of Women.* Unfortunately for him, Elizabeth I came to power just as the work was published, and Knox got himself a monstrous shellacking.

First Blast is quite a title, but it's not my favorite so far in the *Britannica.* My favorite title comes from a book written by Robert Fitzroy, captain of the HMS *Beagle,* the boat that Darwin took to the Galapagos. It's called *Narrative of the Surveying Voyages of His Majesty's Ships* Adventure *and* Beagle *Between the Years 1826 and 1836, Describing Their Examination of the Southern Shores of South America and the* Beagle's *Circumnavigation of the Globe.*

I haven't read *Narrative of the Surveying Voyages of His Majesty's Ships* Adventure *and* Beagle *Between the Years 1826 and 1836, Describing Their Examination of the Southern Shores of South Americana and the* Beagle's *Circumnavigation of the Globe,* but I hear it's quite good. I wonder if my sister-in-law Alexandra's book club might want some copies of *Narrative of the*—okay, I'll stop cutting and pasting Mr. Fitzroy's title. I spent a good minute or so punching it into my computer, so I thought I'd get the most out of it. But you get the idea: It's long. Almost as long as the entire text of the *Mahabharata* (the Hindu sacred book that comes in at a hundred thousand verses).

And yet, I have to like it. No cutesiness or coyness or irony or false advertising. Fitzroy doesn't try to dazzle you with wordplay, he just tells it like it is. You know exactly what you're getting. I've noticed a lot of old-time titles do this. There are a lot of *Narratives of* and *True Stories of* that go on for a paragraph summing up the book. And when I write another book, I'm going to call it *Occasional Reflections on Several Subjects,* which is the title used by Anglo-Irish chemist Robert Boyle for his book of moral essays. I love that one, too. It's the best one-size-fits-all title in the history of publishing.

Kyd, Thomas

A freelance writer I know pitched me an article today. He wants to write about a fringe director who remade *Raiders of the Lost Ark*—but had kids playing all the starring roles. A prepubescent Indiana Jones, an eight-year-old Nazi, and so on. I file it under "Eerie Echo of the Past," number 341. It's the exact same concept as children's companies, groups of children who put on plays by the likes of Shakespeare and Ben Jonson and Thomas Kyd in the 1600s. They came to be loathed by adult acting troupes, because audiences apparently preferred seeing cute miniature humans recite iambic pentameter to watching their fully grown counterparts.

Still, the article's not right for *Esquire.* I send him a brief rejection e-mail. I decide to spare him the Shakespeare stuff. The poor guy is already getting his idea squashed; he probably doesn't want a history lecture too. In general, I'm trying very hard to be more selective in what knowledge I impart. I've started to realize that not everybody appreciates brilliant 17th-century parallels.

L

La Rochefoucauld, François de

Perhaps the greatest writer of *maximes* in French literature. Among them: "Crimes are made innocent and virtuous by their number." "Virtues are lost in self-interest as rivers are lost in the sea." You've got to like *maximes,* the 17th-century literary equivalent of bumper stickers.

Lacoste, René

Some things in this world have gotten better, but one thing has definitely gone south: sports nicknames. I first noticed it when my fellow *Esquire* editor Andy "Hammering Homunculus" Ward mentioned this in the pages of our magazine, but the *Britannica* drives the point home.

What happened to names like Cool Papa Bell (a baseball player in the twenties)? Or the Bounding Basque (a tennis pro) or the Galloping Ghost (Red Grange)? Why can't we come up with nicknames like the Game Chicken (a 19th-century prizefighter)? Nowadays, we've got A-Rod and Shaq and "Hey, dildo!" They've got all the spunk and appeal of farmer's lung (a pulmonary disorder resulting from dust inhalation, related to pigeon breeder's lung and cheesewasher's lung).

René Lacoste was from the golden age of nicknames. A Parisian tennis player in the twenties, known for his methodical style, he helped lead the French to six Davis Cup victories. They called him the Crocodile. The American press gave him his reptilian nickname, partly for his tenacity and partly because he won a set of fancy crocodile luggage in a bet.

I hadn't known about Lacoste the tennis player. But I did know the shirts, which the *Britannica* discusses at the end of the entry: Lacoste, it says, founded a line of "sportshirts and other items of apparel with his 'crocodile' emblem (although somehow changed to an alligator)."

This is odd, I thought. What happened? Why did the crocodile suddenly switch to the alligator side? Did Lacoste's marketing department discover a big difference? The public finds alligators intelligent and sexy, but crocodiles lazy and untrustworthy?

I should have kept reading my *Britannica*. The Lacoste alligator is not a profound epistemological mystery along the lines of "Is there a God?" or "What is the definition of evil?" or "Why is David Pelzer allowed to publish books?" But I kind of wanted to find out the truth. Growing up, my mother had outfitted me with dozens of Lacoste shirts (often paired with bold plaid pants that would embarrass a Connecticut dentist), so there was a personal angle. Plus, I had been reading for four hours straight, and my eyes were about to start bleeding.

I riffle through Julie's bureau drawer and find her periwinkle Lacoste shirt. I study the emblem. I know from my trusty *Britannica* the difference between alligators and crocodiles: in crocodiles, the fourth tooth in each side of the lower jaw projects outside the snout when the mouth is closed. Is there protrusion? I can't tell, because the reptilian bastard has his mouth open. Great. Next, I check the Lacoste Web site. The Web site does indeed call the logo an alligator—but is suspiciously mum on its crocodile past. Hmm. Have I stumbled onto a cover-up?

I decide I need to do some old-fashioned reporting; I need to talk to someone at Lacoste. I call up the New York headquarters, and am connected to Gigi, a nice Southern-accented woman in charge of media relations. Before I can finish asking my question, she stops me: "It's a crocodile."

But the Web site says . . .

"Well, then the Web site needs to be fixed," she says. "It's definitely a crocodile. It's always been a crocodile. It's a croc!"

This is very disconcerting for a man who's trying to know it all. I'm up to my snout in conflicting sources. If I can't know for sure about the silly Lacoste icon, what does this say about knowledge as a whole? My best attempt at a conclusion: the Lacoste emblem is a crocodile, but Americans think of it as an alligator. I'll have to be satisfied with that. I'm just hoping Joe Camel isn't a llama.

Langley, Samuel

A Connecticut-based inventor who finished a heavier-than-air machine nine days before the Wright Brothers. When he launched it from a catapult, it got snagged and crashed into the Potomac River; if not, many think he would have gone down in history as the first. How many times a day you reckon he thought about that snag? Probably every hour for the rest of his life.

Langley belongs to another heartbreaking niche of historical figures, just as sad as George Darwin and his band of loser relatives: the close-but-no-cigar crowd. One snag meant the difference between centuries-long fame and almost total obscurity. Langley can commiserate with Elisha Gray, who filed papers with the patent office on February 14, 1876, for his telephone device—just a couple of hours after Alexander Graham Bell filed his. Gray really should have rearranged his schedule: first, the patent application, *then* the grocery store.

language

Today I've got Sunday lunch at Grandma and Grandpa's. Once a month, my parents and I drive up to my grandparents' house in the suburb of Riverdale, where we spend the afternoon eating chicken and roast potatoes at the largest table I've ever seen. It's huge. My grandfather told me that it was once owned by an obscure Bonaparte, but he could have told me that it used to serve as the main dance floor at the Copacabana, and I would have believed him.

This brunch, we've got two special guest stars, my aunt Jane and her eleven-year-old son, Douglas. Jane's widely acknowledged to be the egghead in my mom's family—a graduate of Harvard, a Fulbright scholar, a speaker of most languages on the European continent (not including Votic, a Finno-Ugric tongue that has fewer than a hundred remaining speakers). Douglas is equally brilliant. I've never met anyone who takes more after-school classes than he does—German classes, chess classes, fencing classes, and classes in something called Lego robotics. I'm still not sure what Lego robotics is—I guess it has something to do with building robots out of Lego blocks. But it's nice to know, if this journalism thing doesn't work out, there is a career to be had as a Lego robotics instructor.

When we arrive, we sit at Grandma and Grandpa's enormous antique walnut table. Down at the other end, Douglas, who has brought his laptop along, is busy playing a word game. "It's just so good to have everyone here!" says Grandma. "Look at my two grandsons! My two smart grandsons!" Douglas nods and gets back to the word game.

The rest of the family talks about the usual fare—jobs and holidays. Fortunately, the acoustics are good enough that I can hear what my family is saying, even though we're separated by an expanse of dark wood.

Grandma starts passing around the bowls of food. "This is less potatoes than usual," she apologizes.

Douglas suddenly stops pecking away on his computer and looks up.

"Hold it!" he says. "That's incorrect!" Douglas takes out a piece of paper and pencil, checks something off, then leans across the table and slides the paper toward Grandma.

I pick it up. It's something called a "grammar citation." It's got a list of grammar infractions like "free gift" and " 'impact' misused as a verb." Douglas has checked off a box that says " 'fewer/less' abuse." Apparently, grandma should have said "fewer potatoes than usual" instead of "less potatoes than usual."

"Douglas has gotten into grammar," explains Jane. "He's an officer in something called the grammar police."

"Word police," corrects Douglas.

"Isn't that something," says Grandma, chuckling.

"He gave a citation to his teacher last week," says Jane.

"What'd she do?" says Grandpa.

"She said, 'Between you and I.'" replies Douglas. He shakes his head, no doubt feeling both sorrow and pity at her pronoun abuse.

"Tell them some other things you've learned in your books," prompts Jane.

Douglas clicks pause on his word game to give us some nuggets. "Well, everyone's heard of antonyms and synonyms. But there's also capitonyms. That's when the meaning of the word changes according to whether it starts with a capital letter."

I'm not understanding.

"Like Herb and herb," says Douglas, "or Polish and polish."

"I never knew that," my father says.

"Good for you, Douglas," says Grandpa.

It's true. That's a damn good fact. I decide I better try to match my eleven-year-old cousin. I search my mental file for some English language trivia.

"Did you know, in Old English, the gh in the word 'light' was not silent? And in some areas of Scotland, they still pronounce it *licht*."

No one seems particularly blown away by my brichtness.

"Also, there's something called miranyms," continues Douglas, unfazed "That's the word in between two opposites."

The adults around the table are confused.

"Like when you have 'convex' and 'concave', the miranym is 'flat,'" says Douglas, patiently.

Right now, I've got a mixed bag of emotions. On the one hand, I'm proud. Here we've got a bona fide prodigy, a fellow athlete of the mind, and he shares my blood. It's quite possible that he really does have the genius IQ that I deluded myself into thinking I had back when I was his age. On the other hand, I'm jealous and threatened. Whenever I try to correct people or throw out bits of trivia, I feel about as welcome as an assassin bug at a Sunday barbecue (the assassin bug, by the way, can shoot a stream of blinding saliva up to twelve inches). When Douglas corrects people or throws out trivia, he gets a pat on a head and a smile. Why do know-it-alls turn from cute to obnoxious as soon as their voices turn and they sprout body hair?

"Or with 'hot' and 'cold', the miranym is 'room temperature,'" continues Douglas.

"Well, on behalf of myself, I find that very unique," I say. I've decided to switch my strategy. I won't compete with Douglas on facts; I'll drive him nuts by mauling his beloved English language. Mature, I know.

Douglas digs out his grammar citation, checks off a couple of boxes, and slides one over to me.

"What'd I get one of these for?" I say.

Douglas gets out another, checks off "dangler" and slides it over.

"But I didn't say nothing wrong!"

Douglas looks at me. He's caught on. "You're just trying to get them, aren't you?"

"No I ain't."

"What is the longest word you know in the English language?" Douglas challenges me.

"'Smiles,'" I say. "Because there's a mile between the first and last letter."

Backed into a corner, I had whipped out a joke I learned when I was Douglas's age. Douglas shakes his head.

"What about 'pneumonoultramicroscopicsilicovolcanoconiosis.'"

I've got to give it to him. He knows his English.

"It's a disease you get from the silica dust when volcanoes erupt. I know how to spell it too." He begins spitting out the letters in a rapid monotone staccato. "*P-n-e-u-m-o-n . . .* " Game over.

Las Vegas

Mormons were the first settlers. Not sure Joseph Smith would approve of today's topless showgirls and liquor. Though he would like the volcano at the Mirage. Everybody likes the volcano.

Lascaux Grotto

A noted French cave with dozens of Paleolithic paintings, including one of a bird man with an erect phallus. I realize halfway through the article that I've been to this cave, though, of course, I'd forgotten its name. (Thanks, Ebbinghaus.)

Julie and I stopped at the Lascaux grotto on our bike tour of southern France a couple of years ago. This was one of those bike tours where you pay a third of your annual salary to huff up hills with a bunch of other helmeted Americans, most of them dermatologists, though with a sprinkling of periodontists to spice things up. We've been on a couple of these tours, and it's always an exercise in humiliation for me. I never train enough beforehand, and end up spraining my knee or ankle, which means I get shuttled from stop to stop in the company van, sandwiched in between the spare parts and picnic supplies. So that's bad enough. But then there's always the eighty-two-year-old retired dermatologist, who rode forty miles without breaking a sweat, who will ask, "How's your knee doing, young fella?" By which he means to say, "What the hell is wrong with you, boy? I've got hemorrhoids older than you, and I still pedaled up those hills, you nelly." At least that's the way I interpret it.

Anyway, I remember pulling up to the Lascaux grotto on our fancy bikes with their—no exaggeration—forty-two gears. (The first successful bicycles in the 1860s, incidentally, had only one gear, and riding them was such a bumpy experience, they were called "bone shakers.") At the cave entrance, we were met by the skinny French anthropologist who was to be our tour guide. He gave us a five-minute course in human evolution—he seemed particularly interested in telling us about humanoid cranial capacity, which has grown over the years from 800 cubic centimeters to 1350 cubic centimeters. He then led us through the tunnel to the prehistoric art gallery.

"Regard the outline of this bull," said our French anthropologist.

The dermatologists all nodded and murmured.

"The horns on this bull are very well defined," he said.

"Where? I can't see it." I said.

"There," he said, pointing. "Those lines."

"Sorry—where, exactly?"

"Don't worry about him," Julie said. "He only has 800 cubic centimeters of cranial capacity."

Our guide laughed his French laugh. *"Très bien,"* he said. *"Très bien."*

I never did figure out which were the horns on that bull, but all the talk of humanoid evolution reminded my tiny brain of something that has haunted me since I was a kid. If humans manage to survive another few thousand years, they'll continue to grow larger and larger craniums. Which means no matter how smart I am, no matter how much I know, how much I read, how much I absorb, how much I think, I'll still be a member of the species that couldn't do differential calculus in their heads. "Oh, look at the way Homo sapiens solved Fermat's last theorem! And it took them only three hundred years. Isn't that cute!"

Which makes me question my current venture. Even if I'm smarter by the end and write a brilliant book about the experience, I'll still be doing the 21st-century equivalent of scrawling bird men with erect phalluses on cave walls.

last words

Another reason I'll never make it into the *Britannica,* in addition to the fact that I'm not an Arctic explorer or a Swedish botanist: I can't talk like these guys. I don't have the conviction, the passion. This is clearest to me when I read about the last words of great men. Like Georges Danton, a leader of the French Revolution who was beheaded for opposing the extremist faction. When he was about to be guillotined, Danton told the executioner, "Show my head to the people. It is worth the trouble." As opposed to what I would have told the executioner: "Holy fuck! Holy shit!" Or if you want to get technical, "Holy *merde*!"

Danton has plenty of company. Men like Giordano Bruno, an Italian philosopher and astronomer in the late 1500s, who went beyond the Copernican heliocentric view of the universe, instead arguing that space contained a multiplicity of worlds like the earth. For this, the Catholic Church gagged him and burned him at the stake. When the judges read

Bruno his sentence, he told them: "Perhaps your fear in passing judgment on me is greater than mine in receiving it." How can he be that cool under pressure? He's just been told that he's going to be flambéed, and he responds with a noble, coherent, brilliant quotation. Again, I believe my reaction would be, "Listen, I was just kidding about that multiplicity of worlds stuff. Just joking around. Only one world. I take it all back."

learning

There is a short section on IQs in the *learning* section. It says that high IQs "are strongly associated with the 35-yard dash and balancing on one foot." This is one of the most strangely specific pieces of information in the encyclopedia. Why a thirty-five-yard-dash? I've never even heard of that. Why not a fifty? Why balancing on one foot? What about tether ball? Is that strongly associated with high IQ? Because that would make as much sense. Also, it seems totally counterintuitive; what happened to the stereotype of the sickly weakling genius? But most of all, it seems unfair. It seems wrong that nature makes people smart *and* fast and well balanced. Can't nature divide those things equally among her brood? Since I don't have the highest IQ—as evidenced by the Mensa test debacle—I should at least be able to do that balancing crane stance in kung fu.

lector

I had to skip my morning *Britannica* reading today. A handful of the *Esquire* editors were required to show up at the ungodly (for us) hour of 9 A.M. to make a presentation to the magazine's advertising staff. We are supposed to present our plans for *Esquire*'s future issues. Sounds relatively simple. Problem is, I've never been a great speech giver, and I'm moderately stressed out about my presentation.

I've been half hoping the *Britannica* would help me with my oratory. And the volumes are, in fact, packed with information on classical rhetorical devices. My favorite is one called "aposiopesis"—the deliberate failure to complete a sentence, as in "Why, you . . ." or "Why, I ought to . . ." (possible Business Idea: print T-shirts with the motto "Aposiopesis makes me want to . . ." and sell them to rhetorical scholars for a killing). But outside of sputtering fathers in fifties sitcoms and classical debate lovers, aposiopesis wouldn't seem to be very useful in modern society.

I'm also a fan of inversion, the transportation of normal word order, as in the first lines from Samuel Taylor Coleridge's poem "Kubla Khan": "In Xanadu did Kubla Khan / A stately pleasure-dome decree." There's something great about that sentence—slightly disorienting, but majestic. Yet when I tried to write something with inversion for today's presentation, it just came out weird: "In the pages of our magazine will appear women with little clothing." I sounded like a perverted Yoda.

In the end, I settle on three rhetorical devices: anadiplosis, or repetition; asyndeton, or lack of conjunctions (as in Caesar's "I came, I saw, I conquered"); and antithesis, the juxtaposition of two opposing ideas (as in the phrase "Life is short, art is long").

I put on a suit—my Gucci wedding suit, the only suit I own—and go down to the Trump Tower, where the meeting is being held. I speak right after my boss, David Granger, which is always problematic, since he's a good speaker, getting as worked up as a Baptist preacher.

I put down my notes and begin: "This year, the front of the magazine will get smarter. The front of the magazine will get funnier. The front of the magazine will get better in every way." I pause, letting my anadiplosis and asyndeton sink in. I felt self-conscious as I was saying it, as if I was reciting lines from a stilted Jacobean play. But I continue with an antithetical flourish: "*GQ*'s front section is good, but *Esquire*'s is great. *GQ* is moderately interesting, but *Esquire* is indispensable."

The ad staff is paying attention. Some are taking notes!

And that is about all I can muster, rhetoric-wise. The rest of the speech is free of eloquence and classical devices—just a disorganized and flat-footed list of upcoming articles.

I'd judge my rhetoric a moderate success. But I think it made for a better speech than the usual collection of "um's" and "uh's." Maybe I just have to learn to trust my *Britannica* more. At the very least, my presentation went better than Benjamin Disraeli's maiden speech in the House of Commons, which was so unpopular he had to end it with, "I will sit down now, but the time will come when you will hear me." So I got that going for me.

Leonardo Pisano, aka Fibonacci

Fibonacci was a 13th-century Italian mathematician who invented the Fibonacci series, which goes like this: 1, 1, 2, 3, 5, 8, 13, 21, etc. Each of the numbers is the sum of the two preceding numbers. I look at the sequence again. I know I recognize it from somewhere. It takes me a couple of seconds, but then it clicks: Boggle! It's the scoring system for my favorite find-a-word game, Boggle.

Before we go any further, let me defend poor Boggle. I know professing to love this game is about as cool as admitting that I collect Hummel figurines, but it's truly the best word game ever invented. Scrabble involves too much luck; I'm always getting stuck with a bunch of hard consonants that look like they might spell a Slavic factory town, but nothing in my mother tongue. Boggle, on the other hand, just like chess, is all skill. Everyone's crouched over the same little letter cubes trying to unlock the same hidden words. And I'm not half bad at Boggle; it's one of the few things I can beat my brother-in-law Eric at, mostly because I add an "er" to every word. My strategy is to defend the validity of words like "pillower" with such vehemence that Eric will make some skeptical and condescending noises, but not bother to look them up.

Now in this glorious game of Boggle, depending on the number of letters in each of your words, you are rewarded 1, 1, 2, 3, or 5 points. Voilà! The Fibonacci series. Or at least the start of it.

Somehow, knowing this makes me happy. I'm not sure why. I think it has to do with being able to see patterns in the world, knowing how an obscure math sequence relates to one of my favorite pastimes, unlocking a code, even if that code is about a silly Parker Brothers game.

Thanks to the *Britannica*, I now know not only the name of the Boggle scoring system, but also how such a series was first proposed. Fibonacci gave it in the form of a riddle about randy rabbits. Namely: *A certain man put a pair of rabbits in a place surrounded on all sides by a wall. How many pairs of rabbits can be produced from that pair in a year if it is supposed that every month each pair begets a new pair, which from the second month on becomes productive?* Naturally, I'm jealous of these critters' boundless fertility, not to mention disturbed by the amount of incest involved. But mostly I'm impressed by how this works—the more rabbit couples there are, the more pairs they produce, with the increases occurring at the good old Fibonacci intervals—1, 1, 2, 3, 5, 8, 13, 21, 34, etc. The year-end total: 376.

I now have an unexpected link between lascivious rabbits and Boggle. Even better, I know that Boggle connects in some cosmic way to pinecones and seashells, whch also exhibit the Fibonacci sequence, according to the *Britannica*. It's a nice little quartet: Boggle, rabbits, pinecones, and seashells. Or actually quintet, if you throw in *The Da Vinci Code*. (A friend tells me that the best seller also includes the Fibonacci sequence. She apparently reads for pleasure—wonder what that's like.)

liar paradox
The ancient paradox goes like this: *If the sentence "This sentence is not true" is true, then it is not true, and if it is not true, then it is true.* I feel very lucky I am not stoned, because if I had read this after a bong hit, my head would explode.

life span
Tucked in among the other statistics—like the one about the yearlong life span of small rodents and pine trees that can last for forty-nine hundred years—comes a number that shocks me. It says the average human life span in the 1700s was thirty years. Thirty years! I'm thirty-five. I don't need the *algebra* section to figure out that if I had been a cobbler back in the 18th century, I'd have spent the last five years relaxing in a coffin. Thirty years is nothing—crayfish can live thirty years. This is good information. Useful information. Optimism-inspiring information.

lily
Two errands today, two very different experiences. First, the florist. Julie's taken to calling herself an "encyclopedia widow," so I figure now might be a good time to remind her that I love her, and that I'm willing to spend $45 to back up that fact.

I go to a shop in midtown, a couple of blocks from the office. The first thing I notice is that the florist has dreadlocks that reach down to his waist. I can't imagine that's a huge subset of the population: florists with dreadlocks. Sort of like insurance executives with mohawks.

When I inform him that I want to order a bouquet, he asks me if I want the flowers in a vase. I reply that I do.

"That's called an arrangement, not a bouquet," he says. His tone is surprisingly hostile, with a little boredom thrown in for good measure. I should walk out right now.

I tell him I'd like a hyacinth. "You know, hyacinth," I say. "Named for Apollo's male lover, whom Apollo accidentally killed while teaching him to throw the discus."

The dreadlocked florist gives a half snort, half harrumph.

"And I'd like some dogwood with that," I say.

"Dogwood doesn't go with that," he says.

I tell him that I was just reading about dogwood, and how in Victorian flower language, a lady's returning a dogwood was a sign of indifference. I just want to check if my wife still loves me.

"Dogwood's tall and hyacinth is short," he says.

I won't describe the rest of the flower debacle—during which I bring up the Japanese flower arranging system, something called the Hogarth curve, and the Madonna lily, a symbol of virginity in the middle ages, all of which he seems disinclined to discuss. He asks me what I want to say in my card.

"These flowers are bisexual, but I am straight, and I love you," I say.

He keeps his pen poised, but doesn't start to write, instead glaring at me over his granny glasses. Yes, I've neglected to mention he was a dreadlocked florist with granny glasses.

"Because most flowers are bisexual," I say. "Angiosperms are bisexual."

He has already decided I am a moron. Now I am also a homophobe.

Errand two is a stop at Supercuts for a haircut. My barber is named Steve, a man who has a serious collection of earrings on his ears, but neither dreadlocks nor granny glasses.

I take my *L* volume out of my bag. As he snips, I read about lighthouses and lightning rods, my hair dropping into the crease between the pages. Steve wonders what I am doing. I tell him.

"What a great idea!" he says. "We should all do that."

Encouraged, I inform him that Roman households often had a barber on staff. Like a butler. They offered haircuts to guests, like we offer them a glass of wine nowadays.

"Wow," he says. "I love that!"

Maybe he is just being polite, but I think he is genuinely interested.

I tell him that archaeologists have discovered a five-thousand-year-old frozen corpse that showed signs of the first haircut, then segued smoothly to Hollywood, pointing out that Greta Garbo's first job was in a barbershop.

"I knew Mariah Carey worked in a salon," he says.

Steve has been kind and receptive and supportive, and I want to hug him. I give him a $10 tip instead, which I think he much preferred.

limerick

Another reason to be happy—the following poem:

A tutor who taught on the flute
Tried to teach two tooters to toot.
Said the two to the tutor,
"Is it harder to toot,
Or to tutor two tooters to toot?"

That's just good, clean, non-Nantucket-related fun.

Lloyd Webber, Sir Andrew

I didn't need the *Britannica* to tell me about this man, the Ray Kroc of musical theater, the man behind such McMusicals as *Jesus Christ Superstar* and *Phantom of the Opera*. At *Entertainment Weekly*, I had to edit a faux-weepy homage to *Cats* when the producers announced that after 7,485 performances on Broadway, Rum Tum Tugger was going to that kitty-litter box in the sky. I think I probably used that phrase, come to think of it.

But my most significant Andrew Lloyd Webber memory has to do with a play even campier than *Cats*: *Starlight Express*. For those who missed it, *Starlight Express* was the one about trains. The characters had names like Rusty and Dinah the Dining Car, and the actors played the trains by zipping across the stage on roller skates. As far as skate-based theater about modes of transportation goes, *Starlight Express* is among the top five.

I saw *Starlight Express* when I was about fifteen years old. My mom and I had flown to London on a special mother-son bonding trip. After a busy day of examining torture instruments in the Tower of London and getting mocked for ordering ice in our drinks (the waiter brought us our ice cubes in a pail labeled "Yank Bucket"), we went to the theater. *Starlight Express* sounded like harmless fun.

We watched Greaseball skate and sing about depots and the station, and then we clapped dutifully.

"So what'd you think?" my mom asked, when we got outside.

"Well, it was a little heavy-handed, I thought."

"How so?"

And here I explained that, in my opinion, *Starlight Express* was actually an extended political allegory. The old steam train was meant to represent slavery. The diesel train was laissez-faire capitalism. And the evil electric train—the one with the lightning bolt on his costume—was fascism. I can't remember the proof I had for my thesis, but I remember being pretty convincing. At the end of my lecture, my mom nodded her head. "That's interesting," she said. "I never thought of it that way."

This was a huge moment in my life as a know-it-all. Now, it's possible I might have overanalyzed Lloyd Webber, and there's a chance that Mom was just being polite. But I don't think so. I think my mother—a very smart woman with a master's degree and a lifelong *New Yorker* subscription—was actually impressed with my analysis. And that felt great.

That's the feeling I want to get back. I want the world's hidden meanings to leap out at me like a Chinese jumping mouse. I want to see the grand arcs and the big picture. I want to shock people with the incisiveness of my analysis. On the other hand, I don't really want to see any more musicals about trains.

Los Angeles

The *Britannica* quotes the following joke: The suicide rate in Burbank is so low because living there makes suicide redundant. Well, it's better than the Japanese gag about the monkeys and the moon.

Louis XIV

Louis XIV was not a particularly likable character. Here was a man with a Trump-sized ego who poured the nation's riches into building a palace while French peasants ate clumps of dirt for dinner. But Louix XIV had one thing going for him: he tried to ban biological weapons.

According to the *Britannica*, an Italian chemist came to Louis XIV with plans for the first bacteriological weapon. Louis XIV refused. He never developed the weapon, never used it against other European nations. But even more impressive, he paid the chemist an annual salary to keep the bioweapon a secret from the world.

Good for you, Louis. *Très bien*. He was abiding by the Geneva Convention 250 years before it was created.

It was a nice idea, but of course, no one—not even the divinely appointed Sun King—could keep bioweapons a secret forever. Information has a way of getting out. Which is good when it's the perfect recipe for oatmeal raisin cookies, but bad when it involves death by chemical asphyxiation.

And now, I live in a world where some horrible bioweapon may soon infect our subway system, and the Homeland Security Department warns us every couple of hours to duct-tape our nostrils. These thoughts about the inevitability of bioweapons depress me. The Louis XIV entry has set me off on a dark and disturbing train of thought. I've got to cut it off. I've got to suppress it just as Louis XIV suppressed primitive bioweapons. Julie's right: embrace optimism. Remember, life expectancy was thirty years in the time of Louis XIV. So I'm lucky to be breathing at all.

LSD

Lysergic acid diethylamide is derived from the ergot fungus on grain, especially rye. It can be absorbed readily from any mucosal surface, even from the ear.

This makes me nervous. I know it's irrational—I don't have a kid yet, I may never have a kid, but what if I do and he starts dropping LSD? What if he starts stuffing his ears with hallucinogens?

The thing is, I now have regained a handle on some of those questions my kid may ask me. I know how hot the sun is (ten thousand degrees on the surface, 27 million at the core). I know how airplanes fly (Bernoulli's theorem). I even know the answer to that old chestnut "Why is the sky blue?" (dust in the atmosphere scatters the smaller blue rays of the sun).

But I realize that's the easy stuff. What about sex and rye fungus and rock and roll? I used to laugh at the Tipper Gore types and their conniption fits about naughty lyrics or recreational drugs. Now I kind of see their point. What should my yet-to-be-conceived kid be allowed to watch? Are those threesomes on MTV's *Real World* okay? And do I have to stop cursing around the house? And how can I stop him from taking ecstasy while visiting random colleges? I know how that ends up.

A friend of mine recently told me that parents at bar mitzvahs nowadays are forced to hire extra security to keep an eye on the kids. The reason: oral sex. It's so rampant that unless you watch these thirteen-year-olds closely, they'll slip off to a corner and drop their pants. At the rate things are going, my kid will lose his virginity as soon as he stops breast-feeding.

If Julie ever gets pregnant, I'm buying a leash for the kid and not removing it till he gets his master's degree.

Luciano, Lucky

Even before reading the *Britannica,* I knew quite a bit about the history of the mafia. I knew, for instance, that Luca Brazi sleeps with the fishes and that Tony Soprano should have spent less time at the Bada Bing and more time working on his marriage.

Okay, so I could use a little help.

Happily, the *Britannica* is packed with colorfully evil real-life mobsters. Perhaps the best tale—worthy of Mario Puzo himself—is that of Lucky Luciano. A native of Sicily who moved to New York City as a kid in 1906, Lucky was a precocious little menace, already mugging and extorting at the impressive age of ten. In his teens and twenties, he broadened his skill set to include bootlegging, prostitution, narcotics—classic mafia stuff. He earned his nickname, Lucky, both for evading arrest and for winning at games of craps. Not to mention his luck at being one of the only mafiosi to live through one those notoriously unpleasant "one-way rides." In October of 1929, Luciano was "abducted by four men in a car, beaten, stabbed repeatedly with an icepick, had his throat slit from ear to ear, and was left for dead on Staten Island."

After shaking that off, Luciano killed his boss Joe Masseria at a Coney Island restaurant, and by the early thirties, he had been promoted to *capo di tutti capi*. The fun ended in 1936. Luciano was busted for his brothel and call girl empire, and sentenced to prison for up to fifty years. Still, he continued to rule from his prison cell.

So far, we've got a lively if slightly standard mobster yarn. But the next part is where things get interesting. In 1942, the luxury liner *Normandie* blew up in New York harbor as it was getting converted to military use for World War II. Sabotage was suspected. The Allies needed New York harbor to be safe, since key provisions were shipped through there. So navy intelligence made the trek to Luciano's prison cell and asked his help. Luciano—who still controlled the waterfront and the longshoremen's union—gave the orders. Sabotage on the docks ended. As a reward for his war efforts, Luciano's sentence was commuted, and he was deported to Italy, where he kept himself busy with drug trafficking and smuggling aliens to America. He died of a heart attack in 1962.

I love this tale—the heartwarming friendship between the navy and the mobster. I guess the moral is that sometimes, for the greater good, you have to suck it up, hold your nose, and ask for help from the dark side.

lumbar puncture

Lumbar puncture is the official name for a spinal tap. This is a good way to sound pretentious, especially if you're referring to the beloved Rob Reiner mockumentary. I've collected many, many ways to sound pretentious—some of which have actually leaked into my everyday language. At work the other day, I made unironic use of the phrase "died without issue," a phrase I'd never heard of six months ago (it means died without kids). In case you too want to sound pretentious, here are five strategies that could come in handy:

1. If someone asks you the time, respond with this quote from Valéry: "Anyone can tell you *what time it is*. But who can tell you *what is time?*"

2. Call cottage cheese by its alternate name, "Dutch cheese."

3. After a long flight, complain about "circadian rhythm stress" (what your hayseed friends call "jet lag").

4. Refer to the Vietnam War as the "Indochina Wars."

5. Do *not* use the word "bildungsroman" when talking about a coming-of-age novel. Yes, it's pretentious. But it's not *really* pretentious. Try these: *Kunstlerroman,* a novel that deals with the formative years of an artist. *Erziehungsroman,* a novel of upbringing. *Entwicklungsroman,* a novel of character development. "I think *Harry Potter* is a fabulous *Kunstlerroman!*"

Lumière, Auguste and Louis

Two French brothers who owned a camera factory. In 1895, they made a film called *Workers Leaving the Lumière Factory*—an aptly named documentary that shows workers shuffling out the door of the factory. It's considered the very first motion picture. Which gives me Movie Idea Number Four: Do a remake of *Workers Leaving the Lumière Factory* with Hollywood's A-list stars playing the workers. Tom Hanks, Russell Crowe, Tom Cruise all filing out a door, wearing black hats—box office gold!

M

Madonna

The *Britannica* just added Madonna to the edition this year, and you could tell the editors wrote the entry while wearing one of those sterile full-body suits people use when containing an Ebola outbreak. It's wedged in between write-ups for the first Madonna and British legal historian Thomas Madox, and contains sentences like this one: "Her success signaled a clear message of financial control to other women in the industry, but in terms of image she was a more ambivalent role model." In *Britannica*-speak, that roughly translates to: "Madonna is a whore. A very dirty whore."

The entry did teach me some Madonna facts, including her middle name (Louise) and that she was a member of Patrick Hernandez's disco revue in Paris. Not that I know what that is, but I'll be sure to bring it up next time I see a Madonna video.

Whenever that is. Reading about Madonna makes me miss pop culture. I'll get back to you someday, pop culture. I promise. It's just this *Britannica* is so damn long. Did they have to cover every single Nobel Prize winner and African canyon and South American capital? Couldn't they have left out a few? Who would have noticed?

Mahler, Gustav

He had a mother fixation that manifested itself in a slight limp he unconsciously adopted in imitation of his mother's lameness. The man most in need of therapy in the *Britannica* so far.

majuscule

Everyone keeps asking when I'm going on *Jeopardy!* And I have to say, I'm starting to feel pretty good about my chances. I've been watching my old pal Alex Trebek give the clues and I've made huge strides in my ability to shout out the proper questions before the contestants (especially if I use the pause button on my TiVo).

In fact, I may just be too smart for my own good. The other night, I watched Alex give the following $100 clue: "This is another term for uppercase characters, such as the ones that start a sentence."

I knew that. Easy. "Majuscule!" I shouted out, confidently. "What is majuscule!" "Majuscule" is the official name for uppercase letters and "minuscule" is the name for lowercase letters.

One of the contestants twitched his thumb and rang in. "What is capital letters," he said.

"Correct," said Alex.

Oh, yes. That's right. Capital letters. I should have known that. I was reminded of that woman at the Mensa convention who kept saying "interstices" when the word was "gap." I felt like a tool. But also, quite superior.

If I am eventually going to try out for *Jeopardy!* I figure it'd be good to get some advice from an expert. So I track down one of the all-time big money winners, a five-time champion named Dave Sampugnaro, who I found on the Internet (his e-mail handle is jeopardyboy). He agrees to meet me for coffee. Dave is a nice man with a goatee, wire rim glasses, and an abundance of nervous energy that, during our meeting, keeps his leg bouncing and his hands busily twisting a straw wrapper. "I haven't read the entire encyclopedia," he tells me when we sit down. "But when I was five I read the *Information Please Almanac.*"

Nowadays, when Dave isn't at his day job—he works at IBM—he spends his time collecting. He collects antique license plates, soft drink thermometers, presidential signatures—and most of all facts. The man is a fact machine. Our meeting is like a boxing match with factoids.

Dave tells me that Ulysses S. Grant's wife was cross-eyed and posed for paintings only at a concealing angle. I counter with my classic about René Descartes and his cross-eyed fetish. He responds with the nugget that James Buchanan was nearsighted in one eye and farsighted in the other, so he'd look at visitors with his head cocked to the side. I rally with a bit about a cousin of James Buchanan who invented a submarine that allowed him to walk on the bottom of the Mississippi River, where he found a fortune in lead and iron. After which he pounds me with the fact that Abe Lincoln was the only president to hold a patent—it's for a device that lifts boats over levees.

The conversation is fast and wide-ranging and slightly exhausting—but exhilarating. No eye rolling here. No awkward silences. Dave loves facts as much as, maybe more than, I do, and he's just bursting to spout them and drink them in.

Dave warns me that *Jeopardy!*'s not an easy experience. "I was so nervous in the greenroom, I was shaking. I tried to pick up a glass of water and I was spilling it everywhere." And that's if you get on. Dave tried out no less than seven times over eight years before getting the nod. Hopefuls have to take a ten-question test, then a harder, fifty-question test, then have an interview with the producers to see if they are camera-friendly—and even if they pass those they might not get called.

There aren't too many secrets to success, Dave says. Go with your first instinct when answering clues. And be passionate about knowledge—you should never think of studying as a chore. Facts are your friends.

Speaking of facts, he's got plenty more: "You know, at one time there was only one bathroom in the White House and the president had to wait his turn if someone was in there."

When I get back to my office, I start to think about Dave's eight years of auditions. Jesus. I figure I better start now. So I call the *Jeopardy!* publicist to see when the next auditions might take place—and that's when I get an unpleasant surprise. The publicist says that I'm no longer eligible, since I've met Alex Trebek. What? It's not like Trebek and I play Yahtzee every Saturday afternoon. I doubt he'd recognize me in a lineup of other skinny white journalists. And I, for one, mistook him for a Mexican gardener. Doesn't matter. *Jeopardy!* is *The New York Times* of game shows, and there can be no appearance of impropriety. As far as they're concerned, my two-hour interview with Trebek put me in the inner circle next to his wife and mother and Merv Griffin. Answer: This is hugely frustrating. Question: What are the overly strict *Jeopardy!* rules?

Maybe I should look into *Who Wants to Be a Millionaire?* I can win more money and no one will see how bad my handwriting is.

mammals

Elephant copulation lasts twenty seconds. That should make a lot of men feel better.

Mann, Horace

In his final speech, the educational reformer told students: "Be ashamed to die until you have won some victory for humanity." Good wisdom. Great wisdom even. I have to remember that.

manure

The *Britannica* isn't a Farrelly brothers movie, but it does have more than its fair share of scatology. And thank God for that, because I desperately needed to expand my knowledge of waste products.

You see, when I married Julie, I became uncle to her brothers' kids— four adorable, squeaky-voiced children under ten. Not having much experience with the Nickelodeon crowd, I initially had some trouble connecting with them. But then I hit upon a secret. Two words, to be exact. My entire relationship with my nieces and nephew was forged with the phrase "monkey poop." For five years, I have worked this phrase into every conversation I have with them.

"What would you like for your birthday?" I'll ask Andrea, age seven.

"Gameboy pinball!" she says.

"Well, I was thinking of getting you fifty-seven pounds of monkey poop. Would that be okay?"

"Nooo!!!" she'll scream, running away. "No monkey poop!"

My monkey poop joke has been my biggest hit, my equivalent of Bill Cosby's dentist routine. I think my nieces and nephew were just happy to have found an adult who is less mature than they are. And yet, after five years, even something so brilliant as monkey poop began losing its freshness. I needed some new material. The encyclopedia was there to help.

One Sunday, all the kids and their parents made one of their day trips to the city, and used our apartment as headquarters.

"What's for lunch?" I ask Natalia, age nine.

"I dunno," she says.

"You think Aunt Julie will be serving whale poop?"

"Whale poop?" she asks.

"Yeah, whale poop is delicious."

"Uh-huh."

"Seriously, a lot of people do eat whale poop."

"Yeah, right."

"You don't believe me?" I take out volume *A,* and turn to *ambergris.* I show Natalia the definition: a foul-smelling substance found in the intestines of whales that, when dry, takes on a sweet aroma, and is used in spices and perfumes. She is duly impressed. She runs into the kitchen.

"I'd like some whale poop, please! On French bread!"

Who said the *Britannica* doesn't have practical knowledge? This is killer material. Next, I impress my nieces and nephew with stories about fossilized dinosaur poop (it's called coprolite). I segue into the best method for storing manure (stack it, so that it doesn't leach nitrogen), which wasn't quite as big a hit. But I redeem myself with the casebearing beetle. When it's threatened, it pulls its legs inward and disguises itself as caterpillar droppings.

"Everybody, pretend to be caterpillar poop!" I shout.

We all drop to the floor and pull in our arms and legs.

"Hey, are you by any chance caterpillar poop?" I ask Natalia.

"No, it's me! Natalia! Fooled you."

Julie's sister-in-law Lisa walks into the room to see the five of us on the floor in little balls.

"What's going on here?" she asks.

"Shhh," says her daughter, Allison, age five. "We're pretending to be caterpillar poop."

Lisa looks at me. She is not amused.

"I thought we discussed this. We would not be making monkey poop jokes anymore."

"But this is caterpillar poop," I say. "Totally different."

masochism

The term "masochism" was derived from Leopold von Sacher-Masoch, an Austrian novelist who wrote extensively about how he enjoyed being beaten and subjugated. Poor Masoch. He's no Sade. Everyone still talks about the Marquis de Sade—his works are read, movies are made about him, biographies glorify his memory. But Masoch gets nothing, except the sullying of his family name. On the other hand, if anyone likes being ignored, it's probably Masoch. Pay no attention to me! Yes, ignore my writings! Just tarnish my name!

If the *Britannica* has taught me anything, it's to be more careful. I don't want to turn into an unseemly noun or verb or adjective someday. I don't want to be like Charles Boycott, the landlord in Ireland who refused to lower rents during a famine, leading to the original boycott. I don't want to be like Charles Lynch, who headed an irregular court that hung loyalists during the Revolutionary War. I can't have "Jacobs" be a verb that means staying home all the time or washing your hands too frequently.

mechanics

Two days ago, as I was tapping a golf ball around the *Esquire* art director's office floor, I wondered to myself: Why do golf balls have all these dimples? And here's the answer: the dimples create turbulence around the ball, which reduces the drag as it flies through the air. (Some scientists also think that bathing suits with rough surfaces help make swimmers go faster, but this is still controversial.) Sometimes the *Britannica* has exquisite timing.

mechanics, fluid

An insight! A potentially life-altering insight. Gasoline should be purchased on very cold days. The colder the gas, the lower the volume, the less expensive the gas itself. So go to Exxon when you're wearing your fleece and gloves; or if that's not possible, at least go in the morning, when it's cooler.

Does everyone know this?

I had my epiphany while looking at all the equations and diagrams for fluids and their expansion. I knew gases expanded, but had forgotten fluids did as well. I thought of the various fluids in my life—orange juice, water, gasoline—and then I made that nimble mental leap. I took my science and applied it hard.

I wonder how many other hints and secrets and insights are lurking in the encyclopedia, waiting for me to unlock them. It makes me nervous that I haven't been thinking enough.

memory

In a Sherlock Holmes story I read a long time ago, Watson is shocked to discover that his detective friend doesn't know the planets of the solar system—or even that the earth orbits around the sun. Holmes could distinguish 140 types of tobacco by their ashes, but he doesn't know the planets. Holmes explains to the baffled Watson that his mind is like an attic. There's room for only so much lumber up there. So he stores the lumber that he'll find useful in the catching of thieves—information about the coloration of different tobacco types, for instance. Planets are of no use to him. In fact, he's annoyed at Watson for telling him about the planets, and he promises to do his best to forget them.

I've remembered this story for years. Naturally, I forget the name of the story—but the anecdote has stayed with me.

I've thought about Sherlock a lot recently, since I'm trying to cram a lot of lumber into my own mental attic. What's the capacity of memory? Is it really an attic? Or can it stretch indefinitely like a nice pair of sweatpants? And perhaps more important, how can I make sure whatever I stuff in there stays in there.

Hoping for help, I read what the *Britannica* says about memory, and though I do learn that the opposite of déjà vu is called jamais vu (a false unfamiliarity with a situation, as when you walk into your apartment and feel like you've never been there before), I still feel I could use more instruction in memory techniques. But where? As you may recall, my first brush with adult education was not a pleasant one. It was the speed-reading seminar from Hel (a Norse version of hell where it is eternally cold, a temperature that seems more hellish to me). So I'm not eager to jump back in. That said, I did pick up a Learning Annex catalogue that advertised a course called "Gain a Photographic Memory in 1 Night," from world-renowned expert Dave Farrow. Farrow's write-up says that he's in the *Guinness Book of World Records* for memorizing the order of fifty-two decks of cards shuffled together randomly. Fifty-two decks. Not fifty-two cards. That's 2,704 cards. It can't be argued; that is an astounding feat. I need to meet this man, so I give adult education another chance.

When I arrive at the community college cafeteria a couple of weeks later, Dave is decked out in his blue suit and blue tie, pacing at the front of the class and nodding his head at students as they trickle in.

A bearded man cracks the door open. He's wearing a red beret and plaid pants. "Is this the memory class?" he asks.

"You remembered!" says Dave jovially.

"Huh," says the man. "You looked better in the catalogue picture."

I feel bad for Dave. Having a stranger insult your personal appearance is a hard thing to forget, even for nonexperts like me. I want to tell Dave that he looks just fine—he kind of resembles TV's James Van Der Beek— and besides, he shouldn't take criticism on his physical appearance from a guy in a red beret and plaid pants.

Maybe because I sympathize with Dave, I decide I like him from the start. He's Canadian, for one thing. Canadians are hard to hate (though there was talk of annexing their country after the Civil War). Dave ends most of his sentences in exclamation points and he reminds us repeatedly that we're going to have a lot of fun. To inspire us, he tells us his hard-luck tale of battling three learning disabilities (ADD, dyslexia, and another I'd never heard of). And now look at him!

"If you know how to use your gray matter, you can remember phone books of information!" His techniques will give us memory power we never dreamed about! We can do it! Amen!

Oh, and by the way, we really should buy the home study course, which he happens to have on sale right here for $129. Yes, adult education strikes again—another infomercial disguised as a class. The home study course pops up every couple of minutes, sort of like a salesman's version of Tourette's. He could be talking about anything—food, books, Ireland—and all of a sudden, there it is, the home study course, back to say hi. I made a game of counting its recurrences.

The other game—and I wasn't alone in this one—is busting the man who memorized 2,704 cards for every tiny memory lapse. It's a petty thing to do, and a nice Canadian like Dave shouldn't be subjected to such small-minded nitpicking, but it sure feels good. At one point, Dave mentions how he was talking to one of the students on the way up in the elevator, and—

"Stairs!" shouts a man from the back.

Dave stops. "Excuse me?" The guy is leaning back in his chair, his hands locked behind his head.

"Stairs," he says.

"Oh yes, that's right, we took the stairs. The elevator's broken." The class snickers.

Dave's class actually covers some of the same territory as the god awful speed reading class. But since I like Dave better, I pay attention when he sings the praises of visualization. To remember a fact, he says, you create a little picture in your head. For instance, to remember my name—A.J.—the class comes up with Ajax, and visualizes me washing with Ajax soap. It was vaguely disconcerting having the whole class imagine me doing the dishes or washing my tub. I hope they imagined me with my pants on.

Regardless, Dave's system seems to work. We memorize the class names, a string of random words, and the properties of various types of glue, giving ourselves a hand after every victory.

At the break, I tell Dave about my project. "I'm reading the encyclopedia from A to Z and trying to learn everything in the world. You think I can remember everything?"

"Absolutely. With the techniques in the home study course, you can definitely do it!"

"But the encyclopedia's 65,000 entries—"

"You can do it! I memorized 2,700 playing cards in two days. In fact, after you do it, you can give me a testimonial!"

On the one hand, I'm heartened. But on the other hand—a much bigger hand—I'm a little annoyed. I wanted Dave to say, "Wow, not even I—world-renowned memory expert—could attempt such a feat. You are the king! There's just not enough room in my attic!" But the home study course it is. I give Dave my credit card, which kind of makes me nervous, seeing as he can probably memorize the digits without effort.

Back in my living room, I listen to CD number two of Dave's Memory Wiz system, the one where he explains how to memorize definitions. "Let's have fun with this," he says. The fun definition we are going to memorize involves the properties of the anti-neutrino particle. The anti-neutrino sounds sort of like "ant" and "newt", so Dave urges us to visualize an ant carrying a newt on its back. Okay. Now we learn the anti-neutrino is defined as a subatomic particle (now picture the ant and newt driving an atomic submarine). It also has no mass (visualize a priest on the submarine waving his arms to indicate that there will be no communion today) and is emitted during beta decay (the priest also happens to be holding a Betamax that is in desperate need of repair). Voilà! Simple as that.

It's a fun little picture. And it makes me want to take a nap. This memorizing thing is going to be harder than I thought. Still, I figure I should give it a whirl, and not just because I paid $129 for the home study course. I flip back a couple of pages. Here's a good one to try: melee. Melee was the precursor to soccer and was played with inflated bladders or, by the British, with the head of an enemy Dane; by the 11th century, many melees were played on Shrove Tuesday.

Okay. Here goes: "melee" sounds sort of like "melon." I'm picturing a melon in the shape of a soccer ball, and this melon really has to go to the bathroom (that's the bladder). And now it's stuffing a raspberry Danish into its head (Dane's head). Now it's carrying a shovel with two dates (Shrove Tuesday).

Dave's system is no doubt a good one. But the thought of creating fun little pictures for each of the 65,000 entries makes my head feel like it's been kicked by an 11th-century Englishman. I'll probably return to my current system—which consists of squinting my eyes and looking really hard at the page and hoping a bunch of facts stick to my cerebral cortex.

No disrespect to Dave, but I figure it'd be nice to consult another memory expert, maybe one from a school that doesn't have its catalogues on street corners. I force my pride deep into the pit of my stomach and ask my brother-in-law Eric. He's currently a psychology grad student at Columbia University, after having mastered and gotten bored with, successively, foreign diplomacy, computer programming, and investment banking. He allows me to accompany him to a class, though he does make me sit in the back and ask that I stay silent. Afterward, I spend a few minutes talking to his cognition professor, David Krantz, a man with a flower-print shirt and serious glasses.

My main question is, how much can one man remember? And for this, Krantz doesn't have a precise answer. He won't say, "Humans can store two-point-three million facts," or, "You can memorize everything in A to Q, but then you won't be able to squeeze another fact in." Apparently, annoyingly enough, human memory can't be quantified that way.

Instead, Krantz tells me that "memorization is a business where the rich get richer."

Meaning?

"The more you know about a topic, the more you'll be able to remember."

In other words, I'll get richer and richer in history, pop culture, literature—but my quantum physics and chemistry knowledge, which were at poverty levels at the start, will barely climb to the lower middle class by the end. I guess after reading thousands of pages I'd sort of figured this out, but still, it's a little sad to hear it from an expert. I can fill in some holes in my education—but only the shallow ones. The deeper ones I can only sprinkle dirt on.

metric system

I'm a convert to the metric system. I feel un-American even typing those words. I feel like I just admitted that I prefer a nice Linzer torte to apple pie or that I'm too busy to go to Shea Stadium because I have to watch Manchester United on the telly. But I've come to the realization that, kilogram for kilogram, it's just a better measurement system.

I knew very little about the metric system. All I knew was that I resented it creeping into my life—with its liters of Pepsi and ten-kilometer races. Not that I did ten-kilometer races, or bought grams of cocaine, but

I did drink the occasional Pepsi, and I didn't like it coming in foreign amounts. Now I say, bring on the metric system. I'm ready for it.

The thing that got me was the exhausting variety of weights and measures out there. Every few pages I'd run into another one—the chaldron, the chain, the link, the wine gallon, the ale gallon, the corn gallon, the Queen Anne's gallon, the gill, the cubit, the avoirdupois ounce, the troy ounce, the cord, the Old London mile, the Irish mile, the Scottish mile, the libra (from which the abbreviation *lb.* comes), and on and on. And that's not to mention the ways people cooked up these measurements—no doubt after a few gills of whiskey. Like the rod: "The 'rod' was once defined as the length of the left feet of 16 men lined up heel to toe as they emerged from church." What? What's a church got to do with it? Do men's feet change size when they leave a good sermon? And there's the inch. One of the first definitions was the breadth of a man's thumb at the base of the nail. Scientists, however, refined that to the breadth of three men's thumbs—one small, one medium, one large—divided by three. Later, it became the length of three grains of barley. But you might prefer the competing definition of twelve poppyseeds. Exhausting.

Diversity is good in ecosystems and stock portfolios, but in weights and measurements, uniformity is kind of nice. I've come to see the metric system as the Starbucks of measurement systems. Yes, Starbucks is annoyingly ubiquitous—but there's a reason for that. The Frappuccinos are delicious. So stop trying to fight it.

There's plenty to like about the much-despised metric system. It was born during the French Revolution, which automatically makes it cooler. And I knew it was rational—but I didn't know quite how rational. The French scientists defined the meter as one ten-millionth of the distance from the North Pole to the Equator. And the kilogram was designed to be the weight of one thousand cubic centimeters of water. Then there are those prefixes. I was familiar with the "kilo" and "cento" and "nano," but I was happy to learn about the outer reaches, the "peta" and the "exa" and the "tera." I started dropping them into conversation. I'd pop my head into my boss's office. "I just want a picosecond of your time. Maybe just a femtosecond."

Of course, as with everything lovable, the metric system has its flaws. It turned out the weight of a cube of water was too hard to measure. So that's no longer the definition of a kilogram. No, a kilogram is now defined as the weight of a hunk of metal sitting in this building outside of

Paris. This was shocking to me. There's an actual kilogram—a master kilogram, they call it—a platinum-iridium cylinder in a town called Sèvres. I had read about how the ancient Egyptians kept a master cubit of black granite against which all cubit sticks were measured. Apparently, we haven't moved past that.

It gave me Movie Idea Number Five: *The Great Metric Caper*. A bunch of professional thieves—perhaps with Donald Sutherland as the old guy in for one last big job—swipe the master kilogram and plunge the world's weights and measurement system into chaos. Maybe they hold the master kilogram for ransom. And there's got to be a good scene where the Asian thief played by B. D. Wong uses the master kilogram as a jujitsu stick.

Regardless, the master kilogram seems to teach like a profound lesson. In the end, the world hinges on physical things. You can theorize all you want, make abstract arguments for days on end, but eventually you just have to roll up your sleeves and carve yourself a hunk of metal.

Michelson-Morley experiment

Julie wants to see the Einstein exhibit at the Natural History Museum. I agree to go, though I trudge over there with a bad attitude. Maybe it's a rebellion against my father—who has reverence for all things Einstein-ian—but I've always been a little skeptical of Einstein. Yes, he was smart. But was he *that* smart? Was he really a thousand light-years ahead of Dirac and Bohr and all those other neglected shlubs who will never have their faces on T-shirts or children's videos? Was he so smart that he should be synonymous with intelligence itself? I remember being annoyed when a book came out a couple of years ago by a guy who drove cross-country with Einstein's brain. Einstein's legendary brain. Enough already. "I'm going to write a book about driving across the country with Darwin's pancreas," I told Julie at the time. "And after that, I'm taking the bus with Newton's lower intestines."

"You gotta do what you gotta do," she replied, her all-purpose response for when she thinks I'm engaging in crazy talk.

Since embarking on my quest to smarten up, I've gotten even more jealous of Einstein and his unceasing good publicity. Will anyone ever say that I'm as smart as Albert Einstein? Probably not. What about someone saying I'm as smart as Alfred Einstein, his cousin, a noted music historian who also gets a nice write-up in the *Britannica*? Maybe not even that. So I walk into the museum's exhibit with a grudge.

The first room in the exhibit is filled with domestic relics of the man himself. A couple of pipes that Einstein puffed upon, a compass he fiddled with, a little puzzle he figured out as a kid. In a glass case, I find a letter he wrote to his wife in an attempt to save his doomed marriage. It read: "You will make sure that I get my three meals a day in my room. You are neither to expect intimacy nor to reproach me in any way."

Ha! That's not so smart. That's not so smart at all. I may not have a Nobel Prize on my mantle, but I know you don't write an ultimatum like that to a woman and expect it to work. That's about as likely to work as aeromancy (predicting the future based on atmospheric phenomena).

I wander over to another little plaque. This one says Einstein refused to celebrate birthdays. As he explained: "It is a known fact that I was born, and that is enough." This is good. I go fetch Julie, knowing she'll disapprove. Julie loves birthdays. She manages to stretch her own birthday into a series of celebrations she calls a birth week, and which she's threatening to expand to a birth month.

"Einstein hated birthdays," I say. "Pretty dumb, huh?"

"Wouldn't be my choice," she says. "But then again, I'm not busy solving the mysteries of the universe."

Not quite the outrage I was hoping for.

The next room in the exhibit is devoted to Einstein's physics. I decide it's time I understood them once and for all. How hard can they be? Over the years, I've had sporadic flashes of comprehension. When I was about ten, my dad explained to me that, under the special theory of relativity, those people who reside on the highest floors of apartment buildings live longer than those who make their homes on the lower floors. This is because the earth's rotation makes the higher floors move through space faster than the lower floors, just as the tip of the Ferris wheel is going faster than the hub. Relativity says time slows down as you go faster. So odd as it may seem, you actually age less if you live in the penthouse. About a trillionth of a second less, but still, it's something. This always made me envious of my friends who lived in penthouses. The lucky bastards. As a kid, I remember spending many afternoons at Jonathan Green's twenty-ninth-floor apartment, and not just because we enjoyed tossing cantaloupes off the balcony and watching the splatter patterns. No, I was actually lengthening my life.

So anyway, that was my introduction to relativity. Over the years—in high school physics classes and the occasional pop science book—I expanded my knowledge, though not as much as you might think. And since I haven't gotten to the *R*'s yet, the *Britannica* hasn't helped me much. (The *Einstein* entry dealt with his life—his bad grades in geography, his love of sailing —but not his theories).

Julie and I shamelessly eavesdrop on a tour for a visiting high school group. The tour guide—a nice Asian man who took frequent sips from his plastic cup of water—is trying to spice Einstein up for his teenage audience. He says things like, "Einstein was as famous as Justin Timberlake, J. Lo and Ashton Kutcher combined." The kids seem impressed, if skeptical.

Our guide explains something called the Michelson-Morley experiment, which proved that a beam of light projected from a moving object does not go faster than one from a stationary object. Light's a weird animal, he says. As counterintuitive as it may be, it doesn't behave like a Frisbee or softball tossed from a moving pickup truck. It behaves like nothing else.

"Einstein said the speed of light is the same relative to any observer," says our guide. "That's the special case of relativity. If the speed of light is the same, what changes? Time."

Whenever I feel that I'm understanding something profound, I get a little head rush that starts in the back of the neck and shoots toward my forehead. I love that head rush—I used to get it all the time back in my golden intellectual days. And right now, I'm getting a powerful one. The special theory of relativity clicked. I get it. See? That Einstein wasn't in another league from me. If I had been presented with the same data, I might well have come up with the same theory. Right?

On the other hand, the general theory of relativity, which we tackle next, is a bit more complex. The guide talks about how the universe is like Jell-O with an unappetizing fruit cocktail mixed into it—bananas, pineapples, strawberries, you name it. "That's the general theory of relativity," he says. The high school students nod politely. "Space is like the Jell-O. Space is beautiful. We are the blobs of fruit. We mess up space. We bend space. We are the blobs." The Jell-O metaphor isn't quite working for me. No head rush this time. Maybe it's true—I'm no Einstein.

The room we're in has a bunch of his original papers on the wall—papers scribbled with equations and notations that are light-years over my head. Well, at least I know that Berserkers fought naked. You think Einstein knew that? Probably not. Did he know that Hawthorne was obsessed with the number 64 or that Caravaggio killed a man during tennis? Doubt it. As the general theory of relativity slips farther from my grasp, that cushions my ego just a bit.

"You had enough?" I ask Julie. She has, so we increase our life span by walking home at a quick clip.

migration

Julie's going to Seattle this Wednesday to visit her college friend Peggy. A nice little five-day jaunt. She made the reservations several months ago—back when we were confident she'd be plumped up in second trimester by now. But she's not. Still zero signs of any in utero action. Insanely frustrating. Julie and I agreed that she shouldn't be held hostage by our never-ending fertility woes. Plus, she's 90 percent sure that she ovulated on Tuesday, and won't be releasing a single gamete while in Seattle. So off she goes in a cab to JFK Airport.

And that's when I begin to worry. What if she's wrong? What about that 10 percent chance that she is, in fact, ovulating on Wednesday or Thursday or Friday? Should we gamble with this? Should we risk never having a kid because I wanted to stay in New York and Julie wanted to go kayaking with her old pal?

By Thursday midafternoon, I'm on the phone with an airline ticket agent doing some serious damage to my Visa card in exchange for a round-trip weekend reservation to Seattle. I'm migrating. That's the way I think of it. I am migrating thousands of miles to spawn. I'm not so different from the North American eel, which, after fifteen years of paddling around in streams, suddenly sprouts enlarged eyes, turns from yellow to silver, and swims hundreds and hundreds of miles down the streams and out into the ocean and all the way to the warm waters of the Sargasso Sea (east of the Caribbean), where it does its reproductive business.

That's me on Friday evening, with enlarged eyes, sitting in the aft of an American Airlines jet and migrating to another time zone. (Incidentally, Charles Lindbergh was the first pilot on what would become American Airlines).

I get to Seattle by midnight—but the migration isn't over. I have to take a cab to the ferry, which will in turn take me to the obscure hippyish island on which Peggy lives. The ferry, it turns out, doesn't run all that often after midnight. So for an hour and a half, I'm stuck sitting on a dock with a couple of in-lust teenagers, an angry-looking burly man who resembles an extra in a sixties motorcycle gang movie, and an oddly well-appointed middle-aged woman. It's too dark to read my trusty *Britannica*. So I'm left staring at my fellow cast of ferry waiters.

The teens grope some more. The angry man seethes. And the middle-aged woman applies some lipstick. I hope for her sake the lipstick is not made from cinnabar, like the red war paint of 19th-century Indians in California. Cinnabar is mercury ore, and the Indians' red war paint—unbeknownst to them—actually made them sick from mercury poisoning. Maybe that'd be a good way to stop wars, I think. Camouflage paint that makes everyone sick.

Well, it's not a particularly profound thought, my cinnabar rumination. But I have the pleasant realization that I'm not bored. I'm sitting here with nothing to do—no books, no TV, no friends, no deck of cards—and normally I'd be going out of my gourd, but I'm not. I'm fine. I've got my war paint to think about. Thanks to the *Britannica,* my brain is like a playroom, lots of little toys to keep me occupied. Or, to switch metaphors, my rambling trains of thought now have much more interesting landscapes out their windows.

When I finally get to hug Julie hello, it's 3 A.M. And my migration isn't quite over. I still have to spawn. After a fourteen-hour door-to-door trip, I have no interest in spawning whatsoever. But if those eels can do it after swimming hundreds of miles, I can make the effort after a ferry ride. This had better work.

Milton, John

The British poet went blind because he read too late at night while at school. That's something I've learned: scholarship is dangerous. There's a platoon of men who've gone blind (sometimes in both eyes, sometimes in one), who've gotten curvature of the spine, who've suffered exhaustion from too much reading. It makes me feel like my quest—despite its couch-bound nature—is actually treacherous, which gives me a macho thrill.

mime

Poor mime. Everyone loves to mock the mime. Zima, Carrot Top, mime—these are the prefab punch lines of my adulthood. And admittedly, mime is not my favorite form of entertainment. But maybe mime would get a little more respect if people learned of its glorious past. Well, actually, it's not-so-glorious past. More like it's lascivious and demonic past.

Mime started in Greco-Roman times and—well, maybe I should let the *Britannica* explain: "Though only fragments exist, it is clear that the usual mime plot, while free to indulge in biting topical allusion, centered principally on scenes of adultery and other vice. Evidence exists that acts of adultery were actually performed on the mime stage during the Roman empire. Execution scenes with convicted criminals in place of actors are on record."

So there you go. Live sex acts, actual executions—I have to say, that does sound more interesting than a guy in white face paint wrestling with an invisible umbrella.

minimalism

In my defense, I'm exercising a lot of willpower. Julie and I were having lunch in a little town outside Seattle, and her friend Peggy—observing the darkening clouds—said: "Look at that moody sky."

I did *not* say, as I was tempted to: "You just committed the pathetic fallacy" (which is when you assign emotions to inanimate objects). This wasn't easy. People need to realize that.

miscellany

A new trivia book is coming out called *Schott's Original Miscellany*. It's a slim and charming volume that features, among other things, the complete list of Elizabeth Taylor husbands, a glossary of waitress argot, and a catalogue of rock star deaths. The publishing company wants *Esquire* to cover it, so they've invited me—and a handful of other journalists—to dinner with the author, a British bloke named Ben Schott. I figured, why not? Schott and I can trade trivia, maybe have a little brain-to-brain combat.

The dinner is held at a high-decibel Italian restaurant called Da Silvano in Greenwich Village. Unfortunately, I am seated at the round table at the exact farthest point from Schott. The only way I can interact with him is if I call him on his cell phone, or maybe by engaging in the elaborate greeting ritual of the black-tailed prairie dog, which involves throwing its foreparts vigorously into the air, directing its nose straight up, and uttering an abrupt *yip*.

With Schott out of reach, I'm stuck talking to my table mate, a woman who says she works for a small New York paper. She is unusually attractive for a journalist, with long black hair and a face that wouldn't look out of place in a Tommy Hilfiger catalog. She is also, I decide, completely insane. Either that, or she's more hammered than I've seen anyone since my friend John drank fourteen Olde English 800s in college.

"My mother loves Ben," she confides to me.

"Oh, how does your mother know about Ben?" I ask. I figure this is a fair question, since the book hasn't been released in America, and Ben resides full-time in London. But she chooses not to answer it directly, instead saying this: "My mother loves him so much that she bought a house so she could communicate with him."

She smiles at me and bites her lower lip. As the dinner wears on, I figure out that was sort of her trademark: make a cryptic statement, then smile and chew on her lip. She also enjoys rearranging her hair so that it covers her face completely, giving her a little private time to come up with new cryptic statements.

But anyway, back to her mother, who had me truly perplexed. "I'm sorry, I don't follow," I say.

"She bought a house so she could communicate with him," she repeats.

I still shake my head.

"In Costa Rica," she says. Her tone indicates that she thinks this will clarify things once and for all, and that maybe I should stop asking all these dumb questions.

I don't care how much knowledge I have, there is just no way to process this information. So the dinner is looking to be quite the waste of time. But a couple of hours—and several plates of carbs—later, I do finally weasel my way into a seat next to Ben Schott. So in the end, I suppose I didn't need a semaphore to communicate with him.

Turns out he is a lovely chap. That's what I'd call him, a chap. Very genteel, much like the *Britannica* itself. He is well groomed and sharply dressed, self-effacing, and he seems just pleased as punch to meet me.

We trade some talk about our favorite defenestrations—he likes the second one in Prague that kicked off the Thirty Years' War. Then I figure I'll impress him with some of the Britishisms I've picked up in my *Britannica*. If you recall, I'd already scored a big success in this department with the Coriander/Cilantro Incident of 2003. So I feel I am in safe territory.

"So do you think we'll have an old wives' summer this year?" I ask Schott.

He looks at me much the same way I had looked at my dinner companion after she told me about the Costa Rica house.

"You know, an old wives' summer. Isn't that what the British call Indian summer?"

"No, actually we call it Indian summer," he says.

Oh. That's not good. The *Britannica* said it was called old wives' summer in England—but it's hard to argue that to a man who actually speaks the Queen's English.

"Well, I hope the timothy grass didn't give you allergies this year."

Again, confusion.

"Timothy grass—that's what causes allergies in Britain, right? In America we've got ragweed. There you have timothy grass?"

I can feel him about to turn away to talk to an actual journalist who might be interested in discussing his book. So I quickly throw out a final question:

"I was just wondering—what do the British call those machines in Vegas?"

"Oh yes, one-armed bandits."

"No, fruit machines," I say, frustrated.

"Oh yes, we do call them fruit machines. Because they have fruit on the little displays."

I know why they called them fruit machines, dammit. I wanted to clarify to Schott that I'm not a complete dimwit. But too late—he is off and talking to someone else.

I didn't get to impress him with any other British-to-American translations, so I'm printing them here.

•Our "ladybug" is their "ladybird."
•"Lumber" in Britain refers to old furniture.
•What we call "English" in billiards, they call "side."
•A surgeon in Britain is called "Mr." The honorific "Dr." is reserved for physicians.
•Aluminum in Britain is called "aluminium."

We barely speak the same language, I tell you.

After my conversation with Ben ends, I see him having a chat with mysterious Hair Girl. I can't hear what they are saying, but I can tell from the look on his face that she is up to her old cryptic tricks, perhaps the same ones involving communicative Central American houses. I wonder who he finds more baffling: me or her. Sadly, I'm not sure.

missing links

Julie and I are having some friends over tonight. No particular occasion—though it is Paraguay's Independence Day (May 14), so that's more than reason enough.

"Honey, can you get out the cheese knife?" asks Julie.

I could if I knew where it is. I open five drawers before I stumble on the cheese knife. I pick it up and look at it. And look at it some more.

It strikes me at that moment that cheese knives must have quite a story to tell. No doubt, cheese knives have an inventor. Who was he? What was he like? And what about the titans of the cheese knife industry? Who are they? What are the cheese knife legends and rumors? And there must be an eccentric but lovable cheese knife designer who revolutionized its look, right? And then there's cheese knife science—the blade shape best for cutting cheese, the debate over what metal to use in the blade, and what wood varnish to use on the handle.

And I have read none of this in the encyclopedia.

I am staring at the cheese knife for a good twenty seconds, thinking about this, slack-jawed, like someone who dropped too much bad brown acid at Woodstock.

"Great," Julie says, as she returns to the kitchen. "I'll take it."

"Oh yes," I say, snapping awake. "Uh, here's the cheese knife."

The cheese knife revelation sends me into a mini panic. Everything in the world is packed with facts. Just look around the apartment—the little knob on the cabinet, the toaster, the lipstick on Julie's lips, which are right now asking me for the ice tongs. And ice tongs—they have their own history too.

What do I know of these things? Nothing. I am in the *M*s, and I know nothing.

Montaigne

I like this 16th-century French writer quite a bit. I like that he coined the term "essay," which translates to "attempt," or a little "project of trial and error." That's what I want my *Esquire* articles to be. Little attempts, even if my attempts happen to involve more Wonderbra jokes than Montaigne's attempts. It just takes a lot of pressure off when you call them attempts.

But even better than the origin of the word "essay," I like the story of how Marie de Gournay—a French intellectual at the time—fainted from excitement when she read Montaigne's work for the first time. She fainted from reading. What a great image. We've become far too jaded. I've been intrigued, bored, titillated, annoyed, amazed, but I've never even come close to fainting while reading any book.

Which is sad. I wish ideas could still get people so excited that they fainted. I wish people—including me—had a more visceral reaction to reading. The closest I've come to fainting during Operation Britannica was when I felt queasy after reading about the botfly, which lays eggs in horses' nostrils, and I had to stop eating my ice cream sandwich.

moron

I think I'm starting to lose my sense of humor. I was watching a *Friends* rerun with Julie, and there was this scene with Joey, the show's certified moron (Morón, by the way, is also the name of a town in Cuba). In the scene, Joey observes his costar turn a lock. He marvels at this, and says: "It's amazing how keys open doors." It gets a big laugh. It's supposed to show that he's got the IQ of a candelabra.

But all I can think is that, yes, he's right, it *is* amazing how keys open doors. I think back to the diagram in the *lock* section, with all the pin tumblers and springs, and am proud that I finally understand how keys work. I don't understand keys as well as Joseph Bramah—the famed locksmith who created a lock that remained unpicked for fifty years, despite his promise to reward the picker with £200—but still, I understand them. Joey and I—we both know that keys are amazing.

Morozov, Pavlik

Here we have one of the most odious little schmucks in the *Encyclopaedia Britannica*. A truly horrible little human being. And, I'm afraid, one who reminds me a lot of myself as a youngster.

Pavlik was a communist youth who eventually became glorified as a martyr by the Soviet regime.

The son of poor peasants, Morozov was the leader of the Young Pioneers' group at his village school and was a fanatical supporter of the Soviet government's collectivization drive in the countryside. In 1930, at age twelve, he gained notoriety for denouncing his father, the head of the local soviet, to the Soviet authorities. In court Morozov charged that his father had forged documents and sold favours to kulaks (i.e., rich peasants who were resisting the collectivization drive). Morozov also accused other peasants of hoarding their grain and withholding it from the authorities. As a consequence of his denunciations, Morozov was brutally murdered by several local kulaks.

Morozov was subsequently glorified as a martyr by the Soviet regime. Monuments to him were erected in several Soviet cities, and his example as a model communist was taught to several generations of Soviet schoolchildren.

I know I should have felt sorry for young Pavlik. He was, after all, the victim of Stalin's psychotic brainwashing regime. But I couldn't help feeling a bit of glee when I learned he got his comeuppance, the sanctimonious little fuck.

In Pavlik, I saw the worst qualities of myself as a twelve-year-old. That was the age when believed I was the smartest boy in the world. And like Pavlik, I decided I knew far more than my dunderheaded parents. Plus, like Pavlik, I was a Marxist. Somehow, I had gotten my hands on *The Communist Manifesto*. I understood maybe 14 percent of it, but I did like the catchy saying at the end about throwing off chains. So I declared myself a communist.

Some of my childhood intellectual endeavors make me proud—my analysis of Andrew Lloyd Webber's *Starlight Express* comes to mind. That didn't hurt anyone, and I think I might have been right. But this communist phase makes me cringe. I was so thoroughly convinced of my correctness. Embarrassingly so. I couldn't believe my father worked for a capitalist law firm, exploiting secretaries by giving them only four weeks of vacation a year. If there had been proper authorities, I might have called them and denounced him.

Occasionally, I'd engage my father in a debate. I remember one on the beach in East Hampton, as we walked collecting beach glass. My dad said that Marxism was a nice theory—it would be great if there were no poverty and everyone cooperated. But in reality, communism just didn't work. In reply, I gave him one of the half dozen lines I had memorized. It could have been about how communism would cause the "withering away of the state" or that capitalism contains the "seeds of its own destruction." Something like that.

My dad tried to get me to clarify by asking reasonable questions. It soon became clear to both of us that I didn't really understand what those catchphrases meant. Which only got me angrier and more self-righteous. So I repeated my catchphrase, told him that he should read

The Communist Manifesto, and then stomped off the fascist beach. At the very least, I thought to myself, he'll understand when the revolution comes.

I'm not sure what Pavlik's motivation was. But I'm pretty sure, looking back, that this was the intellectual version of our heated games of Wall Ball. My dad had far more knowledge and life experience than me. But if I could just beat him at one thing—if, say, I could overthrow the socio-economic system he was a part of—wouldn't that be something?

Mosconi, Willie

"When his father forbade him to play pool, hoping that he would pursue a career in vaudeville, young Mosconi practiced with potatoes and a broomstick." I like the image of a dad hoping his son will pursue pie-in-the-face humor. But I am also impressed that pool champion Willie followed his dream by using misshapen vegetables. Another inspiring overcoming-the-odds story.

motion

Julie and I drive down to New Jersey for a little suburban Saturday (we buy lower-temperature gas in the morning, at my suggestion). We're going to visit Julie's brother Eric and his wife, Alexandra. As always, we start the day playing mixed doubles with them at their tennis club.

Eric is infuriatingly good at tennis. It reminds me of that fact I read about in the *intelligence* section—the higher the person's IQ, the better he or she is at the thirty-five-yard dash. Maybe the same holds true for tennis. It seems that nature hasn't heard that you're not supposed to put all your eggs in one basket.

Making things worse, Eric is one of those types with a closet full of the proper equipment. Today, he's arrived at the court in his white-collared shirt, white shorts, and white wristbands, all with a tasteful blue trim. He takes out his latest tennis racket, which is made from some material usually reserved for NASA's Mars exploration vehicles.

We begin our pregame leg stretches.

"You up to *L* yet?" Eric asks. "For 'loser'?" He chuckles. "You must have read about aces in the *A* section. You'll be seeing a lot of those."

"Leave my husband alone," says Julie.

"I'm okay, sweetie," I say. I turn to Eric. "After I'm done with you, you're going to need Vladimir Nabokov to give you some lessons."

"What?" Eric says.

"Nabokov was a tennis teacher before he became a writer. He also appeared as an actor in some German movies."

"Well, you're definitely not up to *T* for 'trash-talking,'" says Eric.

"I thought that was very good, A.J.," says Julie.

Julie doesn't actually believe my Nabokov trivia was an appropriate comeback, but she knows what it's like to be tormented by Eric. She endured a childhood of it, including one particularly vicious fight over the merits of Burger King versus McDonald's.

Regardless, I am feeling more confident than usual. I've come up with a bold new strategy. I've been brushing up on the physics I learned in the *Britannica*, visualizing the mechanics of flying spheres, and I've semiconvinced myself that this will make me a better player. I will see the court in angles and forces and arrows. I will be Master of the Natural Laws of Tennis. I will turn knowledge into power, specifically a powerful forehand.

As we warm up, I tell myself to be aware of the Magnus effect. The Magnus effect is what causes tennis balls with topspin to dive downward. It's actually a special case of Bernoulli's Theorem which we can thank for keeping airplanes aloft, and has to do with a greater pressure on top of the ball than under it. Every time the ball comes to me, I watch that yellow fuzzy projectile spin, understand what's going on, and thwack it back. I am doing it! The Master of the Natural Laws of Tennis is in the house! I am playing as well as—if not better than—my impeccably dressed brother-in-law.

"Nice shot, A.J.!" Alexandra says, after one of my down-the-line Magnus-enhanced forehands.

When the match begins, Julie and I jump out into an early and somewhat surprising lead. We're up 2–0. This causes Eric to walk and talk very briskly.

I keep focusing on my beloved Magnus effect. But I'm not forgetting about the parabola of the lob, discovered by Galileo himself. I'm not even forgetting about how gravity is weaker toward the Equator, so the south side of the court should have a little more bounce. Okay, well, I'm trying to forget that one, because that's probably not going to help me. And I'm trying not to get caught up in the Coriolis effect either, which says that a projectile moving north will drift to the east because of the earth's rotation. That won't likely have a huge effect on my ground strokes. But still, the Master of the Natural Laws of Tennis is thwacking back forehands and backhands, visualizing the projectiles in all their Newtonian splendor. We are winning! After one of my knowledge-enhanced forehands, Eric dumps his volley into the net.

"Eric!" shouts Eric.

That's the word I've been waiting to hear. A sure sign that my Harvard-educated, wristband-wearing, cavity-free brother-in-law is pissed as hell at himself. There's no other thing I'd rather hear, with the possible exception of "the pregnancy test is positive."

That makes the game worth it. And that, sadly, is also the highpoint of Julie's and my own parabola. Because, in the end, Eric and Alexandra beat us. As much as I try to keep in mind the Magnus effect, I eventually fall under the sway of my Piss-Poor Backhand effect. So be it. We have had our moment of glory among the yellow spheres.

motion picture

The first true talkie wasn't the *The Jazz Singer,* which the *Britannica* dismisses as "essentially a silent picture with a Vitaphone score and sporadic episodes of synchronized singing and speech." The first 100 percent talkie: *The Lights of New York,* in 1928. More myth shattering, courtesy of the *Britannica.*

Motion Picture Arts and Sciences, Academy of

This is the organization that gives out the Oscars. I know this well, seeing as I spent several weeks every year at *Entertainment Weekly* writing breathless articles about who was going to win those little gold statuettes. In fact, I have firsthand knowledge of the Oscars.

It happened in 1997, right after the movie *Shine*—the one about the schizophrenic pianist—came out, to much critical acclaim. The actor who played the pianist as a young man was named Noah Taylor, a gawky-looking Australian fellow with a pageboy haircut and thick black Kissinger-style glasses. I'm sorry to report that I also had a pageboy haircut and thick black Kissinger-style glasses, not to mention his narrow face and prominent nose. I looked like Noah Taylor's clone, or at least his older brother.

I found out that Noah wouldn't be attending the Oscars, so I decided to go in his stead and write an article about it. It would be an undercover investigation of what it's like to be a movie star. My conclusion: it's pretty damn good.

At first, I was worried that my little ruse wouldn't work. But as soon as I stepped out of the limo in my rented tuxedo and onto the red carpet, the cameras started snapping. The crowd shouted, "Noah! Noah!" the paparazzi jostled, fans demanded my autograph (I wrote, "Shine on!"). I was touched by how many supporters were outraged that I didn't get a nomination. "There's always next year," I said in my fake Australian accent, which sounded remarkably like the Lucky Charms leprechaun.

I gave interviews to eager reporters (I said I wanted to do a big disaster movie next). Chris Farley told me he was a fan. I got so cocky that I went up to Geoffrey Rush—the costar of *Shine,* and a guy who actually knew what the real Noah Taylor looked like, and said perkily, " 'Ello, Geoffrey! It's me!" I've rarely seen anyone so dismayed. It was clear he had no idea who I was, or who I was pretending to be. He backed away slowly.

In any case, having written about them and attended a ceremony, you'd think I'd know a thing or two about the Oscars. And yet, I realized I don't even know what the word "Oscar" refers to. I'm constantly being surprised by my ignorance of the most obvious things, those things that are right under my prominent nose. Why didn't I ever bother to look up the word "Oscar"? Why didn't I even think about it? It turns out—according to the Britannica CD-ROM, which I dipped into at the office today—there are competing theories as to the origin of the name Oscar. Some say the academy librarian came up with the name, because the statuette looked like her uncle Oscar. But Bette Davis liked to take credit, saying the "backside" of the statue looked like her husband, Harmon Oscar Nelson. "Backside" is *Britannica*-speak for "ass."

Mozart

When he was thirteen, he heard the secret chorus of the Sistine Choir and copied it out from memory. I need a memory like that. Maybe he used Dave Farrow's memory techniques.

mule

Julie's not pregnant. My Seattle trip was a failure. Three thousand miles and way too much money for nothing. When this kid comes, he'd better appreciate what we're doing for him. If he comes. I see the word "sterile" in the write-up of the mule (offspring of a male donkey and a female horse) and the hinny (a female donkey and a male horse) and it kills me.

Mussolini, Benito

I wasn't totally ignorant about Il Duce. A few years ago, I had done some cursory research on the fascist dictator for a TV show I worked on. At the time, my friend Rick and I were writing freelance scripts for something called *Celebrity Deathmatch*, which was one of MTV's more sophisticated offerings. It featured clay figurines of famous people beating each other up and playfully ripping out each other's internal organs. The first match was between Hillary Clinton and Monica Lewinsky. But by the time I got there, the show was running out of both celebrities and new types of internal organs to pluck out (the kidney had been removed far too often, I was told; try the spleen or pancreas). Rick and I were assigned to write a match between two Italian stallions: goose-stepping tyrant Benito Mussolini and Oscar-winning actor Roberto Benigni. So I dutifully read up on Mussolini. I remember being dismayed to learn that he started his career as a journalist. My profession already falls between telemarketers and international weapons dealers in the list of least respected career choices; we don't need murderous World War II leaders on our team. In any case, that's what stuck in my mind. (By the way, in case you're wondering, the death match ended with a stunning upset: Benigni won by tossing Mussolini in the air like a pizza pie. I told you. Sophisticated.)

The *Britannica* gave me a whole new look at Mussolini. Namely, I got a fascinating insight into a bizarre theme that ran through his life: mistresses.

Mussolini grew up poor, his family crowded into two rooms on the second floor of a small, dilapidated palazzo in the town of Predappio. His dad was a blacksmith who, the *Britannica* says, "spent most of his money on his mistress. The meals that were eaten by his children were meager." So Benito must have had some serious issues with Papa Mussolini. And he must have thought that a mistress was a high-heeled incarnation of evil itself. Here was this strumpet drinking pricey Chianti and wearing gold earrings, while Benito was lucky to get a few strings of vermicelli for dinner. An angry young man, Mussolini spent his youth getting into trouble and stabbing fellow students at his school with his penknife.

Then, in 1909, when he was twenty-seven, Mussolini fell in love with a sixteen-year-old girl named Rachele Guidi. Where'd he meet Rachele? On a blind date? At a boccie game? No, he met Rachele because she was the daughter of his father's mistress. Jesus, those are some twisted family dynamics. Marrying the offspring of your father's wicked mistress? (Rachele was a daughter from the mistress's deceased husband). I would *not* want to do the seating arrangements at that wedding. If there was a turn-of-the-century Italian version of *Jerry Springer,* the Mussolinis would have been prime guests.

You wonder if Mussolini, who in his spare time went on to create worldwide havoc and oppress millions, might have learned from his childhood that mistresses are hurtful and wrong. Nope. At the end of his life, when he was strung up by his heels at a gas station in Milan, who was strung up alongside him? His mistress Claretta Petacci.

I wanted to know more about Claretta. I wanted to know if there was something kinky going on there, too, like maybe she was the cleaning lady of his father's mistress. I gave into temptation and went on Google, the *Britannica*'s less trustworthy rival, but one that, admittedly, does have a fact or two not found in the *EB*. Google didn't turn up much on Claretta, but I did find something very strange: Mussolini had another mistress in the 1930s. This woman, named Margherita Sarfatti, came to the United States to try to get Benito some good PR; she eventually got a job as a pro-fascist columnist for the Hearst newspaper chain. And here's the really startling part: she was Jewish.

I guess my point is, Mussolini had some serious relationship issues, for which we can probably thank his father. Try as you might, you can't escape your upbringing; fascist dictators don't fall far from the tree. I'm happy to report my father never squired a mistress around New York. His mistresses were reading and knowledge and big thick books. So I've inherited that weakness—but at least I'm not breaking any commandments, banning free elections, or making staccato speeches.

mutualism

The relationship between two species in which both are benefited. Thank God. I needed a dose of goodness. It hasn't been easy, reading about the natural world. I knew it was a jungle out there, but I didn't know the jungle was quite so violent, bleak, dangerous, deceitful, and cutthroat. Over the last few thousand pages, I've read dozens and dozens of brilliant and creative ways that animals have figured out to kill one another. There's the anglerfish, a fish that snags its prey with its own little fishing rod that comes out of its back. Not to be confused with the archerfish, which knocks its prey off overhanging branches with a stream of spit. Or the ambush bug, which traps butterflies with pincers and sucks out their bodily fluids. And that's just a tiny sampling of the *A*s.

I was particularly disturbed to read about the cuckoo. I knew from Cocoa Puffs commercials that the cuckoo might have a personality disorder, but I never imagined the depth of its depravity. The cuckoo is what is called an aggressive mimic. The female cuckoo surreptitiously lays her eggs in the nests of other species. The unsuspecting mom of the other species—who is fooled because the cuckoo eggs look like her own eggs—will hatch the baby cuckoo, which proceeds to murder its adoptive brothers and sisters by pushing the other eggs out of the nest. The prick.

So you can see, it can get upsetting. Which is why it was so good to arrive at mutualism. Finally, some happy stories in nature, like the sweet tale of the intestinal flagellated protozoans and the termites. The protozoans live inside the termites' stomachs. The two species would never survive without each other, but together, the termites eat the wood and the protozoans help digest it, and they live happily together. The end. Or take the wrasse, a cleaner fish that does a little dance to tell the big fish it's time for some dental work. And the big fish relaxes, opens its mouth, and lets the wrasse eat its leftovers.

I need to focus more on this side of life. As Julie always reminds me, I have to fight my tendency toward pessimism. In general, I don't just see the glass as half empty, I see the glass as half empty and the water as teeming with microbes and the rim as smudged and the liquid as evaporating quickly. Julie is always telling me to look for the good in the world, and she's right. The *Britannica* is a perfect test case. Since these thirty-two volumes present all of life—from the incomprehensibly horrible to the inspiringly wonderful—I just have to find the wonderful and celebrate that. Yes, I realize that for every happy partnership, there's a thousand bugs ejecting toxic saliva at their prey. Still, I'd rather be deluded than depressed.

myrrh

So that's what myrrh is. Frankincense I knew, and gold I was familiar with, but myrrh always mystified me. It's a substance obtained from small trees and was used both as incense and to relieve sore gums. And that's it. I'm finished with the *M*s. I have ingested thirteen of the twenty-six letters finished—I should know 50 percent of all knowledge.

Actually, more than 50 percent. The *Britannica* frontloads its letters, so the *A*s and *B*s and *C*s are longer than they deserve to be—not to mention that the second half of the alphabet has *Q, X, Y,* and *Z,* which each comes in at barely longer than a novella.

N

names

Julie and I have been talking about names for our yet-to-be-conceived child. Julie's both an unflagging optimist and a planner, so she figures we should get started now. She's already got a list in her Palm Pilot—Max, Jasper, Kaya, Maya.

Thanks to the *Britannica*, I've got lots of new ideas. Over dinner one night, I decide to test them out.

"I've got a good name for the kid," I tell her.

"Oh yeah?"

"How about Crippled Jacobs?"

"That's a horrible thing to say," she says.

"No, it's just that many cultures use bad names to scare off demons. Crippled Jacobs or Ugly Jacobs—that kind of thing."

"Uh, no."

"They're called apotropaic names."

No response.

"How about Mshweshwe Jacobs? After the founder of the Sotho nation. He changed his name to Mshweshwe, which is supposed to be the sound a knife makes when shaving."

I mimed a little shaving. "Mshweshwe."

"Probably not."

"What about Odd? *O-d-d*. Like Odd Hassel, a Norwegian chemist who won the Nobel Prize."

"Oh, that one I really like," Julie says. "That one sounds just great."

Napoleon

Finally, I arrive at the little big man himself. In an odd way, I feel like I know Napoleon already. Dozens of bits and pieces about the French emperor have bobbed up in the previous eighteen thousand pages, giving me an unfinished but compelling portrait. I know, among other things:

• A disgruntled Aaron Burr tried to get Napoleon to conquer Florida.

• Napoleon was a Zionist—or at least "thought of establishing a Jewish state in the ancient lands of Israel."

• Napoleon loved ice-skating.

• The Napoleonic Wars were so expensive, England started the first income tax to pay for them.

• A French soldier named Nicolas Chauvin showed such simpleminded devotion to Napoleon, he is memorialized in the word "chauvinism."

• Napoleon used balloons for military reconnaissance, and appointed a man named Nicolas Conté—who also invented the pencil—to be head of the balloon corps.

• Napoleon knew he might want to dump Josephine someday, so when he married her, the crafty emperor made sure there wasn't a parish priest present at the ceremony. This slight technicality allowed him to dispose of her without a sticky divorce.

• Napoleon commissioned a sculptor named Antonio Canova to make a huge statue of himself in the style of a classical heroic nude. (This one I find particularly surprising. Can you see George W. Bush allowing a statue of himself nude? Clinton, maybe. But most of today's leaders like their nipples covered.)

• Napoleon's sister slept with Metternich, the Austrian statesman.

• Napoleon sold the western half of the United States to Jefferson for less than three cents an acre.

It's a bizarre collection of Napoleon arcana, an admittedly idiosyncratic portrait of the man, but I'm kind of proud of it. I like its randomness. Maybe that says something about me—that I'm overly attracted to the quirks of history. Or maybe it's because I'm trying to justify the days and days I've spent reading the encyclopedia. But in true Napoleonic style, I prefer to see something grander in my grab bag of Bonaparte lore. I prefer to think that it proves just how interwoven history is. Napoleon didn't just affect 19th-century European alliances, he affected income taxes and hot air balloons and my parents' private joke during the eighties that my dad was a male chauvinist pig, which led to a rash of pig-related gifts for his birthday every year, including pig salt and pepper shakers.

As for the *Napoleon* entry proper, it's fine. Nothing spectacular. He was a brilliant general, he and the pope weren't the best of buddies, he loved his Voltaire. I'm still, at the end, convinced that the heap of Napoleonic slivers was more revealing.

Nation, Carry

The formidable, nearly six-foot woman who fought for Prohibition by smashing barrooms with her trademark hatchet. According to the *Britannica*, "she also railed against fraternal orders, tobacco, foreign foods, corsets, skirts of improper length, and mildly pornographic art of the sort found in some barrooms of the time." Tobacco and short skirts I can see. But foreign foods? What's so evil about those? I had no idea this was controversial. I'm glad Carry Nation lost, and I live in a world where I can eat my mooshu vegetables with impunity.

national park

Julie and I are spending the weekend in my parents' house in East Hampton. It's a nice house, with tasteful wood floors and a classic porch—and lots and lots of buffalo knickknacks. That's the main decorating motif: 21st-century bison. Buffalo signs, buffalo mugs, buffalo photos, buffalo stuffed animals.

This buffalo invasion is a result of yet another one of my father's practical jokes. It's a story I've heard so many times, I think I can get it right. When their friends the Odells bought a house in East Hampton, my mom and dad hatched a plan. They sent an official-looking note to the Odells— on faux government letterhead—announcing that the Odells' just-purchased land had been claimed by the National Park Service as federal grazing area for the endangered buffalo. My dad threw in some legalese like "eminent domain," and they signed a bureaucratic-sounding name.

The Odells, my parents guessed, would figure out the perpetrators. They didn't. So my parents took it to the next level: they got my aunt—a former actress—to show up unannounced at the Odells'. My aunt was wearing safari shorts and a pith helmet, clipboard in hand, and she demanded the Odells evacuate for the buffalos. Doors were slammed. Calls were made to the police. My aunt retreated.

This is how my parents spend their time.

When the Odells figured out the responsible parties, they retaliated by sending my parents several pounds of bison jerky. This resulted in an escalating buffalo merchandise war. One day, the Odells are going to get really pissed, and my parents will come home to find a bloody buffalo carcass in the living room.

In any case, we arrive in time for Saturday lunch, which entails eating off buffalo plates and drinking out of buffalo glasses.

Naturally, I open with a buffalo fact—how could I not? I point out that the town of Buffalo, New York, was probably not named for the animal, since there aren't any buffalos in Buffalo. The most popular theory is that the name is a mispronunciation of the French phrase *beau fleuve*, or "beautiful river," in reference to Buffalo Creek.

My buffalo knowledge exhausted, the topic somehow drifts to former child stars—I think the connection was a new show with Emmanuel Lewis—and my father chimes in:

"One of the *Brady Bunch* kids became a porn star."

Huh. I thought about that. I wasn't sure that was true. And Julie—she knew that wasn't true. You don't mess with Julie on *Brady Bunch* knowledge.

"No," she says. "I can tell you what they became. None of them became porn stars." And she told us: Cindy was a sneaker designer, Bobby became a cameraman, Marcia had a sitcom a couple of years ago.

Nice one, I think to myself, as she continues ticking off the stars. Good for Julie. My dad may be more knowledgeable than Julie and me about a lot of areas, but Sherwood Schwartz sitcoms is not one of them.

neat's-foot oil
This is a pale yellow oil derived from boiling the feet of cattle. Good Lord. I'm trying to eat an apricot fruit roll here.

nervous system
Much more detail on brain damage. This time, quantified detail. After the age of twenty, humans lose 50,000 brain cells a day to atrophy. You probably lost a couple of dozen just reading that sentence. Whoops! There go a bunch more. I still have enough neurons to do a quick calculation on my Palm Pilot: since my twentieth birthday, about 30 million of my precious bits of gray matter have gone belly up. Thirty million! Sure, I've got a few billion left, but still.

I'm glad I didn't know this back in my carbon-monoxide-obsessed days. But now it's more incentive to keep reading—I've got to compensate for my evaporating cortex.

New Year
In India, there's the ritual boiling of rice. In Thailand, people throw water playfully at one another. Here's one of those rare times that I know more, thanks to my sister's husband Willy, a native of Cuzco: in Peru, on New Year's, women wear yellow underwear.

Newton, Isaac
Before my reeducation, I knew the basic points about Sir Isaac: British scientist, believer in deism, discoverer of gravity, alleged victim of a falling apple. The *Britannica* doesn't fully endorse the apple theory, calling it an unconfirmed legend. But I was pleased to learn that Newton's verified inspiration for his theory of gravity is just as interesting as falling fruit—maybe more so.

Newton's revelation came during a six-year self-imposed exile from British society. It was 1678, and he had just suffered the first of his nervous breakdowns, which caused him to lock himself away in his home. Yes, Newton was a complete nut job, the angriest and nastiest scientist in history. The *Britannica* comes right out and uses the phrase "pronounced psychotic tendencies."

Among his many feuds was one with philosopher John Locke, to whom he sent strange, paranoid letters accusing Locke of trying to "entangle [him] with women." Newton also hated the German philosopher Gottfried Wilhelm Leibniz. The two were in a battle over who had invented calculus, and toward the end of his life, Newton expended an enormous amount of energy discrediting Leibniz—even after Leibniz died. As the *Britannica* puts it: "Almost any paper on any subject from those years is apt to be interrupted by a furious paragraph against the German philosopher. . . . In the end, only Newton's death ended his wrath."

But back to gravity. So Newton had gone AWOL for several years. Up to that point, he had been a traditional 17th-century mechanistic scientist who saw the world as a bunch of billiard balls colliding. There was no such thing as action at a distance. But during his seclusion, Newton became obsessed with occult works about alchemy and magic treatises, many of them in what was called the hermetic tradition, even copying these texts by hand. These occult books talked about substances having mysterious sympathies and antipathies toward one another, forces that could affect something even without touching it.

This unconventional idea allowed Newton to take the intellectual leap. This was his apple. The occult forces inspired him to envision forces of attraction and repulsion that worked at a distance, a breakthrough that eventually led to his theory of universal gravity.

This, to me, is fascinating. Newton—the man who finally gave us a vision of the universe as a rational and orderly place—couldn't have done it without the help of those weird occult books. Is there a lesson there? I think so. I'm going to keep my mind open, try to be more tolerant of unorthodox ideas, because even the kookiest of them can inspire a profound theory. Maybe I shouldn't be so dismissive of the Kabbalah, or tarot cards, or my New Age aunt from Berkeley who swears that staring at the sun for two minutes every morning is good for your health. No, that last one is crazy.

nonfictional prose

It's Sunday morning and Dad invites Julie and me to the beach. My father loves the beach. Or more precisely, he loves sitting on the beach. The temperature doesn't matter. He's not interested in paddleball or Frisbee. He just likes to sit in his beach chair and work. He either works on his twenty-fifth law book or he reads hardbacks—big important nonfiction hardbacks.

Like many in his generation, he is drawn to the real information, the kind with fiber and vitamins and minerals, not the Ring Ding-quality information I fill up on. My dad devours books like Ezekiel. He reads so intently on the beach that my mother once painted him a T-shirt with the following image: his beach hat floating on the ocean. The implication was that he'd be so engrossed in his reading and writing, he wouldn't notice if the tide rose and swallowed him up. I think he might read right through the apocalypse. He'd just brush those raining frogs off the page. He might look up, make a mental note that the ocean had turned to blood, then get back to business.

He's got the same weakness I have—we both love information so much, we tend to choose it over actual experience. Case in point: when we'd go on trips to Europe, he'd bring along his Fodor's. We'd get to the Parthenon, and Dad would read passages aloud from the guidebook about its history—the role of Athena and the Centaurs and the Doric columns. Then he'd lower the book, glance at the decaying big marble building for exactly three seconds, then be ready for his next chapter, uh, tourist attraction. And I'm happy to do the same. Which is what I tell Dad. I won't be able to make it to the beach, but there's an excellent section in the *Britannica* on waves, and how they break when the wave depth equals 1.3 times the wave height.

norms

Julie and I are on line at JFK's Alitalia counter. We're off on a week-long trip to Italy to attend the Memorial Day wedding of our friends Rick and Ilene.

I'm worried that we'll be stopped by security. Won't three clunky volumes of the *Encyclopaedia Britannica* passing through the X-ray machine raise a red flag? It's not exactly the usual vacation-friendly Elmore Leonard paperback. But apparently, Alitalia has respect for scholarship, because we breeze right through.

The flight is an overnight one, and after reading about nonsense verse and Nordic skiing, I slip my *Britannica* into the seat pocket and lie back for a nap. I get about ninety seconds of sleep before it starts. The snoring. Two rows behind us, in row 17, seat D, we've got a snorer. This isn't regular snoring—this is Fred Flintstone–style snoring. It's about the same decibel level as the two-thousand-pound jet engine hanging from the wing. I expect to see the window shades go up and down in its rhythm.

"My God," I say.

"Wow," says Julie, who has pushed her eyeshades up to her forehead.

I turn around. There he is, his mouth agape, a meaty doofus, red-faced and plump as a Tuscan tomato, squeezed into a tight yellow tank top. I'm not alone. I notice a dozen others like myself turned around in their seats, marveling at this acoustic phenomenon. No one within a seven-row radius is sleeping.

A stewardess walks by, and I'm just cranky enough to stop her.

"Can you wake him up?" I ask.

"I'm sorry, that's not our policy," she says, in an Italian accent.

"But no one on the plane can sleep."

"We don't wake passengers up unless there's a safety reason."

"Well, actually, sleep apnea can be quite dangerous. You can lose oxygen to the brain for up to a half minute."

Doesn't seem to register. "You can wake him yourself if you want."

She walks off. Damn. I consider poking the pudgy snorer in the arm and running away, but decide instead on the better strategy of hating him from afar.

Every couple of minutes the snoring stops, and I have a false moment of hope, but then it revs back up again. I'm screwed. All the knowledge in the world can't solve this dilemma. That said, my scholarship does help me in one way: I can now see the snoring situation through a clear historical and philosophical framework.

"This is a classic ethical dilemma," I say to Julie. "Classic."

Julie studies me. She isn't sure if this is going to be more or less pleasant than the sound of the snoring.

"I read about this in the *ethics* section," I continue. "We've got here a clear-cut example of utilitarianism versus deontology."

"Meaning what?"

I explain: the utilitarians believe in the greatest good for the greatest number. So they'd wake him up. If the philosopher Jeremy Bentham were pushing the dessert cart on Alitalia, you can bet your ass that the Snoring Wonder over there would be wide awake, with some espresso forced down his throat for good measure.

But deontologists would let him sleep, because they believe in personal rights. Unfortunately, our flight attendant is a deontologist. Deontologists say that if you're all starving in a lifeboat, you still don't have the right to kill and eat the sickest person.

Julie seems mildly interested—more than average, anyway.

"And which are you?"

"Well, I think we should wake the snoring jackass up. So I guess I'm a utilitarian."

"Huh," says Julie.

"Unless I was the one doing the snoring. Then I'm a deontologist."

Julie laughs. But sadly, I'm not really joking. I'm a utilitarian for other people and a deontologist for myself. Clearly, I could use a little more growing in the morals department. But at least I know how to label the theories. Which makes me feel better.

North Italy

I was hoping that the *Britannica* would be a good substitute for an Italian-English dictionary. I was crossing my fingers that the *Italy* section would tell me how to order my pizza with no anchovies and ask how far to the nearest taxi stand. No such luck. That's not to say the *Britannica* lacks handy-phrase translations—they just aren't in Italian. Just so you know, I've compiled a little phrase book of things I've learned how to say:

English: Let us, each one of us, move indeed to the west across the creek.
Hokan Native American language: *Yabanaumawildjigumma-ha'nigi.*

English: The girl ate mush and three biscuits but she wasn't satisfied.
Traditional Gullah slave language: *Uma-chil' nyamnyam fufu an t'ree roll-roun, but 'e ain't been satify.*

English: You are going to remain lying down.
Haitian Creole: *T-ale reste kushe.*

English: I have good friends.
Esperanto: *Mi havas bonajn amikojn.*

I'm not sure why the *Britannica* in all its wisdom chose those particular phrases to translate. But if I'm ever walking to a Starbucks on the other side of a Hokan reservation and there's a creek in the way, I'm in excellent shape to encourage my Hokan pals to cross it. Also, I can stage a kidnapping in Haiti. But *mi havas no Italian chops.*

This was troublesome. Italy was beautiful and all, and the food was tasty, but I felt helpless, more helpless than I'd felt since this project began. Just finding our hotel in Venice took an exhausting variety of verbal gymnastics and hand signals and maps.

My insecurity only got worse when we met up with our friends Peter and Sharon and their new baby boy, the three of whom jetted down from London, where they are currently living, to join us for a couple of days. Peter—a tall and chiseled tax lawyer—is a smart one. Whenever we play charades, Peter always puts in obscure historical figures instead of the accepted fare of former MTV veejays or eighties pop stars. His Tenzing Norgay—the Sherpa who accompanied Edmund Hillary up Mount Everest—caused an uproar. Naturally, Peter also speaks fluent Italian. At meals, Julie and I would haltingly place our orders, and then Peter would converse with the waiter for several minutes, spitting out rapid vowel-filled Italian, and the waiter would laugh and slap Peter merrily on the back. Then Peter would turn back to us as if nothing had happened. No translation. What the hell was he saying? I worried it was some variation on "Did you notice that the guy I'm with is a hairy little Jew? Check it out. It's true."

As is customary in Italy, we spend a lot of time eating. We sit for hours in restaurants on various piazzas, with Sam, their baby boy—just six weeks old—alternately attaching himself to Sharon's breast and speaking loudly in what sounded like Hokan Native American language.

"Hey, Sam," says Sharon. "Look over here! Look at Mommy!" Sam turned his eyes toward Sharon, but then rolled his head back and began studying the ceiling.

"If you want him to look at you, you should probably wear more red," I say. "Studies show that babies are attracted to the color red."

I look around for a prop. Our napkins are red, so I wave mine in front of Sam's face until his eyes wander over to it.

"See?"

I've been paying close attention to the child-rearing sections, as Julie and I are hoping to have a breast-loving, head-rolling infant of our own soon.

Sharon says she'll think about my tip.

"He's getting enough vitamin K, right?" I ask. "Because infants' large intestines don't have the bacteria needed to produce vitamin K."

"Well, he's breast-feeding."

"Doesn't matter. You still might want to supplement."

"Uh-huh."

"Just a thought. Right, Sammy boy?"

I stroke the outside of his foot.

"You ticklish, Sam?" Sharon asks. "Is Uncle A.J. tickling you?"

"Actually, I'm not tickling him. I'm testing his Babinski reflex." When you gently scratch the outside of an infant's foot, his big toe is supposed to go upward and his small toes are supposed to spread. I stroke the foot, and Sam's toes sort of spread, though the pinky toe seems to do most of the shifting. "See that? The Babinski reflex. Goes away after the fourth month. Looks like Sam's in good shape, so don't worry."

If Julie and I can't have a child of our own, at least I can show our exasperatingly fertile friends that I know more about babies than they do.

After lunch, we go to Peggy Guggenheim's museum. It's a lovely, clean, white modern art museum on the Grand Canal with a yard where Peggy buried her many beloved dogs. They have an elaborate grave for themselves, worthy of Ramses II.

As we walk through the museum, Peter stands in front of the paintings with his hand on his chin for minutes at a time. He is appreciating the art. He is appreciating the bejesus out of this art.

I am jealous. Thanks to the *Britannica*, I am pretty up on my art history, but I still don't have the patience to look at any of the pieces for more than a few seconds each. What is Peter seeing that is so fascinating? Does he know the paintings aren't going to move? They haven't moved in eighty years, and they aren't about to start now. But he sees something in there.

The museum is located in Peggy's former home, and in her living room, there's a famous sculpture called *Bird in Space* by Constantin Brancusi. Created in the 1920s, this abstract work looks more like a very elegant copper carrot than a bird. I happen to know a good piece of trivia about *Bird in Space,* which I decide to share with the art-appreciating Peter.

"You know, Brancusi got in trouble when he tried to bring this to the States. The U.S. government accused him of trying to secretly import an industrial part into the country."

"Really?"

"Yeah, almost got him arrested."

"That's fascinating."

Peter is genuinely intrigued, and seems happy that I taught him something. He is, clearly, far more evolved than me.

number games

It can be a desolate trek, this encyclopedia reading. Yes, I know: I signed up for it voluntarily, which makes it tough to elicit sympathy from friends and family. But it's still a lonely mission. I'm on the bed in the hotel, an hour after Julie has gone to sleep, reading in silence, no music, no TV, just the *Britannica* and me, as I wade through sentences such as this one: "During diagenesis, most of the magnesian calcites were transformed into stable assemblages of rather pure calcite, often along with scattered grains of dolomite." You still there? Good.

I'm tempted to skip. And I have skipped a few times, but I always feel guilty enough to go back to give hoop skirts (or Herbert Hoover or whatever the victim was) a good skim. Or a decent skim. In any case, a man's got to find ways to keep himself amused. I've become a master of this. I've developed dozens of little games. Here are just three:

1. *The Count the Carpets Game.* Every few pages, the *Britannica* features yet another in a dizzying array of carpet patterns. You've got your Bakhtiari, Balochi, Bergama, Bijar, Bokhara, and on and on. It feels like a very well organized Middle Eastern bazaar.

2. *The Spot the Celebrity Look-Alike Contest.* Here's a fun visual game based on the little black-and-white pictures in the *Britannica*. Eighteenth-century French scholar Firmin Abauzit? He looks like Kevin Spacey! Karl Abel, a noted viola player of the 18th-century, is a dead ringer for Drew Carey.

3. *The Worst Ruler Competition.* History is brimming with evil leaders you've never heard of. Early on, there was Jean-Bedel Bokassa, head of the Central African Republic, who, emulating his hero Napoleon, crowned himself emperor in a sumptuous $20 million ceremony that helped bankrupt his country. Though he did find enough money to also kill a hundred students. (On the other hand, he *was* acquitted of cannibalism charges.) Pretty bad. But then, in the *C*s, Bokassa got some tough competition from Chou, king of China in the 12th century B.C. To please his concubine, Chou built a lake of wine and forced naked men and women to chase one another around it. Also, he strung the forest with human flesh. Chou really put some creativity into his evilness, but he's not unusual. Every letter has at least one truly dark-hearted cretin who somehow ascended to head of state.

Once every few hundred pages, the *Britannica* will come to my rescue and surprise me with a game of its own. In the *C* section, you can find an actual unsolved *New York Times* crossword puzzle. Just take your pencil—or pen, if you're a real puzzler—and fill it in right there on the page.

Under *charades*—which was originally the name for a type of riddle, not the pantomime game we know now—I got this brainteaser:

"My first is a Tartar / My second a letter / My all is a country / No Christmas dish better."

You get it? Turk-*E*. Turkey! That's the answer. Ha!

And now, I've reached a thirteen-page section devoted exclusively to *number games,* like this curious pattern, which affords a "pleasant pastime":

$$3 \times 37 = 111$$
$$6 \times 37 = 222$$
$$9 \times 37 = 333$$

And so on. Believe me, after reading about the Permo-Triassic rock strata of the Karoo system, this is fun stuff. Unfortunately, after number games, *number theory* is looming, which I don't expect to be quite the orgy of fun.

numismatics

Back when coins were made of metals like gold and silver, petty thieves would shave off the edges and melt down the valuable slivers. To stop this, mints began putting serrated edges on coins. So that's the real story behind the cool ridges on quarters. Good to know that security measures can also be aesthetically pleasing.

nursery rhyme

My favorite Mother Goose fact thus far: "Jack and Jill" is actually an extended allegory about taxes. The jack and jill were two forms of measurement in early England. When Charles I scaled down the jack (originally two ounces) so as to collect higher sales tax, the jill, which was by definition twice the size of the jack, was automatically reduced, hence "came tumbling after." Kids love tax stories. I can't wait to hear the nursery rhyme about Bush's abolishment of the estate tax.

Nyx

She's the female personification of night. It's about 5 P.M., with Nyx approaching fast, and here I am in an unremarkable hotel room in Venice, perhaps the single most beautiful city in the world, full of gliding boats and striped-shirted men and quaintness around every corner. Instead of taking a predinner walk with Julie and Sharon and Peter to admire the surroundings, I've opted to stay and finish the Ns. Julie feared this when I started Operation Britannica, and she turns out to have a point: I've got a whole new and compelling reason to stay inside. I'm addicted to this thing. But like most addicts, I feel simultaneously drawn to it and repelled by it.

O

oath

Our stay in Venice over, we say good-bye to Sharon and Peter and take a water taxi to the train station. It's a quick trip, five minutes tops, and it should cost the equivalent of $10.

Instead, we get there, and the water taxi driver demands we pay him something approaching the gross national product of Bolivia ($8.2 billion). I shouldn't pay him, but we're late and he's a big Italian man. According to psychologist W. H. Sheldon's classification system, he is an endomorph (with a round head and bulky torso) and I am a wimpy ectomorph (narrow chest, high forehead, long arms). So I give him his ransom and Julie and I climb off.

I wait till the taxi driver pulls away from the pier—until there's a safe patch of murky Venetian water between us—and then I shout at him: "Hey!" He looks up. If there's any time to be an ugly American, this is the time—when dealing with an ugly Italian man who just took most of your savings. It's time to insult him.

Question is, after reading more than half the *Britannica,* are my insults of a higher quality? I've saved up a good one for just these situations. It's called the "bell, book, and candle," an oath formerly used by the early Roman Catholic church to excommunicate a Christian who had committed some unpardonable sin.

It goes like this: "We declare him excommunicate and anathema; we judge him damned with the devil and his angels and all the reprobate to eternal fire until he shall recover himself from the toils of the devil and return to amendment and to penitence. So be it!"

Now that's an insult.

Unfortunately, in the heat of the moment, as I was being ripped off, I had a little trouble remembering the entire bell, book, and candle curse. I knew the word *"reprobate"* was in there, maybe the devil, but I couldn't summon the rest of it. And sadly, I couldn't even come up with the less elaborate backups: "You've got cryptorchidism!" (undescended testicles) or even "You've got dumdum fever."

No, in the thick of battle, there's no time for elaborate insults. So I rely on a standby, and one that probably translates better across the language barrier. I give him the finger.

obscenity

Julie and I checked into the hotel today in Portofino, the site of Rick and Ilene's wedding. We spend the day hanging out by the pool eating our greasy Italian finger food. We're sharing an umbrella with another wedding guest, a blond-haired Minnesota native named Trent. He's a writer for *Newsweek,* and has just spent eight weeks embedded in Iraq.

Trent has plenty of war stories. Like the danger of eating anything other than the food provided by the U.S. military. If you decide to be adventurous in the culinary department—say, by sampling a little local goat meat—you will pay for your bravery for days. That's not to mention another risk to journalists: writing anything that could be seen as anti-American. Trent wrote an article implying that his division was a tad trigger happy. For that, not only was he physically threatened, but he was subjected to a xeroxed anti-Trent newsletter created by the soldiers, a publication that included the witty word jumble "E-A-T S-H-T-I T-R-E-N-T." But the most surprising thing that Trent had to say involved the customs of the American soldiers. The troops, he said, can be a little crude.

"Such as?"

We didn't want to know, he says. We begged to differ. "Well, there's mushrooming."

"Never heard of it."

Mushrooming, explains Trent, occurs when one of our soldiers is asleep, and his buddy wants to wake him up in a creative way. The buddy unzips his pants, takes out his penis, dips it in ketchup, then thwacks the sleeping guy on the forehead, leaving a mushroom-shaped imprint. Hence mushrooming.

Huh.

Julie and I spend a few moments processing this bit of military reconnaissance.

"Now that's something that you don't read in the encyclopedia," says Julie.

"It'll probably be in the 2003 edition," I say.

But it's true. Mushrooming is not in the *Britannica*. I'm jealous of Trent. Well, I'm not jealous of the fact that he ate goat meat or showered less often than I go to the opera. I'm jealous because he was out there in the sandy trenches getting firsthand knowledge. He wasn't reading it secondhand in a wussy book. And the knowledge he picked up was weird, crude, and to my still-adolescent mind, pretty fascinating.

I can console myself, though. At least the *Britannica* does have plenty of its own weird and crude facts. I've learned almost every other bizarre thing men enjoy inflicting on their private parts. They've practiced ritualized bleeding to mimic menstruation. A shocking number have been castrated. An equally shocking number have been partially castrated—the 50 percent deal, officially called "monorchidism." They've inserted pebbles, stuck it with a pin, subincised it (cut the underside) and plain old circumcised it. They've splattered blood from their pierced penises and offered it to the gods. And the men of the Cobeua tribe of Brazil dance around with large artificial phalli, doing violent coitus motions accompanied by loud groans to spread fertility to every corner of the house, jumping among the women, who disperse shrieking and laughing as they knock phalli together.

So at least I have a little sociological context for the practice of mushrooming. Now, instead of just snickering at mushrooming, I can ponder its place in other penis rituals the world over, then snicker at it.

"Does General Tommy Franks mushroom?" I ask Trent.

"I don't think so."

occupational disease

In the past, hatters often became ill because they used mercury salts to make felt out of rabbit fur. The mercury poisoning led to a mental deterioration known as erethism. Hence the phrase "mad as a hatter." Good to know. If I ever have kids, I'll make a little note in the margin of their *Alice in Wonderland*.

olive oil

The wedding itself was gorgeous. A nice traditional Jewish ceremony. Well, traditional except that it was held at a 12th-century Italian monastery. Since I'm pretty well versed in medieval Christianity these days, I can say with 90 percent certainty that monks did *not* wear yarmulkes, especially not monogrammed ones. But I'm guessing they did love a good hora. Who wouldn't?

After the vows, I go on the receiving line to congratulate the happy couple. I shake Rick's hand, then give him a little marital advice I'd picked up from the encyclopedia: Attila the Hun died on his wedding night, perhaps from exhaustion. "So take it easy tonight," I say. "No need to prove anything your first night."

"Great tip," he says. "Thanks."

I tell Ilene that she looks radiant. Then add: "Just so you know, if you ever need an out, the easiest method of divorce comes from the Pueblo Indians. Just leave Rick's moccasins on the doorstep. Simple as that." Ilene says she'll keep that in mind.

The food is delicious and deeply Italian—lots of pasta, lots of bread, lots of olive oil (which, by the way, the ancient Egyptians used as a lubricant for moving heavy building materials; so without olive oil, no pyramids). The only part of the wedding that is not a complete success—at least for me—is the after-dinner dancing. Julie is looking particularly elegant, with a wide-brimmed hat and black gloves.

"Would you care for a dance, milady?" I ask.

"Why, yes sir," she says.

So far, so good. But when we get out on the dance floor, I decide to test out some new dance moves. I leap in the air wildly and move my limbs in a convulsive, jerky fashion.

"What's going on here?" Julie demands.

"Saint Vitus's dance!" I say. "Come on, join in!."

I jump up and wave my arms frantically. Julie doesn't ask for an explanation, which is too bad, because I had one at the ready: Saint Vitus's dance was an ecstatic dance that spread throughout Europe in the middle ages. It was, says the *Britannica*, a kind of mass hysteria, affecting hundreds of people and becoming a public menace. Those afflicted would shout and foam at the mouth. I figured: when in a 12th-century monastery, do as 12th-century Christians would do.

Julie turns her back to me and starts dancing with Rick's friend Ted, who apparently is not afflicted with a medieval seizure. My plan was to spread Saint Vitus's dance through the entire wedding party. Perhaps I should have gone with the tarantella, a medieval dance used to combat venomous spider bites by sweating the poison out.

Olympus Mons

I think I partially redeem myself when we get back to the hotel in Portofino. Our hotel is a fancy affair with a pool boy and wooden hangers—and really crappy air-conditioning. The thing wheezes like a bypass patient in recovery. The room is far too hot to sleep in. It's hot as Al-Aziziyah in Libya (136 degrees). Hot as the interior of Olympus Mons (the largest volcano in the solar system, located on Mars). If the room had any sweat bees—insects that are attracted to perspiration—they'd be all over us. I order up an oscillating fan. No help. I complain to the concierge, who sends up a bellboy to inspect the air conditioner. Oh, it's on, he assures us, and then leaves us.

"You've got to do something," says Julie.

"What am I supposed to do? Fix the air conditioner?"

"Something."

"Sorry, I forgot to bring my power drill."

But she's right. Something has to be done.

A quick but relevant digression: Before we left for Italy, Julie and I rented an old black-and-white movie called *Ball of Fire*. A friend had recommended it to us because it's a romantic comedy about encyclopedias—a genre that doesn't yet have its own aisle at Blockbuster. We loved it. The film—cowritten by Billy Wilder—is about eight professors who live in a brownstone and scribble away day and night on an encyclopedia. These professors, as you might expect, have wire-rim glasses and bow ties and are very adept at bumbling. The only semicool professor is the young one, played by Gary Cooper, who specializes in language. He's writing the entry on *slang*, but realizes he's been locked in this brownstone for so many years, he's totally ignorant of modern-day slang. So Gary Cooper ventures out into the world, and encounters a hotsy-totsy burlesque singer—played by Barbara Stanwyck—and despite her atrocious grammar and her unfortunate connections to the mob, they fall in love.

The movie is a weird mix, at once deeply anti-intellectual and pro-education. The movie's anti-intellectual part is smack-you-on-the-face obvious—these professors have filled their heads with information but neglected their hearts, so they know nothing about life. On the other hand, there are some scenes where learning triumphs—specifically a climactic scene (warning: I'm giving away a key plot twist here) wherein the professors are being held at gunpoint by a bunch of thugs.

The desperate professors think back to the story of the Greek scientist Archimedes, who burned the entire Roman fleet by training a big magnifying lens on the ships. So these dweeby men use the lens from their microscope to burn the wire holding up a painting, which then falls and clunks the villain on the head, knocking him out and allowing the professors to escape.

I found a couple of things about this scene interesting. First, I know from the *Britannica* that the Archimedes story was a myth—he didn't actually burn the Roman fleet—so that felt good. (Likewise, the film's narrator described these men as "knowing what tune Nero was fiddling when Rome burned." I told Julie that actually Nero was not fiddling while Rome burned.) But more important, I was jealous. I wanted to use my knowledge like this. I wanted to use it to capture the bad guy or save the heroine. In my constant quest to put my knowledge to work, I've had only a handful of modest victories, the herb and crab soup incident being the most impressive.

Which brings me back to the air-conditioning conundrum. What to do? I thought back to the history of air-conditioning. I could remember only that the Graumann's Theater in Los Angeles was one of the first places to be air-conditioned. And also that, in the days before electricity, Indians used to hang wet grass mats in the window. If life had sound effects, there would be a loud ding right about now.

I took two big white towels from the bathroom, sprayed them down in the shower, and hung them in the open window. I can't say for sure they lowered the temperature of the room, but I think they did. And regardless, I felt better. I was taking action. I was putting my knowledge to work. I was a hero, just like Billy Wilder's microscope-wielding professors.

onion

We've come back to the United States, but Julie's mind is still in Italy. She's yearning for some more of that pizza. She decides to make it herself, with me as her sous chef.

I chop my eggplant and zucchini. We're both quiet, focused on our chores. Next up, the onion chopping. I peel my onion, take it to the sink, turn on the faucet, and start slicing it under the flow.

"What are you doing?"

"I'm cutting the onion underwater."

"Why?"

"It says in the *Britannica* it stops you from crying."

This was an Heloise-style hint from the *Britannica*—one of those rare useful ones—and I was quite excited to be putting it into practice.

"Nope, too dangerous."

"But it's in the *Britannica*."

"Nope, I'm the executive chef. You're the sous chef."

Here I'm confronted with an unfortunate situation: the *Britannica* versus my wife. Two big sources of authority. Which do I choose? Well, the *Britannica* is pretty trustworthy. However, as far as I know, it can't carry my child or ignore me for several days or throw out the T-shirts that it hates.

So I decide Julie wins this one. The onion will be cut without water and I will cry.

ooze

Ooze, I learn, is sediment that contains at least 30 percent skeletal remains of microscopic floating organisms. You've got to marvel at the specificity of that. Thirty percent; 29 percent and you're out of luck, buddy. You may be sediment, but you're no ooze.

Opium Wars

It's Friday night, and Julie and I have rented a movie. We are frighteningly loyal fans of movies, and this year alone have provided some lucky Hollywood executive with enough cash for three Gucci suits and a Bikram yoga class. Tonight, we rented a movie called *Shanghai Knights*. It's a buddy comedy with Owen Wilson and Jackie Chan set in 1887 England and China.

In the first scene, the villain breaks into China's imperial palace with a bunch of evil members of China's Boxer gang.

"The Boxers were nuts," I tell Julie. "They were called Boxers because they thought their boxing training would make them impervious to bullets."

"Not now, honey."

I sort of shrug and go back to eating my Indian takeout chickpea dish.

A few minutes later, Sir Arthur Conan Doyle shows up as a character. He's working as a detective at Scotland Yard, where Jackie Chan has been thrown in jail. Conan Doyle at Scotland Yard? I don't think so.

"Actually Sir Arthur Conan Doyle was a medical student before he became a writer."

"A.J., please."

I'm good for the next half hour. But then, the villain reveals his plan to take advantage of China's Opium Wars. That's too tempting. I read about the Opium Wars a few days ago, and they were a memorable tale. One of the causes was a crusading Chinese official who dumped confiscated opium into the ocean to try to squash the drug trade. He was considerate enough to write an ode of apology to the gods of the ocean for defiling their home. I thought that was a nice touch, writing a poem apologizing to nature for polluting it. Exxon should start doing this. In any case, the opium dumping—just like the Boston Tea Party before it—really angered the Brits, who were making lots of money from the opium trade. So England started a war with China.

This happened sometime in the 1830s. I can't remember the exact dates, but it was in the 1830s for sure—way before 1887.

"Hey, Julie, the Opium Wars were—"

Julie pauses the movie. "Okay, new policy."

"What?"

"Whenever you give me an irrelevant fact, it's a fine of one dollar."

"Come on."

"A one-dollar fine."

"These facts were relevant," I say.

Julie thinks for a second.

"Okay, a one-dollar fine for any irrelevant fact, and a one-dollar fine for a relevant fact that interrupts a movie."

"This is crazy."

"I've got to do something."

opossums

Opossums have thirteen nipples. Good to know. Also, the notion that the opossum gives birth through its nose probably comes from the female's habit of putting her face into the pouch to clean it just before giving birth. I had never heard of this notion. I was simultaneously illuminated and disillusioned.

opposites

I'm dyin' here. That's my fellow editor Andy's favorite phrase to express general anxiety, one he uses several times a week at the start of exasperated e-mails, and it seems applicable right now. I'm dyin' here. To be more specific, I'm still having a hell of a time processing all this information, figuring out what it means. I can't see the forest for the trees, and in this case the forest is the information equivalent of the Siberian boreal forest, which makes up about one fifth of the world's forested area, so that's a lot of goddamn trees.

I'm looking for answers—and there are answers. That's not the problem. The problem is there are too many answers, thousands of answers, and they all seem to conflict with one another. I'll come up with a thesis, and pat myself on the back for my incisiveness, and then a couple of hours later I'll decide my thesis is absurd, and that the exact opposite thesis is correct. Then I'll switch back to the first.

I'll give you an example. I'll decide that the *Britannica* provides evidence to back up the old saw that patience is a virtue. For instance, ticks wait on twigs for weeks, months, sometimes *years,* for a mammal to pass underneath. And then they drop onto the fur and suck happily away on the blood. So be like the tick. Good things come to those who wait.

But then I'll read something that supports the opposite side, the importance of being impulsive, making quick decisions, of following that other old saw, "Just do it." For instance, Napoleon. He lost at Waterloo because he waited too long to attack. He waited till the afternoon, when the sun had dried the mud from the overnight rains, but by that time the Brits had received reinforcement. Historians agree: he should have just done it.

So what the hell should I do? Should I be patient? Or impulsive? I want a guide, someone to tell me this is right, this is wrong. I watched a little of Dr. Phil the other day, the blunt-talking TV host. Maybe I need a Dr. Phil for the *Britannica.*

orgasm

They can be experienced from infancy. What? Did I have orgasms when I was an infant? Did I smoke a tiny cigarette afterward?

oyster

Oysters can change sex according to the temperature of the water. I always knew there was something emasculating about warm baths.

Ozma, Project

Project Ozma was an attempt by some American astronomers to find intelligent life in the universe. It took place in the sixties, was named for the princess in *The Wizard of Oz*—and was a spectacular failure. For the past couple of weeks, I've been conducting my own search for intelligent life here on earth. Since I've announced to the world that my goal is to become the smartest man in the world, I figure I should suss out the competition. Which is why I called a man named Ron Hoeflin.

Ron is the founder of four high-IQ societies—HiQ, if you really want to sound cool. HiQ societies are clubs for those brainiacs who make the average Mensa member look like a knuckle-dragging, drooling Australopithecus. Mensans must score in the top 2 percent on the IQ test. That's nothing. Kids' stuff. Ron started the Top One Percent Society, which is for, naturally, the top 1 percent. His One-in-a-Thousand Society is for the top 0.1 percent. The Prometheus Society is for the top 0.003 percent. And the mighty Mega Society is for the top 0.0001 percent. Ron's IQ varies depending on which test he's taking, but he clocks in at 190 on a good day.

I found Ron because he was profiled in *Esquire* a few years ago. Ron later wrote a letter to the editor listing the various egregious mistakes the writer made in the article—Ron uses Wite-Out, *not* Liquid Paper; his father was a ballroom dance instructor, *not* a ballroom dancer, and so on. I'm already nervous about meeting him. I vow to myself to take meticulous notes.

Ron greets me at the door of his Hell's Kitchen apartment. It's tiny, even by New York standards, but his rent is lower than his IQ: $150 a month. Ron lives there with his two cats, Big Boy and Wild Thing, and a radiator that clanks louder than the bassist at your average Metallica concert. On the walls are a series of futuristic drawings of women with pronounced biceps, wearing G-strings and wielding swords.

"They're from a fantasy calendar," says Ron. "I got tired of seeing all my narcissistic diplomas up on the wall."

Ron's fifty-nine years old, a bear of a man with graying hair and smudged glasses. He's legally blind, but he can see things up close, which forces him to read with a magnifying glass. He grew up in the suburbs of St. Louis, memorized pi to two hundred decimal places as a kid (he still remembers the first fifty digits) and eventually got a Ph.D. in philosophy from the New School for Social Research. He makes his modest living putting together newsletters for HiQ societies. As he'll tell you himself, he's shy and awkward, not exactly a social butterfly, barely even a social caterpillar; he reminds me of Dustin Hoffman's idiot savant in *Rain Man*, but without the idiot part. I like him immediately.

He seems interested in my encyclopedia project. Turns out he's an obsessive reader too. Every day, without fail, Ron reads philosophy at the Wendy's on Eighth Avenue and Fifty-sixth Street over an iced tea, a Caesar salad, and a chicken sandwich. Why Wendy's? "It's got good lighting, and it's more social. Even though I don't talk to people, there are people around me, which I like." It was there that he read the entire *Encyclopedia of Philosophy* in 420 days, about ten pages a day. "Some articles on logic," he tells me, "were just so technical, I couldn't finish them."

Sweet Jesus! This is wonderful news. Even a verifiable megagenius like Ron has trouble finishing entries. Next time I'm mired in text about vector bundles and Möbius strips, I've got Ron's confession to comfort me.

Ron has been working on a book called *To Unscrew the Inscrutable: A Theory of the Structure of Philosophy*. At one point it was nearly four thousand pages but now he's shaved it down to a fifth of that, about 748 pages. He shows me some of it. The idea—as far as I can figure, and I'm probably wrong about this—is that all philosophical systems can be categorized by a number. So his Chapter 2 covers two-part systems like the yin and the yang and the wave particle duality in quantum physics. His Chapter 3 covers the Christian Trinity and Freud's tripartite system (ego, id, and superego). And so on. It sounds smart. He's talking quickly, scribbling diagrams of squares inside circles, shooting off on tangents, dropping phrases like "anticipatory goal object" and "root metaphor" and "superstring theory," and I'm saying, "Right, right, right," because I don't want to look like a moron, but the truth is, I have no idea what he's talking about and no way to judge whether it's a good theory.

Ron tells me that, after ten years of work, he's just recently finished writing the book, and is ready to print it out, but his printer is broken, and he can't afford a new one. This makes me so sad that I want to hug him, which he'd probably hate.

He asks me what I've learned in the encyclopedia. I figure I should give him a philosophy fact. "Did you know that René Descartes had a fetish for women with crossed eyes?" I say.

"Well, my mother died on exactly the same date that Descartes did. February eleventh."

I nod. We listen to the Chopin in the background. Several seconds tick by. "So how would you define intelligence?" I ask him.

"That's a very difficult question," Ron says. If he has to be pinned down, he tells me, it probably has to do with trial and error, learning from mistakes, moderating our thoughts and actions like a thermostat, like the painter who dabs paint and, if it doesn't look good, dabs in a new place.

"Do you think I can become smarter by reading the encyclopedia?"

"Depends what you mean by smarter. You could say a computer can get smarter by feeding it more information. But in terms of hardware, there's not much hope for humans. You're stuck with the brain you were given."

It's not quite what I was hoping for, but it's not a terrible answer. I've always preferred software to hardware. At least I can improve the programs in my brain.

I ask him about geniuses. Is there anything to the stereotype that geniuses have psychological problems?

"Well, yeah," he says. Ron clicks on his computer to show me exactly what problems he suffers from. On the screen pop up the results of his personality test, with a bar graph showing the different aspects of his character.

"See? I zoomed all the way to the top on the sensitivity scale. I'm too sensitive."

Ron is shockingly open. I've been a journalist for almost fifteen years, and this is the first time someone's whipped out a personality test to show me exactly where all his flaws lie. If only the celebrities I interviewed at *Entertainment Weekly* had done this. I would have loved for talk show host Bill Maher to quantify for me exactly why he's such a huge jackass. Again, I want to hug Ron, but instead I go with an attempt to bond: "I'm very antisocial as well."

"At least you're married. I never got married."

"There's still time," I say. Ron hasn't had a girlfriend in a some time, though at one point he dated professional genius and *Parade* columnist Marilyn vos Savant. I make a mental note to have Julie fix him up with an attractive woman with an IQ bordering 200.

It's about 4 P.M., time for Ron to go to Wendy's to do his daily philosophy reading. He's dabbling in feminist tracts, but he's not too impressed. On the walk to Wendy's, he tells me that he heard you can raise your IQ by six points if you take a sauna right before your test. Perhaps that's the secret. I should abandon this encyclopedia and just take a sauna. So much more efficient! Ron smiles weakly. I shake his hand good-bye.

I'm a big fan of Ron's. He seems sweeter and more humble than those Mensans I met at the Staten Island convention. He also breaks my heart. On the subway home, as I flip through a copy of the Mega IQ test written by Ron (three xeroxed pages of absurdly difficult analogies and spatial problems), I make a note in my Palm Pilot to buy an advance copy of Ron's book to help him pay for a new printer. And I come to the ingenious conclusion that maybe it's not such a good thing to be the smartest man in the world—something I knew back when I thought I was the smartest boy in the world. Maybe it's better to be dumb and happy.

P

pachycephalosaurus

In my periodic check on how I'm faring, I stack the *Britannica*s up on the office floor. Look at how that pile has grown, I chuckle to myself, shaking my head proudly. It's really getting up there. Seems like yesterday when that cute little stack was barely up to my ankle. And look at it now! As I dive into the *P*'s, it's shot to above my belly button, like I've been rubbing the covers with somatotropin growth hormone.

So I'm getting there. I'm not Ron Hoeflin, but I'm no pachycephalosaurus (a dinosaur with a thick mass of solid bone grown over its tiny brain, also known as the "bone-headed dinosaur").

Paige, Satchel

Here was the hardest-working man in baseball. Before his major league career—which began when he was surprisingly old, in his late forties—Paige barnstormed the country, traveling as many as thirty thousand miles a year, pitching for any team willing to meet his price. Any team at all. He played for various teams in the Negro League, Central America, the Caribbean, and South America, and "wearing a false red beard, he also played for the bearded House of David team." That was a baffling sentence. This was one of those rare times I felt compelled to do some additional detective work. Bearded House of David team? An Internet search revealed that the House of David baseball team was made up of the members of a Michigan-based apocalyptic cult who all wore long beards. A baseball-loving cult with excessive facial hair. My journalist's mind is trained to find trends, put things in folders with other facts. But after much thought, I can honestly say that a bearded baseball-playing apocalyptic cult does not belong to a category. It is a trend of one.

Paine, Thomas

When Thomas Paine died, most American papers reprinted an obituary from the *New York Citizen* that said: "He had lived long, did some good and much harm." Today he's a beloved Revolutionary War hero; back then, the majority thought him a scoundrel.

His life had more ups and downs than the upper Ural mountain range. He failed at an impressive number of jobs—he once tried to invent a smokeless candle, which sounds like a pretty good idea, but it didn't take off. His marriages ended badly.

On the other hand, the man could write a pamphlet. His *Common Sense* series was a huge hit—the first sold 500,000 copies; a later one was read by George Washington at Valley Forge and launched the phrase "These are the times that try men's souls." Paine refused to take profits on it so that cheap editions could be sold.

Things went sour after the war when Paine wrote a defense of the French Revolution. His ideas were solid—relief for the poor, pensions for the aged, public works for the unemployed, a progressive income tax. But in England, where he was living at the time, it got him charged with treason. Things worsened when he wrote another pamphlet attacking organized religion. Though he made clear in the pamphlet that he was a deist and believed in the Supreme Being, he still got charged with being an atheist.

And that's how he died—broke, drunk, and seen as an infidel. Oh, and his skeleton was later lost en route to England. It took decades for his approval rating to climb. Point is, you just can't predict your reputation in history. I guess you just have to write your pamphlets and hope you eventually get understood.

parallelism

My aunt Carol is visiting from Connecticut. She's got a lot of competition, but if I had to choose, I'd probably say Carol is the single smartest person to share my DNA. And she's not just smart—she's a bona fide intellectual. She's like those characters in Woody Allen movies who wear turtlenecks and talk about Rilke—except she doesn't wear turtlenecks and she's completely unpretentious. Carol studied with Paul de Man and currently holds a job as professor of German literature at Yale. She's published books on major thinkers like Walter Benjamin and Claude Lévi-Strauss. I haven't read all her books (sorry Carol) but I do love having them on my bookshelf, since, just like the *Britannica,* they add much-needed gravitas to my room.

This trip, Carol has given me another serious book: Jean-Paul Sartre's *Nausea,* which she says is very appropriate to my current life. I'm flattered she thought of me. When I get home, I open it up to the page where Aunt Carol has left a pink Post-it. I begin to read: Sartre's narrator is at the Paris library. He's observing a character called the Self-Taught Man, who spends a lot of time in the stacks.

> [The Self-Taught Man] has just taken another book from the same shelf, I can make out the title upside-down: *The Arrow of Caudebec, A Norman Chronicle* by Mlle Julie Lavergne. The Self-Taught Man's choice of reading always disconcerts me.
>
> Suddenly the names of the authors he last read came back to my mind: Lambert, Langlois, Larbaletrier, Lastex, Lavergne. It is a revelation; I have understood the Self-Taught Man's method; he teaches himself alphabetically.

It is a revelation to me as well. A fellow adventurer through the alphabet. This is wonderful news! Sartre goes on: "He has passed brutally from the study of coleopterae to the quantum theory, from the work of Tamberlaine to a Catholic pamphlet against Darwinism, he has never been disconcerted for an instant. There is a universe behind and before him."

Couldn't have said it better myself.

I flip forward, skimming. The Self-Taught Man seems like a good guy. He's for universal love, he admires youth, he's a humanist. I like him. I wish I could dive into the book and have a conversation with him over some unpasteurized cheese at the café.

I skip to the end of the book. Ah, here's the Self-Taught Man again, back in the library, where he belongs, with his beloved books. He seems to be having a conversation with two young boys in the library. Huh, what's this about? Now the Self-Taught Man is putting his hairy hand on the smooth palm of a little brown-haired boy. Uh-oh. Now, writes Sartre, the Self-Taught Man "timidly began to stroke" the boy's hand.

Jesus H. Christ! The Self-Taught Man is a child molester. This is unbelievable. There's more.

The Self-Taught Man's "finger passed slowly, humbly, over the inert flesh . . . he had closed his eyes, he was smiling. His other hand had disappeared under the table. The boys were not laughing any more, they were both afraid."

Dammit!

First I read about Bouvard and Pécuchet, two doofuses who blow up their own house. Now comes the Self-Taught Man, who spends his afternoons timidly stroking little boys under the table. I can't believe the hostility my quest—or similar ventures—engenders from major thinkers. I'm just trying to read the encyclopedia here, people. Just trying to make myself a little smarter. Does that make me a card-carrying member of NAMBLA? What's next? Is someone going to accuse me of having body parts in my freezer or of selling plutonium to Syria?

I went on the Web. Turns out Sartre used the Self-Taught Man to represent rational humanism, a philosophy he considers bankrupt. What a mean-spirited jackass. Just because he disagrees with a point of view, he links it to pedophilia. Plus, I happen to prefer rational humanism to his absurd Marxist-inflected existentialism.

I called up my aunt to ask if she was implying anything about my sexuality. She said, no, she had read *Nausea* decades ago and had forgotten about all about the Self-Taught Man's boy-fondling behavior. Which makes me feel a little better.

"In fact, Henry and I were just talking about your quest," says Carol. Henry also teaches at Yale, and is also frighteningly smart, the author of dense books about Hegel's theory of time and Kafka's theory of the state. "Henry was saying that this is a very American quest. It's very American and democratic, the idea that you can improve yourself. It's a noble idea."

Now I feel a lot better. That's the first time someone has called me noble. So Sartre can go straight to existential hell.

Paris

The storming of the Bastille was surprisingly lame. When the mob forced open the doors, the prison had been largely unused for years and was scheduled for demolition. It "held on that day only four counterfeiters, two madmen and a young aristocrat who had displeased his father." Seven people? That barely qualifies as a storm. More like a light drizzle. Couldn't they have stormed something a little more impressive?

passenger pigeons

These birds—which, judging by the picture, were much better looking than the chunky gray head bobbers that coo and cluck on my windowsill—officially became extinct when the last known representative died, on September 1, 1914, in the Cincinnati Zoo. Humans hunted passenger pigeons into nonexistence. But in the 1800s, there were billions of them. This I know. Way back in the B's under *animal behavior*, the *Britannica* printed a remarkable passage by Audubon that I haven't been able to get out of my mind. It said:

> The air was literally filled with pigeons; the light of noonday was obscured as by an eclipse; the dung fell in spots not unlike melting flakes of snow . . . the people were all in arms. . . . For a week or more, the population fed on no other flesh than that of pigeons. The atmosphere, during this time, was strongly impregnated with the peculiar odour which emanates from the species. . . . Let us take a column of one mile in breadth, which is far below the average size, and suppose it passing over us without interruption for three hours, at the rate mentioned above of one mile in the minute. This will give us a parallelogram of 180 miles by 1, covering 180 square miles. Allowing 2 pigeons to the square yard, we have 1,115,136,000 pigeons in one flock.

My thoughts after reading that passage, in no particular order: People are terrible, I can't believe we killed so many pigeons . . . Thank God I wasn't around when that flock was flying overhead—those dung snowflakes sound nasty . . . Did any of the 1.1 billion pigeons think to himself, *I'm really special. I'm not like these other losers?*

Well, in somewhat of an order, I guess. Because that last one haunted me especially. Reading about massive numbers of a particular species does that to me. I pride myself that I'm an individual, that I'm unique. But I doubt that a Venusian scientist would be able to distinguish me from the other 5 million Manhattanites who converge on midtown every day to sit in front of computer terminals and talk on the phone. I'm just one member of a huge nonflying flock.

The *Britannica* points out that passenger pigeon flocks are the second largest social unit in history, topped only by desert locusts. Third place? Modern-day China. Locusts, pigeons, and China: that seems vaguely insulting to the Chinese people, to be classed with locusts and pigeons. But I guess it's only insulting if you refuse to accept that humans are animals.

patch box

A rectangular box used as a receptacle for beauty patches in the 18th century. Back in the days of Louis XV, says the *Britannica*, black patches of gummed taffeta were popular with chic women (and men) who wanted to emphasize the beauty and whiteness of their skin. The smart set had plenty of patch designs to choose from. For the understated, there were the simple spots. But the truly fashionable had patches in the shapes of stars, crescents, elaborate animals, insects, or figures. Placement was also important, seeing as these patches had their own language: a patch at the corner of the eye symbolized passion, while one at the middle of the forehead indicated dignity. Women carried their patch boxes with them, in case they wanted to slap on a fresh one during the royal ball.

This is good to know, seeing as I have my very own patch. Apparently I was born about 250 years too late, since I've always thought of it as a big ugly mole, not as a fashionable accessory that enhances the whiteness of my skin. My beauty patch, sadly, isn't in the shape of a giraffe or spider— just the regular old spot. But it is on my face. It's on the right side of my nose, which makes me wonder what my patch would symbolize to a courtier in 18th-century France. Probably *"Je suis un jackass."*

I love learning the lengths that humans will go to make themselves attractive to potential mates. The French in particular were good at this. In addition to carrying her box of patches, a stylish gal in the court of Louis XIV needed to affix a *fontange* (tower) to her head. This was a complex wire frame, often in the shape of a fan, that held her hair, along with artificial curls, dangling streamers, ribbon, starched linen, and lace. A huge tower of hair and black splotches on her face—va-va-voom.

Of course, if I'm tempted to feel superior when reading this information, I need only think back to my own attempts at preening in high school. They weren't pretty. They involved not only several increasingly goopy types of hair gel, which was bad enough, but also something much worse: an ear clip. This was a little silver band that attached to the middle of my ear. The ear clip was for those milquetoasts like me who lacked the backbone to get their ears pierced. It was something you could remove before going to Thanksgiving at Grandma's, much like the gummy taffeta of the 18th century.

patriotism

We're out at my parents' house in East Hampton for July Fourth. I come down to breakfast and announce my big July Fourth fact: John Adams and Thomas Jefferson both died on the same day—July 4, 1826, fifty years after the founding of the country. Jefferson died at noon, his last words being, "Is it the Fourth?" Adams died later in the afternoon, his last words being, "Thomas Jefferson still lives." He was wrong.

Been holding on to that one since the *J*'s. Feels good to get it off my chest.

perception (of time)

I'm thirty-five years old, which isn't young, but it won't qualify me for any special rates at the Boca Raton Denny's either. Still, it's old enough that I've started to notice something disturbing, a phenomenon my grandparents talk about a lot: time has sped up. The years are vanishing more and more quickly, the calendar days flipping by faster than a falcon in full dive (150 mph).

The *Britannica* has an explanation for this: elderly people find time shorter because they notice long-accustomed changes less frequently.

I'm not 100 percent sure what this means. Which long-accustomed changes in particular? They notice the daily setting of the sun less frequently? The changing of the seasons? The rhythms of the body? The Buckingham Palace guards? Regardless, I get the gist. Old people adapt to stimuli. To put it bluntly, old people are less perceptive.

I wonder if I can fight this change. Can I stop the acceleration of time by remaining observant? By keeping my mind open to changes and filled with wonder at the world, instead of tuning it out? That would truly be an accomplishment. I vow to try, though I know it's about as likely as stopping the sunset.

Perry, Matthew

Ever since my banishment from *Jeopardy!* I've been checking the *Who Wants to Be a Millionaire* Web site every day for audition times. There haven't been any. Just an apology from the producers and a photo of an agonized man who has apparently just lost a lot of money—I guess it's supposed to be amusing, but it just increases my frustration.

The prime time version—the one with Regis Philbin—has long since been canceled. I'm just trying to get on the syndicated version—the one that runs in the afternoon every day, around Oprah time, and is hosted by a woman named Meredith Vieira, who doesn't shout nearly as much as Regis.

Finally, after several weeks, the agonized man face is gone. Auditions! Here in New York! I sign up for a Tuesday night, not knowing what to expect. Coincidentally, an intern at *Esquire* tried out on Monday night, and when he shuffles in on Tuesday morning, I pump him for details. They aren't inspiring. He failed, as did almost all of the one hundred hopefuls, and he warns me that the audition quiz will "pound your brain and ego." So I'm already on edge when I arrive at the ABC studios on the Upper West Side.

I'm not relaxed by the situation there. For forty-five minutes, all of us potential millionaires stand outside the building in the rain.

"This is fun, huh?" I say to the wet woman next to me.

"Yeah," she says. "This sucks. Final answer."

We both have a chuckle. She's wearing loose black clothing and has a middle part in her hair that wouldn't be out of place at a Renaissance fair. Her face reminds me of an attractive Broom-Hilda, the cartoon witch.

"So what do you do when you're not trying out for quiz shows?" I ask.

"I'm unemployed right now. That's why I'm here."

Jesus. Did I learn nothing from my Mensa experience? Remember: do not ask about occupations at gatherings where above-average IQs are involved. Still, my guilt over the faux pas is tempered by relief, because I have a realization: this middle-parted woman should get my spot. I'm just here to get my ego massaged; she actually needs the money. She's got utility bills, phone bills, maybe some kids with middle parts. She deserves a chance more than I do—that's just basic marginal utility economics. So if I lose, I'll just tell all my friends and family, "Oh, I took a dive for a friend in need."

And then she takes out her BlackBerry pager. Shit. There goes my excuse. Anyone with a BlackBerry pager isn't sleeping on vents in Central Park or waiting in line at soup kitchens, unless those soup kitchens are serving twenty-three-dollar bowls of bouillabaisse with sprigs of parsley. Now I've got no reason to throw the test. Pressure's back on.

My BlackBerry-owning friend tells me that this is her second day of trying to audition. Yesterday, the *Millionaire* folks gave her the wrong time to show up, then treated her with all the dignity of a used napkin. I shake my head. We speculate that they treat us badly because they feel threatened by our intellect. It's a good feeling—the feeling of being part of an oppressed but brainy minority.

After forty-five minutes of waiting—during which, for some reason, I start mentally reviewing vice presidents on the chance that they will play a major part in the *Millionaire* quiz (Hubert Humphrey, George Dallas, Charles Warren Fairbanks)—we are ushered into a huge room. The room has posters of actual millionaires—ABC stars like Drew Carey.

The *Millionaire* helpers pass out the quizzes and the official *Who Wants to Be a Millionaire* number 2 pencils to the hundred-plus hopefuls. We have eleven minutes to answer thirty multiple choice questions. Now go!

The questions are of midlevel difficulty. They aren't like the disturbingly simple hundred-dollar questions on the show, the ones like "What color is an orange?" but they also aren't the million-dollar variety, like "What was the name of Cardinal Richelieu's pet cockatoo?"

I dive in.

What does not follow a straight path?
    (a) the Equator
    (b) the Tropic of Cancer
    (c) the International Date Line
    (d) the meridian

I knew it! I knew it thanks very much to the *Britannica*, which had a map of the International Date Line taking a jog to the west so that it would avoid the Aleutian Islands. I'm feeling good, feeling cocky.

Which planet cannot be seen with the naked eye?
    (a) Mercury
    (b) Saturn
    (c) Jupiter
    (d) Neptune

Again, the *Britannica* to the rescue. I know my planets. I remember the poor telescope operator Challis whose claim to fame is that he failed to discover Neptune. Neptune's the tough one to find. Neptune it is.

I zip through the rest. And here's the weird part: the questions that leave me baffled mostly focus on my former safe haven, pop culture.

What country is Latina pop star Shakira from? Not a clue. If I were keeping up with my *People* magazines instead of burying my nose in the *Britannica*, I would know.

This is big. I've officially made the switch in where my gaps lie. As I've started to fill in holes in history and science and literature, new holes have opened up in pop culture. I make a guess about Shakira's native land (it's Colombia) and am finished a good four minutes before they tell us, "Pencils down!"

"So how'd you do?" I ask my unemployed BlackBerry owner.

"Pretty well," she says. "I didn't know the one about Captain Matthew Perry."

"Commodore Matthew Perry," I correct her.

"Yes, Commodore Perry. I didn't know which country he opened up to trade."

"That'd be Japan," I say, suppressing the urge to pat her on the head. "Did you think it was the Republic of Courteney Cox?" I chuckle.

She doesn't react.

"Because, you know, the actor on *Friends* is named Matthew Perry as well," I say. "And he's going out with Courteney Cox on the show."

God, I can be a condescending schmuck. Meanwhile, the other end of our table has become very noisy. A fierce debate has erupted over the question "Which advertising character is known for lying?" The correct answer is fast-talking eighties car salesman Joe Isuzu, but one man is arguing that Madge—the Palmolive lady—was also a stinking liar. Madge refused to admit that her soft hands were the result of submersion in Palmolive. A lie.

But the argument will have to wait. The tests have been graded by *Millionaire*'s speedy computer. We were each assigned a number—mine is two—and the emcee begins calling out the winners.

"Number three!"

The crowd claps grudgingly for number three, who stands up and takes a deep waist bow.

"Number eighty-six!"

More halfhearted applause.

As he reads off number after number, I start to doubt myself. Maybe Shakira screwed me. "Number fourteen!" Maybe after months of stuffing my head, I'm still so ignorant I can't get an audience with Meredith Vieira. "Number two."

Thank God! *"Yes!"* I shout, as I jump up and do a Rocky fist pump. I'm as happy as Lindbergh landing at Paris (his prize: $25,000).

There are about fifteen of us winners—my BlackBerry friend among us—and we are instructed to migrate to the back of the room. Our crucible isn't over. We still have to clear another hurdle: the interview. We are smart enough, but are we interesting and presentable enough? Do we have enough personality and basic hygiene? Are we semiattractive?

I am just as nervous about passing the telegenic test as I was about the knowledge quiz. It reminds me of a particularly humiliating episode in my career. This was about ten years ago, back when I was in my midtwenties and trying to sell my first book—an analysis of the eerie similarities between Jesus and Elvis. One of the publishing companies said they loved the book, but they had just one request: could they see a photograph of me?

"Why do they want a photograph?" I asked my agent. "Is this normal?"

"They just want to make sure you're presentable, so you can go on talk shows. Just to make sure you don't have three heads."

So I went to a photographer at a department store near San Francisco, where I was living at the time. The photographer put me in front of some oscillating fans so as to tousle my hair just right, gave me some flattering upward lighting, and snapped a few dozen pictures. I sent them in.

A week later, my agent calls. "I'm sorry, they've decided to pass."

As you can imagine, this was not the best news for my ego. Apparently, I wasn't good-looking enough to be an author. An author. I wasn't asking to be a soap opera actor or a news anchor or a Gucci model. I just wanted to sit in my room alone and write books. But apparently I wasn't even attractive enough to do that. Did Nathaniel Hawthorne have the ladies' hearts aflutter? Did Herman Melville have killer abs? Maybe so.

In any case, I'm hoping that the *Millionaire* folks are a little more liberal. The interviews are one-on-one affairs, and mine is with a young brunette named Wendy.

"So how would your friends describe you?" she asks.

I hate that question. What am I supposed to say? That they think I'm wildly entertaining and shockingly intelligent? "I guess they'd describe me as lanky."

She seems confused. "That's all they'd say?"

"Maybe lanky and brown-haired."

She knits her brows. Uh-oh. This is not going well. I learn my lesson, and answer the rest of her questions in as orthodox a manner as possible. My delivery, however, is not ideal. I spend the remainder of the interview mumbling and shifting my eyes. Instead of the effervescent game show contestant that I should be, I come off as if I've just been arrested for shoplifting marital aids.

Wendy takes out the Polaroid.

"Okay, say 'cheese'!"

I thought it'd be funny to say "Emmentaler cheese, which is what the Swiss call Swiss cheese, which gets its holes from the carbon dioxide that is formed while it ferments at seventy-five degrees." But I don't. I just say "cheese." Which is probably a good thing.

pet
It's believed that the ancient Egyptians used geese as guard animals.

Petrarch
I'm completely ignorant of this man, but he sounds like someone I should know about. Here's what I learn: He's a 14th-century Italian poet famous for his chaste love of a woman named Laura. He first spotted Laura on April 6, 1327, at the Church of Saint Clare in Avignon, when he was 22 years old. He loved her, says the *Britannica,* almost until his death, even though she was out of his reach. And from this love sprang the poems that made Petrarch's name.

Oh boy. Another one of these guys. There are at least a dozen such fellows sprinkled through the encyclopedia. Like Dante, who dedicated most of his poetry to a woman named Beatrice, whom he loved and worshiped since he saw her at age nine, even though he never got so much as a single peck on the cheek. Or Byron, obsessed for decades with his cousin, who had spurned him as a young man.

What's the word we have today for men like this? Oh yes. "Stalker." If they were around now, Beatrice and Laura would slap restraining orders on their respective obsessors. Perhaps something like "Mr. Petrarch is forbidden to come within one hundred yards of Laura. In addition, he is forbidden to write sonnets, octets, epics, couplets, limericks, or haiku that name or allude to Laura in any way, most especially ones that compare her to a summer day."

And what about the husbands? Yes, these yearned-for women were, in many cases, married, but you never get these schmos' side of the story.

Beatrice, the daughter of a noble Florentine family, got married to a man named Simone. If he didn't, Simone needed to have a little conversation with Dante:

"I can't help but notice that you keep writing love poetry to my *wife*. Well, you see, I married her, which makes her my *wife*. You know what you might want to try? Writing some poems about the sunset. The sunset isn't fucking married."

I know I shouldn't be thinking these thoughts. I know they make me sound like a philistine. I know I'm looking at the long and marvelous history of romantic love through my shallow 21st-century lenses. I'm supposed to be smartening up. Shouldn't I marvel at the depth of their emotion? Shouldn't I be inspired to read their love poems?

Instead, I just want to tell them to shut their cake holes and get over it. I want to tell them to go on Dr. Phil and get their head chewed off. I want to tell them what I tell my friend John, who is still hung up on his college crush, a woman who later went on to star in an Adam Sandler movie. "John, you can't have her. It's over. Sign on to match.com and find yourself a new woman. Okay?"

Of course, Petrarch and Dante probably didn't have match.com available. They'd have to settle for something more primitive, like video dating services. But you get the idea.

philosophy

I studied philosophy for four years. But I'd trade everything I learned for this passage, originally written by a scholar named Robert Ardrey and quoted in the *Britannica*:

But we were born of risen apes, not fallen angels, and the apes were armed killers besides. And so what shall we wonder at? Our murders and massacres and missiles, and our irreconcilable regiments? Or our treaties whatever they may be worth; our symphonies however seldom they may be played; our peaceful acres, however frequently they may be converted into battlefields; our dreams however rarely they may be accomplished. The miracle of man is not how far he has sunk but how magnificently he has risen. We are known among the stars by our poems, not our corpses.

Amen. That's great stuff. If ever I was going to faint like the woman who read Montaigne's essays, this would be the time, because that is a powerful set of sentences. That has been the major and ongoing battle as I read the *Britannica* and live my life—the battle to find the bright side, which is something I'm not constitutionally inclined to do. Never has the case been stated better. Of course, I don't like poems. But I'm happy to substitute that we are known among the stars by our movies, books, a great joke, a comfortable pair of shoes, a beautiful and towering building—and not by our corpses.

Phryne

I now know far too much about odd legal proceedings. I know about the 9th-century trial of Pope Formosus. He didn't do so well under cross-examination, seeing as he was—I believe this is the technical term—dead. His successor—Pope Stephen VI—hated Formosus's policies so much, he had Formosus's corpse exhumed, propped up on a throne, and put on trial. Shockingly, Formosus lost. As punishment, his fingers were cut off and his corpse was thrown into the Tiber River.

I also know about the Burmese practice known as "Ordeal by divination," in which two parties are given candles of equal size that are lighted simultaneously; the owner of the candle that lasts longer wins the case. And I know about the medieval practice of "appeal to the corpse," which allowed the dead body to point out the murderer.

So I know some things. But nothing could prepare me for the trial of Phryne. Phryne was a famous prostitute in ancient Greece. Her name means Toad—a sobriquet she picked up because of her sallow complexion.. Phryne was phenomenally successful at her job; she made so much money she offered to rebuild the walls of Thebes. But she was also controversial, as prostitutes tend to be.

Phryne was on trial for blasphemy, a capital offense. Things were looking a bit bleak for Phryne, so she employed an interesting defense. In the words of the *Britannica,* Phryne tore her dress and "displayed her bosom, which so moved the jury that they acquitted her." That's what the *EB* says. She flashed her tits and she got released. I believe in legal circles this is called the "Greek Whore Gone Wild defense."

Now, I don't need the *EB* to teach me that your average heterosexual man loves looking at boobs. I've worked at a couple of magazines that based their economic model on this fact. I've received an e-mail from my previous boss expressing outrage that Jodie Foster's nipple had been digitally erased from a photo. So I know.

Still, this is surprising historical evidence. Men really will do anything after looking at a lady's top shelf. A pair of breasts are mesmerizing enough to be a powerful weapon. No doubt, Phryne's were particularly impressive—they were green, for one thing. And earlier in the *Britannica,* I read that jury duty lasted an entire year in ancient Greece. So the guys were probably desperate for a little variety.

But I wonder if lawyers today could make this work. It could revolutionize the profession. "Yes, my client poisoned her husband and chopped him into chunks the size of croutons and fed him to her Rottweiler. We admit that. But gentlemen of the jury: have you seen her rack?"

pigeon

I know I just talked about passenger pigeons. But I've reached the entry on the nonpassenger kind, the regular old pigeons who are, right now, as always, strutting on the windowsill of my office.

After reading about them, I lay my volume on the glass table and spend a good five minutes observing the three-dimensional version. Their characteristic head bobbing when they walk from one end of the ledge to the other. The skin saddle between the bill and the forehead. Their little orange eyes. The way they dive their bill into their feathers to preen, which I have learned spreads skin oil to the feathers.

They're remarkable. They may be flying rats, as my mom calls them, but they're remarkable flying rats. Plus, they're monogamous for life—and when one dies, the surviving spouse accepts a new mate only slowly—which makes me empathize with them all the more.

As I stare dumbfounded at the three pigeons head-bobbing their way along the ledge, I have that "whoa" feeling, as if I've just done some bong hits, like that freshman in *Animal House* who said, "You mean, our whole solar system could be one tiny atom in the fingernail of some giant being?" Three hours of heavy reading will do that to me, send my mind into a different state. I find myself being blown away by pigeons.

Earlier, I was concerned that all this reading was bad for my relationship with the world. I wondered if I wasn't like John Locke's blind man, who learned all about the concept of scarlet but remained totally clueless as to its true nature. Maybe. But I've decided it can have the opposite effect too. It can enhance my relationship with the world, make me marvel at it, see it with new eyes.

And those eyes are constantly shifting. When I read about the hydrosphere, I see the world as a vehicle for water—the rain, the evaporation, the rivers, the clouds. Then I'll read about energy conversion, and see the world as a collection of ever-shifting quanta of energy. There are infinite numbers of ways to slice the universe, and I keep seeing cut after cut. Recently, I tried to trace the role of pumpkins through history (the highlight being the Pumpkin Papers, which were documents from alleged spy Alger Hiss that were hidden in pumpkins). Pumpkins might be slicing it too thin. Perhaps gourds would be better.

Pirandello, Luigi

The Italian playwright, creator of *Six Characters in Search of an Author*. Pirandello said in 1920: "I think that life is a very sad piece of buffoonery; because we have in ourselves, without being able to know why, wherefore or whence, the need to deceive ourselves constantly by creating a reality (one for each and never the same for all), which from time to time is discovered to be vain and illusory. . . . My art is full of bitter compassion for all those who deceive themselves; but this compassion cannot fail to be followed by the ferocious derision of destiny which condemns man to deception." Good Lord. That's a bleak paragraph. That is just the kind of thinking I'm a sucker for—that life is just a sad piece of buffoonery. But it's not healthy. I've got to fight it, wash it out of my mind with thoughts like Robert Ardrey's on the miracle of man. Is Ardrey's point of view just pitiable self-deception? I hope not.

planetary features

Julie comes into my reading room.

"Honey," she says, "look at this. What do you think is going on?"

She lifts her shirt to reveal a rash that has taken over a good part of her stomach.

"Looks like the Great Red Spot on the surface of Jupiter."

"What?"

"The Great Red Spot. It's this strange big red cloud on Jupiter, like fifteen thousand miles long. Scientists don't know what causes it, but they think it's a storm or maybe a—"

Julie pulls her shirt down and walks out. Not another word. Just walks out of the room and shuts the door a little too hard. Uh-oh. Not good. When she's peeved, Julie argues with you, gives you sass, lets you know exactly what's annoying her.

But when she's furious, she clams up and walks right out of the room. When she's furious, she goes scarily silent and retreats to another place until she calms down.

This is a furious.

I probably should have known this is not the best time for a fun fact. I already pushed Julie to the breaking point this morning. She suggested that maybe we have a picnic in the Central Park—it was such a nice day. I told her no thanks. I could see the park from the window in the reading room.

So that didn't go well. And now this.

I try to go back to reading. I start in on *Plateau Indian* and *platform tennis*, but it's not working; I'm too distracted.

Julie doesn't even have to argue with me. I'm arguing with myself, and I'm losing: She doesn't need this now, not with our fertility woes already blackening moods. She doesn't need to hear about an astronomical phenomenon. She needs to hear: "Oh, no. I'm sorry to see that you have a rash. Does it itch? Can I help? Have you eaten anything unusual?" When these facts in my brain push out my ability to empathize, then maybe I've got to reassess. When I'm too busy parading around my knowledge to ask about the health of my wife, that's bad news.

A couple of days ago I was congratulating myself on my appreciation for pigeons. But now I feel like doing some penance. I feel as though I should flagellate myself like a 14th-century Christian (before the practice was condemned by Pope Clement VI). Instead, I go to the bathroom and fetch a tube of Lanacane anti-itch cream.

I crack the door of the bedroom, where Julie has retreated. Her fury has melted to sadness. I hold out my peace offering, a yellow tube of ointment.

"Sorry."

"I really need you to be here for me."

"I know."

Plath, Sylvia

What *is* it with writers and suicide? I knew about Plath before I read the *P*s—and I knew about Hemingway before I read the *H*s. But man, what an army of company they have. Writers are drawn to self-destruction like hawk moths to the Madagascar orchid (the insect has a remarkable nine-inch nose that it uses on the orchid's long nectar receptacle). I tried to start a body count every time I read another self-destructive writer, but it got so high I'd need scientific notation.

A French writer I'd never heard of hanged himself from a lamppost. A Peruvian did it in a deserted classroom. A Japanese poet finished himself off with his mistress at a mountain retreat. They throw themselves down stairwells, they leap from bridges. One Hungarian writer weighted his clothes down with stones and jumped in a lake, foreshadowing Virginia Woolf, who will do the same in another few thousand pages.

And that's not to mention the writers who tried to commit suicide and failed. Among them: Joseph Conrad, Maxim Gorky, Guy de Maupassant, Eugene O'Neill. Pretty impressive list, actually. If I plan to continue this writing thing, I better tell Julie to hide my razor blades and remove the shoelaces from my sneakers.

I find the whole phenomenon a bit baffling. As far as jobs go, writers have a pretty sweet deal. You make your own hours, the dress code is remarkably lax. You rarely strain your back, you don't have your phone calls recorded for training purposes, and you don't have to intentionally lose to clients at golf. And the ladies like you.

These writers need to buck up and suck up and keep the nooses off their damn necks. I haven't read about a lot of coal miners committing suicide (okay, there aren't quite as many coal miners who get write-ups in the *Britannica,* but you get the idea).

Plato

More philosophy. I get to Plato as I sit on an Acela train that's whizzing quietly and efficiently toward Philadelphia. It's Friday, and I'm with Julie—who is, thankfully, rash free—on our way to visit her brother Doug for the weekend.

I read the fable about Plato's cave just as the train emerges from a tunnel. Weird, I think to myself. I'm coming out of a cave just as I read about coming out of a cave. Well, maybe not that weird. These coincidences happen all the time. I read the *fatigue* entry as I huffed away on the Stairmaster. I read about the Julian calendar while watching a miniseries about Julius Caesar. I read so damn much, these overlappings are bound to happen. If the tunnel hadn't happened, something else might have—some guy might be eating a Greek salad in the next row, or slightly less likely, drinking a glass of hemlock.

In any case, I'm reading Plato and I have to say, I'm not impressed. His theory of forms seems absurd, even infuriating. Plato wrote about the existence of another world, apart from the physical world, a world filled with ideal forms. Somewhere, there's an ideal man, stone, shape, color, beauty, justice. Somewhere, there's the Platonic ideal of a bottle, of a chair.

Seems like a bunch of what they used to call hogwash. Problem is, reading the *Britannica* is a very un-Platonic experience. Over the last 21,000 pages, I've watched everything change and evolve—men, stones, beauty, everything. How can there be an ideal form of a chair? Which of the dozens of chair styles would you choose to represent this ideal? The 18th-century ottoman? The 19th-century cockfighting chair? And what of beauty? Anyone who says that it's eternal needs to take a look at the stone cutting they show in the *Britannica* representing Helen of Troy, the great beauty of her day. She looked like a drag queen in need of a nose job. Today, that Helen of Troy wouldn't make it past a local Miss Broccoli pageant, much less Miss Universe. She wouldn't launch a dinghy today.

Yes, there are a few constants among the thousands of changes. Like Planck's constant, a physical law that says that radiation emitted from atoms remains steady. And I'd like to think that "Thou shalt not kill" is a moral constant. But you won't find them in some outlandish otherworld of ideal forms.

Likewise, I hate Plato's theory of knowledge. He resides on the knowledge-is-internal side of the spectrum. Like his teacher Socrates, Plato said that men already have all the knowledge in the world, they just need to have it drawn out of them. This, in my opinion, is more of what they used to call claptrap. I'm on the empiricist side of the knowledge debate, the side that says it all comes from the senses. I don't trust internal knowledge. Of course, there's a little rationalization going on here. I've just spent the last eight months getting knowledge through my senses. If it's true that the most important knowledge is interior, then I'm a moron.

Regardless of whether I'm right or wrong, I have to give myself credit: this is a big improvement over my interior dialogue during the Aristotle entry. Remember that one? The one that went something like: "Hey, he likes hot young girls." "Yeah, that's cool."

plumbing

Allow me to present Sir John Harington, another in the *Britannica*'s continuing series of unsung heroes, and one who got his own two solid paragraphs back in the *H*s. I'm stunned I haven't heard of Harington. This guy invented a device that affects my life just as much as Edison's lightbulb or the Wright brothers' airplane, something every American uses several times a day, not counting that drunken Sigma Chi pledge who repeatedly peed on my duvet cover freshman year of college. And yet I'd never seen Harington's name.

At one point, I'd heard Thomas Crapper invented the flush toilet. Then I was told that was a myth—which it is—but I never learned the real identity of the man behind the can. Finally, here he is. And what a likable rascal he is.

The first thing to strike me is that Harington is no shlub; he's the godson of Queen Elizabeth I of England and a member of her court. But as befits the father of the toilet, he wasn't exactly the most pristine courtier. In his twenties, Harington distributed among the ladies of the court a "wanton tale" by the 16th-century Italian poet Ariosto. Elizabeth was not amused. She banished her godson, imposing on him a punishment that doesn't qualify as cruel, but it sure is unusual. She ordered him to translate Ariosto's notoriously long epic poem, *Orlando Furioso*. Beats becoming a prison bitch, I guess.

After doing his homework and returning to court, Harington invented the flush toilet and installed one for Queen Elizabeth in her palace. You'd think he'd get a parade. Not so much. He had the gall to write a playful book about his invention called *The Metamorphosis of Ajax* (a pun on "a jakes," which was Elizabethan slang for a water closet). As the *Britannica* says, Harington's book described his toilet "in terms more Rabelaisian than mechanical," and he was again banished from court. Exasperated—at least I would be—Harington went on a military expedition to Ireland, which finally got him knighted. A moderately happy ending for Sir John. I think Harington has my favorite résumé in the *Britannica*—even better than Goethe's: plumber, translator, wit, army officer, royal godson, scoundrel. I don't know how history overlooked him. What does a guy have to do to get some respect? A forgotten military jaunt to Ireland gets him knighted, but revolutionizing the bathroom doesn't? And don't think Harington gets respect whenever we call the bathroom a "john." That name came about independently. We really should be calling it the Harington.

Poe, Edgar Allan
He married his cousin when she was thirteen. Sort of the Jerry Lee Lewis of his day but with more interest in Gothic imagery.

pop quiz

We're back from Philly, and my mom has sent Julie and me an e-mail. For years, my mom refused to get e-mail, saying she thought it was a waste of time, but now that she's gotten it, she's become a frighteningly enthusiastic forwarder of lawyer jokes, Jewish jokes, wacky haiku, and other things with smiley emoticons at the end of them. This e-mail is a collection of trivia called "Think you know everything? Think again." So admittedly, it's pretty relevant.

After the Great Red Spot debacle, I've been very good recently about refraining from inserting unwanted facts into conversations with Julie. But this time I have license. Julie wants to quiz me. As I lie on the couch, my *Britannica* resting on my chest, she reads off her Macintosh screen.

"All right. A dime has how many ridges around the edge?"

"Two hundred and forty-four," I say.

"No. A hundred and eighteen."

"What did Al Capone's business card say he did?"

"Phrenologist."

"No, used furniture dealer."

"Who invented the words 'assassination' and 'bump'?"

"Well, Assassins were an Islamic sect. They were named for the hashish they smoked to get into a frenzied state before acts of war."

"No. Shakespeare. What is the longest one-syllable word in the English language?"

"Makalakamakai," I say. No doubt Alexander Woolcott would have had the exact same answer had this question been asked at the Algonquin—and had "makalakamakai" been a one-syllable word.

"No, 'screeched.' Which winter was so cold that Niagara Falls froze over?"

"Nineteen thirty-two," I say confidently.

"Yes," says Julie. She looks at me. She seems genuinely impressed, even amazed.

"How did you know that?"

Frankly, I guessed. Pure plucked-from-thin-air speculation. But there is no way I am going to tell Julie that. I am going to take full credit for this one.

"I just know a lot," I say. "I know so much sometimes I don't even know how much I know."

Powhatan

Powhatan was an Indian tribal leader and the father of Pocahontas. I went to Camp Powhatan in Maine for three summers—and until very recently received the *Pow-Wow Newsletter,* keeping me apprised of such vital information as the construction of a new outhouse facility near Bunk 14—and yet somehow I was able to remain ignorant of the identity of Powhatan himself. This is a little embarrassing. I probably should have paid attention to my history textbook or at least gone to see Disney's *Pocahontas.* That might have helped.

Powhatan, says the *Britannica,* was "a bright and energetic ruler, but he was also noted as being cruel." This is appropriate, because we campers were both energetic and cruel, as well. But mostly cruel. We were a real bunch of prepubescent schmucks. I'm thinking in particular of our treatment of Rob Blonkin, a frizzy-haired twelve-year-old from upstate New York who suffered from numerous twitches, most notably one involving excessive puckering, which immediately qualified him as our scapegoat (the original scapegoat, of course, was burdened with sins and thrown over a Jerusalem cliff).

We developed several methods of mental torture. In one, we'd go up to Rob and say, very quickly, "Hi, Rob. How you doing, Rob? Bye, Rob"—then walk away. This would leave him sputtering in frustration, still formulating his response of "I'm fine." In another method—our most sophisticated and evil—we'd sing "All Around the Mulberry Bush" in a particularly menacing manner, which, without fail, caused Rob to burst into tears. No one knew why. It was a Pavlovian thing, I guess; we'd start by growling, "All around," and by the time we got to "Pop goes the weasel," Rob's cheeks were wet.

I'm not proud of this behavior. Those summers were my lowest moments as a moral being. (During the school year, I was more likely to be the one sprouting tears from bullies who were making fun of my acne, of which there are fifty different types, by the way.) I don't have an excuse. Maybe I was so focused on being the smartest boy in the world. Looking back, maybe I should have tried to be the most moral boy in the world. Maybe I should have said, "Hey, instead of making Blonkin cry, let's have a bake sale and donate the money to farmers in developing countries."

One thing is for sure: if Julie and I ever have a boy, I'm not sending him to an all-male camp. Exclusively male environments lead to trouble.

The *EB* talks about the increased incidence of aggressive behavior in small groups of isolated men, such as polar explorers and prisoners. No doubt about that. Polar explorers, prisoners, and predominantly Jewish summer camps in Maine and Vermont. But I digress. Back to the books.

precedent

I've never met someone else who read the *Encyclopaedia Britannica* from *A* to *Z*. There've been a couple of people in the same ballpark, reference-book-wise. My mother-in-law, Barbara, for instance, has read almost the entire Manhattan phone book. She loves it. Thinks it should be on Oprah's book club. She tells me she started to read it when she was a kid visiting her grandparents. They were just over from the old country, spoke no English, and spent their days eating chicken fat and weeping. "So what do kids do when adults are crying?" says Barbara. "They read the phone book, of course." She says this emphatically, as if it's a perfectly logical syllogism. Who am I to question it? So ever since childhood, Barbara has devoured a few letters whenever she has some free time. "I learn some very interesting things," she says. I once asked her what exactly she's learned. "Well, I learned that a man I know who works with Spike Lee lives in the building next to yours." That kind of thing.

And every couple of weeks or so, I run into someone who confesses to being an encyclopedia dabbler. One man told me how his mom stashed the *Britannica* in the kids' bathroom growing up. She was hoping to fill her children's minds while they voided other parts of their bodies. Problem was, this guy would remain seated on the toilet reading about Faulkner and flamingos and flounders for hours, while his siblings banged on the door outside and suffered bladder distress.

But these are amateurs. I've never met anyone who's completed the alphabetical marathon that is the great *EB*. (Incidentally, the modern marathon gets its distance—26 miles and 385 yards—because the British Olympic committee in 1908 wanted it to go from Windsor Castle to the Royal Box in London Stadium.) I've never met anyone who has attempted to read every word. I know they're out there. Or at least they were in the past. George Bernard Shaw read the complete ninth edition at the British Museum. Physicist Richard Feynman consumed an entire set. C. S. Forester—the author of the *Horatio Hornblower* series—also read the *EB*. And he read it twice, which I suppose makes him twice as smart as

I will ever be. It's not clear whether Aldous Huxley—the author of *Brave New World*—read the entire thing, but he carried half-sized volumes with him on trips, calling it the best travel reading around.

These guys were no slouches, and that made me feel good. After polishing off *Z*, maybe I'll come up with a revolutionary theorem in astrophysics or at the very least, write a respected nautical novel. But these names were also unsatisfying. I wanted someone living, someone with whom I could swap war stories.

I called the *Britannica* headquarters and spoke to the publicist Tom Panelas. As you might expect, Tom was the smartest publicist I had ever encountered. In all my years talking to publicists for Paul Reiser and Bruce Willis and the like, I had never heard the adjective "Borgesian." Tom used it. He also knew all about Huxley's *Britannica* habit—and added that Huxley died on November 22, 1963—the exact same day as C. S. Lewis and John F. Kennedy. Good to know.

Tom told me there had been other faithful readers over the years— that's what we're called, "faithful readers"—but he didn't know if any of them were still alive. (He assured me that there isn't a causal relationship. My head won't explode.) He promised to investigate further.

A couple of days later, Tom called with an update. The only other person currently reading the entire *Britannica* is a guy in a small town in China. He wrote a couple of fan letters awhile back, but the letters are gone, and the *EB* folks have no way of contacting him. On the other hand, there's one living American who read the *Britannica* from *A* to *Z* decades ago, when he was a kid. His name is Michael DeBakey. As any fan of surgical breakthroughs knows, DeBakey has since gone on to become a world-famous heart doctor—he implanted the first artificial heart in 1963—and to merit his own four paragraphs in the *Britannica*.

I phoned up Dr. DeBakey and was surprised when the esteemed ninety-five-year-old physician got on the line. DeBakey has a wonderful Louisiana drawl and a warm way about him. I think I'd feel comfortable having him reroute my aorta, even if he's seen a few dozen birthdays.

"When I was a child," DeBakey says, "my parents allowed us to take one book out of the library every week. I came home one day and said there was a wonderful book at the library—but they wouldn't lend it to me. My parents said, 'What is it?' And I said, 'It's the *Encyclopaedia Britannica*.' So they bought a set. I was about ten or twelve years old, so it must have been 1919 or so. By the time I went to college, I had finished the whole thing. I had four siblings, and all of us would rush through our lessons so we could get to read the encyclopedia."

I ask him, as a man who has survived the voyage from *A* to *Z*, if he has any advice for me.

"You have a job and a family," says Dr. DeBakey. "You only have a limited amount of time. The thing you want to do is skip over the topics you aren't interested in."

I don't want to be rude, so I jot down his wisdom and thank him. But my actual reaction is: What? I can't do that. I'm trying to achieve something here. Trying to finish something consequential—if simultaneously ludicrous—for the first time in my life. I can't run fourteen miles of marathon, and take a cab through the neighborhoods that don't appeal. I've got to be—as Alex Trebek says—curious about things that don't interest me.

procrastination
I'm pissed at myself. I just spent forty-five minutes Googling my ex-girlfriends and ex-crushes. That's just information I don't need. I don't need to know that Noel Dawkins is a consultant on an indie movie called *Dead Sexy*. Or that Rachel Zabar still holds the record for the 1600-meter dash at the Dalton School. Or that Kathleen Murtha—probably not even the Kathleen Murtha I know—wrote a letter of recommendation for a California roofing service. This is an unhealthy addiction, this Google, a waste of my time and brain space. Those forty-five minutes could have been spent any number of ways: reading the *Britannica* would have been nice, or hanging out with my wife, or maybe sorting our rubber bands by size and color. As Dr. DeBakey points out, I have a limited amount of time. So that's it: No more inconsequential Googling, I tell myself. Though I know that vow will be unbroken for maybe three days, max.

It's been a constant battle to dam the data flood that comes with being a 21st-century American. I'm trying to keep my mind relatively free from non-*Britannica* information, on the Sherlock Holmesian theory that there's only so much room in the mental attic. And I have made a little progress. I've cut way down on the *New York Post;* no more updates on Kirsten Dunst's canoodling behavior for me. I trimmed back on my *New York Times* consumption—only the important articles about world events; no more whimsical stories about the trend for upscale luaus.

Proust, Marcel

It wasn't a madeleine. In real life, Proust's memories were sparked by a rusk biscuit, which is basically another name for zweiback toast. He changed it when he wrote *Remembrance of Things Past*. What's wrong with zweiback? I'm just guessing, but I smell a corrupt product placement deal with the madeleine industry.

Public school

I was lucky enough to go to a fancy private school. But my dad—he was a pure public school kid. He took the subway every day from the Upper West Side of Manhattan to Bronx Science, a public school for gifted children, mostly middle-class Jewish kids at the time.

I know a good amount about my dad's education after high school. I know about his many, many diplomas. He's told me how engineering school battered his eyesight with its microscopic charts on steam pressure. He's told me about how, during law school, he operated some of the earliest computers—the ones with punch cards and vacuum tubes that sprawled over several basketball courts. He even wrote a paper on how computers could influence the legal field, modestly proposing that computers be the judge, jury, and—since they were already electric—executioner. So I know about his college days.

But the high school era—that's sketchy. So as part of my continuing effort to figure out the origin of my mania for knowledge, I figure it'd be good to get a few more details on my dad's formative years. The next time I see him—it's at a benefit thrown by my grandfather—I corner my dad.

My dad, of course, is reluctant to answer seriously. But I press him. "It's for my encyclopedia project," I tell him, cryptically. Well, he says, there's not really much to tell. His favorite subjects were math and science. He had a ducktail haircut.

And how was he as a student? Top 5 percent? Top 10?

He shakes his head. "Oh no. Top seventy-eighth percentile."

What? Is this a joke?

"No. I was in the seventy-eighth percentile."

"How'd that happen?"

"I had a rule. I only did homework on the subway to and from school. If I didn't finish it on the subway, it never got done."

This was a weird revelation. My dad as a slacker. It's strange to discover your dad's flaws, even if they're small and forty-five years old.

Somehow, it makes his twenty-four books seem less intimidating. Even slow starters like my dad can end up accomplishing great things.

Puccini

Julie convinced me to go to the theater. I try to go to the theater about once per Juglar cycle (the eight-year financial cycle of global recession). The genre just doesn't appeal to me. I grew up on movies and TV, so whenever I'm at a Broadway show, I keep waiting for the director to cut to a new scene. Where's the montage? Where's the extreme close-up featuring the actor's huge, unblinking eyes? Instead, I'm looking at the exact same sawed-in-half house for an entire excruciating hour.

But Julie tells me that if I'm trying to become smarter, I should engage in some highbrow cultural activities. And she's right. So I found myself sitting in my red faux velvet seat at the Broadway production of the opera *La Bohème,* waiting for the show to start.

"So is it what you expected?" says Julie.

"What?"

"The inside of a Broadway theater."

"I *have* been to a couple of shows before."

"Now, remember, there won't be any previews. It's just going to start right in."

"Okay, okay. Very good."

"And no yelling at the screen," she said. "Because these are live actors, and they can hear you."

Mercifully, the lights go down and the show begins. It's not a bad show. The plot line is okay—a love story with a little consumption thrown in. But now, a couple of weeks later, as I read about *La Bohème*'s composer, Giacomo Puccini, I've become less impressed. The problem is, Puccini's life contained more high drama and surprising twists than his operas. Why didn't Puccini just write some librettos out of his diary? Here's what he could have put to music:

In the 1880s, says the *Britannica,* Puccini caused a scandal when he fled from his Italian hometown of Lucca with a married woman named Elvira. His affair with Elvira— whom he eventually married—was juicy, but it was only Act I. In 1908, "Elvira unexpectedly became jealous of Doria Manfredi, a young servant from the village who had been employed for several years by the Puccinis. She drove Doria from the house, threatening to kill her. Subsequently, the servant girl poisoned herself, and her parents had the body examined by a physician, who declared her a virgin. The Manfredis brought charges against Elvira for persecution and calumny, creating one of the most famous scandals of the day." Elvira, says the *EB*, was found guilty, but Puccini paid off Doria's parents to keep Elvira out of prison. After that, Puccini's marriage was "in name only."

Murder threats, poison, adultery, trial, young servant girls—what more do you want? That's one lesson the *Britannica* drives home every day: truth is better than fiction.

punctuation

The Greek interrogation mark became the English semicolon. Bizarre, no;

Pythagoras

Here I encountered one of the quirkiest men in the encyclopedia. He seemed so harmless—the inventor of the perfectly rational geometric theorem that bears his name. But not counting his admirable work with triangles, Pythagoras was a complete and total wacko. He founded a religious brotherhood in ancient Greece—and by religious brotherhood, I mean a fringe cult. According to the encyclopedia, members of the brotherhood were told to "refrain from speaking about the holy, wear white clothes, observe sexual purity, not touch beans, and so forth."

That's what it said: do not touch beans. The *Britannica* offered no explanation for this edict, which it listed as if it was just another run-of-the-mill commandment, along the lines of "Do not kill your parents." It didn't say whether that meant all beans, or just certain beans like kidney or pinto. Just those four words. Sometimes I'm inspired to venture into non-*Britannica* sources to clarify a point—but in the case of no-bean-touching, I decided to accept it and move on.

Legumes aside, Pythagoras also had a complex set of beliefs about the spiritual qualities of mathematics and the holy attributes of certain numbers. The brotherhood was way into math. Fanatically so. The brothers allegedly drowned one of their members because he pointed out the existence of irrational numbers, which didn't jibe with the Pythagorean worldview.

All this was interesting enough, but it wasn't the most notable lesson I took away from the Pythagoras sections (he is featured in his own write-up but also gets some ink in the *philosophy* entry). The most notable lesson came when I was reading about the Pythagoreans' love of something called a *gnomon*. This square was constructed out of dots or pebbles, and was meant to represent certain numbers. The number 16, for instance, looked like this:

```
.  .  .  .
.  .  .  .
.  .  .  .
.  .  .  .
```

A perfect square. Using the *gnomon*, the Pythagoreans figured out the square root. The square root of 16? That would be the four dots at the bottom of the square. In other words, the square root is actually a *square root*. The word "square" in the phrase is not just some coincidence.

This was a revelation to me. Did everyone know this? Is this so startlingly obvious that I should I be ashamed I had never made the connection? Maybe. But I'm happy, at least, that I understand it now.

I've come to realize that dozens of words and phrases have been detached from their origins, and the *Britannica* is helping me put them back together. "Cupboard" is a place to board cups. "Holiday" is a holy day. "Fiberglass" is a fiber made from glass. "Marshmallow" was originally made with the marshmallow root. I keep these facts in a computer file that I've labeled, wittily enough, "Duh."

Pythagoras was a loon and bean hater, but I'm glad I know about him and his perfectly sensible square roots.

Q

qa

This word—a Babylonian liquid measurement—could be the best Scrabble word I've encountered in my life. So already the Qs are shaping up to be helpful. I'm very much looking forward to this Q chapter, which clocks in at a gloriously short thirty-nine pages. A little grapefruit sorbet between the rich courses of *P* and *R*. A few pages of Arab leaders followed by *quail* and *quicksand*, and boom, you're done. A breeze.

I will read every word of Q. I make that pledge because, well, I've been bad. In the last handful of letters—namely *M, N, O,* and *P*— I did some felony-level skimming. Not a huge amount, but enough to make me feel guilty. The *Macropaedia* entries on *optimization, plate tectonics, plants,* and *Portuguese literature*—those took the heaviest hits. Earlier in the alphabet, I'd breezed through some paragraphs, going too fast for full comprehension—but now I've progressed to another, more disturbing level of skimming. With this method, I unfocus my eyes and try to take in the whole page at once. I rationalize to myself that since I *see* every word on the page, even if I don't *process* every word, I am still—by some definitions—reading every word. I know. Very Clintonian. I feel like going on TV and making an apologetic speech to the American public.

So I'm here to reform myself in the Qs.

Quaker

Originally, the word "Quaker"was an insult. It was coined to make fun of the members of the Society of Friends for trembling at the word of God. As George Fox, founder of the society in England, wrote in 1650,

"Justice Bennet of Derby first called us quakers because we bid them tremble." Despite early derisive use, the Friends adopted the term themselves. Now, of course, it carries no negative connotation.

I love these stories—the ones where an underdog group co-opts an insult and makes it their own. It's got a great mischievous Bugs Bunny feel to it. I loved when the gay movement stole the word "queer" and took all its power away from the seething homophobes. And the *Britannica* is packed with other examples: A journalist came up with the term "Impressionism" as a jeer, but Monet and his pals stole it as their own. A group of Oxford students in the 18th century were derisively called "Methodists" because of their methodical habits of study and devotion. Muckraking was originally an insult derived from John Bunyan's *The Pilgrim's Progress*, which referred to the Man with the Muckrake "who could look no way but downward," always searching for worldly gain in the cow dung, never bothering to look to heaven. The early crusading journalists stole it and made it their own. Me, I'm still trying to figure out how to co-opt my eighth-grade nickname, Douchebag.

quarantine

Ships in the Middle Ages were isolated for thirty days; the period of time was later increased to forty days, to equal the amount time that Jesus was in the wilderness. Not exactly the product of rigorous logical thinking. I wonder how many total days were wasted because they decided the ship-Jesus thing was a handy metaphor.

quill pen

It's Sunday, and I decide to take a tour of the museum at the New-York Historical Society. Not only is it about fourteen steps from my apartment, but they have a great permanent exhibition of antique furniture, Revolutionary War costumes, and paintings of old New Yorkers signing historic documents (the best quill pens, by the way, were made from the second or third outer feather from the left wing of a crow).

Our guide is a prim lady named Nancy with straw-colored hair, a tiny pocketbook, and a bad case of hay fever. You can tell she used to be a teacher—her tone is a mixture of kindness and condescension, with a little I'll-send-you-to-the-vice-principal sternness thrown in. I'm joined by about a dozen fellow tour takers, most of them pushing sixty.

Our first stop is a series of Audubon paintings of North American birds. The Historical Society has the largest collection of Audubons in America, explains Nancy, having snapped them up from his estate soon after his death. I know I should probably keep my trap shut and nod politely, but I feel compelled to speak up. I've got some Audubon information, and that information wants to be free.

"You know," I say, "Audubon was quite the bastard." Nancy seems startled. "What I mean is, Audubon was a literal bastard. Illegitimate."

"Oh yes," she says, relieved. "Yes, he was illegitimate." Nancy acts as if she knew about Audubon's birth heritage, but I'm not convinced. I continue: "Also Jean Genet and Alexandre Dumas were bastards. Lots of bastards running around throughout history."

I chuckle, and look around for approval from the crowd. I don't get it. The other tour takers are regarding me warily, as if I might decide to take off my pants or lick the glass display cases. I have miscalculated. I was working blue before I had gained their trust.

Nancy leads us to a painting of colonial businessmen in their wigs and three-corner hats.

"Does anyone know when the first stock exchange in New York was?" she asks.

I don't know, but I think I'll offer up a related fact: "The first stock exchange was under a tree," I say.

"Yes, that's true," says Nancy.

I'm feeling semitriumphant—the head of the class—when I hear a deep voice. It belongs to a fellow tour taker, a man in a gray sweater who's even taller and skinnier than I am.

"A buttonwood tree," he says.

Who the hell is this guy? I don't like him at all. First off, he raises his right index finger when he talks, like he's hailing an imaginary cab. What kind of person does that? And second, that seems just crass, this naming the variety of tree just to top me. And third, what in God's name is buttonwood?

"Yes, it was a buttonwood tree," she says. "But then it moved to a coffeehouse, the Starbucks of the day." And it was 1792, by the way.

Nancy—in between sneezes—leads to a painting of Peter Stuyvesant, the peg-legged Dutchman who was an early governor of New York.

"Anyone know where Suriname is?"

Suriname. Damn—I should know. Though I'm not up to the Ss, so I sort of have an excuse. Uh-oh. Manute Bol in the gray sweater is raising his index finger again. "It's in South America, near Brazil."

He is correct. A small country on the northern coast of South America, formerly known as Dutch Guiana.

"Very good," says Nancy. She proceeds to tell us what is, admittedly, a great fact. In 1667, the Dutch engaged in perhaps the worst deal in real estate history: they traded Manhattan to the British in exchange for Suriname. It seemed like a good idea back at the time, since Suriname had lots of sugar plantations. But unfortunately for them, Suriname didn't become the commercial center of the Western Hemisphere. The *Suriname Times* didn't become the newspaper of record for the free world.

I'm feeling threatened. I need to redeem myself. We get to a painting of Peter Minuit, who bought Manhattan for that famous sum of $24. Here I see my chance. I raise my finger—a deft satire of Mr. Buttonwood Tree over there—and say: "Actually, the Indians got paid a lot more than twenty-four dollars. More like $120."

Which is true. The *Britannica* said that Minuit bought Manhattan for sixty guilders, which equaled about a pound and a half of silver. For some reason, I had decided to click on Google and see what a pound and a half of silver would sell for today. The total: One hundred twenty bucks. So the Indians were ripped off slightly less badly than most people think, and I had successfully wasted five minutes of my life.

Nancy refuses to be rattled. "Yes, some people say that it was more in the range of a hundred dollars." I hear at least one "Isn't that interesting?" from the crowd. I flash a smug smile at my competition.

A few paintings, a couple of statues, and an antique chair later, Nancy pauses to ask a question. "Now who knows when was the first insanity plea in U.S. history?"

"The Stanford White trial!" My decibel level is alarmingly high—more suited to, say, alerting my fellow colonists about approaching Redcoats—but I'm just so pleased to know the answer. Stanford White, the colorful and lady-loving New York architect, was killed by a jealous husband.

Nancy smiles and shakes her head. "A lot of people think it was the Stanford White trial. But actually, it was a Civil War general named Daniel Sickles."

What a sucker. I have fallen right into Nancy's trap. Perhaps it's punishment for my Peter Minuit hubris. Stanford White is the wrong answer, but it provides her the segue she needs: White designed Madison Square Garden, which had a statue of the Greek goddess Diana on top. White's assassin—a man named Harry Thaw—thought that White modeled the Diana statue on his wife, and went ballistic.

"And the irony," says Nancy, "is that Diana is the goddess of what?"

Diana, Diana . . .

"She's the goddess of chastity," says my rival.

I spend the rest of the tour silently sulking in the back, beaten. By the end, the bald guy is giving mini lectures on the lampposts of New York, explaining that you can still spot olde-style lampposts on the Upper East Side at Sixty-second Street.

"You know a *lot* about New York," marvels Nancy. She loves him. She'd like to take him home and make him wear nothing but a stovepipe hat and have him whisper to her about Tammany Hall.

What a bastard, and I'm not talking about the Audubon kind. I'm jealous, I'm discouraged, and most of all, I'm troubled: am I as annoying to the rest of the world as this guy is to me?

quiz show

Still no word from *Millionaire*. I guess I wasn't good-looking enough for daytime television.

quodlibet

Julie and I are up at our friends John and Jen's house for a Saturday summer barbecue and some quodlibet (free-ranging conversation on any topic that pleases us; Louis IX, for instance, allowed his courtiers to engage in quodlibet after meals). It's not an ordinary Saturday, though. At 1 P.M., the nurse at our fertility clinic was supposed to call Julie's cell phone to let us know if she's pregnant. Right now it's 1:45. No call. I'm flipping out.

I'm trying not to read anything into the thundering silence of Julie's cell phone, but that's an impossible task. Too nervous to socialize with John and Jen, Julie and I have wandered over to a hammock in their yard. They must think we're antisocial schmucks. So be it. As they grill some shish kebab, Julie and I lie silently in the hammock, rocking back and forth, staring at her Nokia.

I trot out some calming-the-nerves material—all the reasons to be thankful, whether or not we have a child. Life expectancy in ancient Rome was twenty-nine years, so we're lucky to be breathing at all.

"That's a good way to look at things," she says.

Maybe it's because we're vulnerable, or maybe it's because my speech didn't involve planetary storm systems, but that information goes over well. No one-dollar fines here. I'm sort of helping, or at least helping to pass the time.

The race does not go to the swift, I tell Julie, nor the battle to strong, nor bread to the wise, nor babies to those who would make really good parents and read Dr. Seuss to them every night, but time and chance happen to them all.

And . . . the phone is chirping!

"Hello," says Julie.

The nurse apologizes for calling late—the blood-testing machine was broken for thirty-five minutes. Okay. Maybe we could hear about the blood-testing-repair anecdote another time. Maybe now would be a good time to tell us: is Julie finally pregnant?

Julie gives the thumbs-up. Yes! My seed has found purchase. The mitosis has begun. If she were a hamster, she'd be in labor right now. This is a great day. We hug hard, happier than we've been in days, weeks, months, years. We say nothing for several minutes. I have finally been rendered silent.

R

---

rabbit

Still can't believe Julie's pregnant. Maybe that stuffed rabbit—the symbol of fertility— finally kicked in its magic. I'm delirious. Of course, I've also got a whole universe of new things to worry about: miscarriage, Klinefelter's syndrome (when there's XXY instead of XY chromosomes), cri-du-chat syndrome (congenital heart disease that causes a high-pitched cry like that of a cat). Horrible.

No, I've got to think good thoughts: Julie's pregnant.

raccoon

It washes its food before eating. My new favorite animal.

raspberry

Our friends Paul and Lisa are staying the weekend—they live in Washington these days. Paul tells us over dinner that he just got in an argument with his uncle over the definition of a fruit.

I have to break it to Paul: his uncle was right. A fruit is, botanically speaking, anything with seeds. So yes, tomatoes are fruit. Paul is no shlub, intellectually speaking—he graduated from Yale Law School—but for some reason, he has never heard the widespread classic about tomatoes being a fruit.

But that's baby stuff. I know something that will really freak him out.

"What about this one," I ask Paul. "Is a strawberry a berry?"

Yes . . . he ventures.

"Nope. A strawberry is not a berry. Neither is a blackberry or a raspberry."

"What are they?"

"They're aggregate fruits. *Aggregate fruits*." I repeat this as if I am a professor and Paul is taking notes for a quiz. "So what is a berry?" I continue in my postdoctoral tone. "I'll tell you. A banana is a berry. So is an orange. So is a pumpkin."

Paul is, in fact, impressed, if a little confused. So what's the definition of a berry?

"Botanically speaking, a berry requires a single ovary with lots of seeds," I say.

At this point, I am hoping they will stop asking questions, because I have reached the frontier of my knowledge about berries.

"How do you tell if it's a single ovary?" asks Julie.

"Very carefully," I say. Ancient joke, as old as the Fig Tree chert fossil from South Africa (3.1 billion years old, the oldest on record). But I don't know what else to say.

"That's insane," says Paul. "Wouldn't it be easier to just change the definition of 'berry'? I mean, it's gone beyond any usefulness. A pumpkin as a berry? What about eighteen-wheel trucks—are they berries?"

"No, I don't believe so."

"What about tables and chairs? Are they berries?

"No, I believe those are legumes," I say.

The truth can be controversial.

Rasputin

An illiterate peasant, Rasputin rose to become a powerful mystic and adviser to the Russian czar and the czarina. It was his death, though, that struck me most. Rasputin was well hated by the aristocrats in the czar's inner circle, who resented the sway he had over the czarina (she believed Rasputin knew how to treat her son's hemophilia). In 1916, a group of conspirators decided to murder him. And what a murder it was. This was a man who did not go gentle into that good night. First, Rasputin was given poisoned wine and tea cakes. That didn't kill him. So a frantic conspirator shot him. Still Rasputin didn't die—he collapsed, got up again, and ran out into the courtyard. There, another conspirator shot him again. Not dead yet. Finally, the conspirators bound Rasputin and threw him through a hole in the ice into the river, where he finally died by drowning (they hoped).

His was among the more unusual expirings. But just one of dozens, hundreds, thousands I've read about over the months. I've read about blues singer Robert Johnson, who died after drinking strychnine-laced whiskey in a juke joint. And Marie Blanchard, an aviation pioneer who died when her hot air balloon was set ablaze by fireworks. Explorer David Livingstone died of hemorrhoids(!); poet Henry Longfellow's wife's dress caught on fire; the Greek philosopher Peregrinus Proteus threw himself into the flames of the Olympic Games; the French revolutionary Jean-Paul Marat was stabbed in his bath by a female assassin. Samuel Johnson said, "The frequent contemplation of death is necessary to moderate the passions." Well, be assured: my passions are quite moderate. I know that at any minute I could leave the building for a whole number of reasons. I could keel over from uremic poisoning, like Jean Harlow. Or slightly less likely, but still within the realm of possibility, I could be thrown out of my window by eunuchs and then eaten by dogs, like the Bible's Jezebel. It's memento mori after memento mori.

But then there's the biggest memento mori of them all: when someone in your family dies. We got a call a couple of days ago from Julie's mom that her aunt Marcia had passed away. Today was the funeral.

I didn't know Marcia well—maybe met her three times—but I learned from the speeches at the memorial service that hers was an extraordinary life, with a childhood spent under the floorboards of a chicken coop in Poland, hiding from the Nazis. All the speeches had the same theme: Marcia was a giver. When Marcia was sick in the hospital with cancer that was eating away at her body, a friend called with some troubles; Marcia asked how *she* could help the friend. Or more precisely whispered it, because she was in such pain she couldn't talk. It reminds me of that Horace Mann quote: "Be ashamed to die until you have won some victory for humanity." Marcia seemed to have won some victories for humanity. Nothing on an epic scale, but small victories, every day.

After the service, we drove out to the cemetery in Long Island, alternately tailing and losing the hearse in traffic. When we got there, we all took a silent turn with the shovel, tossing a couple of heaps of cinnamon-colored dirt onto a pine box at the bottom of the grave. Nothing will make you contemplate death like the soft thud of earth on a coffin. It's such a final sound, that thud. That thud is worth a thousand entries about death.

We drove back to Manhattan to sit shiva. In the car, the dings in my mind continued as always—*Bavarian corpse cakes are a food placed on dead bodies to soak up the deceased's goodness*—but they were faint and hollow, and I mostly ignored them. When we got to Julie's uncle's apartment on the Upper West Side, I busied myself by making two huge urns of coffee. I shoveled scoops of coffee into the filter, the soft thud reminding me of the other soft thud at the grave site. But the coffee project made me feel better. I needed to keep busy. I'm addicted to work, whether it's reading the *Britannica* or making coffee. And at least this work provided a clear, caffeinated benefit to others.

After a couple of hours, we said good-bye. We had another rite of passage to attend. My sister, the night before, had given birth to a seven-pound baby girl, Isabella, at Cornell Medical Center. It's a nice twofer for my parents, Julie's pregnancy and Beryl's delivery.

When we got to the hospital, Beryl's husband, Willy, was cradling Isabella in his arms while Beryl ate yogurt in the bed, tired but giddy. The birth wasn't easy—Beryl had a cesarean section. But still, Isabella was healthy.

"She looks like an old Chinese man," said Beryl. It's kind of true. She does look like she'd be at home in an opium den or paging through Mao's *Little Red Book*—but she's an adorable, gorgeous old Chinese man.

It was a weird day—death and birth. And at the end of it, when I got home, I couldn't bring myself to read a single page of the *Britannica*.

razor

Prehistoric ones were made of clamshells and sharks' teeth. Egyptian razors were made of gold, which probably cost slightly more than my Mach3, but not much.

Reed, Walter

I recognized Walter Reed from the famous hospital that bears his name. But I didn't know he was the man who solved the yellow fever mystery. During the Spanish-American War, when hundreds of soldiers were dying of yellow fever, Reed went down to Cuba to try to figure out how the disease was spread. Previous suspicions had focused on infected bedsheets and uniforms. But some scientists—including Reed—now thought insects were the culprits. Reed eventually proved yellow fever was indeed transmitted by mosquitoes, thus saving hundreds, thousands, who knows how many lives. Which is great. He deserves much praise.

But I think at least a couple of smaller hospitals should bear the names

James Carroll and Jesse Lazear. These long-forgotten men were the two scientists who worked with Reed and who volunteered to be bitten by infected mosquitoes. Carroll suffered a severe attack and survived; Lazear died. It's one thing to come up with a scientific theory, it's another altogether to get yourself dosed with a fatal disease to help prove it. I can't even imagine what that must have been like for Carroll and Lazear. What went through their minds when they stuck out their arms and let those little fiends feast on their blood? On the one hand, they no doubt wanted the mosquito hypothesis to be true—but on the other hand, if the hypothesis was true, they'd have a fatal disease coursing through their veins. These were great, brave men.

religion

I didn't grow up with an overabundance of religion. I'm officially Jewish, but I'm Jewish in the same way that the Olive Garden is an Italian restaurant. Which is to say, not very Jewish at all.

I never saw the inside of a Hebrew school, had no bar mitzvah, and wouldn't know a gefilte fish if it bit me on the finger. Until recently, my family celebrated Christmas instead of Hanukkah—though, to be fair, we did sometimes have a Star of David on top of our Christmas tree.

My family had melted right into that pot. You want to talk assimilation? My family are members of something called the Maidstone Club in East Hampton. This is a club for those who enjoy tennis, golf, speaking with their jaw locked, and debating which of their ancestors stepped onto Plymouth Rock first. This could be the Waspiest organization in America. I can't swear on it, but I'd guess there are at least five unironically named Muffys on the membership roster. My friend John always urged me to wear a pink-and-green plaid yarmulke to the dining hall, maybe one with whales embroidered around the edges. Sadly I never did.

Perhaps my closest brush with true Judaism came via a girlfriend, Rachel Zabar. Not that Rachel was particularly religious. She wasn't. But she was Jewish royalty. Her father owned Zabar's delicatessen, the most famous Jewish deli in the world, the white-hot center of whitefish.

Everyone said the same thing: "Bet you get a lot of free lox. Eh? Eh?" Then they'd elbow me in the ribs, thinking they were making a very original sexual innuendo. Yes, I did get free lox. I also got to attend a Zabar seder, where both of the Zabar brothers—Rachel's father and her uncle—brought matzoh from their respective stores, and you had to choose your allegiance by which matzoh you ate.

In any case, that—and watching Woody Allen movies—is about as religious as I've gotten. As for my belief system, thanks to my relatively God-free upbringing, I'm agnostic. The word "agnostic", by the way, was coined by the great and honorable evolutionary thinker T. H. Huxley, who died in 1895, fittingly, midway through a defense of agnosticism. Agnostics like to point out that there's no empirical evidence for or against God. In fact, it's impossible to even conceive of the evidence that would convince a true agnostic. The *Britannica* asks readers to imagine thousands of people are watching the night sky, and the stars suddenly rearrange themselves to spell out the word "God." Would that constitute evidence? The *Britannica* says no. But let me tell you, if that happened, I'd be in a temple strapping on tefillin before you could say "potato kugel."

But as of this writing, the stars haven't spelled out "God", or even something close, like "Thou shalt not kill," or "Never pay retail." So I'm left to ponder these things without definite proof. I'm probably just rationalizing my own beliefs, but the *Britannica* does seem to offer support for agnosticism. You read about dozens and hundreds of religions, all claiming to be the one true religion. And you get scientific explanations for biblical miracles—the rivers of blood during Moses' time were probably the result of excessive heavy rains mixing with the red soil and red algae of North Africa.

The *Britannica*, at least, has made me feel less egregiously ignorant about the religion I was born into. It's been an excellent substitute for Hebrew school. Finally, I know what this Purim is. I know who Esther is, and I know that a haftarah is not half a Torah, which I actually thought it was.

Do I consider myself more Jewish after reading all this Judaica? Yes and no. I've found more reasons to be impressed with Judaism than I anticipated. I've also found more things that I really dislike about my religion. In the spirit of Talmudic dialogue, I figured I should talk my learning over with a three-dimensional rabbi.

A friend's rabbi agrees to see me. He has asked me to meet him at that well-known center of Semitic studies, the Au Bon Pain in Greenwich Village. When I arrive, I couldn't be happier with the way he looks. His chin sports a long gray beard, about the size of a cafeteria tray. Very rabbinical. It reminds me of the facial hair I've seen in pictures next to 19th-century people in the *Britannica*. Perhaps Theodor Herzl? The rabbi is wearing a tweed jacket, big wire-rim glasses, and a yellow tie.

I get a sesame bagel, which I figure is appropriate. The rabbi just has some coffee. We start with some small talk about our mutual friend, but he soon cuts us off. "Well, I could schmooze you all day, but I know your time is short," says the rabbi. "Why don't we get to your questions?"

Straight to business. I like that.

I figure I should ease into our debate—give him a couple of things I like about Judaism before attacking my own millennia-old heritage. I tell him I admire Judaism's love of scholarship. I quote the *Britannica*, which says that scholarship in Judaism is an "ethical good."

The rabbi nods his head, his beard bobbing up and down right above the table's surface.

"It's more than an ethical good," he says. "It's a tool for survival. The emphasis on telling a story—that's one way to express yourself Jewishly."

I've never heard Judaism used as an adverb, but I like it.

I next praise Ecclesiastes.

"What do you like about it?" he asks.

I get nervous, as if I am going to fail his test. I babble as Jewishly as I can. I say that I think Ecclesiastes is wise and true: you can't be guaranteed of anything, so you should enjoy the good things that God has provided.

He agrees it is wise—I have passed the test! "We shouldn't be focused on the completing of a task. When you're going from *A* to *Z*, if you make it to *Z*, great. But if you don't, it doesn't mean you're a failure."

"Very appropriate," I say.

He smiles wisely. "Some Orthodox Jews read a page of the Talmud every day. After seven years, they complete their study, and there's a big celebration at Madison Square Garden. You know what they do the next day? They go back to page one."

Dear Lord. I hope I don't go back to *a-ak* when I finish this.

"Another thing I like about Judaism is that there's very little asceticism," I say. This is something I read way back in the *A*s and it had stuck with me.

When I bring up asceticism, the rabbi embarks on a long verbal detour about Cain and Abel and participating in the community. It is a little off the point I am trying to make. I am trying to say that I think it is cool that Judaism allows you to have sex. But now that seems a bit too sleazy a point to pursue. So I decide to change the topic.

"Okay, now to the things I don't like about Judaism," I say.

"Okay," says the rabbi.

"Well, there's halitza," I say.

"Halitza?"

"Yes, you know, halitza. According to the Bible, if a woman's husband dies, she must marry his brother. Halitza is what the widow must do to get out of the marriage. The widow pulls a sandal off her brother-in-law's foot and spits in his face."

"I know what halitza is. What's your question?"

"My question is, well, don't you think that's crazy? I mean, first requiring a woman to marry her dead husband's brother. That's crazy. And then with the sandal and the spitting?"

"I'm still not sure what you're getting at," says the rabbi.

His tone isn't offended, just confused. I realize my question wasn't the best phrased in the history of Jewish debate. So I try to explain again: halitza is a bizarre and unsavory ritual, one I could never support, and it comes straight from the Bible. Since other Jewish rituals—circumcision, Passover—come from the same source, why should I give them any more validity?

The rabbi nods his head and stays silent for a solid fifteen seconds. Either I've made him think, which would be good, or I've really ticked him off.

"First, halitza is not practiced anymore."

"That's good," I say.

"We don't practice it because it's demeaning to human beings. You have to distinguish between rituals that are demeaning to human beings versus rituals that are life-affirming."

A good point, and a distinction that seems reasonable. And yet, Jews—like those in all religions—still seem to practice many non-life-affirming rituals. In the Orthodox synagogues, for instance, men and women are not allowed to sit together. That, to me, doesn't seem life-affirming.

"Have you ever heard of the two rabbis Shammai and Hillel?" asks the rabbi.

I shake my head.

"These were two famous rabbis, and they disagreed about everything. One said the mezuzah should go horizontal, the other thought it should go vertical. Which is why it's diagonal to this day. Anyway, a man went to Shammai and said, 'Tell me about Judaism while standing on one foot.' Shammai said, 'Get out of here.' So the man went to Hillel and asked the same thing. Hillel stood on one foot and said, 'Do unto others as you would have them do unto you. That is the essence of Judaism. All the rest is commentary.'"

I like that story. It's a story told well and Jewishly, a fine conclusion to my Talmudic debate.

My conversation with the rabbi lasted a couple hours—admittedly not quite equivalent to several years at Hebrew school, but longer than I'd ever spent one-on-one with a religious figure. At the end, I'm still agnostic. And yet, there is wisdom in Judaism—so I'll just pick and choose the parts I like and hope I don't go to Jewish hell (known officially as Gehenna). I'll choose to follow the Golden Rule. I'll choose Ecclesiastes. I'll choose to go to seder, but more to be with my family than because I find the ritual meaningful. I'll choose to stay married to Julie, who knows all the Jewish rituals cold, and who will give our kid a proper dose of ethnic identity.

As we leave Au Bon Pain and walk to the subway stop, I throw out my final Semitic fact—that I am a descendant of a noted Jewish scholar. He was an 18th-century genius named Elijah ben Solomon, also known as the Vilna Gaon, the Wise Man of Vilna.

The rabbi seems impressed, almost startled. "That's quite some yichus." I am flattered, once he explains that "yichus" means "lineage." I feel like a very minor star, as if maybe I should autograph a yarmulke. "He was the original know-it-all," says the rabbi. "I hope that he would think you were following in his footsteps." Oy. That's a lot of pressure. No one's calling me the Wise Man of New York City.

I had brushed up on the the Vilna Gaon before my meeting. According to the *Britannica*, he revolutionized Jewish study by expanding its boundaries. He argued that a complete understanding of Jewish law and literature required a broad education—the study of mathematics, astronomy, geography, botany, zoology, and philosophy. He was also violently opposed to the mystical Hasidic movement, which he thought of as unscholarly. I ask the rabbi about that. "Yes, that's a battle that rages even today. Some people have a great hunger for what we would call the touchy-feely side of spirituality. The Vilna Gaon didn't like the touchy-feely side. He didn't like those who got in touch with God through dance and music."

For better or worse, I've inherited the Vilna Gaon's worldview. His and my dad's. I don't think I had a choice. I was fated to be the obsessive scholar. I was genetically bound to be the wary-of-emotion, intellect-worshiping reader that I am.

Renoir, Jean

It's the weekend, and I'm feeling sick once again. Got flulike symptoms. I'm moping around the house in my polar-bear-themed pajamas, drinking my Tropicana orange juice and shooting extremely expensive cold medication up my nose. Julie thinks I'm sick because of a lack of sleep. Then again, she thinks every health problem is caused by a lack of sleep. If I twisted my ankle or got pistol-whipped by a gangsta rapper, she'd blame it on my not getting the proper eight and a half hours.

Regardless of the cause, I feel terrible and achy and generally unsettled. But I'm trying not to wallow. Nowadays, I'm trying to think more positively about my frequent illnesses, trying to see the silver lining. There's always a silver lining—that's what the *Britannica* has taught me. When the volcano Krakatoa erupted in 1883, it caused tremendous, unprecedented devastation. But it also threw so much dust into the atmosphere, it caused the most beautiful red sunsets around the world for the following year.

Well, maybe that's not such a relevant example. But there are plenty of instances—dozens, even—when getting sick was the best thing that could happen to a guy. The great Latin American writer Jorge Luis Borges was a decent if unremarkable writer until 1938. That was the year when he banged his head, suffering a severe wound and blood poisoning that left him near death, devoid of speech and fearing for his sanity. Best thing that ever happened to him. The *Britannica* says this experience seems to have "freed in him the deepest forces of creation." After that, Borges did his best work. Frida Kahlo began painting while recovering from a horrible bus accident. Henri Matisse took up the brush while recuperating from a bad case of appendicitis. Jean Renoir spent time recovering from his World War I leg wound in moviehouses, where he fell in love with the medium.

The key is to take advantage of the free time your health problem creates, to use it as a chance to explore some unknown creative alleyway. So far, this weekend, the alleyways I've explored have been pretty unimpressive. I doodled a bit in my spiral notebook, tried to think of some Big Ideas and failed, stacked five Cheerios in a column without tipping it over. Maybe this isn't my breakthrough illness, so I go back to reading my *Britannica*.

reproduction

The bandicoot male has a two-tipped penis, and the female a double-slotted vagina, so they can have a little orgy without sending out invitations.

revelation

Another thing my dad and I have in common: bad cholesterol. Without Lipitor, we'd both have cholesterol approaching Avogado's number (6.0221367×10^{23}). Now I've also started to take aspirin every night. I can't remember when I decided this would be good for my heart—after reading a *Newsweek* article? after talking to Julie's father, a fellow high cholesterol sufferer? But it seems like the right thing to do. (Aspirin, by the way, was originally made from the bark of the willow tree.)

When we're on the phone, I tell my father about the aspirin habit. He's not opposed, but suggests I should consult Dr. Mackin.

"I'll think about it," I say.

But I won't. And the main reason I won't is that the *Britannica* has systematically, relentlessly eroded my faith in the authority of doctors. That's what will happen when you read about page after page of bloody and bloody ridiculous medical history. I knew about leeches and bodily humors, but that's just the start. I'm still unsettled by trepanning—the primitive practice of drilling a two-inch hole in the skull to let out the evil spirit. I'm sure during the heyday of trepanning, the chief resident for trepanning at Lascaux Grotto Hospital was very authoritative and assured his patients in a condescending tone not to worry about a thing. We're professionals here, he said, as he smashed their skull with a rock.

Okay, so that's too easy. But medical history in the postscientific age isn't much more heartening. Here's a quote that took me aback: "I believe firmly that more patients have died from the use of [surgical] gloves than have been saved from infection by their use." That's from one of the leading medical experts in the early 20th century weighing in on the surgical glove controversy—a controversy I didn't even know existed. In my encyclopedia, I wrote a little note in ballpoint pen next to that quotation: "Doctors don't know shit."

That was an overreaction, of course. They do know a little shit. I do believe in science and double-blind studies. But I also have much less faith in the infallibility of these self-aggrandizing guys with diplomas on their wall. Plus, I can feel myself getting a little cocky. I've read about medicine, so I know this stuff too, right?

Cocky, that's the word. In the last few weeks I'm not sure where, maybe the late *Os*—I started to feel my ego expand. I started to feel secure. I realized this when I did a little gedankenexperiment—a thought experiment. I imagined myself at a dinner with such established big brains as Salman Rushdie and Stephen Hawking, and I could see myself holding my own. (The good part is that I will never actually find myself at such a dinner, so there's no way to disprove my thesis.)

The thing is, I don't feel intellectually adrift as I used to. I feel that I have a handle on the map of all knowledge—and even if there are some details missing, I at least have the outlines of the continents and islands. When I go to meetings at *Esquire,* I've got this bedrock of confidence that wasn't there pre-*Britannica.* Sure, they may talk about the football game I know nothing about, with names of Jets and Falcons that I couldn't spell. But for every running back I've never heard of, I've got a handful of Portuguese explorers or Parisian archbishops or whatever in my mental pocket. I know they're there if I need them.

Rice, Dan

We all know the cliché—politicians are a bunch of clowns. Well, here we have an actual, bona fide clown/politician. Dan Rice was perhaps the most famous clown of the 19th century. He started his circus career, says the *Britannica,* when he bought a half interest in a trained pig. He then switched over to a short stint as a strongman before settling on clowning and horse tricks. The 1860s were Rice's glory days, the decade when he toured the country for a then amazing salary of $1,000 a week (not so far from my own salary, come to think of it), recognized by his trademark white beard. He got so popular, President Zachary Taylor made him an honorary colonel. And here's my favorite part: in 1868, he ran for the Republican nomination for president. He didn't win, which is sad. I would have liked to read history textbooks about the Pie in the Face Incident involving the French ambassador.

riot

You only need three rambunctious people to legally qualify as a riot. That's all. So Julie, our kid, and I could hold our very own riot.

Robert-Houdin, Jean-Eugène

Robert-Houdin was a French conjurer, the founder of modern

magic—a man so revered that a Jewish kid in Wisconsin renamed himself Houdini in his honor. My favorite Robert-Houdin fact: in 1856, the French government sent him to Algeria to combat the influence of the mystical dervishes by duplicating their feats. I like the idea of magicians being called into war service. Maybe we should have air-dropped David Blaine into Iraq. A really dangerous part of Iraq. A minefield, perhaps.

Robespierre

Out to lunch with Dad again, one of our semiregular workingman meals at a midtown deli. Dad is already seated when I get to the restaurant, chewing on one of the complimentary pickles they leave in a bowl on the table.

"Be careful of that. Pickles have been linked to stomach cancer," I say. "Pickled foods and salt both increase your chances of gastric cancer." I'm not really concerned about my father's health, which would have been nice. I'm just trying to show off.

"I'll only have half," my dad says.

"Also, Jewish women after menstruating are forbidden to touch pickles."

As soon as I said that one, I wished I could take it back. That is just a rule of life, along with "shower every day" and "wear sunscreen": Do not discuss menstruation with your father.

Luckily, Dad kind of ignores me. Which is better for both of us.

"So I've been reading about your profession," I say.

"Oh."

"Yes, they had a nice section on lawyers in the *Britannica*. Did you know that Saddam Hussein, Vladimir Lenin, and Robespierre were all lawyers?"

"A lovely group of people," says my dad.

Sometime before our sandwiches arrive, my dad spots a colleague across the dining room—a man I've never met. He asks me to go up to the guy's table and say, "Hi, Barry," to see the reaction.

I feel even more uncomfortable than when I brought up the Jewish menstruation taboo. I just can't do it. Dad looks disappointed.

rock tripe

A monthly story meeting at *Esquire*. It's five of us in the conference room, with the editor in chief, Granger, at the head of the table, taking occasional notes.

My fellow editor Brendan is pitching a story about living "off the grid," away from civilization.

"Getting your own generator is just the tip of the iceberg," says Brendan.

"Actually, the tip of the iceberg can be pretty large," I offer.

"What?"

"A tip of the iceberg doesn't have to be small. In some iceberg formations, fully half of the iceberg is above water. So it's not a very accurate cliché."

Brendan thanks me with a glare, then finishes his pitch by talking about solar energy. Granger likes it, as evidenced by his scribbling pen.

A few seconds of silence follow, so I figure maybe I'll jump in now.

"I've got a good one," I say.

Granger's listening.

"I think we should do something on an unsung hero of our country," I pause dramatically, then: "Lichen."

"The fungus thing?"

"Part fungus, part algae, and all-American."

The faces of my colleagues indicate that they don't quite follow. So I explain: George Washington's starving troops ate lichen off the rocks at Valley Forge. Lichen saved our country. If it weren't for lichen—or more specifically rock tripe, a type of lichen—we'd all be playing cricket.

Someone says that they actually think we should bolster our coverage of ferns instead. Everyone laughs. Someone else says that nothing can beat Norman Mailer's article on peat moss.

And on it went. Back in the safety of my office, I give lichen some more thought. I honestly don't think it would make a bad article. Everyone likes an unsung hero. Granger's always asking us for ideas that haven't been done before, and I can almost guarantee *GQ* hasn't scooped us on lichen.

Originally I was thinking big—a two-page spread on lichen, a list of its other uses (perfumes, litmus, food dyes), a lichen recipe, the top ten varieties of lichen, a celebrity lichen angle that I hadn't quite figured out yet. But after the reception at the meeting, I'd settle for a little box. I e-mailed Granger restating my case. Just a little box, I say.

He e-mails me back: "Fine."

After two years at *Esquire*, I've mastered Granger's e-mail code. "Great" means he loves an idea. "Okay" means he likes it. "Sure" means he couldn't care less. And "fine" means he hates it, but he'll let you do it to shut you up.

A few days later, I have written up a little salute to lichen and squeezed it on the bottom of a page. I've even had the art department call in a lichen photo. Let's just say it's not quite as attractive as Penelope Cruz. It looks not unlike a skin ailment. But it's a proud moment—lichen is getting its due. When the article comes out, lichen will take its place next to Paul Revere and the guy with the fife as a Revolutionary War hero. I love when my knowledge has an impact on the outside world.

rodeo

The inventor of steer wrestling was an African-American cowboy named Bill Pickett. He would tussle a steer to the ground and bite the steer's upper lip in a "bulldog grip." Jesus. Makes rodeos today look like PETA conventions.

Rubens, Peter Paul

This much I knew about Rubens: the adjective "Rubenesque" may sound smart, but it's something to avoid when trying to compliment a date. The *Britannica* had a little more for me. I learned that Rubens, the 17th-century Flemish painter, was prolific and inventive, his style partly influenced by our old friend Caravaggio. But their similarities end with their work. In his personal life, Rubens is the anti-Caravaggio. As the *Britannica* puts it: "The father of eight children—this prosperous, energetic, thoroughly balanced man presents the antithesis of the modern notion of struggling artist." Yes! That's comforting. Rubens will be my role model. Now I know: I don't have to yell and scream and throw artichokes at waiters to qualify as an artistic genius. I don't have to kill a man on a tennis court. So forget the tantrums. I just need some talent.

S

Sabbatarians

My God, I'm exhausted. I keep thinking about that scene in *Cool Hand Luke* in which Paul Newman shoves hard-boiled egg after hard-boiled egg into his mouth. I think I know how he felt after that forty-third egg. Same way I felt after I ingested that twenty-seventh Lithuanian poet.

And now I'm confronted with *S*. The killer. At 2,089 pages, the single longest letter in the *Britannica*. It's like Heartbreak Hill in the Boston marathon. I look at the *S* volumes on my mustard-colored bookshelf. So silent, so thick, so smug. I take a deep breath and I march ahead into the *S*s, right into the Sabbatarians—a term sometimes applied to Christians who believe the weekly holy day should be Saturday rather than Sunday. For me, neither Saturday nor Sunday this week will be a day of rest. It will be a day of *S*s.

Saint Elias Mountains

The Saint Elias Mountains are a mountain range I already know depressingly well, having seen them up close for far too long. When I was growing up, my parents took my sister and me on a trip every summer. They wanted to show us the world, and they did such a thorough job, I now feel happy to do any additional traveling by watching the Discovery Channel, much to Julie's dismay.

But anyway, when I was a freshman in high school, my parents took us on a trip to Alaska, where we visited Glacier Bay National Park, bordered by the Saint Elias Mountains.

It's a huge park—five thousand square miles—about four thousand times the size of Central Park, though without as many Rollerbladers or drug dealers. And it's spectacular, even for someone like me, who, as Woody Allen says, is at two with nature.

One afternoon, my sister and I rented a kayak (a craft, by the way, that was invented by Greenland's Eskimos and was originally made of sealskin over a whalebone frame). The man who rented it to us looked harmless enough, if overly familiar with the workings of a bong. My sister and I paddled out into the glorious bay—oohing and ahhing at the mountains and the seals that poked their noses out of the water. We saw no one else—no other kayakers, no campers, nothing to indicate humans existed at all. Just wilderness. And then, as planned, half an hour later, we started to paddle back. Problem was, we seemed to have made a wrong turn. The place where there was once a channel of water had now become a beach. (We found out later that the bong-loving kayak rental guy had forgotten to mention that the low tides would drain our channel.)

So Beryl and I just made a right turn and started paddling, figuring we'd find a way back eventually. Not the best philosophy, but our navigation skills weren't honed to a sharp edge, seeing as going from Eighty-first to Seventy-sixth Street doesn't generally require a compass.

We paddled and paddled some more. We passed the minutes singing TV theme songs—*Diff'rent Strokes, Brady Bunch.* We started on *Gilligan's Island,* but decided that a song about an ill-fated nautical adventure was too appropriate, so we stopped. We talked about which of our classmates might be most upset by our deaths. I liked to imagine that Rachel Yassky might throw herself on my coffin and have to be dragged off. That was a nice thought.

After an hour or two, we ran out of songs and conversation, so the only sound was the paddles splashing in the water. That, and the occasional howl of an unidentified but no doubt ferociously carnivorous animal.

We didn't want to go on land alone. The hotel owner had told us an unpleasant story that had effectively removed that option. I can't remember the details now, but it involved a grizzly bear, a pack of butterscotch Life Savers, and a detached torso. It got cold. And dark. And it started to rain. We were scared—though not overly so. Maybe it was New York overconfidence, but we weren't panicked.

Our parents, back on land, were making up for our panic deficit. They were terrified. Because it was now night, the park rangers couldn't send out search planes till morning. Worse, the rangers let slip that if

Beryl and I stayed outside all night, we would freeze to death. So my parents had to stay up wondering if they had kids anymore.

At about 1 A.M., Beryl and I heard something over the sound of our chattering teeth. Men laughing. We shouted. They shouted back. We paddled toward their voices. We found out later they were the only campers in hundreds of square miles. They were nice men, up from California to relax and fill their lungs with fresh air. The first question they asked us was, "You got any cigarettes?" Beryl and I got a decent night's sleep—the California men lent us a nice dry tent and assuaged our worry about the bears—and we awoke to the sound of the search-and-rescue seaplane buzzing overhead.

I still remember the look on my dad's face when he stepped off the plane and saw me and my sister. It flooded with relief. I'm not just throwing that phrase around—I could see the relief wash over his face.

That night shook my dad up good. You can joke with him about most things, but not that night. I think it changed him, too. He liked having us nearby before then, but after that, he became obsessed with physical proximity. Nothing pleases him more than having us in the room, watching TV, even if no one's allowed to talk except for those fifteen seconds when we're fast-forwarding through commercials. After that, he wrote me a note so uncharacteristically earnest and emotional, a note all about how proud he was of me, that I can't even think about it without tearing up.

In any case, I bring all this up because I'm starting to get a glimmer of what it felt like for Dad. Julie had cramps the other day, and it freaked me out. I would put that in capitals and italics with a couple exclamation points, but you get the idea. I've been a worrier my whole life. This, however, was a whole new level, a quantitatively different type of distress. Thankfully, Julie turned out to be fine, but I'm starting to understand the man in a Slavic folktale who plucked out his eyeballs for fear he might inadvertently give his children the evil eye.

Salieri, Antonio

Here's the flipside of Thomas Paine. History has given Paine a big fat wet kiss, but poor Salieri has gotten a drive by. What'd he do to deserve his status as the embodiment of mediocrity? Not much. In his day, the *Britannica* says, he was a respected composer, even a revered one. And far from despising Mozart, he was a Wolfgang friend.

Unfortunately, a man named Rimsky-Korsakov thought it'd be fun to write an opera called *Mozart et Salieri* (1898)—based on no historical evidence—in which Salieri is eaten up by jealousy and poisons Mozart. Then a few decades later, the play with the same theme. Yeah, artistic license and all that. But what about poor innocent Salieri? Just doesn't seem fair.

Sartre

Here he is, the author of *Nausea*. The man who practically accused me of pedophilia. I scan the entry for weaknesses and find that Sartre was cross-eyed. First Descartes and his fetish, now this. I've got to ask: what is it with French philosophy and crossed eyes?

Schmeling, Max

I knew about Schmeling—the Aryan boxer, Hitler's champion in the ring, the Great Nazi Hope. A real villain. Or so I thought. After reading Schmeling's life history, I'm not so sure. I'm not going to name my kid Schmeling Jacobs, but I also don't think he's the soulless incarnation of evil. The *Britannica* does that a lot. You realize that, yes, there are a few black-or-white hats in history, but most are somewhere in the charcoal or slate range.

Schmeling gained fame from his bout with Joe Louis in 1936. Schmeling was clever. Before the fight, he studied slow-motion films of Louis and found a weakness—Louis always dropped his guard after delivering a series of left jabs. Thanks to that information, Schmeling knocked Louis out. By the time of the rematch in 1938, Joe fixed his bad habit and flattened Schmeling—dealing a nice blow to Aryan propaganda.

But here's the odd part: the man touted as the Aryan boxer "openly associated with Jews," had a trainer who was Jewish, and shielded two Jewish boys in his Berlin apartment during Kristallnacht. His refusal to abandon Jewish friends got him in trouble with the Nazi regime. Instead of giving him favored treatment like other celebrities, they assigned Schmeling to the dangerous parachute forces, where he was injured in 1941.

After the war, Schmeling briefly returned to boxing, then opened a Coca-Cola franchise in Germany. Later, he gave financial aid to the widow of his former nemesis, Joe Louis. So there you go: he's not about to be sainted—he did fight for the Nazis—but he also shielded Jews and helped out Joe Louis's widow.

school

I figure it's time for a nostalgic field trip. Since I used to be under the impression that I was the smartest boy in the world, and seeing as I'm trying to recapture my former glory, maybe it'd be illuminating to return to the scene of the crime. Maybe I'll get some insights from a trip to the Dalton School, where I spent thirteen years improving my brain, from kindergarten right on up to graduation.

My guide for this adventure is sixth-grader Abbey Bender. Abbey is the daughter of my old English teacher Steve Bender, the one who suggested I read that snotty Flaubert book. I trust Abbey—she's smart and funny, and when I asked her what I should know before my big day, she told me not to wear a miniskirt. Good advice.

I get to school ten minutes early—a years-old habit. And I find Dalton has changed plenty since the days I spent here trying to make turkey tetrazzini stick to the cafeteria ceiling. Macs have popped up everywhere, the elevators actually work, and all the white Upper East Side boys dress like rap stars. That's what strikes me most. I feel as if I've walked into a school teeming with four-foot-tall Eminems: baggy pants, white headbands, Allen Iverson T-shirts hanging down to their knees. They're missing some diamond jewelry and Glock semiautomatics, but otherwise, they've got it cold.

My first class is science, with Dr. Fenton, who does not look like a rap star. He looks like a charming British fellow, which he is, with his beard flecked with gray and his tie stuffed in his shirt pocket so it won't flap about and find its way into a Bunsen burner. Dr. Fenton tells us that we're going to do some chemistry today. Chemistry. I can handle that, I think. I try to recall my chemistry facts from the *Britannica*, but only come up with the story of Fritz Haber, the German chemist who had a scheme to pay for the fatherland's World War I reparations by extracting gold from seawater. There is, in fact, gold in seawater, but not enough to make his scheme successful. I decide to keep this nugget to myself.

Dr. Fenton gets out a coil of magnesium.

"Can you burn magnesium?" asks one of the tiny hip-hop artists.

"It's illegal to burn it," says Dr. Fenton. "It might scar the retina."

"Can you eat it?" asks another kid.

"No, that's not a good idea either."

I like the way these kids think. But seeing as the really fun things have been ruled out, we have to settle for observing Dr. Fenton drop bits of magnesium into a container of hydrochloric acid.

"Now watch what's happening," Dr. Fenton tells us. The acid bubbles and hisses and burps out a smoky vapor. My fellow students and I—who are all wearing fluorescent green safety goggles that would be at home at a San Francisco rave—watch intently, scribbling notes. "Now how do you explain what's happening?"

Uh-oh. I'm hoping Dr. Fenton won't call on me, because I'm really not sure what's happening. Something involving covalent bonds, perhaps? Noble gasses? Electroplating?

"Do you have pH strips?" asks a particularly skinny kid. "Because if the hydrochloric acid . . ." His voice trails off.

"Please continue," says Dr. Fenton.

"Because if the hydrochloric acid is the stuff being released in the vapor, the solution should be getting less acidic."

Dammit! That 12-year-old bastard is good. Dr. Fenton runs off to get some pH strips, which he dips into the solution. We talk some more, and there's another suggestion that we eat the solution.

It's time for me to assert myself. I raise my hand. I'm genuinely nervous. "What if the magnesium is still in the liquid?" I ask.

"Are you saying the magnesium is *in* the liquid, or *turns into* the liquid?" asks Dr. Fenton.

I'm not honestly sure. I dodge the question. "Either one."

Dr. Fenton nods. I'm glad I spoke up, because my hypothesis—vague as it was—turns out to be the right one. Dr. Fenton shows us that the magnesium does dissolve in the liquid, and hydrogen is released. Yes! Plus, at the end of class, to prove that the gas is indeed hydrogen, he creates an explosion. It wasn't a Jerry Bruckheimer–style explosion; it was more of a pop about as loud as a bubble wrap. But a crowd pleaser nonetheless.

After Dr. Fenton dismisses us, I decide to give myself a grade: B. I couldn't have come up with the chemical equation ($Mg + 2HCl \rightarrow MgCl_2 + H_2$), but my instincts were right.

Abbey's next class is English. Good. This is what I happen to do for my salary, this English language, so I should be able to shine. Our teacher, Ms. Cornog, an attractive woman in capri pants, announces that today is a special day. "It's the Grammar Jamboree!"

The class is a small one, eight kids including me, and we split into two teams of four for a grammar-themed showdown. I'm on a team with two rowdy rap artists and a shy girl. Ms. Cornog will hold up a sentence writ-ten on a piece of oak tag, and if it's your turn, you have to tell her the grammatical term for the underlined word. Ms. Cornog holds up a poster for Sophie: "The cat dragged Frank to safety."

"Noun," says my teammate Sophie. High fives all around.

Ms. Cornog flips the next poster. "The sun shone, yet the day was cold."

"Conjunction!" shouts Jack, before Ms. Cornog can read it out loud. In celebration, Jack does the dirty bird.

And now Ms. Cornog turns to me.

"Yesterday, she saw twenty bears." Uh-oh. That seems tricky. Why couldn't I get the damn cat? I know what a freakin' cat is. Okay, I can do this. Yesterday is a day, which is a noun.

"Noun."

"Sorry," says Ms. Cornog. "It's an adverb."

My team lets out a groan.

"Aren't you a writer?" says Jack.

"Well, you see, there are people called copy editors who work with the grammar. So actually, writers don't need to know grammar too much."

Maybe that wasn't the best thing to say. I look at Ms. Cornog. She looks pissed off, which, by the way, is an adjective.

"You're now on scoreboard duty," says Jack. "You think you can han-dle that?"

That I can handle, and handle well. But when Ms. Cornog lobs me another grammar question, I incorrectly answer that "with" is a conjunc-tion—it's a preposition, apparently. My teammates slap their foreheads and wonder if I'm maybe better suited to kindergarten.

When the final Grammar Jamboree question rolls around, my team trails 23–25, thanks entirely to me. But now, Ms. Cornog introduces a lit-tle spice. We can wager as many points as we want. My teammates want to gamble eighteen. I say no. Let it all ride! We do, and—after parsing a sen-tence about Chauncy and a slippery surfboard—we win! The other team didn't wager enough. I'm a hero! I may be bad at parts of speech, but I did teach them about gambling. So that's at least something.

I give myself a D.

Time for history class. Our teacher is Ms. Springer, who wears an untucked denim shirt, glasses on the tip of her nose, and calls the kids "sweety pie" and "darling," except when one of the boisterous boys won't pipe down, at which point she says, "Hey, Zach! This is your life passing by."

Today's topic is Rome.

A boy named Alex raises his hand. Ms. Springer calls on him.

"Have you seen *Gladiator*?" he asks.

"You bring up *Gladiator* every time we talk about Romans," says Ms. Springer. "Yes, you know I've seen *Gladiator*."

Alex makes the point that Russell Crowe's character was a farmer at one time, and therefore . . . and therefore . . . well, that seems to be the extent of his point. Still, it's hard to argue with.

"Okay, class," says Ms. Springer. "What does *arete* mean?"

"Quest for excellence!" they shout. Damn. How could I have forgotten that? I knew that at one point.

"The Greeks were interested in *arete*, and the Romans were interested in dominance." Or as she puts it later, "The Greeks were wonderful. The Romans were savages."

Ms. Springer is wise, I've decided. "You're young," she tells the class. "You are going to live through a lot of war. People are going to say that it's a war to make peace. I want you to think back to your sixth-grade history class. Because they've been saying that since Roman times."

I wonder if my own sixth-grade teacher said anything that I should have remembered all my life. I wonder if—well, I wonder if that girl in the first row could possibly make *any more noise*. She is hoovering handfuls of Honeymade chocolate graham crackers, and every time her fingers dive in for some more, she crinkles the bag at disturbingly high decibels. Finally, Ms. Springer suggests that "sweetheart" put the bag away till after class. These kids have it good. I don't remember ever being allowed to snack during class, even if I snacked silently.

The kids, like those in my other classes, know a lot, and not just about Russell Crowe's character. They know about Assyrian kings and Virgil's *Aeneid* and several other things that I should know but don't. Though I did get a round of applause by saying what *res publica* means. So I give myself a C+.

In conclusion—that's how I ended my elementary school essays, so I figure it fits—I came away with three things from my time travel adventure. First, I got more alarming evidence of the Ebbinghaus curve. From magnesium to *arete* to conjunctions, I've lost even more information from my school days than I expected. Second, I got a better glimpse into the origins of a young know-it-all. I can't say for sure whether any of those mini Eminems I met think they're the smartest boy in the world, but I recognize their cocksure swagger. It's the swagger of boys who are consistently told how smart they are, who have yet to get drop-kicked by recessions and failed relationships. And third, I realize—way too late, as it turns out—how fun school could have been. As confident as I was of my intellectual abilities, I still spent most of my time worrying. I worried about grades, my appearance, the effects of that nefarious carbon monoxide. I neglected to realize that I was spending five days a week learning amazing things. That was my job. *Learning.* I guess I should stop looking at the *Britannica* as a self-imposed homework assignment and just embrace the joy of learning. Relax. Remember, A.J., this is your life passing you by!

Scrabble

The game is available in braille. That's a nice fact. This makes me feel better about humanity for some reason. I can't really explain why.

script

Dammit. Julie watched *The West Wing* and told me that President Bartlet stole my great July Fourth fact about Jefferson and Adams dying on the same day. Now it's common property.

selection

A regular day at work editing an article on a new BMW and another on a pouting TV star. A regular day until about three in the afternoon. That's when I get the following message on my voice mail: "Hi, this is Matt from *Who Wants to Be a Millionaire.*" Sweet mother of God. I call him back and it's what I both hoped and feared. I've been chosen. I've been called to the big leagues. The show will tape on December 16. A few short weeks to prepare. I immediately get a stress stomachache.

Seven Wonders

A real letdown. I don't think even half of the seven qualify as genuine wonders. The pyramids, yes, they are, in fact, wondrous, but some of the others—well, let's take a look. The Colossus at Rhodes did not bestride the harbor. That was a myth. It was pretty big—105 feet—but there was no bestriding going on. It just stood with its legs closed on one side of the harbor. So I'm already disappointed. The Hanging Gardens of Babylon were not hanging at all. Just terraced gardens on a bunch of ziggurats. Sort of a fancy roof garden. Again, not impressed. And the Mausoleum of Halicarnassus—it didn't do much. It was just a big rectangular building. I, for one, am not sure I'd call that a wonder. Whoever came up with the Seven Wonders of the World concept—that was a great PR mind.

sharks

Menstruation can increase the likelihood of a shark attack. Another reason to be happy Julie's pregnant.

Shaw, George Bernard

Before I started reading the encyclopedia, my most impressive piece of Shaw knowledge was his quote about marriage: "When two people are under the influence of the most violent, most insane, most delusive and most transient of passions, they are required to swear that they will remain in that excited, abnormal and exhausting condition until death do them part." I remembered this because, for a couple of years there, every time I attended a family function at my grandparents' house, my grandfather would break out *Bartlett's Familiar Quotations* and read Shaw's passage out loud, giggling until he shook. Then Grandma tore out the page and the recitations stopped.

Shaw, I learned, was an odd man. A failed writer in his twenties, he became a pamphleteer, a music critic, an opera buff, a peacenik, a vegetarian, and a socialist, before getting around to completely revolutionizing English drama. He also had an apparently celibate marriage—how the *Britannica* knows this I can't say—which helps explain his quote about the institution. But my favorite Shavian fact was this one, which I actually learned back in the Cs: the great dramatist got nekkid for a photographer. In 1906, at the request of Alvin Langdon Coburn, the first art photographer, Shaw sat for a nude photo in the pose of Rodin's *Thinker*. George Bernard Shaw, centerfold.

This is heartening news for the thousands of men and women who have peeled their clothes off for a cameraman. So what if Vanessa Williams exposed some skin? So what if Madonna and Burt Reynolds went buff? The modern world's greatest playwright did too.

I am personally heartened because, sadly, back when times were tough, I too posed naked. It happened in my second year at *Esquire*. We had asked the actress Mary-Louise Parker to pose nude in our pages—a request we make of many talented young actresses—and she said she'd do it, but only on the condition that the editor of the piece also pose naked. The editor happened to be me.

This was unsettling. The only thing more unsettling was that when my boss heard about the idea, he thought it was absolutely brilliant—and suggested I be photographed with caviar spread over my nipples, the way we shot an Italian actress the year before. So, in order to keep my job, a few days later I found myself at a dim, hangar-sized studio being shot for a "classy" black-and-white photo. There were no Russian fish eggs involved, but I did have to sit in an awkward cross-legged yoga position to cover up what the Irish photographer called my "chopper." He also kept telling me to "sooook in yer goot," which I eventually figured out was a request to conceal my mini beer belly. Sadly, all the cute young female assistants displayed monumental indifference to my naked form, which to them apparently held as much allure as a wicker table.

The really anxiety-producing part was the reactions of friends and family. When I told my mother, she looked at me the way I imagine John Walker Lindh's mom did when he told her he'd chosen a career in the Taliban military. Several people recommended I invest in some bottles of Nair body hair remover. And colleagues told me this was the end of my serious journalistic career, as if I ever had one.

In any case, I wish I had had the Shaw fact in my arsenal back then. That would have made me feel much more comfortable. But since I still occasionally get mocked for taking off my pants for a photo, I finally have an answer at the ready: "Well, it didn't seem to hurt George Bernard Shaw's career." Now all I have to do is write a few brilliant plays.

Sinology

I'm not what you'd call a relaxed father-in-waiting. I'm overprotective, constantly stressed. Julie's much better about dealing with this whole pregnancy thing than I am, and she's got the little added difficulty of hormonal seesaws and a growing human being in her body.

I get nervous if Julie carries anything heavier than, say, a bottle of Liquid Paper. I hate it when she's out pounding the New York pavement or, worse, riding the Stairmaster in our extra bedroom. She swears to keep her heart rate low, but I still hover nervously nearby, checking to see if she starts huffing too heavily. Personally, I wouldn't object if she spent the rest of her pregnancy in bed.

I think I'd be even more neurotic—if that's possible—if not for one reassuring fact. Namely, that the wife of Mao Zedong accompanied him on the Long March while she was pregnant. The Long March—a roundabout trek from east to west China—was a grueling, six-thousand-mile ordeal over eighteen mountain ranges and twenty-four rivers. If Mao's wife and baby survived that, I figure it's probably okay for Julie to walk to the Fairway supermarket eight blocks away.

Mao's wife survived the Long March, but their marriage didn't. A few years later Mao dumped his devoted wife and married an actress. I tell Julie to watch out—I'll probably marry Renee Zellweger soon.

sleep

I won't be getting a lot of this once the baby comes out—which doesn't trouble me too much. I've always hated sleep. I see it as a waste of time, one-third of my life vanished with nothing to show but a bunch of ever-larger drool stains on my pillows. Julie, on the other hand, loves her shut-eye. She's a champion sleeper, polishing off twelve hours on a weekend night with no effort at all. She'd rather sleep than do pretty much any activity—read, watch TV, listen to her husband discuss the various competitors to the Dewey Decimal System. And when she wakes up after a solid dozen hours, she makes that satisfied postnap smacking sound that I used to think was the exclusive trademark of Yogi the bear after he finished his hibernation.

She'd better savor those twelve hours now. We'll soon be suffering from hyposomnia (little sleep)—which is the preferred term to "insomnia" (no sleep), because, technically, almost everyone gets a little sleep. High-pitched screeches will soon jolt us out of sleep. This, I learn, is actually considered quite dangerous by certain cultures. The Tajal people of Luzon believe that the soul leaves the body during sleep and goes to a special dreamworld, which is why they "severely punish for awakening a sleeping person."

When I tell Julie this, she approves, as I predicted she would. "Now that's a good law," she says. "Those Tajal people have their priorities straight." And as I should have predicted, the next morning, when I clink my cereal bowl a bit too loudly on the counter, Julie shouts from the bedroom, "Don't make me come out there and punish you!"

Julie likes the Tajal people, but I've got to prefer the Kamchatka. The Kamatchka believe that dreams demand fullfillment, sort of a literal "make all your dreams come true" rule. Here's the sentence that got me: "Among some natives of Kamchatka a man need only dream of a girl's favour for her to owe him her sexual favours."

You have to admit, that's a pretty interesting idea. In my case, this would have come in extremely handy in high school. I can imagine any of dozens of conversations like this one:

"Hey Isabel, you busy after school? Well, you might have to cancel that. Because I kind of had a dream about you last night. So why don't you come on over wearing a very tight meter maid's outfit? And maybe bring some pancake batter. And why don't you invite your sister Alison along. Sorry, but I did dream it. See you then!"

Of course, there is a little downside to this fulfill-your-dreams idea, which the Iroquois Indians apparently got to see up close. They had a similar dream philosophy to the Kamatchka, and as the *Britannica* says, "One Indian was said to have to have dreamed that 10 friends dove into a hole in the ice of a lake and came up through another. When told of the dream, the friends duly enacted their roles in it, but unfortunately, only nine of them succeeded."

So maybe that's not the best idea. Maybe I should focus instead on creative dreaming. The *Britannica* lists all sorts of people who have used their dreams to help them work. Samuel Taylor Coleridge wrote "Kubla Khan" after composing it in his dream (he had fallen asleep while reading about the Mongol conqueror). Robert Louis Stevenson, author of *Dr. Jekyll and Mr. Hyde,* said that his writing was helped by "little people" in his dreams. A German chemist figured out the structure of benzene by dreaming of a snake with its tail in its mouth.

Excellent. Sleep doesn't have to be a waste of time. I'm going to use those eight hours to finish everything in my in-box. To quote Lorenzo de' Medici, who was berated by a friend for coming to work late: "What I have dreamed in one hour is worth more than what you have done in four."

Over the next few nights, as I'm falling asleep, I promise to do some creative thinking. Namely, I decide to think about how I can turn my encyclopedia facts into a great poem or a new scientific theory. But the only dream I can remember involved Benedict Arnold retiring to a Florida condo, the kind with shuffleboard and bookmobiles. I think my "little people" need to be fired.

snails
They can actually jump quite rapidly, by a violent flexing of their foot. Good for snails—smash that slow-as-snail stereotype to bits.

snorkel

I've got an idea: maybe names of objects should be reassessed every fifty years or so. If they're named after something evil, then they get a new name. The word "snorkel" came from the ventilating tube used by German submarines in World War II. That's pretty evil. And "sandwich"—well, we all know about the earl of Sandwich, but I didn't realize he was such a miscreant. He was a bribe taker, a backstabber, a gambling addict (the eponymous sandwich came from his snack while he was at the gaming table for twenty-four straight hours), an enemy of American independence, and a terrible tactician to boot. We should come up with an American name for it. Maybe after Robert Morris, underappreciated financier of the American Revolution. Give me a ham and cheese Morris.

socioeconomic doctrines and reform movements

My favorite reform movement leader is a Frenchman named Fourier, whom this *Britannica* entry matter-of-factly describes as "more than a little mad." In Fourier's utopian vision, humans would live in cooperative groups, called "phalanges," where they would "cultivate cabbages in the morning and sing opera in the evening. . . . Love and passion would bind men together in a noncoercive order."

His anticapitalist plan called for not just social but natural and cosmological transformation: wild animals will turn into anti-lions and anti-tigers, serving mankind, and the ocean will be changed into lemonade. It's a lovely vision and, of course, completely bonkers. In reality, as we all know, the ocean will be changed to tomato juice.

Fourier didn't convert me. I'm still a capitalist. But I will say that reading the *Britannica* has stirred up quasi-radical political feelings I haven't experienced since those dreaded Marxist days in high school. For the last few years, I've been mostly successful in cocooning myself in the comfortable first world, with its abundance of chain stores and restaurants and catalogues. When most of your reading consists of celebrity autobiographies, you can go for long periods without confronting the horrors of famine. You shouldn't underestimate my ability to come up with blinders. But here, every day, I read about countries where the average annual salary barely breaks double digits, where the life expectancy hovers in the forties, where thousands of children die of dysentery. I can't help but grapple with this stuff again. I can't help but realize the world needs saving. I should be more like my sister Beryl, who spent several years in Peru working in shantytowns, sort of a one-woman Peace Corps. She's got a powerful moral sense, and she don't need no *Britannica* to awaken it.

Solomon

I knew he was wise. But I didn't know that he was so busy. The biblical king had seven hundred wives and three hundred concubines—sort of the Larry King of his day.

sound

That old question—if a tree falls in a forest, and no one hears it, does it make a sound?—hasn't kept me up at night in a long time. But it's still good to know the unequivocal answer: yes. Yes, it does make a sound, says the *Britannica*, because a sound is defined as a mechanical vibration traveling through the air or another medium at a frequency to which the human ear is sensitive. So a falling oak makes a pretty serious sound, even without an ear around. Done.

Spanish-American War

Roosevelt's charge up San Juan Hill is a good yarn, as is William Randolph Hearst's warmongering yellow journalism. But my favorite fact about the war is this one:

"Spain declared war on the United States on April 24, followed by a U.S. declaration of war on the 25th, which was made retroactive to April 21."

Now that's a handy trick—retroactive declarations. If my boss ever fires me from *Esquire*, I figure I'll just say, "Well, that's nice. But I quit, retroactive to last Tuesday. And I'm retroactively telling you to go screw yourself."

America's retroactive declaration is a fine example of the impeccable logic I've noticed throughout the history of warfare. True, men in wartime sometimes act nobly—but more often they act like tantrum-throwing kids. Geopolitics reminds me of fourth grade, except that the titty twisters and swirlies more often result in death.

To prove my point, I've been keeping a list of my favorite absurdist wars, wars worthy of a Joseph Heller novel. There's the Pastry War. This was an epic clash between Mexico and France that began when a French pastry cook living in Mexico City claimed that Mexican army officers had damaged his restaurant. I feel bad for the men who died in this war. There's just not a lot of dignity to losing your life over dessert, even if it's a really good éclair. And then there's the War of Jenkins's Ear. This one—between England and Spain—started because a British sailor named Jenkins claimed his ear was cut off by the Spanish coast guard. He even presented the remains to Parliament. And that's not to mention the Pig War, which occurred between the British and the Americans in 1859 in the San Juan Islands over a marauding British pig in an American potato patch. And finally, the Beer War, which had nothing to do with keggers or the classic tastes-great/less-filling debate, but happened in 15th-century Germany over a beer tax.

speech disorder

Julie's cousin Andrew visited our apartment the other night. Andrew—a lawyer and film professor—is one of the best talkers I know, so his revelation that he was a star of the Columbia debate team made a lot of sense.

"You should take them on, smart guy," Andrew told me.

This is not a bad idea. The debate team—that'd be a nice and rigorous test of my intelligence. If I can beat the vaunted Columbia team, who's to say I can't take down my brother-in-law?

Now I'm not exactly a veteran debater. The only official experience I've had was a particularly disastrous appearance on CNN's *Crossfire*. The topic was "Are movie prices too high?" (apparently, it was a slow news day over at CNN). I had written an article on box office prices for *Entertainment Weekly,* so I was chosen to represent the point of view of the consumer. I knew the show was called *Crossfire.* I'd seen an episode or two, and was aware that it had a debate format. But somehow I thought, since the subject was the movies, this was going to be more along the lines of a fun and friendly chat. Maybe host John Sununu would tell us about his favorite Bond villain or quote lines from *The Godfather.*

Instead, as soon as the red light appeared on the camera, Sununu began barking at me. The man seemed genuinely upset with me, as if I had just fondled his teenage daughter's breasts or urinated on his BMW. Prices too high, are they? So you don't like capitalism? You want the government to regulate movie prices? What the hell's the matter with you, boy? I felt as if I was one of those shell-shocked shlubs at the McCarthy hearings. So how long have you been subscribing to *Pravda,* Mr. Jacobs?

The producer in my ear tried to help. He'd say, "Now might be a good time to defend yourself." Or, "Feel free to jump in." Or, "Please, just say something." With me on, it wasn't so much crossfire as receive fire. When I did get around to responding, the main thrust of my argument was that the new movie *Lost World*—the sequel to *Jurassic Park*—cost $9 to see, but still kind of sucked. Socrates I wasn't.

When I got to work the next day, my colleagues couldn't even muster a fake "You did great!" Instead, I got: "Are you all right?" "You looked stunned out there." "At least you have your—well, I guess you don't have that . . . um, okay, see you later."

The Columbia students seemed a lot more polite than John Sununu. When I called them up, dropped Andrew's name, and explained my plan, they seemed to think it was a capital idea. I was told to show up on a Tuesday night at Columbia.

I expected somehow a grand debating coliseum, but the actual debate is held in an institutional-looking room on the fourth floor of the student center. The debate's topic is "The death penalty can be justified." I am given a teammate—it's a two-on-two affair—and we are assigned the pro-death-penalty side.

The first debater is a tall senior named Evan, who steps up to the podium and delivers an excellent seven-minute speech. He enunciates, he projects, he talks about the Rousseauian social contract and cost-benefit analysis, about rehabilitation and individual rights and several other grand philosophical ideas. Damn, he's smooth.

"Hear, hear!" Evan's teammate bangs his hand on the table. This is a clever trick, the "Hear, hear!" Very debaterly. Also, I learn the phrases "point of order" and "on this side of the house," both useful ones. And best of all, if you stand up to make an objection, you must put your hand on top of your head. (This dates back to the British Parliament, where the members had to make sure their wigs didn't fall off.) Throughout the debate, these college kids constantly pop up with their hands on their skulls to interrupt one another, reminding me of very articulate chimps.

My teammate, Gary—who is a fast-talking, energetic senior—is a particularly good objector. When he rebuts points, he presses two of his fingers on his neck as if he's taking a pulse. I'm not sure whether this is proper debate procedure, but it looks kind of cool. Gary makes some excellent points about how there needs to be another level of punishment besides prison. "Hear, hear!" I say, banging my hand on the table. "Hear, hear! Hear, hear!" I've got that down.

But unfortunately, the rules of debate procedure say that I too must make an argument. When I get to the podium, I grab the sides of it, since that seems to me stern and decisive. I look down at a piece of paper on which I have scribbled some death penalty facts. I begin: "In Mesopotamia, under the Code of Hammurabi, the first legal code, bartenders could be executed for watering down the beer. Watering down the beer was a capital offense."

I pause. An interesting start—but I'm not really sure where to go with it. How about this: "Am I suggesting that we should execute bartenders on the Upper West Side for watering down cosmopolitans? Not necessarily. But I am saying that you can bet that the beers in Mesopotamia were pretty damn strong."

The crowd was very gracious, if a bit skeptical about my innovative logic. There were no "hear, hear's," but at least there were no vegetables hurled in my direction. There were even some polite chuckles.

"Let's turn to ancient Rome. In ancient Rome, the punishment for parricide—the murder of your father—was getting thrown in the river. But you didn't just get thrown in the river alone. You were thrown in the river in a bag that also contained a dog, a rooster, a snake, and a gorilla."

I pause again, partly for dramatic effect, but mostly because I am trying to figure out what conclusion to draw. "What am I saying? Well, I'm not saying that we should throw modern-day criminals in the Hudson with a bunch of animals. But I am saying that Roman fathers felt pretty safe."

I've got more time to fill, so I look down at my scrawlings. "Let's talk beheading," I say. "In ancient times, beheading was seen as a privilege of the upper class. Then came the French invention of the guillotine. This made beheading much more practical. Now everyone from king to peasant could be decapitated. One man proposed a steam-powered guillotine to make beheading even easier. But that never got implemented." Uh-oh. I seem to be wandering off point. I don't help matters when I start in on the topic of benefit of clergy, the 16th-century capital punishment loophole. I pronounce studying Latin a good thing and thank the audience.

I return quickly to my seat. In support of myself, I bang my hand on the table and say "Hear, hear! Hear, hear!"

My opponent Max takes the stand and proceeds to pick apart my points without difficulty. He points out that Iraq is hardly a model of justice, so I shouldn't be citing the Code of Hammurabai in glowing terms. He points out there are plenty of other ways to deter people besides throwing them into a river with a dog and a rooster. Then, he and Evan conclude with a flurry of facts about xenophobia, torture, and zero gain—all from the last chunk of the alphabet. Having fun at the old man's expense. I have to be flattered.

These kids were smart. Smarter than I was in college, and quite possibly smarter than I am now. At least they are better at forming a logical argument. That wasn't so good. I had genuinely gone into this experiment hoping to dazzle them with some syllogisms and QEDs. I had the proper weapons and ammunition, but I didn't know how to aim and fire, so I ended up spraying a bunch of cannonballs into the water. Still, at least I made a loud bang. And it sure was better than my Ishtar of a CNN debate.

spice trade

I promise myself not to take cinnamon Pop-Tarts for granted. Or Big Red gum or Quaker Oats cinnamon-and-spice-flavored oatmeal. As a 21st-century American—an upper-middle-class New Yorker with massive chain stores dotting my neighborhood—I live in a place and time of huge bounty. I live in a consumer culture where everything is available—probably cinnamon-flavored reindeer sausage, if I look hard enough on eBay. I've got to appreciate this, I decide. The encyclopedia makes that clear.

Because four hundred years ago, I'd have had to spend my monthly salary to get a pinch of cinnamon. The spice trade, I learn, was a big morass of deceit and corruption, sort of like the drug trade nowadays. One of its prized substances was cinnamon, which was more valuable than gold. To discourage competitors, spice traders spread tales that cinnamon grew in deep glens infested with poisonous snakes. They also said that the cassia spice grew in shallow lakes guarded by winged animals.

If I put my cinnamon into a mug of hot chocolate, I promise not to take the chocolate for granted either. The conquistador Cortés introduced chocolate to Spain—but Spain kept it secret from the rest of Europe for more than a hundred years. So that's it. No more entitlement. I pledge to appreciate chocolate and cinnamon as I've never appreciated them before.

sporting record

Sixty-six solid pages on the topic of *sporting record*. There are forty-five sports covered, from archery to yachting—and let me tell you, this is a tough read, an endless stream of names and scores and dates.

You want to know who was the Tiger Woods of badminton in the 1920s? That would be J. F. Devlin of Ireland, a master of the shuttlecock. The winner of baseball's first World Series in 1903? The Boston Pilgrims.

Maybe if the Red Sox renamed themselves the Pilgrims, they'd break their little curse. The Canadian Football League, I notice, has a team called the Ottawa Rough Riders as well as a team called the Saskatchewan Roughriders, which could be a record of its own for lack of imagination.

I do like reading the names of champion horses. Like Gay Crusader from 1917. Or Pope from 1809. Or the strangely modern-sounding Skyscraper, which took a British Derby title in 1789. It reminds me of the time, back when I was a know-it-all wiseacre kid, that my grandfather bought a share in a racehorse. I was particularly excited about the prospect of naming the horse. I submitted a long list of potential names to my grandfather—all of which were designed to trip up the announcer and confuse anyone listening to the race on radio. Names like "Three Furlongs" and "Muddy Conditions" and "By a Nose"—that kind of thing—so that the announcer would have to say, "It looks like By a Nose by a nose." Looking back, it's remarkable what a jackass I was. Thankfully, my family overruled me.

sports
More ammunition for those dreaded sports conversations at work: The first basketball game—played with a soccer ball and peach baskets— took place in 1891 in Springfield, Massachusetts. The score was 1–0, thanks to a midcourt basket by William R. Chase. I assume Chase immediately got a multihundred-dollar cream soda endorsement.

Stalin, Joseph
If there's one ironclad rule I've learned about government, it's this: never trust a politician with the nickname "Uncle." You've got Uncle Joe Stalin, who won't be receiving saint status anytime soon. There's Ho Chi Minh, whose nickname was Uncle Ho. And for the trifecta, you've got Paul Kruger, the founder of South Africa's nefarious Afrikaaner nation, also known as Uncle Paul. So if you see an uncle on the ballot, do not be tempted to vote for him. He is not actually your uncle. He will not tell you funny jokes and pull nickels out of your ear. Instead, he may try to have you purged. Just to be safe, stay away from politicians named Papa as well.

Star-Spangled Banner, The
Francis Scott Key's poem was originally called "The Defence of Fort M'Henry." Not quite as catchy. Also, the melody was taken from a British

drinking song. Which is odd, since Key wrote it during the War of 1812 against . . . the British. First rounders, now this. We love to steal our most patriotic things from our former enemies.

Stravinsky, Igor

I actually knew about Stravinsky very early on in my life. I was about twelve. I was taking piano lessons from a Denise, a nice, frizzy-haired, thirty-something bachelorette who would come to our apartment to teach me *Für Elise,* Bach's variations, and, to keep me interested, the theme from *Star Wars.* Despite the minor point that I showed no musical talent whatsover, I somehow decided I needed to take it to the next level. I needed to become a composer.

So one week, I spent hours every afternoon plonking around on the piano in our foyer, scribbling down notes, erasing, scribbling some more. Finally, on Friday, Denise came, and I played my opus for her. It sounded like a combination of a traffic jam on Madison Avenue, a fax machine, and weasels in heat.

"Good for you, A.J.," she said. "You're experimenting in atonal compositions."

"Yes, I'm very interested in atonal compositions." Of course, I had no idea what atonal compositions were; in fact, I was trying desperately to write tonal compositions. It's just that my ear was 100 percent tin.

"It reminds me of Stravinsky," she said.

"Ah yes, Stravinsky," I replied, nodding my head. Denise was being exceedingly nice. She didn't want to discourage me, but the only way it could have reminded her of Stravinsky is if Stravinsky had accidentally sat on the keyboard.

That's how I first learned of the Russian master. Then, in college, I expanded my knowledge of Stravinsky by four words: *The Rites of Spring.* An atonal composer who wrote *The Rites of Spring.* So that's about where I stood.

From the *Britannica,* I learned two important things. First, it's *The Rite of Spring.* Only one rite. So I'd been sounding like a jackass all these years when I made the occasional allusion to Stravinsky (and sadly, I had made an occasional allusion). Second, *The Rite of Spring* was enough to cause an "opening-night riot" when it debuted at the Théâtre des Champs Elysées on May 29, 1913.

Stravinsky's score—with its "scandalous dissonances and rhythmic brutality"—caused an uproar among the chic Paris audience. The commotion was so loud, the ballet dancers couldn't hear the orchestra in the nearby pit. But the dancers kept dancing anyway, urged on by the choreographer, who stood on a chair in the wings, shouting and miming the rhythm.

I love this. I can't believe that less than a century ago, a ballet with some discordant notes could cause an actual riot. (If they heard my composition, by the way, they would have burned the theater down.) Nowadays, audience members at the ballet rarely riot. They are often too busy falling asleep. Or if they are really upset, they leave after the first act to get a nice pasta dinner somewhere. But they don't riot.

It makes me feel nostalgic for when you could shock people with art. It was so easy back then. A couple of notes too close on the scale, a little sex, and presto, outrage! Now, good luck shocking the audience. You go to the movies and watch teenagers having sex with parakeets or whatever, and you just won't be treated to an uproar, a commotion, or even a man standing on a chair. Being a true artist used to be a lot easier, not counting that tuberculosis business.

stuttering

I will not overcorrect my child. That's a promise. "Stuttering tends to appear when a child's parents anxiously overreact to normal pauses and repetition—which may also explain the tendency of the stutterer to be an only child or to have no siblings close in age."

That's some solid parenting advice, which is good, because the creature inside Julie is becoming more and more human.

Yesterday, Julie and I were at Mount Sinai Hospital to get an ultrasound. The nurse paints some molasses-colored liquid on Julie's stomach, then places the end of a microphone-like gadget on top of that. She sticks the gadget in hard, indenting Julie's stomach, and making me nervous. But there it is, there's the baby.

"Can you see an organ?" I ask.

"Oh yes, you can see the heart," she says, pointing to a little pulsating blip. "And that black spot is the liver."

"No, I mean *the* organ." I want to know whether our kid will be a future reader of *Esquire* or of *Cosmo*.

"Oh, I see," says the nurse. "Let me get a better view of that." She clicks a couple of buttons on the big humming ultrasound machine, switching to a new point of view. "Oh yes, there's an organ there. You've got a boy."

The screen shows what appears to be a white blobby peninsula off the mainland. It's not a bad-sized peninsula. Maybe it's just my imagination, but I could swear the nurse was impressed. She made a face that looked to me like "If I were single and thirty-five years younger . . ."

But in any case, a boy. A boy who will not stutter. Julie and I aren't sure how to react. The Jacobs name will continue, that's one thing. But boys have a tendency to destroy more property than girls, and decorate the opposite wall with more lunches. But let's not quibble here—we have a child. A beautiful child with a thumping heart and a black spot for a liver and an organ that could qualify him as the Milton Berle of fetuses.

Julie gets dressed, and we go to pay the bill. While we're waiting, I look out the window at the collection of softball fields. I guess I'm going to have to relearn how to swing a bat.

"That's a pretty park," I say. "Which park is that?"

"Uh, that's a little park called *Central* Park."

"Oh."

"Where did you grow up, again?"

Damn. She's got a point. The *Britannica* hasn't helped with my sense of direction.

Suez Canal

Just over a month till my *Millionaire* appearance, and I'm handling the pressure well. By which I mean I can't sleep, can't think straight, and eat only when I force food down my gullet. I'm not making nearly as much progress through the alphabet as I should. Instead, I'm spending my nights studying, reviewing, preparing. I feel as if I'm about to take the SATs again—but this time in front of millions of judgmental home viewers.

Several times a day, I panic because I think of a topic that I have only a wobbly grasp on. In my pocket, I have an ever-growing list of these subjects—Plutarch, major bridges, pints versus quarts, Asian capitals, Russian nobles, Sir Walter Raleigh, Sir Walter Scott, Sir Francis Drake, robber barons, zodiac, Bayeux tapestry, Suez Canal (built in 1869, separates Asia and Africa). It's like a syllabus from the College of Crazy.

Since this project began, I've often felt that I've been swimming in facts. But now I feel as if I'm immersed in them, drowning in the damn things. I had a weird sensation the other day. I was walking home from work up Central Park West, and I started to see the world as a collection of moving, pulsating, caroming facts. It was like that scene in *The Matrix* where Keanu Reeves's character visualizes life as a stream of zeroes and ones. Same thing for me, but mine were facts about tires and lights and cement and awnings, all bouncing off one another. I'm losing it.

I envy all those other, regular folks on *Millionaire*. They haven't just spent the last year of their lives reading the encyclopedia. They haven't declared to their friends and family and coworkers that they know almost everything there is to know. Their potential for humiliation? High. Mine? Stratospheric. (Note to self: study the levels of the atmosphere.)

My confidence veers wildly. In my good moments, I just know I'll be pocketing a seven-figure check. I fantasize about my victory speech. Maybe I'll demand my winnings be given to me in one hundred $10,000 bills, the ones with Chief Justice Salmon Chase on the front. In my darker moments, I'm sure I'm going to muck it up on the hundred-dollar question. What if they ask about nursery rhymes? I don't know my Little Jack Horner's thumb from Little Miss Muffet's tuffet. Or what if they ask about zebras or Zanzibar? I mean, the timing of my *Millionaire* appearance is good—I'm near the end of my alphabetic journey—but it's not perfect. They could still trip me up with a yak fact.

I'm annoyed at myself for placing so much emphasis on my performance. I know I'm relatively smart, I know I know a lot. Why do I need public proof of this? But I do. So I've been watching *Millionaire* every day, scrutinizing it—an activity that's not good for my already shaky psyche. If Meredith asks the contestant a question that I know—and I do know most of them—it drives me batty. Why didn't *I* get that one? My brain contains only a couple of million facts—and that's another one I won't get asked about. But if I don't know the answer— that's even worse. And there are those facts I just don't know—facts that aren't even in my beloved encyclopedia. The official name of the drumroll in taps? A muffled ruffle. That's not in the *Britannica*. A new flavor of Life Saver? Blackberry. That ain't in there.

When I'm not hogging the TV watching my *Millionaires*, Julie watches this show on MTV about the life of a blond pop star named Jessica Simpson. Jessica's become Public Imbecile Number One. Julie told me about how, on the very first episode, Jessica asked her husband whether tuna is a chicken or a fish. She can't figure it out. Her surprised husband informs her that tuna is, in fact, a fish. Well, she responds, if it's a fish and not a chicken, why does the container say "Chicken of the Sea"?

At first, I chuckled. Yes, very funny. Jessica's got a brain the size of a midget moth (wingspan three millimeters). But then I started to feel bad for Jessica. Or as bad as you can feel for a repulsively wealthy pop star. We all have those knowledge gaps, right? I once announced that I was never going to eat cheese again because it was made from cow pee. Okay, I was six years old when I said that. And I think it's an honest mistake—confusing milk and urine. But still, those two months of mockery that ensued from my classmates, they leave a scar. More recently, I mixed up former baseball commissioner Peter Ueberroth and fat British actor Peter Ustinov, which led to a round of ridicule at work. Ueberroth and Ustinov—the walking encyclopedia has stumbled. Ha!

What if I stumble on national TV? I could become the Jessica Simpson of my peer group. You can ingest facts for seventeen hours a day, every day of your life, and you'll still have gaps. It's just a matter of where the gaps are hidden and whether you can drive a truck through them, or a Segway scooter. That glorious cockiness I felt a couple of weeks back? The feeling that I could hold my own with Stephen Hawking? Gone. Vanished like the dodo bird (of which the only remnants are a head and foot at Oxford, a foot in the British Museum, a head in Copenhagen, and a handful of scattered bones).

T

Taiping Rebellion

This was a Chinese upheaval in the mid–nineteenth century that "took an estimated 20,000,000 lives."

I read that sentence again. And again. It took 20 million lives. Holy shit. I try to process that enormous number. That's four hundred stadiums full of human beings. That's more than ten times the population of Manhattan. The Taiping Rebellion occurred about the same time as our own Civil War, which was horrible and bloody—and took less than seven hundred thousand lives. About 4 percent of the Taiping total. And I've barely even heard of this rebellion.

I feel like an ignorant Westerner. Even with my liberal education, I learned next to nothing about the other side of the world, so that doesn't feel good. But I also have another, stranger reaction. I feel angry at the *Britannica*. The *Britannica* just states that 20 million died in its typical deadpan tone. Shouldn't there be three exclamation points after it? Shouldn't it say, "took an infuckingsane 20 million lives"?

There's a disconnect. The *Britannica* is completely dispassionate, which I've always thought was one of its strengths. But how can you be dispassionate with crazy information like this? How can you try to deal with the horrors of human behavior as if you're talking about tectonic plates? The *Britannica*'s tone lulls you into thinking that the world is rational, but entries like this one just stop you cold.

The details of the story are sad and bizarre. The rebellion started with

Hung Hsiu Chuan, a peasant from a small town in southern China. His early life was a disappointment—he took the Confucian civil service exam several times, but failed repeatedly. After the third failure, he suffered a breakdown, and experienced a vision in which he saw an old man with a golden beard, who told him the world was overrun with evil demons and presented him with a sword.

After the fourth failure, Hung found a book that was written by a missionary, basically a Chinese-language *Christianity for Dummies*. He read the book and decided that the golden-bearded man in his vision was God, and he was the new Jesus Christ. Hung didn't have the best grasp of Christianity—he ignored the kindness and humility of the Christian God and instead focused on his vengefulness— but that didn't stop him from declaring himself Heavenly King.

His message—a mix of primitive socialism, spiritualism, and Puritanism—struck a chord. He demanded an equal distribution of land; the abolition of gambling, prostitution, and opium smoking; and an end to the repressive Manchu rulers.

He started out with hundreds, then thousands of followers. As the rebels passed through the countryside, says the *Britannica,* whole towns and villages joined them, till their ranks swelled to more than a million. Taiping followers were both men and women, but no sexual relations were permitted. Oh, except for the Taiping leaders, who had huge harems. That's Cult Leader 101—always have a huge harem for yourself.

Hung took Nanking and made the city his capital. He became increasingly erratic, and began killing off his lieutenants—one for demanding that Hung be whipped because he had kicked a concubine, another for just being generally haughty. In 1860, the Taiping troops failed to take Shanghai, which was defended by a Western-trained army. (One of the leaders of the anti-Taiping forces was a fearsome and ruthless man named General Tso, now reduced to a chicken entree.) Then in 1862 Nanking was surrounded. Hung—who had withdrawn to his harem—committed suicide, and Nanking fell in 1864.

It's an amazing tale. I imagine the million stories that have gone untold—what life was like if you were one of Hung's lovers, how the world looked from inside besieged Nanking. But above all, I'm disillusioned with the *Britannica.* I'm not sure it's equipped to deal with just how crazy people are.

terrorism

More horrible human behavior. Nearly two solid pages on the history of murdering innocent people.

The entry is one of the most disturbing—and oddest—in the encyclopedia. It starts with terrorism in biblical times, then ticks off terrorism through the centuries, ending with four sentences on September 11. It was a disorienting feeling, to read just a few sentences on September 11.

I happen to know from the *Britannica* publicist that the encyclopedia was at the printer when the World Trade Center towers fell. They had to pull the books off the presses and insert a couple of paragraphs. I'm sure next year's edition will have much more on the attack.

So maybe it's not fair to draw any conclusions based on this edition. Still, seeing the September 11 attack in historical context had a calming effect. It gave me hope that, as my parents' friend said, this too shall pass. I don't mean to trivialize September 11, which was probably the most awful thing I've witnessed in my lifetime. But seeing it among the thousands of other horrible—and great—events gives me hope that we can overcome it.

My reaction was, ironically, the exact opposite of the one I had to the Taiping Rebellion. The dispassionate tone I found so outrageous a few entries ago, I now found soothing. Such is the mental whiplash of reading the *Britannica*.

Tesla, Nikola

Our pregnancy books say that I should talk to my gestating boy so he'll get used to my voice. Tonight, I decide to read to him about electronics pioneer Nikola Tesla, the main rival of Thomas Edison and the inventor of alternating current. Embryos love electronics pioneers.

I lean toward Julie's stomach—which has just recently started to swell, and now resembles the gut of a man who drinks too many Budweisers on the weekends. I begin to read:

"He was quite impractical in financial matters and an eccentric." I'm using my best singsongy, reading-to-kids voice. I hope he likes it. "He was driven by compulsions and a progressive germ phobia."

"Just like Dad!" says Julie.

"Yes, just like Dad." I continue with the Tesla bio: "Caustic criticism greeted his speculations concerning communication with other planets, his assertions that he could split the Earth like an apple, and his claim of having invented a death ray capable of destroying 10,000 airplanes at a distance of 250 miles."

I look up at Julie. "Is he kicking?"

She shakes her head. No movement.

"He's probably rapt with attention."

"Yeah, that's probably it."

I realize I can't wait for this boy to come out. I can't wait for him to fall in love with learning and knowledge like the rest of the Jacobs men. The poor guy.

theater

In the 19th century, theaters featured a genre called "the racing drama," where live horses galloped on treadmills set into the stage floor. The chariot race from *Ben Hur* was staged this way in 1899. Too bad this was discontinued. Even I'd go to the theater to see that.

thing

In medieval Iceland, the parliament was called a thing. If I ever hang out with Icelandic historians, I'm prepared for some serious punning: "all things considered," "wild thing," "ain't no thing." I should call my Mensa friends—they'd appreciate that.

thinking

I've been thinking a lot about thinking lately. Or more specifically, I've been thinking a lot about thinking and knowledge and intelligence, and the relationship among the three. It comes back to that old question that my aunt Marti put to me—will stuffing my head with knowledge actually make me smarter, or is this a yearlong fool's errand?

I decide to contact one of America's foremost authorities on intelligence, a Yale professor named Robert J. Sternberg, who also wrote the *Britannica*'s entry on *intelligence*. The perfect source. I e-mail Dr. Sternberg that I am reading the entire *Britannica* in my quest to become the smartest person in the world. I want to talk intelligence with him. A couple of days later, my computer gives its telltale "pling" to indicate that an e-mail has arrived. It's from Dr. Sternberg. He says: "I have read your e-mail. If you are familiar at all with my theory of intelligence, then you will know that I would not view this quest as worthwhile, nor would I view it as turning you into the smartest person in the world. Quite the contrary, I think it is a waste of time. Best, Bob."

Well. Dr. Sternberg may claim to know about intelligence, but he could learn a thing or two about etiquette. He's what I might call a complete Dutch airplane (a total Fokker).

A second e-mail from Dr. Sternberg suggests that I read up on theories of intelligence. In spite of the snooty tone, I decide to do just that. I buy a couple of Dr. Sternberg's own books, namely the ones called *Successful Intelligence* and *Handbook of Intelligence*. The first thing I learn is that intelligence is notoriously hard to define. As a concept, it's as slippery as a pig covered in white, brown, yellow, bone, and garbage grease. Different cultures have different definitions. In Zimbabwe, intelligence means "to be prudent and cautious." In the Taoist tradition, humility is a key part of it. In Zambia, intelligence is linked to "cooperativeness and obedience." And the Western emphasis on verbal ability is far from universal— one African tribe thinks of reticence as wisdom.

Even in our own culture, the perception of intelligence is constantly shifting. The first "scientific" intelligence theorist was a man named Francis Galton, a cousin and friend of Charles Darwin. He believed intelligence meant better sensory discrimination, so he devised a test that measured, among other things, how well we hear high-pitched whistles, guess the weights of objects, and smell roses. Since Galton and his roses, there have been dozens and dozens of attempts to define it. One recent theorist broke intelligence down into such categories as muscle intelligence, musical intelligence, and kinesthetic intelligence (how well you move). Another theory boasted no less than 150 categories.

Perhaps the most famous intelligence theorist is Alfred Binet, a French psychologist who invented the precursor to the modern IQ test in the early 1900s. He devised his test to try to weed out mentally retarded children from regular classrooms. Dr. Sternberg thinks the IQ test is defective because it tests only one type of intelligence—analytical intelligence (the ability to solve problems). It neglects creative intelligence (the ability to come up with new problems) and practical intelligence (the skill of incorporating solutions into real life). I've got to like Dr. Sternberg for his IQ bashing, seeing as I did a belly flop on the Mensa IQ test.

On the other hand, I don't appreciate the harsh tone he takes toward what some call crystallized intelligence. Crystallized intelligence is the accumulation of knowledge—the kind of intelligence that I happen to be soaking up from the *Britannica*. Sternberg seems to hold crystallized intelligence in lower regard than fluid intelligence, which is the ability of people to mentally adapt to the situation and remain flexible when reasoning and problem solving. Most modern theorists agree flexibility is a major key to intelligence.

Fine. I'm all for flexibility. But here's one thing Dr. Sternberg should consider—the more knowledge I accumulate, the more I see the importance of flexibility. The two are linked. Flexibility is one of the major lessons of the *Britannica*. The Romans became a seafaring power because they were flexible—they adapted their land tactics to naval warfare by having their troops board the enemy's boats. Alexander the Great conquered the much larger Persian army because his soldiers were more mobile. Britain beat France in the Hundred Years War because the French were too heavily armed and couldn't move quickly. In warfare, in economics, in math, flexibility always wins out.

My second problem with Dr. Sternberg is that my greater pool of knowledge allows me to come up with more creative solutions to problems. I have more examples to draw on, more metaphors I can make. To give an example: I was recently typing on my Macintosh laptop, and the battery started to overheat. It seemed in serious danger of turning into a bubbling gray soup. Most people have probably already figured out a solution, but I'm not a very handy person by nature. I recently had to call the building handyman to open our washer/dryer. So my insight took longer. And it came in a roundabout way—thanks to my knowledge of machine guns. I remembered that machine guns, when they first were invented, got so hot they had to be cooled by water. A soaked Macintosh didn't sound like a good idea. But what about the fan? I trained one of our oscillating fans on my computer and, voilà, saved my laptop.

I e-mail Dr. Sternberg with my argument. Thanks to the *Britannica*, I have in fact become more intelligent by his definition, as evidenced by the computer battery incident. Dr. Sternberg writes me back speedily. He starts his e-mail: "Great story!" All right! So maybe he's not such a Fokker after all. He continues: "I doubt that any of the great contributors in history—in the arts and letters, sciences, music, business—became great contributors because they read this or that encyclopedia." Damn. Well, that doesn't seem necessary—especially the detailed list of areas in which I won't contribute greatly. He goes on: "If it were me, I could think of many more useful ways to spend my time. But perhaps the encyclopedia will work for you, as the Bible or the Koran has worked for others. It gives one a certain security that is lacking in other methods." So he ends it on an upbeat, if slightly condescending, note.

Dr. Sternberg didn't really address my argument. Still, I have to admit: the man is intelligent. His theory about the encyclopedia-as-Bible is an insightful one. I've thought the same thing over the last few weeks. (See? I'm just as smart as Sternberg!) Consider: I read the *Britannica* every day, like a ritual. I criticize it here and there, but overall I take what it says as gospel. And most of all, the *Britannica* gives me a sense of stability and peace; the world may shift at a scary pace, but these paper-and-ink volumes have a permanence about them. When I look at them, I feel safe. Maybe that feeling is just as important as feeling smart.

time

The hour has not always been sixty minutes. In ancient civilizations—Greek, Sumerian, Roman, and so forth—daylight was divided into twelve hours. Thus, depending on the season, the length of an hour oscillated between about forty-five and seventy-five present-day minutes. I like this system. At least during winter, no Andy Rooney.

Tolstoy

I'm a big fan of the *Britannica*'s coverage of great books. It's like the Cliffs Notes—but the summaries are even shorter and the level of shame while reading them is slightly lower. No need to trudge your way through all the characters and dialogue—the *EB* will give you the whole book in a paragraph, along with a neat little moral. A beautiful time-saver. I'm not really kidding; I do find it helpful.

Consider its coverage of *Anna Karenina*, a book I never got around to finishing. Or starting. The *Britannica* gives an elegant description of Anna's brother Stiva, who is "genial and sybaritic." It says, "Stiva, though never wishing ill, wastes resources, neglects his family and regards pleasure as the purpose of life. The figure of Stiva is perhaps designed to suggest that evil, no less than good, derives from the small moral choices human beings make moment by moment."

Though I can't be sure it's an accurate analysis of the book, this sentence in the *Tolstoy* section strikes me as a profound one. It's a gem of a sentence, the wisest one I've seen in hundreds of pages. I'm reading about Tolstoy at a little Formica table at a deli, eating a low-fat muffin. I mention this because, when it is time for me to go, I am about to leave the used napkin on the table. But then I think, that's the kind of small moral choice the *EB* is talking about. That's what Stiva would do. So I pick up the napkin and throw it away. I know, I'm a saint.

Over the next few days, I adopt a new mantra, my own version of "What would Jesus do?" I tell myself, Remember Tolstoy. (Incidentally, speaking of Jesus and Tolstoy: the Russian novelist published a "corrected" version of the Gospels in which he referred to Jesus as "the man Jesus." Not that it's relevant.) When leaving my office, I make sure to turn off the lights. Remember Tolstoy, I say. When I borrow a sweater from *Esquire*'s vast closet of clothes to be used in photo shoots, I return it the next day. It's not enough to be moral about the big things, I decide. It's not enough that I refrain from murdering and robbing banks and giving PowerPoint presentations. I've got to be mindful of my smallest decisions.

We'll see how long this lasts. It crosses my mind that, as I approach the end, I'm scrounging for profundity, desperately searching for meaning. Maybe I am. But for now, I'm pleased with my new and improved Tolstoyan self.

training

As my son gets ready to make his out-of-the-womb debut, I go to Mom and Dad's apartment to pick up some of my own childhood toys— a big yellow Tonka truck, a Lego set, a pillow in the shape of a football. (That last one makes me nervous. What if it sways him to become a football player? I won't know what to say to him, except for Teddy Roosevelt's influence on the development of the forward pass.) While I'm over at the apartment, my dad does something surprising. Astounding, even. He asked me for help with their new DVD player.

This had never happened before. He's the engineer and I'm the mechanical imbecile. It's as if Bob Woodward called me and asked for tips on investigative journalism. "I just want a lesson from someone who's used it," he says. I had indeed used it. I pop in the *Casablanca* DVD and show him the fast forward, the pause, how to negotiate the menu—basic stuff he probably would have figured out in about four seconds without my aid.

"You know how Bogart got that stiff lip, right?"

"I think it was a war injury," says my dad.

"No, it was a wooden splinter, weirdly enough. Also, it's thought that Bogart originated the phrase 'Tennis, anyone?'"

Dad is busy testing the remote control. I felt good. Important. Here was my dad asking me for assistance. He wasn't too proud. Maybe someday I'll ask my son for tips on how to set up the holographic toaster.

triumphal marches

I am taking a break from my studies and I flip on my old pal the E! channel, a network devoted to twenty-four-hour breathless coverage of Hollywood. I hadn't watched this channel in months.

It seems stranger than I remembered it. The correspondents use an overabundance of hair gel and superlatives ("greatest, sexiest, hottest"). They move their facial features a lot. They talk about these events as if they have the historical importance of the Berlin airlift. I begin to feel a little ill, as if I've eaten some bad chicken marsala or something. Which I think might be a good sign, actually.

The E! channel is covering a story that involved Bruce Willis walking down a red carpet. He was smiling, perhaps winking, allowing his ecstatic public to touch his hands, his team of publicists and agents and hangers-on in tow.

Not long ago, I had read about the Romans and their official triumphal marches, and this seemed a weird modern echo, but without the slaves in chains, at least not visible ones. The Roman triumph was given when a general had slain at least five thousand of the enemy. That was the minimum. The victorious general, says the *Britannica*, rode on a chariot festooned with laurel, wearing a purple-and-gold tunic and toga, clutching a laurel branch in his right hand and an ivory scepter in his left.

But here's the part that fascinated me: "A slave held a golden crown over the general's head while repeatedly reminding him in the midst of his glory that he was a mortal man."

Brilliant. That's exactly what we need on our red carpets. We need some production assistant following behind Bruce Willis, whispering in his ear: "You're a mortal man. You're just some putz with good orthodonture who says lines from a script. You are not a god." We need some enforced humility in today's society. It seems to be a lost virtue.

triumvirate

A couple of more weeks till *Millionaire,* and I'm still cramming like Thomas Jefferson on a bender (as a young man, he studied fifteen hours a day, practiced violin for three, and spent the remaining six eating or sleeping).

I take time out to choose my lifelines. These are the folks who will be waiting by their phones to help me in case Meredith asks me a stumper of a question. My friend Mike offered to be my lifeline for any and all juice-related questions (he works for a smoothie company). A nice offer. But in the end, I settle on Ron Hoeflin—he of the nosebleed-altitude IQ—and Dave Sampugnaro, the five-time *Jeopardy!* champ.

Also Eric. Yes, my brother-in-law and nemesis (the original Nemesis, by the way, was a Greek goddess of vegetation who had sex with Zeus-disguised-as-a-swan). I struggled with this one, but I figure we're talking about a million bucks here. A million bucks would soothe my ego just fine. The man just knows too much information *not* to be a lifeline. I accepted this a couple of weeks ago when, in response to his mom's question about the historical accuracy of *Ben Hur,* Eric gave a startling century-by-century history of the Roman Empire—from the first triumvirate (Julius Caesar, Pompey, Marcus Crassus) right on up to the death of the Holy Roman Empire. I tried to keep up—I threw in a reference to the Visigoths and another to the Ostrogoths—but Eric just trampled me. I went home and checked on his facts. Sadly, they were all correct.

Soon after, I pop the question. "Eric, would you do me the honor of being my lifeline on *Millionaire?*"

"You want me as a lifeline?"

"Yes."

"Well, if I help you win a million, what kind of financial remuneration will I get?"

I think for a second.

"Well, I'll give you ten percent of my winnings. But if you screw up, you have to reimburse me for the entire amount that I lost."

In that case, Eric said, he'd do it for free. Julie beamed. She was proud of my hard bargaining.

I figure I'd put Eric to work early. I had noticed a quirk in the way *Millionaire* pays out its reward money. In the fine print of the ream of documents they sent me, it said that $250,000 is paid in one lump sum—but $500,000 and $1,000,000 are paid out over ten and twenty years, respectively. If you factored in inflation and lost investment opportunities, could $250,000 actually be a better deal? I hope so. I figure that would be a great moment in *Millionaire* history: I stop at $250,000 and explain to Meredith the intricacies of amortized payments. So I ask Eric—the former investment banker—to crunch the numbers.

He e-mails back that $1,000,000 over twenty years came out to $540,000 in today's dollars. That's before taxes, mind you—but it is still more cash than the other options. Damn. Now I really have to try to win the million.

Trotsky, Leon

Julie's breasts have ballooned up so much that she walks around the apartment holding them in place with her hands. It's very distracting when I'm trying to read about trolls (they burst into flame when hit by sunlight) and Trotsky (killed in Mexico by an axe murderer).

Trump, Donald

I am watching an HBO documentary with Julie, and the *Britannica* makes a surprise cameo. Not a flattering one, though. The documentary is called *Born Rich,* and follows the frivolous lives of a bunch of young heirs—the heir to the Johnson & Johnson fortune, the daughter of Donald Trump (he owns more than twenty-five thousand apartments, by the way). These privileged tools were each sitting on some serious coin. Add up their trust funds, and it'd rival Pizarro's collection of treasures (the conquistador collected a ransom of twenty-four tons of gold and silver for the Inca emperor Atahuallpa—whom he then killed).

Anyway, the documentary features some guy from an obscure branch of the European ruling class. He has a superior accent, well-oiled hair, and a nice chunk of his parents' textile fortune. He spends much of his leisure time—which he has in abundance—ordering around his personal tailor; he tells us he found improperly positioned lapels "vulgar." Truly the most odious of heirs. Then at one point, he shows the viewers his eleventh edition of the *Encyclopaedia Britannica* and explains that this was the last time the *Britannica* was good. Since then, it had "become for the *masses.* Now, the *Encyclopaedia Britannica* is, you know . . . *sheeet."* What a putz. What right does he have to insult my beloved *Britannica?* Read 28 million words of it, then come back and talk to me.

This guy—whose name I don't remember—is a walking argument for the sweeping revision of inheritance laws. The *Britannica*'s inheritance section says that primitive food gatherers destroyed a person's belongings—his weapons, his bowls—upon his death. Also, the Papua of New Guinea burned the hut of a dead man. Maybe we could learn something from this. Maybe we should burn the Jaguars and Nokia cell phones of these people's parents when they die. Or at least redistribute them.

It's possible our whiny aristocrat doesn't like the current edition because it points out that proinheritance arguments have lost a lot of force. Nowadays, you don't need inheritance to guarantee the continuance of business. In general, business is handed from CEO to CEO, not from father to son. So the economy would presumably keep humming if Ivanka Trump had to start driving a Hyundai and eating at KFC. The world's economy wouldn't suffer if this European nitwit had to join the masses he finds so sheety.

Tunguska event

This was an "enormous aerial explosion that, at about 7:40 A.M. on June 30, 1908, flattened approximately five hundred thousand acres of pine forest near the Podkamennaya Tunguska River, central Siberia, in Russia. The energy of the explosion was equivalent to that of ten to fifteen megatons of TNT. Uncertain evidence of various kinds suggests that the explosion was perhaps caused by a comet fragment colliding with the Earth."

I had more than a passing acquaintance with the Tunguska event. For a couple of weeks there, when I was eight or nine, I was obsessed with it. I had read about the massive Siberian explosion in a collection of unsolved mysteries, and I can now recall the black-and-white drawing of thousands of trees splayed out on the forest floor. I looked it up in other books after that. I knew all the theories—that the Tunguska event was really the result of a UFO doing target practice, or that it was a chunk of antimatter that somehow took a left turn and sailed into our atmosphere. Naturally, I worried—if it can happen in Siberia, why can't it happen on Eighty-second Street in Manhattan? Who's to say that I won't be vaporized in the Upper East Side event?

And then, when that didn't happen over the next few weeks, the Tunguska faded from my memory. In the past twenty-six years, until just moments ago, I had given absolutely zero thought to the Tunguska event. I guess unexplained Siberian explosions don't come up too much in celebrity journalism.

turnip

It's Halloween today. In the British Isles, the Halloween jack-o'-lantern used to be made from a turnip, not a pumpkin. The savages.

By the way, another good thing about Julie being pregnant: she's too tired to go out. No pumpkin carving. No turnip carving. No costumes. (In the past couple of years I was enlisted to be Colonel Sanders, then Colonel Mustard from Clue, so who knows what colonel I'd be this year?) Instead, we get to stay inside and watch something scary on TV. We opt for a show about former child actors going out on dates.

tutelage

My friend Jamie has invited me to speak to an adult education class he's teaching. Finally, after enduring the speed-reading and memory fiascoes, a chance to be on the other side of the adult education table. This time I will be the one pontificating.

It's a writing class. There are about a dozen students who want to shed their real jobs and join the lucrative field of writing, where you can earn lots of money if your name happens to include both the words "Stephen" and "King." The students seem nice enough. One has spent a lot of time as a ski bum and wants to go into magazines, another wants out of her hellish PR job.

I decide to start with some good writing advice I'd culled from the encyclopedia. I printed my speech on little index cards to make myself look organized and professional. I begin reading.

First, I tell them to be aggressive. The poet Langston Hughes was a busboy at a hotel in Washington, D.C. While in the dining room, he slipped three of his poems beside the dinner plate of established poet Vachel Lindsay. The next day, newspapers announced Lindsay had discovered a "Negro busboy poet." The moral: get your writing in people's face—no matter how you do it.

Second, I tell them they can write anywhere. If you have a job at the Gap, steal a few minutes and write some lines in the sweater section. No excuses. Hugh Lofting wrote *Dr. Doolittle* while in the trenches of World War I. Amid exploding grenades and gas masks and rats, he created a lovely little story about talking animals that he sent home to amuse his children. Be like Hugh. Write everywhere.

Then I tell them that if you write with style and passion, you can make any topic interesting. Any topic at all, as William Cowper proved.

Cowper was a poet whose friend challenged him to write a long discursive poem about a sofa. He did, and it was a smash success. Personally, I'd rather read a footrest-based novel, but I can see the allure of sofas.

Jamie's students all nod politely. But I notice a remarkable lack of movement of their pens. Every time I look up from my speech, all the pens are still lying on their desks. Notes are conspicuously not being taken.

Then one of them asks if I know anyone at *The New Yorker*.

Well, yes, I reply.

"How do we e-mail them?" he asks.

I don't feel comfortable giving out my *New Yorker* contact's name, but I tell them that all e-mail addresses at *The New Yorker* are made with an underscore between first and last names.

This time, the pens in the classroom begin scribbling: first name_last name@newyorker.com. That they find interesting.

typewriter

I haven't touched one of these since my mom's electric Remington back in the early eighties, a machine that hummed so loud it drowned out anything resembling a coherent thought. It was like trying to write my high school essays about Huck Finn or the Whiskey Rebellion on the tarmac at La Guardia. Still, I feel I should pay some attention to typewriters, since I spend most of my day pecking away at the typewriter's electronic descendant.

I learn that Mark Twain was an early adapter, submitting the very first typewritten manuscript to a publisher. Those antediluvian typewriters were the size of pianos, and also had only capital letters. In 1878, typewriters finally introduced lowercase letters. Yes, the shift key was born—but mind you, it wasn't an easy birth. The shift key had to do battle with a rival, the double-keyboard machine, which contained twice the number of keys, two for each letter, a small and a large. After many years, the shift key won out thanks to the invention of touch typing.

I take a minute and look at the shift key on my Macintosh PowerBook G3. Good for you, shift key. I'm glad you trounced that evil double-key method. CONGRATULATIONS! There, I just used you. Thanks again.

That's a nice thing about reading the *Britannica*. I'm constantly learning to appreciate things that I didn't even know deserved appreciation. The lightbulb and the theory of relativity—they get more good PR than Tom Hanks's visit to a children's hospital. But it's the little things, the forgotten mini revolutions that need our thanks.

U

ukelele

The Hawaiian ukelele is adapted from the Portuguese machada and is quite unsuited to indigenous musical forms. In other words, Don Ho's "Tiny Bubbles" is not an ancient Pacific island chant. Disillusioning.

umlaut

It's time for my haj. Time to make the pilgrimage to the *Britannica* HQ. These thirty-two volumes have consumed the last months of my life, and I'm desperately curious to see their birthplace.

Well, the real birthplace is Edinburgh, Scotland. I won't be going there. But since the 1930s—when the *Britannica* was owned, briefly and improbably, by Sears Roebuck—the offices have been located in Chicago. I haven't been to Chicago since my days at *Entertainment Weekly*, when I visited the city to report on another highbrow cultural institution, *The Jerry Springer Show*. If I had to guess, I'd say the *Britannica* trip will involve slightly fewer lesbians wrestling in chocolate pudding. Julie wants to come—she has friends in Chicago—so we book a flight.

"You know, it's not called the Windy City because of the wind," I tell her. "It's because the early Chicago politicians were full of wind, as in hot air. That's how it got the nickname."

"A dollar, please."

I've lost about $20 so far on fines for irrelevant facts. But this one I'm going to fight.

"That's not irrelevant. That's useful meteorological information. I'm saying it's not as windy as you might think. Don't pack a windbreaker."

Julie shrugs, gives me that one.

The morning after we arrive in Windbag City, I wake up, put on a blazer so I look all professional, and go meet the *Britannica*'s publicist, Tom Panelas, for breakfast. As a journalist, it's part of my job to think of all publicists as soldiers of Satan. But with Tom, that's not possible. He's a burly man with a booming, from-the-diaphragm voice and an easy laugh. As I mentioned before, Tom is smart—he's got a frightening vocabulary and range of references. I remember once, while talking to Tom on the phone, I mentioned my birth date for some reason—March 20, 1968—and Tom said, "That was right between the Tet offensive and MLK's assassination," which simultaneously dismayed me about my birthday and impressed me greatly with Tom's memory. He unabashedly carries three or so pens in his shirt pocket. He'll tell the occasional intellectual joke. Like: "René Descartes walks into a bar. The bartender says, 'Yo, René, how you doing? Can I get you a beer?' 'I think not,' replies Descartes. And then he disappears." After which joke, Tom will immediately apologize.

The only time I saw Tom even slightly rattled was when I mentioned an article that claimed that, at one time, the domain name encyclopaedia-britannica.com had been swiped by another Web site—one that featured blond women doing things you probably wouldn't even find in the *reproduction* section of the encyclopedia. Linking *Britannica* and hardcore porn—that made him a little nervous. And he wanted to make quite clear any problem like that had long since been remedied.

In any case, Tom has scheduled a packed day for me, a breakneck tour of the *Britannica*'s highlights. So off we go. It is an odd feeling walking off the elevator and into the offices. I've been reading the Britannica so much, it has become this disembodied mountain of knowledge. It seems somehow delivered from on high, whole and intact, like Deuteronomy. I almost forget there are people who put it together, people who put on their pants—often corduroy pants, it would turn out—one leg at a time.

But there are indeed editors, and they are indeed mortal. Also quiet. This could be the quietest office in America. Tom has told me that, at one point, the company that owned Muzak also owned the *Britannica,* which meant the office was constantly bathed in soothing cheesified versions of Simon and Garfunkel. But no more. All I hear is the click-clack of of computer keyboards and an occasional polite, low discussion of Gothic architecture, or what have you.

The offices are clean and clutter-free, not counting a smattering of highbrow cubicle knickknacks, like the foam rubber brain issued by the *Britannica* a few years before. The office walls are appointed with a taste-ful selection of *Britannica* lore: a Norman Rockwell–painted ad showing Grampa reading a volume to his eager granddaughter; the first timeline (not the first timeline in the *Britannica,* mind you: the first timeline, which appeared in the third edition); and some of the original engravings for the 1768 edition—most notably some extremely disquieting images of old midwifery contraptions that look like something you'd find alongside a ball gag in an S&M closet. And so on.

My first stop is with the two top editors—Dale Hoiberg and Theodore Pappas. Dale studied Chinese literature, and his office has a print of Confucius on the walls. For some reason, Dale reminds me of the father on the eighties puppet sitcom *Alf*—a fact I decide to keep to myself. This is not the place for that. Theodore has a mustache and a blue vest and a tie and is very precise. You get the feeling his CD rack does not in-discriminately mix classical and jazz. Both Dale and Theodore are very kind, in that gentle academic sort of way.

I immediately decide I like them, partly because they seem very curi-ous about me. What's not to like? I tell them my quest is going well. Their thirty-two-volume work is a great read, if incredibly challenging.

"The math sections," I say, "are my bête noir."

Bête noir? I can't believe that came out of my mouth. Who talks like that? I realize I'm more nervous than I thought I would be. I'm so desper-ate to impress these guys, to prove I'm no lightweight, that I've resorted to the injudicious use of absurd French phrases.

When we start talking specific things I've learned, somehow the first fact that springs to mind is one about embalming. In particular, the tale of the crafty widower who kept his wife aboveground so as to inherit her money (see *embalming*). I'm a little embarrassed that—out of all the thou-sands and thousands of facts in the *EB*—this is the one I share. On the other hand, at least I don't tell them the one about the five-butted abalone.

"I found that embalming story fascinatingly morbid," I say, trying to recover by using a well-placed adverb.

They chuckle graciously. They didn't know about that one.

Didn't know about it? That takes me aback. Somehow, I assumed that the editors of the *Britannica* would have a handle on pretty much everything in the encyclopedia. They edit the damn thing, right? Well, if I give that notion more than three seconds' thought, I would realize it is moronic. The editor in chief couldn't possibly read or remember all his books' 44 million words. But hearing it in person—getting proof that I have at least one piece of knowledge Dale and Theodore don't have—well, it's a huge relief.

Emboldened, I decide to forge ahead. "I've got to say, the accuracy is remarkable. I found very few errors in the *Britannica*."

They seem pleased.

"But I did find some."

I tell them about how Robert Frost is listed as a Harvard graduate even though he dropped out, and about a backward quotation mark. I watch their faces for shock or hostility, but they just seem curious. They want to fix them. Theodore actually takes notes. This is a huge feeling of power, a strange and great sensation. Can you imagine? I am going to have an impact on the esteemed *Encyclopaedia Britannica*. It has always seemed so imposingly static; to be able to change it was unthinkable, as likely as changing Teddy Roosevelt's chin on Mount Rushmore. But here I am, doing it.

"Also, my wife is upset there's no mention of Tom Cruise."

Again, Theodore jots down a note. This one is much more of a long shot. But Theodore did say they want to beef up the pop culture coverage, to make the *Britannica* more accessible without sacrificing the gravitas or dumbing it down. Man, if I got Tom Cruise in, I would be golden with Julie. I could forget a half dozen anniversaries, but I'd always have that.

I spend an hour chatting with Dale and Theodore—during which I start to understand a smaller and smaller percentage of what they are saying, since they begin to discuss the theory of databases. I also, embarrassingly enough, have to ask what the word "ligature" means—it's when two letters are smushed together, like the *a* and the *e* in the official title of the *Encyclopaedia Britannica*. (I've used the nonconnecting *ae* in this book, partly because I can't figure out how to get the ligature on my Macintosh keyboard.)

But there is much more to see, so Tom hustles me out of Dale's office. He shows me the illustration department (I particularly like the disemboweled laser printer being used as a model). And the animation department, which makes short movies for the *Britannica* CD-ROM (I comment that the video of a dragonfly eating its prey reminds me of a Bruckheimer movie, a reference I immediately wish I could take back). I am whisked to the indexing department, which is still riding high from its

Wheatley Medal, the Nobel for index people (I get them to show me how they indexed the concept "index," since I still enjoy a little postmodernism). I talk to some fact checkers (and learn about the time they were confirming the population of a tiny Scottish town, and they called up some guy in the town, who told them, "If you hold the phone a second, I can count," and he went out and counted). I meet a handful of editors (each has an area of expertise, and assigns the articles out to specialists in the field). I visit the library (a book on Indian treaties, a Malay-to-English dictionary—generally, the oddest collection of books I've encountered).

And then Tom has a surprise for me. The wily folks at the *Britannica* are going to put me to work. They want me to really understand how this encyclopedia is built, so they're going to have me lay a couple of bricks myself. I'm led to a cubicle, which is all set up for me with two red pencils, a highlighter, a stack of books, and a *Britannica* mug. And I am left alone, in the silent *Britannica* offices, listening to the clacking keyboards of other employees.

My first task is to fact check an article on the history of sports. I can do this; I spent several months as a fact checker at the *New York Observer*. I start by trying to confirm that sumo wrestling uniforms were designed in 1906, not the Middle Ages as many assume. I scan the table of contents of my stack of books. No sumo there. I start clicking though Web sites, spending several tantalizing minutes at one Drexel University page before coming up empty. I begin to sweat. Not metaphorically, but actual perspiration, at least a sponge worth. I get that panicked, I'm-flubbing-this feeling I haven't gotten since the Mensa test. I want to dazzle these *Britannica* folks, show that I'm worthy of reading their book. And I'm failing.

After forty minutes—during which time I confirm exactly two of the fifteen facts—I switch to my next task: editing. I've been given an article on international criminal law, and been charged with adding "meaningful cross-referencing." This I can do. Cross-referencing is the art of adding "see *such-and-such*" at the end of a sentence. If there's a mention of broccoli, I'd add "see *vegetables*"—that kind of thing. I start adding cross-references with near giddy enthusiasm, filling up the page with red pen marks, trying to compensate for the fact-checking Chernobyl. International airspace? See *sovereignty*. Now that's what I call "meaningful cross-referencing."

After twenty minutes, I'm called back to Theodore's office, where I boast about all the references I crossed. He seems moderately pleased.

"Was there anything you would have changed in the international law article," asks Theodore. "Any big suggestions?"

Damn. I was so busy with my meaningful cross-referencing, I didn't devote any brain space to the grand picture of whether this was actually a good article. See *moron*.

"Maybe, um. Well, it could have talked more about the history of international criminal law. Like, did they have the concept in ancient Greece?"

I kind of think this isn't a half-bad answer. But it isn't the right one.

"Did you feel that there could be more examples of international criminal law?" asks Theodore. "To bring it down to the reader?"

Shit! That is the right answer.

"Yes," I say, going into ass-kissing mode. "Definitely a great idea. Like Slobodan Milosevic. When I think of war criminals, that's who I think of."

"Well," says Theodore gently, "we want to make sure we're not just a newspaper. We've got to take the long perspective."

Jesus. Screwed up again. I was chasing the headlines like some hack journalist instead of thinking like a *Britannica* editor.

Soon after, I have to leave to catch a flight back to New York.

As Julie and I sit in the airport, my humiliation fades. That wasn't what I'll remember most—they were too kind to make my failure sting. What I'll remember most is the refreshing, genuine, unfettered *enthusiasm* of the *Britannica* folks. I've never seen people get so excited about diacritics—those little lines and accents on letters, the umlaut, the tilde, that diagonal slash through the *L*. Dale talked about a database called Information Management and Retrieval System the way teenage boys might discuss Christina Aguilera's cleavage. He was *into* it. They love information—reading it, digesting it, and most of all, organizing it.

And you get the feeling the *Britannica* staff believes—perhaps naively, perhaps a little pretentiously, but sincerely and strongly—that they are engaged in a noble pursuit. It's not just a business. To them, it's not the same as selling deodorant, which is what a lot of publishing is nowadays.

At one point during our conversation, when I was speaking in sentence fragments and "uhs" and "ums" as those in my generation tend to, Theodore stopped me cold by reciting a quotation. People in my social circle just don't recite quotations, unless they're from *Fletch* or *Spinal Tap*. Theodore's quotation was a dedication in a 1940s edition of the *Britannica* that he thought was relevant, and it went like this: "To the men, women, and children of the world who, by increasing their knowledge of the earth and its people, seek to understand each other's problems and through this understanding strive for a community of nations living in peace, the *Encyclopaedia Britannica* dedicates this volume." Word.

university

The first one was in Bologna, Italy, in the 11th century. When universities began, teachers charged fees for each class, which meant they had to appeal to the students. Now that's a brilliant idea that needs to be resuscitated. Open classes up to the free market! Set up a ticket booth outside Psychology 101 and Advanced Statistics and watch the professors scramble to spice things up. I think that would improve education immensely. At the very least, I'd get to see the nap-inducing course I took on the *The Faerie Queen* flop like an academic version of *Gigli*.

urine

Dalmatian dogs and humans have strangely similar urine (they're the only two mammals to produce uric acid). This could be useful if I ever smoke pot, apply for a government job, and have access to Dalmatians. Regardless, the unexpected connections continue to amaze.

utility

It's official. I made my dad proud. He was at a benefit last night, and he told an acquaintance that his son was reading the encyclopedia from *A* to *Z*. The guy refused to believe it, figuring it was just another Arnieism. Another one of my dad's practical jokes.

So this morning, I got on a conference call and confirmed that, yes, I am reading the encyclopedia. My dad was delighted—I had helped him pull off a practical joke. Or actually, an anti–practical joke. If there's one thing that my dad likes better than a well-played canard, it's when he tells an outrageous truth that nobody believes.

I'm honored. I may not have impressed my dad with my knowledge yet. But the quest itself came in quite handy.

Uzziah

The last of the *U*s—a king of Judah for fifty-two years in the 8th century B.C. As I reach the end, I keep trying to impose some sort of plot on the *Britannica*. I keep hoping that there will be some sort of resolution at the end. I know that's deluded, but a man's got to dream.

V

vaccine

Brunch at Grandma and Grandpa's. The talk at the meal is of a tremendous feat of publishing: *The Complete Family News*. The *Family News* is my grandmother's two-page newsletter, published monthly since 1950, with a circulation of about twenty-five loyal readers. My aunt Jane has tracked down most of the five hundred total issues, xeroxed them, and bound them in a massive, Britannica-sized volume.

It's fascinating reading, at least for those in my gene pool: births, marriages, job accomplishments, details about which baby sucked the toe of which other baby—which sounds a little kinky now that I type it in, but did actually happen.

The *Family News* doesn't have a tremendous amount of scandalous information. It's sort of like *Pravda* under Khrushchev, but with fewer stories about heroic factory workers. You won't read about cousins getting downsized or kids experimenting with hallucinogenic mushrooms.

But still, it's great to flip through. Julie's been particularly fascinated by the coverage of my first few years of life. This consisted almost exclusively of the announcement of which disease I had that month. I had, in no particular order, an ear infection, "the grippe," an eye infection, "the germ," and something called "the croup."

"I told you I get sick a lot," I say. "I'm not a hypochondriac."

Grandma has been reading it herself. She says she was surprised, when reading about my parent's courtship, that my father was so young when he entered college.

"How old were you again?" she asks.

"I was sixteen," he says.

"Wow."

I take the opportunity to make my requisite passive-aggressive remark—namely that both Cotton and Increase Mather entered Harvard when they were twelve. "The Mathers were also pioneers in smallpox vaccinations," I added. "Which was controversial at the time. An angry opponent threw a bomb in Cotton's window."

For his part, Dad says he was struck by something else when reading *The Complete Family News*.

"What's that?" says Grandma.

I prepare for whatever silly joke is to follow.

"I was struck by how much you two have accomplished," says my Dad. "It's really remarkable how many great things you've done, and how you've made the world a better place."

Huh. I was not expecting that. A genuine emotional moment from my dad. I've seen it a few times—more and more in recent years, it seems to me, most notably after the kayaking incident. I've read about something called a "joking relationship" that exists in some societies—it's a way to keep a safe distance. But Dad has broken through the joking relationship. This is admirable. Maybe I need to do the same, like the famous follow-the-leader goslings studied by ethologist Konrad Lorenz.

Van Buren, Martin

Amid all the castrations and blindings and beheadings and bribes and other discourteous means of attaining power, Martin Van Buren is a refreshing commander in chief. The eighth president of the United States proves that sometimes—not often, but sometimes—it pays to be nice.

In 1828, Andrew Jackson appointed Van Buren (along with his huge muttonchops) secretary of state. It was a strange year in Washington, the year the city became embroiled in a scandal that would be called Peggy-Gate if it happened today. Peggy Eaton—who got a few sentences back in the *E* section—was a humble gal, the daughter of a tavern keeper. But she had the audacity to marry out of her class, getting hitched to Jackson's secretary of war, John Eaton. Rumors about her alleged misconduct swept Washington, and snooty Washington hostesses snubbed her at their parties. The anti-Peggy brigade was led by the wife of Vice President John Calhoun—a fact that outraged President Jackson, who considered himself a man of the people. Jackson had originally favored Calhoun to succeed him as president, but thanks to the Peggy Eaton affair, Jackson soured on Calhoun.

There was one man in the cabinet, however, who was gracious to Peggy Eaton: Martin Van Buren. And he became the Jackson favorite. Jackson made Van Buren vice president in 1832 and supported him for president four years later. It's a weird path to political power—being nice to a blue-collar woman. But it's a heartening one.

Of course, Van Buren was a pretty bad president. And Peggy Eaton, after the death of her husband, married an Italian dancing master who defrauded her of her money and ran off with her granddaughter. So the story's not exactly a fairy tale. But I try to ignore that part. Be nice to people—that's the takeaway here.

Vassar College

Just a couple of days till *Millionaire*. I'm still freaking out, still making arbitrary lists of things I've forgotten. Which are the Seven Sister schools? What's the biggest volcanic eruption (it was Mount Tambora in Indonesia in 1815, not Krakatoa). Who are King Lear's three daughters? Which one of Shakespeare's kings was a hunchback? I know they're going to ask that. Oh, yes. Richard III.

vegetarianism

My aunt Marti calls me at home tonight and asks what I am doing.

"Just hitting the books," I say.

That doesn't go over so well. She scolds me for the violent metaphor—no need to use the word "hit."

"Okay, I'm performing gentle acupressure on the books," I say.

She seems to like that better.

I love Marti, but a conversation with her always includes a list of what I'm doing and saying wrong, and how it supports the phallocentric power structure. She's got some opinions, my aunt. There's liberal, there's really liberal, then there's Marti, a few miles further to the left. She lives out near Berkeley, appropriately enough—though even Berkeley is a bit too fascist for her.

I haven't talked to Marti since Julie got pregnant. I break the news to her as gently as I can, and apologize to her for contributing to the over-population problem.

"That's okay," she says. She'll forgive me. But, she points out, I can help minimize the damage to the environment by raising the child vegan.

Marti herself is beyond vegan. Animal rights are her passion (even if she thinks the concept of rights is too Western), and she spends a good part of the year flying around the country attending vegetarian conferences. I could take up quite a bit of space listing the things that Marti doesn't eat: meat, of course, and chicken, fish, eggs, dairy (she likes to call ice cream "solidified mucous"), but also honey—she won't eat honey because the bees are oppressed, not paid union scale or something. You'd think she'd like soy, but she believes the soy industry is corrupt. She recently took her diet to a new level by becoming a raw foodist, meaning she eats only food that's uncooked, because it's more natural.

Despite her dogmatic beliefs, Marti is very sweet and funny, and her stridency is always tempered with an ability to laugh at herself. So talking to her is always fascinating—though no matter how hard I watch my tongue, I still get in trouble. She doesn't like sexist language, naturally, but she also objects to antianimal language. I once got scolded for calling someone a pig. Pigs are fine animals, she pointed out. My grandmother was recently complaining about George W. Bush, and made the mistake of calling him a "lemon."

"Nothing wrong with lemons, Mother," said Marti. "Don't be fruitist." She said the word "fruitist" with a little bit of irony—but not a lot.

Whenever I tell Marti about what I'm reading in the *Britannica,* I can count on her to tell me what it got wrong, what it neglected to mention. I told her early on about Francis Bacon. "Did it mention he was a sexist?" she asked.

"No, that didn't make it in."

She was unimpressed.

This time, I tell her I have just read an article she might find quite interesting—the one on vegetarianism.

"What'd it say?"

I tell her how it mentioned that Pythagorus, Plato, and Plutarch were vegetarians. Voltaire praised and Shelley practiced vegetarianism, and Jeremy Bentham had a great quote about animals: "The question is not, can they reason, nor can they talk, but can they suffer?"

Oh yes, she likes that one.

I say, would you like to see the article? I make it sound all innocent. But mostly, I am just looking forward to seeing how many inevitable faults she will find with it, from its factual inaccuracies to its use of too-masculine typeface.

I fax it to her, and she doesn't disappoint. There is, indeed, plenty wrong with the *vegetarianism* entry. It neglects the long-standing association between meat eating and maleness. It overplays the motivation of vegetarians to remain pure and conquer animalistic passions—radical feminist vegetarianism doesn't buy into the conquering-of-the-animalistic-passions argument. And why mention only Peter Singer but ignore feminist philosophers on vegetarianism?

The lesson is, the *Britannica* can try to be dispassionate and fair, but it'll never please everybody; it'll always have inevitable biases. In fact, for a while there, attacking of the *Britannica* became a cottage industry. Well, maybe not an entire cottage, but a small structure of some kind. According to the book *The Great EB*, in the late 1800s an Alabama journalist named Thaddeus Oglesby wrote a bile-filled book entitled *Some Truths of History: A Vindication of the South against the Encyclopaedia Britannica and Other Maligners*. Oglesby was furious about such passages as this one in the ninth edition: "The few thinkers of America born south of Mason and Dixon's line [are] outnumbered by those belonging to the single State of Massachusetts." That is, in fact, kind of rude. Oglesby may have had a point.

Then, in 1935, a man named Joseph McCabe—a former priest turned crusader against Catholicism—wrote his own book, called *The Lies and Fallacies of the Encyclopaedia Britannica*. McCabe argues that the eleventh edition was commendably honest in its treatment of Catholicism, but by the fourteenth edition, the church had pressured the editors to chop out the unflattering bits. Gone are the references to Pope Innocent VIII's many children and vast corruption. Gone are the passages about the church castrating boys for choir (McCabe makes the ham-handed point that the *Britannica* itself was castrated). I read McCabe's book—it was short, and took only an afternoon. It's an experience I don't recommend, but he does make a compelling case.

After reading almost the entire Britannica, I think the 2002 edition has done an admirable job at striving for objectivity. That said, it still has a handful of pet topics that get excessively glowing treatment. Chamber music comes to mind. The *Britannica* has an unseemly soft spot for chamber music, about which it writes: "It probably gives the most lasting pleasure to more music lovers than any other kind of music." I think a rebuttal by the a cappella community is in order.

vehicle

I am working on a year-end wrap-up for *Esquire,* and I read a news article about activists who torched a car dealership containing twenty new Hummers—those cruise ships of the highway. The perpetrators spray-painted the words "Fat, lazy Americans" on the burned metallic carcasses.

I filed it under "Eerie Echo of the Past," number 425. Way back in the *C*s, I read about coaches—those opulent, four-wheeled, horse-drawn carriages that first appeared in the 1500s. In short, the SUVs of the day—and about as popular. The *Britannica* describes this surprising, long-forgotten controversy: "Poets derogated coaches as ostentatious vehicles employed by wantons and rakes . . . Bostonians attacked coaches as works of the devil. . . ." A German noble forbade them in an edict.

I was happy to make the Hummer-coach connection. But even happier that I still remembered something from the *C*s.

vending machines

Another in the *Britannica*'s pile of unsung heroes: the coin-operated vending machine. The vending machine became popular right before World War II as America was building up its defense. The factory owners installed them so that workers could pull twelve-hour shifts without taking a full meal break, instead stuffing themselves with snacks from the machines. We owe vending machines thanks. Without them, we might be eating bratwurst and sauerkraut out of coin-operated machines.

ventriloquism

The Eskimos and Zulus are both adept at the art of ventriloquism. I like that these sub-Saharan and Arctic peoples are linked—the brotherhood of man, you know. And I like it even better that they're linked by bad jokes from talking dummies.

vexillology

So far, journalism seems to be working out okay for me as a career. But it's good to know I have options. The EB is teeming with ideas for new careers. In some ways, it's a huge thirty-three-thousand-page version of *What Color is Your Parachute.* Here, my top seven:

1. *Pamphleteer.* This used to be a very popular profession. Lots of pamphleteers were needed to engage in pamphlet wars. In one notably

ruthless pamphlet war, the Puritans attacked Episcopalians as "profane, proud, paltry, popish, pestilent, pernicious, presumptuous prelates." I like both alliteration and short books. So this would be a perfect job for me.

2. *Abbot of Unreason.* I just think this would look cool on an embossed business card. In medieval Scotland, the "Abbot of Unreason" was the man who organized the elaborate Christmas festivities, complete with a mock court that paid homage to him. In England, he was called the "Lord of Misrule," also cool.

3. *Limnologist.* A person who studies lakes. I like the idea that there is a job devoted solely to the study of lakes. But honestly, I can't decide between limnologist and all the other fun ologists in the encyclopedia. Perhaps it'd be better to be a vexillologist (one who studies flags), or a psephologist (studies elections). What about an exobiologist (studies extraterrestral life), a martyrologist (no need for an explanation), a selenographist (studies the moon), a sigillographist (studies seals—the wax kind, not the swimming kind)? Hard to choose.

4. *Whale ritualist.* Among the Nootka Indians of the Pacific Northwest, this was the man who performed ceremonies that caused dead whales to drift ashore. It's probably not a fast-growing sector—maybe only half of the Fortune 500 companies require a whale ritualist. But still, it just seems like a good specialty to have.

5. *Printer's devil.* Ambrose Bierce was one, as was *New York Times* owner Adolph Ochs. I'm not sure what they do, but any job with "devil" in the title has to be good.

6. *Pretender to the throne.* I had to be impressed by the three men named Dmitry the False, each of whom claimed to be Dmitry the son of Ivan the Terrible, who had died mysteriously when he was a child. They looked nothing like one another, nor particularly like Dmitry himself, but they didn't let that get in the way of claiming the Russian throne. That's the main skill set here: chutzpah. So what if I'm Jewish? That shouldn't stop me from claiming to be the long-lost Bush cousin.

7. *Supreme Court justice in the 19th century.* These guys worked seven or eight weeks a year, with a comfortable forty-four weeks of vacation, not counting sick days and personal days. I'm guessing, though, they got squat for paternity leave.

And then there are some of the worst careers in the world:

1. *Professional bone picker.* If you're in the Choctaw tribe and you die, your corpse is picked clean a by a professional bone picker, a man or woman with special tattoos and long fingernails.

2. *Member of the Opposition.* I'm not talking about the British Parliament. The Opposition is the official name of the team of white guys whose job it is to lose to the Harlem Globetrotters. I just think that might get a little frustrating after the 4,323rd straight loss. The coach for the Opposition would be even tougher. "You guys are going to lose, and you'll lose without any dignity at all!"

3. *Lenin's corpse keeper.* Lenin remains embalmed, and his corpse needs, according to the *Britannica,* "periodic renewal treatment."

Victoria

Queen Victoria forbade knocking, insisting on gentle scratching. But she did like one sound; a previous entry mentioned her bustle that played "God Save the Queen" when she sat on it. Sort of a royal whoopee cushion.

vinaigrette

In the 18th century, everyone smelled like salad. A vinaigrette—which was used to battle body odor—was a small gold container with a sponge soaked in vinegar and lavender.

vital fluid

It's here. My day of reckoning, my version of D-Day (the real D-Day was officially called Operation Overlord, by the way). I figured that by now I would achieve a Zenlike calm. I was wrong. I wake up early with both a stomachache and a headache. I spend a few minutes double-checking my Greek dramatists and African rivers, get a good-luck hug from Julie, and hop a cab to the ABC studios on the Upper West Side.

"Welcome to *Who Wants to Be a Millionaire,*" says the greeter, a smiley young woman named Amy. She leads me up a flight of stairs to the windowless greenroom.

Here I learn that *Millionaire* contestants are treated somewhere between A-list celebrities and Guantánamo Bay prisoners. Amy strips me of my cell phone, my Palm Pilot, my reading material. Contact with the real world is verboten. Contact with entertainment or information of any kind is verboten. On the other hand, enjoy the free crudités!

The greenroom is filled with eight of my fellow inmates. There's a trucker-turned-DJ from San Francisco, a CPA from Massachusetts, a couple of teachers from the Midwest. The vibe is part we're-all-in-this-together convivial, part cutthroat competitive. And jittery—knuckles are cracked, legs are bounced, actual groans are emitted.

I, for one, am desperate for reading material. This textual cold turkey is killing me.

"Maybe we could study the labels on the Poland Spring water bottles," I say.

"That was a question once," says a big blond teacher from Michigan.

"What was?"

"They asked a question about where is Poland Spring made."

"Really?" I say.

"Yes," she says.

At which point the long-haired college sophomore from Philadelphia bursts into song. "Poland Spring—what it means to be from Maine." She stops singing. "That's their ad campaign," she says, by way of clarification.

She will prove to be troublesome.

"Actually," says one of the other contestants, "they recently changed their ad campaign." Good for him. I don't know if he's right, but I like that he's shown up the show-off.

These people are no slouches, knowledgewise. They know their bottled water, for one thing, and most are obsessive learners from way back. But they also aren't omniscient. One woman has never heard of the airline Jet Blue—which makes me feel a lot better for some reason.

We are soon herded downstairs to the studio—a circular theater with a heavy-handed futuristic metallic design. And in the middle, the Hot Seat. This is the official contestant chair—and it is *not* to be trifled with. The Hot Seat isn't actually hot in a temperature sense, but it can be quite dangerous: it's tall and swivels quickly. The stage manager gives us lessons on how to mount the Hot Seat properly— plant your butt on the chair's edge, pull up with the arms, rotate into position. We all practice. We don't want to do a faceplant like that old lady a couple of weeks back.

Back in the green room, the *Millionaire* lawyer gives us a lecture. She warns that it's a federal offense to cheat. Throughout the presentation, the college sophomore from Philly laughs nervously—I'm talking minutes-long nonstop laughter. Hee-hee-hee! It's a one-woman claque gone insane.

The executive producer comes to give us her shtick. Like all the other *Millionaire* staff, she tells us to have fun out there. But she also tells us something that sounds like the exact opposite of fun: that the questions have gotten a lot harder than they used to be. Viewers were getting bored. Dammit! What's wrong with boredom? Let the schmucks be bored. This is my self-esteem on the line.

The waiting is torture, a mental version of the strappado (a machine used by the Inquisition that lifted heretics by a rope tied to the hands). Lunch, more waiting, the crowd files in, more waiting, a comic warms up the audience, more waiting.

Finally, the first victim—a surgeon with well-coiffed hair—is called to that fast-swiveling Hot Seat.

"Good luck!" I say, as she is whisked away.

"Go get 'em!"

"Win that million!"

In other words: Botch it up soon so we can go!

The rest of us inmates watch the proceedings on the greenroom's closed-circuit TV. Eight of us sipping our Poland Springs from Maine, all trying to blurt out the answer before the contestant. I have some shining moments. I know that Venezuela was named after Venice (the explorers saw some coastal houses on stilts, which reminded them of the Italian city). I also know where the axilla is.

"It's in the ear," says one contestant.

"No, it's the armpit," I correct him.

"You sure?"

"I'm sure. We did an article on weird fetishes in *Esquire*. And axillism was sex with the armpit."

In retrospect, maybe I shouldn't have revealed that particular piece of information. Amy looks frightened.

A producer periodically appears with a clipboard to announce the next contestant. The former truck driver goes. The teacher goes. The guy who guards the Rockefeller Center Christmas tree goes. The rugby coach goes. They all go—except for me, the laughing Philly girl, and the Harvard graduate/waiter. The taping is over.

"Come back tomorrow at eleven forty-five," Amy tells us, trying to smile.

I sleep at least two or three hours and return to the greenroom to a whole new group of inmates. Today's troublesome character is a fiftyish man who refers to himself as an "opinionated son of a bitch." He shares his opinions on Britney Spears (not a fan), former mayor Rudy Giuliani

("Sieg heil!"), George W. Bush (he mimes cocaine sniffing), a *Millionaire* producer (she looks like a Victoria's Secret lingerie model). When not giving his opinions, he asks us trivia about the periodic table.

A biologist with a hearing aid throws out his own question: name the four actors who were killed in the duel in *High Noon*.

Everyone shakes their heads.

"Ian MacDonald, Bob Wilke, and Sheb Wooley," he says. "And did you know Sheb Wooley also wrote the song 'Giant Purple People Eater'?"

"That's only three—whose the fourth?" asks another contestant.

"I forget the fourth."

"That's the one they're going to ask on *Millionaire*!" I say.

He shoots me a glare.

And then the producer with the clipboard comes into the room and calls my name. "Yes!" I say a little too loudly.

"Good luck!" say the others. I know what they mean.

I am led down to the set, which seems more aggressively futuristic and metallic than ever. The crowd is clapping double-time—they have been told it looks better on TV. My mom, dad, and Julie are in the audience, though they've been seated behind me so they can't signal me. The absurdly dramatic music plays. The lights flash. My palms are as damp as Cherrapunji (the Indian town with a record 366 inches of rainfall in one month). I climb into the Hot Seat—and, despite my lesson, I manage to stumble.

I've got to say, Meredith Vieira is exactly the opposite of the scary studio—she's calming, maternal, all smiles. Either she's a great actress or she really, sincerely wants you to win that million. We chat for a bit. She tells me to relax and take my time.

"You ready?"

I think I am.

The $100 question: What is the meaning of the phrase "Bon voyage"?

"I've forgotten ninety-nine percent of my high school French," I say (I figure start out humble, get the audience on my side), "but I remember this one percent. It's C, 'good trip.' Final answer."

Applause. Yes! I have avoided complete and total humiliation. I'm on my way. In fact, I zip through the first batch of questions: the Quaker is a logo for oatmeal; nuns live in a convent (though also a nunnery, I point out); hydrogen sulfide smells like rotten eggs; an ampersand means "and"; Sophia Loren is from Italy. More applause.

I'm loving this! I'm ticking off the letters flawlessly, a Ninja of knowledge. This Hot Seat is one of the few places on earth where you can't be too much of a know-it-all. And maybe, in fact, I do know everything.

Or not. The $8000 question throws me: What current *Law & Order* cast member has been on the show the longest?

Shit. Maybe all those South American capitals and Japanese shoguns have elbowed out my TV trivia. I'm not sure of the answer—could be Jerry Orbach, could be Sam Waterston.

"I'd like to ask the audience," I say. I get to do this only once, but I figure now's the time. Back in the greenroom, one of the producers had told us about the Colombian version of *Who Wants to Be A Millionaire,* in which the audience purposely votes incorrectly just to torment the poor contestant. But I trust these fine Americans—two of whom happen to be actual nuns—so I go with them. Seventy percent of them think it's Orbach. They are right.

"Thank you, audience!" I say.

The $16,000 question: Lilliputians are from what novel? All right. I know this. I'm back in the zone. "That's C,—*Gulliver's Travels.* Final answer."

I don't mention to Meredith that Gulliver put out a fire at the Lilliputian castle by urinating on it. (I also keep to myself some other weird fire/urine connections from the *Britannica*: Freud said that pyromania and bed-wetting are linked. And urine was used to extinguish Greek Fire—an ancient napalmlike weapon. My mind goes to curious places even under pressure.)

"*Gulliver's Travels* is correct!"

I'm sitting pretty, loving this, ready for my $32,000 question. It pops up on my monitor: What component of blood is also known as erythrocyte?

Erythrocyte. I stare at the word. I search my brain and search some more. Nothing. I could spend days scouring every dusty corner and obscure cranny of my cerebral cortex. I just don't think the word is in there. Damn.

My choices are white blood cells, platelets, red blood cells, serum.

Still don't know. Erythrocyte, erythrocyte. I'm annoyed at myself, but I'm still pretty calm. I've still got my lifeline, so I'll be fine.

"I'd like to call my brother-in-law Eric," I say.

He was a biochem major at Harvard. This is just the kind of thing Eric will know.

"Okay," says Meredith. "Let's call Eric."

After three rings, Eric answers. Meredith tells him I've won $16,000—Eric seems legitimately impressed—and that now I need his help. As instructed, I don't waste time with hellos. I just read him the question.

"What component of blood is also known as erythrocyte? Red blood cell, white blood cell, serum, or platelets?"

Eric emits a sound somewhere between a hmmmm and a groan. Whatever it is, it is not a good sound. It is a bad sound—and a shocking one. This is crazy. Eric doesn't know? That just doesn't compute. That's like the pope not being a Catholic. That's like the kami not being Shinto. I lost a couple of seconds trying to reorient myself.

"Erythrocyte?" he says.

"Type it in!" I say. "*E-r-y-t-h-r-o-c-y-t-e.*"

I am telling him to Google it—it's a dirty little secret of *Millionaire* that the lifelines often use a computer. The crowd titters at my boldness.

"Tell me the choices again?" he says.

And then, before I can list *A* or *B* or *C* or *D,* time runs out.

Meredith gives me a sympathetic smile.

"I thought he knew everything!" I say.

The crowd laughs, but I wasn't kidding. I really did.

Now I panic. Now I feel alone out there. I swivel a bit in my chair, swivel back. I still have something called a fifty-fifty, where two of the answers are randomly taken away. I use it. I am left with serum and red blood cells. Serum, red blood cells. Red blood cells, serum.

"Well, you'd think I'd have heard the scientific name for red blood cells," I said. "I can't believe I wouldn't have. I'm going to say serum." I pause. "Serum. Final answer."

Meredith looks genuinely pained.

"Another word for 'erythrocyte' is '*red blood cell*'."

I sink my head into my hands. That's it. My little moment in the melodramatic lighting is done. Meredith cuts to commercial. I dismount the Hot Seat and am brought backstage, where I'm greeted by Julie, my mom and dad, who all say they're proud of me—at least I think that's what they're saying. But mostly, I'm hearing "You did a great *erythrocyte*! The crowd really *erythrocyted* you." That's all I can think of. Erythrocyte. I will never forget that word. They hand me my check—my winnings have plunged all the way down to $1,000.

When I get back to the office, I call Eric.

"You owe me thirty-one thousand dollars!" I say, sort of jokingly.

"You're the writer," he responds. "You should have known it!"

Eric tells me he did Google it, but ran out of time before he could comb through the results. He didn't mention whether or not, after he was cut off, he shouted, "Eric!" I hang up. For the next twenty-four hours of my life, I spend all of my mental energy coming up with the ways I should have known "erythrocyte." First, of course, I should have remembered it from the *Britannica*. I looked it up, and it's right there in the *E*'s: "Erythrocyte: also called red blood cell or red corpuscle." The cells are biconcave and appear dumbbell-shaped in profile. They are flexible and assume a bell shape as they pass through tiny blood vessels. They contain hemoglobin. Why didn't I remember that? I should have paid more attention to the biology sections. I should have put vital fluids on my list of things to study.

Not only that, but I knew that "cyte" means "cell." I should have figured it was either red or white blood cells. I should have told Eric to use *Britannica*, not Google. I should have had a psychic blood expert in the audience beaming me information telepathically.

So that's it. My dreams are trampled—I won't be lighting my Macanudo cigar with hundred-dollar bills. I won't be popping open a magnum of champagne—or a jeroboam (equal to four bottles), a methuselah (eight bottles), a salmanazar (twelve bottles), a balthazar (sixteen bottles), or a nebuchadnezzar (twenty bottles). But as the hours wear on, I become more and more at peace with my $1,000. First, it'll pay for two-thirds of my *Britannica*— about letters *A* through *P*— which is something. And I didn't look like a *total* jackass out there—that erythrocyte was an obscure question. So obscure, Eric Schoenberg—the Trivial Pursuit champ, the Harvard biochem major, one of the most well informed men in America—didn't know it either. Eric knows a lot—he knows more than me, I can admit that. But he doesn't know *everything*. No one does. And now there's proof on nationally syndicated television.

W

war, technology of

A soul-crushing ninety-eight pages. It's a crescendo of ever-more-sophisticated ways that humans have figured out to kill one another. Spears, ramparts, catapults, crossbows, guns, machine guns, missiles.

One passage struck me in particular. It was about the dropping of the second atomic bomb—with the weirdly endearing nickname of Fat Man—on Nagasaki, on August 9 in 1945:

"The B-29 spent 10 minutes over Kokura without sighting its aim point; it then proceeded to the secondary target of Nagasaki, where at 11:02 AM local time, the weapon was air-burst at 1650 feet with a force of 21 kilotons."

I had no idea that the Japanense city of Kokura was the primary target. I'd never even heard of Kokura. But what a strange fact. Imagine how many lives were affected because of this. Seventy thousand dead in Nagasaki and thousands of people spared in Kokura because of cloudy conditions.

I think about those ten minutes when the plane was buzzing over Kokura. All those people going about their day —making phone calls at the office, playing with their kids, eating their meals— totally unaware that a bomb of unimaginable destructive power was hovering overhead, ready to vaporize their bodies. But they survived because the bomber couldn't spot its *X*.

It's something that I've learned over and over again: luck plays a huge part in history. We like to think that it's the product of our will and rational decisions and planning. But I've noticed it's just as often—more often—about seemingly tiny whims of fate.

To take another example from World War II there's the July Plot to assassinate Hitler. This took place in 1944, and was orchestrated by a group of German conspirators led by an officer named Claus von Stauffenberg. As the *Britannica* says:

"Stauffenberg slipped from the room, witnessed the explosion at 12:42 pm, and, convinced Hitler was killed, flew to Berlin . . . [but] an attending officer had nudged the briefcase with a bomb to the far side of a massive oak support of the conference table, which thus shielded Hitler from the full force of the explosion."

Hitler survived because an attending officer was tidy and wanted the briefcase out of the way. History was changed by the size of an oak table.

Wells, H. G.

Here's another one who married his cousin. Along with contracting gout, marrying your cousin seems to be a favorite pastime of historical figures. Over the last few months, I've been keeping a list of cousin lovers, and here's just a sampling: Charles Darwin, Henry VIII, Edgar Allan Poe (with his thirteen-year-old cousin, if you recall), Sergey Rachmaninoff, and now, the newest member of the club, H. G. Wells.

I went back to check on Rachmaninoff because I wasn't positive about him. I was happy to see that, yes, the composer did indeed marry his cousin. But strangely, I noticed something else about him: Rachmaninoff wrote a symphony based on a poem by fellow club member Edgar Allan Poe. Weird.

Back when I was smart the first time—back in high school—I read a short story by Italo Calvino. It was a fable about a city where people's apartments were connected by threads. The threads were strung from one apartment and across the street or down the block to another apartment. Each thread represented a different kind of relationship. If the people in the two apartments were blood relatives, the threads would be black. If they were in business together, the threads would be white. If one was the boss of the other, the threads would be gray. Eventually, the threads grew so numerous and thick and multishaded that you couldn't walk through the city.

That's what history seems like to me now. There are hundreds of threads connecting everybody in all sorts of ways, both expected and unexpected. It's like a spiderweb (which, by the way, spiders sometimes eat when they're done with them).

wergild

In ancient Germanic law, this was the payment that someone made to an injured party. Most cultures had a similar concept—in the Middle East, it was called diyah. A life was worth one hundred female camels. Loss of one eye or foot was fifty she-camels. A blow to the head or abdomen was thirty-three, and loss of a tooth was five.

Still no sign of my $31,000 wergild from Eric for the *Millionaire* fiasco. But that's okay. He has given me something else. Julie talked to Alexandra, Eric's wife, who told her that Eric felt bad about the *Millionaire* debacle. And not just bad about looking ignorant on national TV. He actually felt guilty about blowing my chances at thirty-two grand. I knew Eric had feelings—he's a loving father and a good son—but I never imagined those feelings would be directed toward me. This was almost more surprising than when he didn't know an abstruse biological term. It made me feel all warm and forgiving. I sent him an e-mail.

> *Thanks for being my lifeline. We didn't win, but we went down fighting.*
>
> > *Your brother (by marriage, not by erythrocyte),*
> > *AJ*

I thought that struck the proper note—familial, sympathetic, but still with a gentle dig at the end.

He wrote back:

> *Glad to be of help. Or rather, no help. At least you don't have to pay a lot of taxes on your winnings.*
> > *Eric*

I almost wanted to write back and tell him that if my kid turns out to be as sweet and smart and fun as his kids are, I'll be a happy man. But there's a limit, you know?

White House

The White House was originally called the President's Palace, but the name was changed to Executive Mansion because "palace" was considered too royal. The building didn't officially become known as the White

House until 1902, under Teddy Roosevelt. Roosevelt, by the way, renovated the second floor to make room for his "children's exotic pets, which included raccoons, snakes, a badger, and a bear."

All pretty good facts. But here's the peculiar part. I was at the office, and I was telling my coworker about the Roosevelt menagerie, and he asked if the bear in question was the Teddy bear. I went on Britannica.com to check, and reread the White House entry. It didn't say. But I noticed the online version had a whole other anecdote that was cut from the print version for space. The anecdote was this:

Apparently, security at the White House used to be shockingly lax. In 1842, Charles Dickens was invited to the White House by John Tyler. Dickens arrived at the mansion, knocked on the door. No one answered. So—and this is what it says—*he let himself in.* Just walked right through the front door and started poking around the rooms unchaperoned. The esteemed British author finally stumbled onto a couple of dozen presidential hangers-on in one of the rooms. He was most appalled that they were spitting on the White House floor, and wrote that he hoped the spittle-cleaning servants were paid well.

Now, that's a good anecdote. I love the print version, but now I wonder what a world I've been missing by ignoring the online *Britannica*.

Winchell, Walter

The famous fast-talking, hat-wearing, pun-loving gossip columnist was born Walter Winchel—just one *l* in the last name. But someone accidentally added an extra *l* to "Winchel" on a theater marquee. Winchel liked it so much he kept it. Likewise, Ulysses Grant had a superfluous *S* inserted into the middle of his name on his West Point papers. He kept it. And a man named Israel Baline changed his name to Irving Berlin after a printer's error rendered it Berlin (not a small error—let's hope that printer switched careers soon after). Here again, luck changing history, though in a much less gloomy and devastating way.

Wise Men

The three Wise Men have been popping up in our lives recently. Or one of the three Wise Men, anyway. Julie and I are considering naming our son Jasper—no particular reason, we just like the name, and Julie nixed Mshweshwe and Ub. Jasper, we learned from one of our many baby name books, is a version of Gaspar, the name of one of the three Magi.

So our son will be named for a Wise Man. Maybe, we figure, it'll make him a Wise Baby. And maybe—here's a shocker—I can even impart a little wisdom of my own to the fellow. I actually think I have some.

The thing is, if I'm really being truthful with myself, Operation Britannica began as a bit of a lark. I figured I'd get some fun facts, have something to say at cocktail parties, increase my quirkiness factor, maybe learn a little about the nature of information. But wisdom? I didn't really expect it.

And yet, surprisingly, wisdom was in there—lurking in those 44 million words. It occasionally hit me over the head (see *Ecclesiastes*). But mostly I got my wisdom from absorbing the *Britannica* as a whole. And the wisdom I absorbed is this:

I finally have faith that Homo sapiens—that bipedal mammal of the Chordata phylum with 1350 cubic centimeters of cranial capacity, a secondary palate, and a hundred thousand hairs per scalp—is a pretty good species. Yes, we have the capability to do horrible things. We have created poverty and war and Daylight Saving Time. But in the big sweep—over the past ten thousand years and thirty-three thousand pages—we've redeemed ourselves with our accomplishments. We're the ones who came up with the Trevi fountain and Scrabble in braille and Dr. DeBakey's artificial heart and the touch-tone phone.

We have made our lives better. A thousand times better. Never again will I mythologize the past as some sort of golden age. Remember: In the 19th century, the mortality rate was 75 percent for a cesarean section, so my friend Jenny might no longer be around. The workday was fourteen hours, which is too long even for a workaholic like me. The life expectancy in ancient Rome was twenty-nine years. Widows had to marry their late husband's brother. Originally forks had one tine, and umbrellas were available only in black, and you ate four-day-old fetid meat for dinner.

For all its terrifying problems, now is the best time to be alive. I'm excited for my son, Jasper, to be born. I can't wait—and not just because he'll be a cool accessory to have on my hip, like a new two-way pager, but because I think he'll like the world, and the world will like him.

The facts in my brain will fade—I know that. But this wisdom, this perspective, I hope will stay with me.

Wood, Grant

The painter of the famous *American Gothic* portrait. I learn that the man and woman aren't a farmer and his wife. The woman is Wood's sister, Nan. And the farmer with the pitchfork? Wood's dentist. It's true, now that I look at him: put a white coat on him, and he screams D.D.S. Plus, he looks at home with that sharp implement, so that's a cue.

Woodhull, Victoria

I figured by this point, after a year of nonstop reading, I'd be pretty well sick of the activity. I figured I wouldn't want to read another book post-*Britannica*. I figured I wouldn't want to read a stop sign or salad dressing label. And yet, when I learn about someone like Victoria Woodhull, I feel like I'd like to dive into an entire biography on her. Odd.

Woodhull was an amazing woman—the first female stockbroker and the first woman to run for president, among other things. Born in Ohio in 1838, she spent her childhood traveling with her family's fortune-telling business. She married at age fifteen, divorced soon after, and moved to New York. There, she befriended robber baron Cornelius Vanderbilt, who was a fan of psychics. Vanderbilt helped her start a stock brokerage firm. (Seems like a good idea—a psychic stock picker.)

In the following years, Woodhull drifted further into fringe causes. She began publishing a reform magazine that advocated communal living, free love, equal rights, and women's suffrage. The eccentric Woodhull wasn't popular with the more staid members of the women's suffrage movement, but they accepted her, at least temporarily, after she pleaded for the women's vote before Congress.

Woodhull's relationship with a reformer named Theodore Tilton led to national scandal. In what seems her sleaziest moment, Woodhull printed rumors that Tilton's wife was having extramarital relations with Henry Ward Beecher. This got Woodhull indicted for sending improper material through the mails. (She was later acquitted.) In 1877, she moved to England—apparently with the financial help of Vanderbilt heirs, who feared she'd try to horn in on the will—where she started a journal of eugenics and offered a five-thousand-dollar prize for the first transatlantic flight.

A curious and fascinating life. I did, in fact, order a Woodhull bio online. There will be at least one book in my post-*Britannica* existence.

X Y Z

X-ray style

This is an artistic technique in which you depict animals by painting their skeleton or internal organs. Mesolithic hunters in northern Europe loved their X-ray style, as did some early aboriginal Australians (*Britannica*'s got a funky-looking picture of an X-rayed-lizard painting from Australia). I'm reading this at night, just a few hours after one of the *Esquire* editors suggested we do an X-ray photo portfolio—an X ray of a guy hitting a golf ball, an X ray of a guy and a woman in bed. Will this be my last eerie *Britannica*-and-life intersection? Could be. I can see those Zs at the end of the tunnel. I'm that close.

yacht

The presidential yacht—a massive boat called the *Mayflower,* built in 1897—saw active service during World War II. I like that—a battling yacht. It'd be good to send Barry Diller's yacht to the Persian Gulf.

Yang, Franklin

A Chinese-born American physicist who won the Nobel in 1957. Yang was born with the first name Chen Ning, but switched it to Franklin after reading the autobiography of Benjamin Franklin as a kid. If you're going to name yourself after someone, Franklin's a solid choice. The founding father has surfaced dozens of times in the *Britannica*, almost always in a flattering light—he founded the American Philosophical Society when he was twenty-one, started the first insurance in our country, discredited a quack named Franz Mesmer who allegedly put people in trances (hence the word "mesmerize"). On the other hand, Franklin did satisfy his libido with "low women."

Year

Today, another Hanukkah/New Year's gift exchange at my parents'. It's been about a year since I started reading the *Britannica,* which is hard to believe. It doesn't feel like a year. It doesn't even feel like a lunar year (twelve lunar cycles, about 354 days, used in some calendars).

We get there early—before Beryl and Willy—which means there's time for Julie and my mom to go to the back room and look at some jewelry designs my mom has been working up.

Leaving Dad and me alone.

"Want to see the latest sonogram?" I ask.

"Absolutely," says Dad.

It's a good sonogram. The spine shows up in bright white, resembling a tiny comb. And you can see his face—Julie and I had an argument over whether he looks more like E.T. or Jason from the *Friday the 13th* series.

I take the sonogram out of the bag and hand it to Jasper's grandfather.

"Good-looking kid," he says, studying it.

"Yeah, he's got the Jacobs nose," I say.

"Any more thoughts about naming him Arnold Jacobs V?" my dad asks.

"Sorry, no."

He nods his head. He knew.

"I have something else you might want to see," I say.

"What is it?"

I dig a piece of paper out of the bag.

"It's a little something I wrote up. Something I'm submitting to the *Britannica* board for inclusion in next year's edition."

My dad takes the paper. He reads it:

Jacobs, Arnold (b. February 26, 1941, New York)

An expert on insider trading and world record holder for most footnotes in a law article. Jacobs grew up in Manhattan, the son of a lawyer and an art teacher. He graduated in the 78th percentile in his high school class—but has the excuse that he only studied during subway rides. Jacobs attended many, many graduate schools that we cannot list for space reasons. With his wife, Ellen Kheel, a fellow collector of buffalo memorabilia, he had two children. He imparted to his son, Arnold Jacobs Jr. (aka Arnold Jacobs IV), a love of learning and scholarship that could be excessive at times—but as far as excesses go, it was a pretty decent one. Jacobs Sr. also impressed his son with his accomplishments, devotion to family, and expertise on Genghis Khan. And perhaps most important, Jacobs Sr. made a great scientific leap when he discovered the speed of light in fathoms per fortnight: 1.98×10^{14}. Jacobs Jr. built upon his father's discovery by calculating the speed of light in knots per nanosecond: .000162.

I watch my dad read it—for what seems like a very long time. Finally, he smiles.

"This is great," he says. "I'm honored."

"Well, we'll see if they accept it," I say.

"Knots per nanosecond?"

"Yeah, I worked it out."

"That's good stuff."

"Yeah, useful information," I say.

"You even got the alliteration down."

"Yeah, I thought it was better than knots per picosecond."

"It's great. It can be the first thing I'll teach my grandson."

I probably won't be joining my father in the really byzantine practical jokes featuring bison statues or lemon Kool-Aid. But I figure, why not join him in a little one about fathoms and fortnights? Why not take his cue, as Lorenz's goslings did, and give him a little praise? I knew he'd love it.

As I approach the Z's, I've finally beaten my dad at something. I finished a mission that he started, and I suppose that's helped me exorcise a demon—specifically the demon of envy, also known as Leviathan in the Bible. Right now, at least for the next couple of weeks, I probably have more information in my cerebral cortex than he does. Am I smarter? Maybe not. Most likely not. Do I know as much as he does about rule 10b-5? Certainly not. But I do know this more than ever: my dad and I are the same. I've learned to stop fighting that fact. I've learned to like it.

yodel

The Swiss do not have a monopoly on this. The pygmies and the Australian Aborigines are also proficient yodelers. On the other hand, their cuckoo clocks are below average.

Young Men's Christian Association

This started with twelve young men in the drapery business in England before blossoming into a Village People song.

Young, Thomas

Proposed the wave theory of light—and was widely disparaged because any opposition to Newton's theory was unthinkable. As George Bernard Shaw said, "All great truths start as blasphemies." See—I got something out of this.

Zeus

I guess it's no big news that men can't keep their pants on. That was clear even in the first hundred pages of the *Britannica*, what with the scores of "dissolute" men and their mistresses. But Zeus is in a league of his own. He deserves a gold medal, or better yet, some saltpetre (well, actually, I learned that saltpetre doesn't dampen the libido; so maybe a cold shower). Zeus was the Wilt Chamberlain of Greek gods, spreading his seed far and wide. Every one hundred pages in my reading, there Zeus would be, making it with another woman or, occasionally, with a man. Sometimes Zeus would have sex as Zeus himself, but more often he'd go in disguise. He's taken the shape of a bull, an eagle, a cuckoo, a dark cloud, a shower of gold coins, and an ant. An ant? He seduced Eurymedusa in the form of an ant. I don't even understand what that means. I have a guess, but I can't imagine Eurymedusa found that pleasant, and she may have required ointment.

Zola, Emile

According to some sources, Zola, as a starving writer, ate sparrows trapped outside his windowsill.

ZOO

The Aztecs had a magnificent one in Mexico that required a staff of three hundred zookeepers. Also, you should know that Londoners during World War II ate the fish out of their city's zoo.

Seventeen pages left. I've got a tingle in the back of my neck. I want to skim, but I force myself to slow down, savor these final entries.

zucchetto

The skullcap worn by Roman Catholic clergymen—the last liturgical vestment in the *Britannica*!

Zulu, the African nation (whose founder, Shaka, by the way, became "openly psychotic" when his mother died, and refused to allow crops to be planted).

My God, seven more pages.

Leopold Zunz, a Jewish scholar.

Zurich ware, a type of Swiss porcelain.

Zveno Group, a Bulgarian political party.

Zywiec

And here it is. I have arrived. The final entry of the *Britannica*'s 65,000 entries, the last handful of the 44 million words. The bizarre thing is, my pulse is thumping as if I were running an actual marathon. I'm amped up.

I take a deep breath to calm myself, and then I read about Zywiec. Zywiec is a town in south-central Poland. It's known for its large breweries and a 16th-century sculpture called *The Dormant Virgin.* Population thirty-two thousand.

And that's it. At 9:38 P.M. on an otherwise unremarkable Tuesday night, sitting in my customary groove on the white couch, I have finished reading the 2002 edition of the *Encyclopaedia Britannica.* I'm not sure what to do. I shut the back cover quietly. I stand up from the couch, then sit back down.

There's no ribbon to break, no place to plant a flag. It's a weird and anti-climactic feeling. The entry itself doesn't help. If the *Britannica* were a normal book, the ending would presumably have some deeper meaning, some wrap-it-all-up conclusion or shocking twist. But everything in the *EB* is a slave to the iron discipline of alphabetization, so I'm left with an utterly forgettable entry about a beer-soaked town in south-central Poland. Zywiec. I guess I knew it wouldn't hold all the secrets to the universe (*zywiec*: a mysterious substance found in badger fur is the reason to go on living!), but still, it's a little disappointing. There's something sad about finishing a huge, yearlong project, an immediate postpartum depression.

I slide the volume back into its space on the mustard-colored shelf, where I expect it will stay for a long time. I wander out to the living room.

"Done," I tell my wife.

"Done for the night?"

"No, done. As in done, done."

She throws open her arms. I get a congratulatory hug and kiss.

"Wait a second," she says. "I have to document this." Julie runs off to the bedroom and reappears with our video camera.

"A.J. Jacobs, you finished reading the *Encyclopaedia Britannica* from *A* to *Z*. What are you going to do now?"

"Um . . ." I shake my head. I really don't know. I'm stumped.

"Are you going to Disneyland?" prompts Julie.

"Yes, maybe I'll go to Disneyland, founded by Walt Disney, creator of Oswald the Rabbit."

Julie clicks off the camera.

"How about a celebratory dinner?" she asks.

"Yeah, why not?" That'll be nice, a dinner with the long-neglected Julie—that is her name, right? "You want to finish your *West Wing*?" I ask.

"Sure."

So I sit on the couch next to Julie and watch the end of *The West Wing*, which is set in the White House, a structure Thomas Jefferson called "big enough for two emperors, one pope, and the grand lama."

I think back to my parents' friend who told me the fable wherein the wise men of the kingdom condensed all the encyclopedia's knowledge into a single sentence: "This too shall pass." That's not a bad moral. If you want a single sentence, you could do worse. What's my sentence? I better come up with one now, because at this very moment, I've got more information than I ever will, before that evil Ebbinghaus curve kicks in.

Frankly, I'm not sure what my sentence is. Maybe I'm not smart enough to come up with a single sentence summing up the *Britannica*. Maybe it'd be better to try a few sentences, and see what sticks. So here goes:

I know that everything is connected like a worldwide version of the six-degrees-of-separation game. I know that history is simultaneously a bloody mess and a collection of feats so inspiring and amazing they make you proud to share the same DNA structure with the rest of humanity. I know you'd better focus on the good stuff or you're screwed. I know that the race does not go to the swift, nor the bread to the wise, so you should soak up what enjoyment you can. I know not to take cinnamon for granted. I know that morality lies in even the smallest decisions, like whether to pick up and throw away a napkin. I know that an erythrocyte is a red blood cell, not serum. I know firsthand the oceanic volume of information in the world. I know that I know very little of that ocean. I know that I'm having a baby in two months, and that I'm just the tiniest bit more prepared for having him (I can tell him why the sky is blue—and also the origin of the blue moon, in case he cares), but will learn 99 percent of parenthood as I go along. I know that—despite the hyposomnia and the missed *Simpsons* episodes—I'm glad I read the *Britannica*. I know that opossums have thirteen nipples. I know I've contradicted myself a hundred times over the last year, and that history has contradicted itself thousands of times. I know that oysters can change their sex and Turkey's avant-garde magazine is called *Varlik*. I know that you should always say yes to adventures or you'll lead a very dull life. I know that knowledge and intelligence are not the same thing—but they do live in the same neighborhood. I know once again, firsthand, the joy of learning. And I know that I've got my life back and that in just a few moments, I'm going to have a lovely dinner with my wife.

ADDITIONAL SOURCES

BROWN, CRAIG. "How the First Fly Guy Went Up, Up and Wa-hey . . ." *Edinburgh Evening News,* December 9, 2003.

COLEMAN, ALEXANDER and CHARLES SIMMONS. *All There Is to Know: Readings from the Illustrious Eleventh Edition of the Encyclopaedia Britannica.* New York: Simon & Schuster, 1994.

FLAUBERT, GUSTAVE. *Bouvard and Pécuchet with the Dictionary of Received Ideas.* New York: Penguin Group, 1976.

KOGAN, HERMAN. *The Great EB: The Story of the Encyclopaedia Britannica.* Chicago: University of Chicago Press, 1958.

KONING, HANS. "Onward and Upward with the Arts: The Eleventh Edition." *The New Yorker,* March 2, 1981.

MARKS-BEALE, ABBY. *10 Days to Faster Reading.* New York: Warner Books, 2001.

MCCABE, JOSEPH. *The Lies and Fallacies of the Encyclopaedia Britannica.* Escondido, Calif.: The Book Tree, 2000.

MCCARTHY, MICHAEL. "It's Not True About Caligula's Horse; Britannica Checked—Dogged Researchers Answer Some Remarkable Queries." *Wall Street Journal,* April 22, 1999.

MCHENRY, ROBERT. "Whatever Happened to Encyclopedic Style." *Chronicle of Higher Education,* February 28, 2003.

OSTROV, RICK. *Power Reading.* North San Juan, Calif.: Education Press, 2002.

SARTE, JEAN-PAUL. *Nausea.* New York: New Directions, 1964.

SHNEIDMAN, EDWIN/ "Suicide On My Mind, Britannica on My Table." *American Scholar,* autumn 1998.

STERNBERG, ROBERT J. *Successful Intelligence: How Practical and Creative Intelligence Determine Success in Life.* New York: Plume, 1997.

——— ed. *Handbook of Intelligence.* Cambridge: Cambridge University Press, 2000.

INDEX

earth *(cont.)*
  search for intelligent life on, 243–46
  time taken by rotation of, 136
  unrestrained outlay of facts about, 68–70
Earth Mother, as fertility goddess, 94
Easter Bunny, background and character of, 94
Ebbinghaus, Herman, "forgetting curve" of, 84, 154, 179, 304, 368
Ebert jokes, 63
Ecclesiastes, 288, 290, 361
E! channel, 330
$8000 question, audience thanked for answer to, 354
Einstein, Albert, 202–5
  see also relativity
embalming:
  Egyptian recipe for, 74
  as loophole in wife's will, 74, 75, 338
Eminems, miniversions of, 301–5
Encyclopaedia Britannica:
  admirable anality of, 128
  alphabetical sequence of, 71, 367
  bloopers in, 127–28
  brilliant quotations helpful in getting into, 180–81
  as bug killer, 163
  card games clarified by, 122
  career ideas in, 348–50
  cat issues of, 78–79
  chamber music as an unseemly soft spot of, 347
  cross-referencing in, 7, 340–41
  dedication of, 341–42
  dispassionate approach of, 322, 323, 324
  diversity of everything in, 120–22
  electronic applications of, 80, 81
  Eleventh Edition of, 5, 80–82, 332
  "erythrocyte" found in, too late for *Millionaire,* 356
  even-handedness of, 143, 300
  excitement about diacritics at, 341
  facts, not that many, missing from, 320
  Fifteenth Edition of, 79
  First Edition and founders of (Macfarquhar, Smellie, and Bell), 78–79, 128
  flexibility a lesson of, 327
  glories of, 4–5
  gravitas added to room by, 249
  great books coverage in, 328–29
  Greek history favored by, 59
  handy-phrase translations in, 229
  hard-to-forget book titles in, 172
  indexing department of, 339–40
  instant wisdom in, 70
  on itself, 77–82
  legal knowledge in, 16
  main sections of, 63
  marginal utility theory in, 124
  material aspects of, 5–6
  medical afflictions found in, 59–61
  as noble pursuit, 341
  nothing evidently left out of, 191
  other readers of, 269–71
  phonetic guides not found in, 169
  physicality of, 164
  purchase and arrival of, 5
  racism in, 82
  randiness of, 9, 11, 38, 169
  randomness of, 9, 71
  reading of, *see* Operation Britannica
  repetition in, 52
  romance in, 32, 44–45, 166
  scatology in, 194
  self-help guidance in, 75–77
  stereotypes broken by, 83
  superior putz's insult of, 332–33
  ten best ways to get into, 88–89
  Thirteenth Edition of, 81
  unauthorized tweaking of, 128
  uneven alphabetical coverage in, 79, 219
  unorthodox uses of, 163–64
  unusual grounds for entry into, 25
  vintage and classic editions of, 79–80
  visit to HQ of, 336–42
  weird and crude facts in, 236
  worldview of, 81–82
"encyclopedia":
  derivation of, 77
  ligature sometimes seen in, 78, 339
encyclopedias, earliest, longest, strangest, etc., 77–78
"Encyclopedia Twit-annica," 128
Encyclopédie (Diderot et al.), 77–78
Engels, Friedrich, ideological dualism of, 82–83
Enlightenment, Eleventh Edition as culmination of, 81–82
entertainment:
  bearbaiting as, 23
  musicals about trains as, 187